**LABOUR STUDIES**
**UNIVERSITY OF WINDSOR**

# THE WESTRAY CHRONICLES
## A CASE STUDY IN CORPORATE CRIME

*edited by Christopher McCormick*

FERNWOOD PUBLISHING • HALIFAX

Editing: Donna Davis and Mary Frances Finnigan
Cover illustration: *The Last Judgment*, by Hieronymus Bosch, a Dutch painter from the 15th century. Shown here is the central panel of a triptych, part of the collection of the Akademie der Bildenden Kunste, Vienna.
Cover design: Chris McCormick
Design and production: Beverley Rach
Printed and bound in Canada by: Hignell Printing Limited

A publication of:
Fernwood Publishing
Box 9409, Station A
Halifax, Nova Scotia
B3K 5S3

Fernwood Publishing Company Limited acknowledges the financial support of the Government of Canada through the Book Publishing Industry Development Program (BPDIP) and the Canada Council for the Arts for our publishing activities.

Le Conseil des Arts    The Canada Council
du Canada              for the Arts

Special thanks go to Stewart Donovan and Breton Books for permission to reproduce "Liscombe Sanctuary." Editorial cartoons have been reprinted with permission from the Halifax Herald Limited and Theo Moudakis of the *Daily News*. Appreciation is also expressed for permission to reproduce excerpts from the *Report of the Westray Mine Public Inquiry*.
Every reasonable effort has been made to acquire permission for copyright material used in this text and to acknowledge such indebtedness accurately. Any errors called to the publisher's attention will be corrected in future editions.

Canadian Cataloguing in Publication Data

Main entry under title:
The Westray chronicles

    Includes bibliographical references.
    ISBN 1-895686-32-6

1. Westray Mine Disaster, Plymouth, Pictou, N.S., 1992.
I. McCormick, Christopher Ray, 1956-    II. Title.

TN806.C22N6 1999    363.11'9622334'0971613    C98-950003-9

# DEDICATED TO THE MEMORY OF

John Thomas Bates, 56
Larry Arthur Bell, 25
Bennie Joseph Benoit, 42
Wayne Michael Conway, 38
Ferris Todd Dewan, 35
Adonis J. Dollimont, 36
Robert Steven Doyle, 22
Remi Joseph Drolet, 38
Roy Edward Feltmate, 33
Charles Robert Fraser, 29
Myles Daniel Gillis, 32
John Philip Halloran, 33
Randolph Brian House, 27
Trevor Martin Jahn, 36
Laurence Elwyn James, 34
Eugene W. Johnson, 33
Stephen Paul Lilley, 40
Michael Frederick MacKay, 38
Angus Joseph MacNeil, 39
Glenn David Martin, 35
Harry Alliston McCallum, 41
Eric Earl McIsaac, 38
George James Munroe, 38
Danny James Poplar, 39
Romeo Andrew Short, 35
Peter Francis Vickers, 38

# LISCOMBE SANCTUARY

in memory of the 26 coal miners
who died at Plymouth, Nova Scotia

A New Glasgow honeymoon couple
kisses for one night only in the luxury
of Liscomb Lodge: here, on Nova Scotia's
Eastern shore, a lonely lighthouse can still
signal codes for late lobster fishermen and
perhaps, too, for the few remaining trawlers
bound with quotas cut for Canso. But rumour
has it that in three weeks only the stars of Asia
Minor will flash for lovers on this coast still
intent on romantic lights.

As a girl, four years back, the young bride,
Sally Doucette, baby-sat bored brothers and
sisters who possessed the natural contempt
for history as they ran, cried and begged to
leave Historic Sherbrooke Village. They don't
care if it's good for them, and only once did
their dark eyes bulge bright and wide with
wonder: "A forge, a forge," cried the bride
in dictionary definition through the roar of
the tiny blast furnace cooking lobster-
red shoes for the great brown Belgians that
steamed and stamped in the dark lonely stalls.

Bored, uninformed, Sally too longed to be back
home, back and busy at McDonald's on the East
River Road where romance, gentle gossip and
Madonna echoed between the stainless steel
fryers on Saturday nights. And where quiet John
MacLellan always ordered the Big Mac special
until Sally gently bullied him to change. Doing
so she won the boast and the five-dollar bet
placed back in the kitchen where the chorus of
co-workers had continually cried it couldn't be done.

Today the honeymooners camp at Ecum Secum
on their return journey from five nights in Dartmouth.
They visit the village now as young adults
and wonder at "so much to see" the strange silence
of absent comforts: cars, radios and tvs. "It's quiet
like Louisbourg," Sally says. John's father had helped
build the fortress, a laid-off Cape Breton coal miner
he resurrected stones blown away by Lord Byron's
grandfather to keep the French forever from
Nova Scotia's coast. John MacLellan, the miner's son,
had only once been underground, and would not go
again because good luck and a friend's bad back at
François Michelin's Trenton plant had saved him
from the Ford seam, or the long nights on the new
dole line of Oshawa.

When the news of the twenty-six came,
they wanted the day postponed, but
family and friends counselled with
comforting clichés, old stoic Scots' sayings
about life not working that way. Now,
in the silence of Sherbrooke Village, John
recalls his father's words from the wedding
afternoon, sitting out back on Doucette's
freshly painted porch, while fiddlers and
dancers from Sydney Mines compete with
a reel from within: "In the old days politicians
knew how far they could push, knew too
there was a line they dare not cross."

Ten miles away in Liscomb
Game Sanctuary the deer
do not know they are safe.
They walk carefully on their
coal black feet, alert to all
things under the stars.
They do not know that the
old dispensation is dead,
so they will not rest in the
still comfort of these crooked
and abandoned fields.

*Stewart Donovan,*Cape Breton Quarry
*(Wreck Cove, CB: Breton,1994).*

# CONTENTS

# LIST OF ILLUSTRATIONS

## Westray Coal Location Map

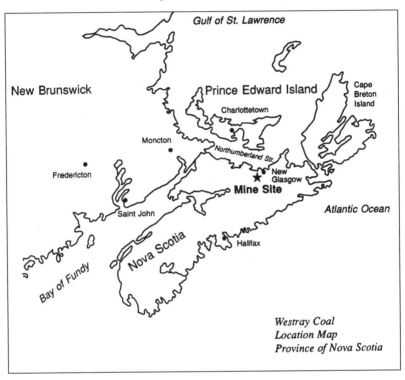

Westray Coal
Location Map
Province of Nova Scotia

8

# ACKNOWLEDGEMENTS

I followed the Westray case from the beginning and was initially dismayed at how the media "got it wrong." The initial coverage was about how the disaster was a tragedy for the families; of course even though it was, I knew that this couldn't be the complete story. I knew that it was too simple to call it an accident, and even though I didn't know then that it was preventable and predictable, I certainly had that feeling. It took me a while to work through this idea, and the media eventually did as well. In 1993, when Shaun Comish's book *The Westray Tragedy* came out, I bought it right away and read it in an afternoon sitting outside in my backyard in the sun. It was a chilling read, and in fact I couldn't bear to read the section containing the biographical information about the dead miners. It was just too much. And, even now, reading some of the accounts in the Inquiry transcript and some of the media interviews of the miners' families still overwhelms me. That's okay—it should. But the emotions I have come to feel in working through this book that you're holding include concern that all the pieces of the Westray story be pulled together and anger that this happened in the first place.

I would like to acknowledge Fernwood Books, first for publishing Shaun's book, but also, of course, for their enthusiasm in this project. They have been most patient during the completion of this book. I proposed the idea in the summer of 1996, I think, and Errol was keen on getting it published as soon as possible. Various life events intruded, including a move from Nova Scotia to teach at St. Thomas University in New Brunswick in the fall of 1997. We rationalized the inevitable delay as giving us time to include the results of the Public Mine Inquiry, the results of the criminal trial, and so on. Well, now everything is done, and it's time to get the book out the door.

I would especially like to thank the contributors for writing chapters for the book and, in some cases, for giving me permission to adapt pieces already written by them for inclusion. I have taken great license to edit their work to make the overall book as smooth and informative as possible while at the same time trying to preserve their different voices. They have been patient regarding the amount of time it has taken to finish this project, and I have been impressed with their persistent encouragements that this important story be told. I hope they like the result. Most importantly, I appreciate how the authors in this collection have tried to honour my request that we tell this story in a way most likely to reach out to the "ordinary reader."

In that vein, I would like to thank the Province of Nova Scotia for giving permission in the Public Inquiry Report to reproduce parts of the same. Excerpts used here have helped clarify and illustrate some important issues.

I would like to thank Stewart Donovan and Breton Books for permission to reproduce "Liscomb Sanctuary" in the frontspiece of this book. I think it is a fitting tribute to the miners and their communities. I would also like to thank Anita Saunders for her help in re-formatting some of the material used in this book, my students for their interest in the story, and all members of my family for their encouragement.

# CONTRIBUTORS

**Shaun and Shirley Comish** have three children and live in Dartmouth, NS. Shaun was a former miner and draegerman at the Westray mine and is author of *The Westray Tragedy* (Halifax: Fernwood, 1993).

**Susan Dodd** is a doctoral candidate in the sociology program at York University in Toronto, Ontario. She is a teaching fellow in the foundation year programme at the University of King's College, Halifax, Nova Scotia.

**Harry Glasbeek** is a professor of law at Osgoode Hall at York University in Toronto, Ontario.

**Sherman Hinze** is a former student of Saint Mary's University, where he completed an honours degree in sociology. He works for the military police.

**Timothy Hynes** is a professor in the department of business administration at St. Francis Xavier University in Antigonish, Nova Scotia.

**Dean Jobb** is a staff reporter at the Halifax *Chronicle-Herald* and an instructor at the King's College School of Journalism in Halifax, Nova Scotia. He is author of *Calculated Risk: Greed, Politics and the Westray Tragedy* (Halifax: Nimbus, 1994).

**Chris McCormick** is an assistant professor in the criminology program at St. Thomas University in Fredericton, New Brunswick, and the author of *Constructing Danger: The Mis/representation of Crime in the News* (Halifax: Fernwood, 1995) and *Criminology in Canada* (Toronto: ITP Nelson, 1999).

**John McMullan** is a professor in the sociology department at Saint Mary's University in Halifax, Nova Scotia. He is the author of *Beyond the Limits of the Law: Corporate Crime, Law and Order* (Halifax: Fernwood, 1992).

**Pushkala Prasad** is a professor in the faculty of management at the University of Calgary, Alberta.

**Trudie Richards** is an assistant professor of public relations at Mount Saint Vincent University in Halifax, Nova Scotia.

**Eric Tucker** is a professor of law at Osgoode Hall at York University in Toronto, Ontario.

**Patrick Whiteway** is director of the Nickel Development Institute, former editor of the *Canadian Mining Journal;* and a former reporter with the *Northern Miner*.

**Gerald J.S. Wilde** is a professor of psychology at Queen's University in Kingston, Ontario.

## CHAPTER ONE

# PREFACE TO DISASTER

*Chris McCormick*

## EXPLOSION!

At 5:20 in the morning on May 9, 1992, a miner working in the Southwest section of the Westray mine was using a continuous miner to cut coal. As he cut into the coalface, the picks on the cutting head struck some pyrite embedded there, causing a shower of sparks. He had seen the sparks before, but this time they ignited some methane gas seeping from the coal seam. He jumped

**Editorial Cartoon. Definition of Westray**

into a wolf (O.E. *werewulf*)

**west** (west) *adv.* at, in, or towards the quarter opposite the east, or where the sun sets at the equinox *n.* that one of the four cardinal points exactly opposite the east; the region or part of a country lying opposite to the east

**west·ing** (westin) *n. (naut.)* a sailing towards the west; a distance thus sailed

**west·ray** (westrei) **1.** *n.* a colossal fiasco; an absurd and complete failure, i.e. mine, trial, inquiry, etc.; successlessness, botchery, a painful or embarrassing debacle, *the Minister of Justice pulled a westray* **2.** *v.t.* to bungle (a piece of work), to fail miserably, *the crown attorney westrayed badly* **3.** *adj.* to become feeble, useless; having no force or effectiveness; lame, *he appears to be a rather westray judge*

**wet** (wet) *adj.* imbued with, covered with or soaked in water or some other liquid; characterized by much rain, *a wet climate;* (of paint,ink, etc.) not yet dried; (of a baby) having urinated in his diaper; permitting or favoring the sale of alcoholic liquors, *a wet state* (O.E. *woet*)

**wet blanket** a person who discourages fun or conversation by his sour mood

**weth·er** (weðer) *n.* a castrated male sheep (O.E.)

Reprinted with permission of Theo Moudakis of the Halifax Daily News down off the miner, terrified at what he saw as he tried to put on his survival equipment. In moments he was dead.

The resulting ignition from the sparks caused a rolling methane flame which traveled away from the working face down the roadway, consuming all the oxygen in its path and leaving deadly carbon monoxide in its place. The rolling methane fire moved both inbye and outbye the cross-cut and continued towards the roof bolter at the face. The flame quickly increased in intensity, fueled by a boom truck located in the intersection and the draft from an auxiliary fan. The flame then propagated into a methane explosion, generating a terrific shockwave which created pressure and increased the air turbulence, causing dust particles to become airborne and resulting in a full-blown coal-dust explosion. Some of the miners in the North mains and the Southwest sections probably heard the explosion and turned around to see the fire coming towards them, covering their eyes if they could get their arms up before the pressure hit their chests and threw them against the walls where they fell, laid low forever; but most of the miners probably died instantly of severe bodily injuries caused by the crushing physical force exerted by the shockwave.

This explosion then moved rapidly through the entire mine, causing death and devastation in a matter of a few seconds. Those miners not crushed in the shockwave were overcome and died almost immediately of carbon monoxide poisoning as the intense methane fire consumed all oxygen.

The rescue teams who went into the mine in the days following the explosion had to wear personal life-support equipment. Any hope they had of finding their comrades alive was gone as they surveyed the terrifying conditions. The force of the explosion had resulted in severe instability within the roof and walls of the mine. Rock was falling from the roof as they worked their way deeper into the mine. The devastation was rampant, as were signs of impending danger. Roof supports had fallen. Heavy steel doors had been blown open. Equipment lay twisted in the roadways. The poisonous air was unbreathable. The ground surrounding the mine openings was grinding and cracking.

No one was found alive.

## REPRISE

The above reconstruction of what might have happened during the Westray explosion is paraphrased from the evidence offered in the *Report of the Westray Mine Public Inquiry* (Nova Scotia, 1997). We will never be completely certain, however, about what caused the death of the 26 miners in the early morning of May 9, 1992.

The Pictou coalfield has been mined for about 200 years, and at the time of the explosion in 1992, Westray was the only operating underground mine (Ryan, 1992). Coal was first discovered in Stellarton about 1798, and the first commercial mine was opened in 1807. The nature of its coalfield with its thick and gassy seams is well-known, and despite covering an area of only about 100 square kilometres it has been a rich source of coal. Coal mining is a labour intensive industry, more so in the past, and communities built up around servicing the many aspects of this primary industry. There are about 25 seams of coal in the Stellarton coalfield, with varying degrees of quality of coal. The Foord seam itself, which Westray was mining, has hosted at least eight mines, including the Storr, the Bye, the Dalhousie, the Foster, the Foord mines, and the Allan. The Allan mine was the most productive mine in the Foord seam and lay just northwest of Westray's workings; during the time it was open it experienced eight methane explosions.

Methane is a natural gas which seeps from the coal and it can spontaneously combust when mixed with oxygen, so fires are a constant threat. With modern technology the concentration of methane in the air can be easily measured and the mine's ventilation system used to disperse the gas. When a methane explosion occurs, however, specially-trained mine rescuers go into these environments to retrieve workers and to attempt to stabilize conditions. Because of the equipment they wear, they are called "draegermen."

> The MacGregor Explosion, 1952
> They found the men strewn around the area. They were partly buried under falls with their feet sticking out, lying across each other or blown some distance away. Their clothes were burned off them; flesh was hanging in rags; blood was coming from their ears and eyes. Some were burned beyond recognition. Steeling themselves, the rescue men went over every body, but there was no life. It was heart-wrenching. They knew every one of the 19 dead.
> (Ryan, 1992: 103)

There have been many fires and explosions in the coal mines over the years with resultant injuries and loss of life. It is estimated that 576 deaths occurred between 1866–1972 and that 625–650 have died from "colliery misadventure" (Cameron, 1974). For example, in the Drummond mine, which is located in the rich Albion seam, sixty lives were lost due to a methane explosion in 1873. In the Foord seam, the Storr mine was racked by fire and explosions in the brief period it was open between 1827–1839. An explosion in the Bye mine (1839–1867) took three lives in 1861, and it had to be abandoned shortly thereafter. The Dalhousie, Foster and Foord mines were sunk between 1850–1869 and were all eventually closed because of explosions due to methane. The Foord "pit," which operated between 1866–1897, exploded several times in 1880, taking a total of fifty lives. Some of these bodies weren't recovered until the 1920s and then later in 1941 when workings were expanded for the Allan mine. The Allan, which was active between 1904–1951, recorded two deaths in 1914, eight-eight in 1918, four in 1924, and seven in 1938.

**Table 1.1. Recorded Coal-Mining Explosion Fatalities,
Pictou County, 1938–1952**

| Year | Mine | Number Killed | |
|------|------|---------------|---|
| 1838 | [Storr] | 2 | |
| 1858 | | 2 | |
| 1861 | [Bye] | 3 | |
| 1872 | Drummond | 60 | closed in 1984 |
| 1880 | Foord | 44 | bodies recovered in 1920s |
| 1885 | Thorburn's Vale | 13 | |
| 1914 | Allan | 2 | opened in 1904 |
| 1918 | Allan | 88 | |
| 1924 | Allan | 4 | closed in 1951 |
| 1952 | Albion Macgregor | 19 | |

Source: Cameron, 1974: 163–253.

## 1987 TO 1991

Various companies had been interested in developing Westray, but it was Curragh Resources which developed the project in November 1987. Westray was the only operating underground coal mine in Pictou County by 1992, and it was probably knowledge of the underground conditions which made other companies reluctant to develop a mine there.

In September 1988, Westray bought out the remaining coal interests in Pictou County that it needed, and signed an agreement with Nova Scotia Power Corporation, which agreed to purchase Westray coal for its generating stations in Trenton. Donald Cameron, provincial minister of industry, trade, and technology at the time and later the provincial premier, committed the province to a mining lease, a loan of $12 million, and a take-or-pay agreement for 275,000 tonnes of coal per year for fifteen years. The cabinet did not approve the take-or-pay agreement until two years later.

In seeking government funding and in preparing development and operating plans, Curragh relied on feasibility and planning studies, some of which were quite preliminary. However, the Department of Natural Resources had approved Curragh's application for the mining lease. The proposed mine was controversial from the beginning but was strongly supported by the provincial government. The combination of Chief Executive Officer Clifford Frame, who

**Figure 1.1. Westray Coal Local Infrastructure**

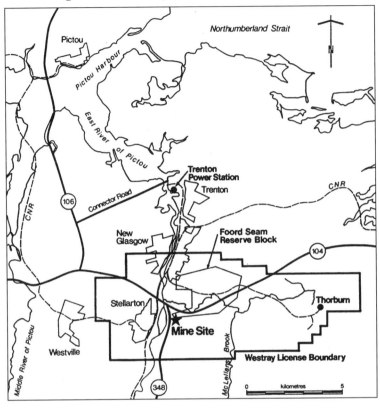

was "uncompromising and abusive," and the "strong and single-minded political backing" of Donald Cameron helped Westray receive tremendous financial support from the public sector with minimal equity investment by the company. Donald Cameron was very much an advocate of the mine and was very influential. In addition to the $12 million provincial loan and the take-or-pay agreement with the province, Curragh secured a federal loan guarantee of approximately $85 million, a direct contribution against interest, and an $8 million interim loan.

In 1989, Curragh's subcontractor, Canadian Mining Development, began driving the main access slopes. In January, the Department of Natural Resources discovered that the tunnel alignment had been changed from the original layout without consultation or approval. Meanwhile, several provincial government departments were engaged in continuing negotiations with Curragh, including the Department of Labour which was concerned about training and certification, equipment approvals, plans for emergencies, and delays in setting up a workplace safety committee. The Department of Natural

**Figure 1.2. Westray Coal Site Plan**

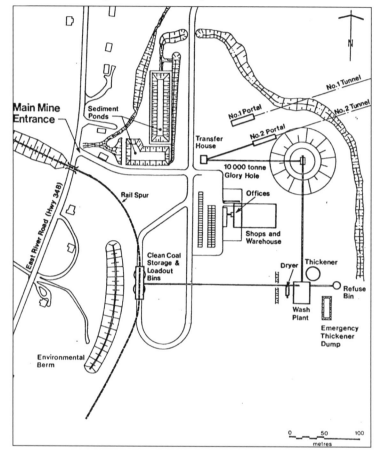

Resources was also concerned that the new tunnel alignment would intersect major geological faults and result in extensive tunnel development through bad ground.

In July 1989, funding for the project was still not finalized and development was suspended. Construction did not resume fully until fall 1990, when the federal government guaranteed financing for the project, less than a year before the mine was supposed to begin shipping coal to the new Trenton power plant.

Roof conditions emerged as a major problem in 1991. Westray took over development in early April 1991, and began using continuous mining machines. The decision to change the original layout of the mine was made so that Westray could tap into the coal seam sooner. The mine thus developed into two distinct sections, the Southwest and the North mains, each with its own crews and supervisors. In the push to reach production sooner, workers without adequate coal mining experience were put into supervisory positions, but were not trained by Westray in safe work methods or in recognizing dangerous roof conditions. Basic safety measures, such as stonedusting, which renders the accumulations of coal dust on the floor non-explosive, were ignored. As the testimony of the miners at the Inquiry showed, if it was carried out at all, it was by volunteers on overtime following their twelve-hour shifts or before a scheduled visit by a mine inspector. For example, at the official opening of the mine on September 11, the mine was "spruced up" and stonedusted.

The new mine was plagued by roof falls from August to October of 1991. Gerald Phillips, the mine manager, minimized the seriousness of the problem and claimed that the falls were controlled, posing little threat to the miners or to production. After the explosion he blamed the miners for the explosion. At the time, however, accounts by the miners revealed near misses and increasing danger. There were approximately 160 employees at the site by October, a large majority of them working shifts underground. Management trivialized the concerns of workers and some quit their jobs. In addition, although the mine inspectors asked the company for roof support plans, as well as stonedusting plans, it repeatedly deferred supplying them. It must be said, however, that the inspectors appeared less than vigilant in enforcing the regulations. Westray is a stark example of an operation where production demands resulted in the violation of the basic and fundamental tenets of safe mining practice.

The new Southwest section was plagued with roof problems, and the level of production and quality of the coal were below expectations. Production remained behind schedule, and the company was not able to meet its commitments to supply coal. In late March 1992, the miners were literally chased out of the Southwest 1 section by rapidly deteriorating ground conditions. In its determination to save equipment, the company put employees at extreme risk during the abandonment.

At 5:20 in the morning on May 9, 1992, the mine exploded.

## A POLITICAL ECONOMY OF CORPORATE CRIME

The events at Westray are an example of corporate crime from the point of view of critical criminology (Taylor et al., 1975; MacLean, 1996; O'Reilly-Fleming, 1996). This approach can contribute to our understanding of Westray by looking at the power relations involved, such as those between owners and workers. These power relations are both material and discursive, and various chapters in this book explore aspects of these relations. In a risk society, risk is seen as pervasive, something to be calculated and regulated. Moreover, risk is someone's responsibility, and to manage uncertainty someone has to bear blame when disaster strikes; yet blaming is relative to the power that can be brought to bear.

Webmark
The NS government's response to the
recommendations of the Westray Mine
Public Inquiry can be found at:
http://www.gov.ns.ca/labr/govupdt.htm

Corporate crime is rooted in the nature of capitalism and can be briefly defined as "the offenses committed by corporate officials for the corporation and the offenses of the corporation itself" (Clinard et al., 1973: 188). There are several main forms of corporate crime, with different victims, as shown in Table 1.2. (Goff et al., 1986). The victims include the state, the public, the environment, the business competitors, or the worker. While some of these categories might overlap (for example, the worker as consumer who also buys the company's products) in general they are mutually exclusive. More importantly for this essay, the worker is subject to particular violence that would not necessarily be suffered by the consumer. While the consumer might be a victim of unsafe products, products that burn or explode, workers are subject to unsafe working conditions, even conditions that might leave them maimed or dead.

A recent example of an environmental crime committed by a corporation is the leaking of methyl isocyanate from a Union Carbide plant in Bhopal, India, on December 3, 1984, which killed tens of thousands of people (Mokhiber, 1988).[1] Another example of corporate crime is the grounding of the tanker Exxon *Valdez* on a reef off the coast of Alaska on March 24, 1989, which dumped 11 million gallons of crude oil and fouled seven hundred miles of shoreline. On March 13, 1991, Exxon agreed to pay $1 billion in criminal and civil fines rather than face trial; this is the largest amount paid as a result of environmental pollution to date.[2] However, when the spill first occurred, the US government announced that it would not pursue charges because it could not afford to; Exxon was then the largest multinational in the world with an annual budget exceeding that of most countries. A former chairman of the company issued a news release immediately after the disaster, claiming that the person responsible was the captain. However when the chairman was testifying before a congressional sub-committee years later, he admitted that he had no factual basis upon which to make that allegation. The captain was, in fact, acquitted of the charge of operating the tanker while drunk. Furthermore, Exxon was operating under lax or inadequate regulation in a very dangerous and fragile environmental area.[3]

## Table 1.2. A Typology of Corporate Crime

| Victim | Crime |
|---|---|
| Consumer | false advertising, harmful products, price gouging, abuse of credit information |
| Environment | pollution, resource mismanagement, destruction of way of life |
| Worker | unsafe working conditions, pension fund abuse, failure to pay legal wages |
| Competitors | price-fixing, illegal takeovers, industrial espionage, influence peddling |
| State | fraudulent billing, tax evasion, bribing of politicians, illegal exporting of products |

Source: McCormick, 1999: 381

Some examples from the mining industry also illustrate how difficult it is to determine whether a "crime" has been committed. At the Canadian-owned Los Frailes mine in Spain, five billion litres of toxic mine waste spilled through a break in a mine tailings pond in April 1998.[4] The parent company, Boliden Limited, announced that it would clean up the waste that subsequently contaminated thousands of hectares of farming land. Environmentalists accused the company of failing to properly maintain the reservoir and of firing an engineer who had predicted the disaster. In 1996, the Canadian-owned Omai gold mine in Georgetown, Guyana, was the site of a massive cyanide spill from a tailings pond;[5] and in 1996, the Canadian company Placer Dome was implicated in an environmental disaster at the Marcopper mine in the Phillipines.[6] In the Omai case, a company called Golden Star, of the Denver Gold Group, had a 30 percent interest in the mine, developed by a Canadian, Robert Friedland, who had himself been sued by the US government for a massive environmental spill of cyanide at the Summitville gold mine in Colorado. When the US government tried to freeze his Canadian assets in order to pay for the cleanup, they were defeated in court.[7] As a sidebar to this story, the initial interest in covering it in the media was occasioned, not by the environmental and corporate details, but by the fact that details of the case were banned from publication.

These cases raise questions as to how regulations can be developed to adequately safeguard the environment (McMullan, 1992), especially since there are reasons to think that disasters are more likely to occur in poorer countries that are heavily dependent on resource extraction. Given the profit incentive to cut regulatory corners, corporate crime is both predictable and inevitable. If that isn't chilling enough, the tendency to blame workers individualizes the problem, shifting blame away from the company. Any political economy of corporate crime should include an analysis of the discourse of responsibility and blame.

As Table 1.3 illustrates, the costs of corporate crime are extensive, ranging from injuries sustained on the job to workplace exposure to environmental pollutants. Not only can a person be exposed to risk at work, but the likelihood of injury on the job is far greater than that of being a victim of crime in the streets. In 1981, for example, the rate of corporate assaults (defined as occupational injuries and illnesses) was twenty-eight times higher than that of criminal code assaults. The rate of corporate deaths was four times higher than the rate of criminal code deaths. For the same year, there were about 1.2 million deaths and injuries caused by corporations in Canada, and approximately a hundred thousand criminal code violent crimes (including murder, manslaughter, infanticide, and assaults) (Ellis, 1987). The majority of these "accidents" are thought to be caused by the negligence of employers (Snider, 1993).

The overall cost of corporate crime is high in monetary terms and in terms of human safety and dignity. Corporate crime is quite varied and can involve damage to property, injury, or loss of human life. Violations of safety standards in the workplace, pollution of the environment by companies unable or unwilling to properly treat waste, and industrial accidents due to negligence can all be classified as corporate violence. It is estimated that in the US corporate crime results in 20 million serious injuries annually, including 110,000 people who become permanently disabled; and 30,000 deaths, ranging from such environmental catastrophes as the collapse of a dam to the long-term development of diseases resulting from industrial pollution (Schrager et al., 1978; Geis, 1984). The total amount of street crime in the US is less than 5 percent of the total yield for corporate crime. The public is gradually beginning to recognize the seriousness of corporate crime, but the media has not done a good job of sensitizing the public to the issues (Clow, 1993).

The cost of corporate crime is high in terms of its prosecution as well. In a report of the Public Prosecution Service Special Prosecutions Unit (Westray), dated March 24, 1998, and obtained under the Freedom of Information Act, it was estimated that to continue with the prosecution of Westray officials on criminal charges would cost in the vicinity of $10 million. While the counsel preparing the report stopped short of saying that the cost was the largest factor in not continuing with the prosecution, they did say that they had no consensus on the likelihood of a conviction and that, if there was one, a community sentence would probably be imposed. Furthermore, they pointed out that the Crown's investigation itself would be open to criticism and that in the overall balance it would probably not be in the public's interest to proceed further.

A final point must be mentioned with regard to the Westray case. The workers were particularly susceptible to being victimized in the workplace. During the 1980s, before the development of the Westray mine, the county's population had declined; average unemployment had almost doubled; and income was about 94 percent of the provincial average. While employment in manufacturing as a percentage of all employment had decreased from 32 percent to 23 percent, service sector jobs had increased. In a county with economic conditions such as this, the prospect of long-term, highly paid employment would have been quite attractive.

### Table 1.3. The Cost of Corporate Crime

10,000 Canadians died from injuries received on the job between 1972 and 1981

Canada has about 500 homicide victims per year, but about 15,000 die from corporate in/action

Failure to remit payroll deductions costs more than bank robbery, extortion and kidnapping

Occupational deaths are the third leading cause of death after heart disease and cancer

Hundreds of thousands of workers are exposed to radioactive and chemical pollutants every year

In 1993 the Canadian Union of Public Employees estimated that 61% of workers were victimized by violence in the previous two years; 43% said that no action was taken after a violent incident

The Canadian Labour Congress (1993) reports that deaths from workplace disease are largely uncompensated

Of those killed in fatal workplace accidents, 97% are men and 3% are women

Women are at risk of reproductive health hazards due to exposure to toxic substances during pregnancy

Source: McCormick 1999: 378

Since Westray, things have not improved. In 1996, the population of Stellarton dropped by over 5 percent, while it increased in Nova Scotia overall. Unemployment in the town is now almost 17 percent, while the provincial average is slightly over 13 percent; the personal participation rate in the economy is 53 percent, while it is over 60 percent provincewide. Average income has dropped to below 87 percent of that in the rest of Nova Scotia, and employment in manufacturing has dropped to below 22 percent. A higher percentage of the population has high school or less than that of Nova Scotia overall, and fewer people have a trades certificate (38 percent as compared to 46 percent) or university education (9 percent as compared to 16 percent). The socioeconomic conditions that made Westray attractive have gotten worse (Statistics Canada, 1996).

## LOCATING BLAME IN THE MEDIA

The coverage of the Westray disaster was massive (McCormick, 1995). In the first week of a two-year period, 14 percent of the total stories on Westray were published. In the first month of that same period, 36 percent of all Westray-related articles were written. The media coverage became the story; with the lack of other news, reporters interviewed reporters and regular mention was made of how many media were represented in Plymouth. The massive media coverage provided details of the explosion, the attempt to rescue the miners, and the suffering of the families. However, much of the initial reporting was not critical nor especially informative; it was emotional and contained phrases such as "the price of coal has been measured in human lives." Excerpts from an editorial from the *Chronicle-Herald* of May 11, 1992, entitled "Tragedy at Westray," are not only full of sentimental phrases but unfortunately come across as an apologetic for the disaster:

> Underground coal mining in Nova Scotia ... has long been a story of *great human courage* pitted against *great natural hazards* ... too often, it has also been a history of hope and fortitude and *heartbreak* in the face of unbearable tragedies. So it was again in Plymouth, Pictou County, this weekend, when a methane bump early Saturday buried 26 miners underground. The scene was the Westray mine ... sunk last year into one of [the] most *treacherous* troves of coal.... The dimension of the tragedy ... was *truly heart rending* ... shifts of draegermen continued to work *tirelessly* to reach the 15 others still trapped underground ... all of Nova Scotia is now waiting and pray-ing ... we share the pain and grief of the families and friends of the men who have perished.... [This] is a terrible reminder of the *enormous sacrifice* made by generation after generation of *brave men* to mine Nova Scotia's deep coal seams.... [This is] *an awesome testament* to the *courage* of those who go down to the deeps. It's a reminder, too, that advanced technology ... hasn't changed the equation. It is still *brave men* toiling in the face of *unseen danger* in the dark. The risks are still there; the men still go knowingly to meet them. And our hearts still mourn when the danger claims these finest of men[8]. (emphasis added)

The sympathetic sentiment behind this editorial is admirable, but in the eulogy it misrepresents the danger—brave men courageously working under-ground, knowing the risks, sacrificing themselves to mine the coal which can turn on them capriciously despite the best of technology. In this depiction we do not get a sense that people most often work out of necessity rather than courageous decision, that occupational safety standards might not be fol-lowed, or that workers often have no choice about working in unsafe conditions. Furthermore, there is no analysis of the politics involved in establishing Westray nor acknowledgment that it was not run perfectly.

The image that readers get from such a depiction is individualistic and romantic—courageous men working on the frontier, pitted against capricious nature—and it provides no way to understand the disaster as anything other than an accident. This explosion was about as accidental as the grounding of the Exxon *Valdez* or the release of gas from the Union Carbide plant in Bhopal, India.

In an editorial appearing after the explosion, this idea that miners live to die underground is called the "Big Lie" (Hambling, 1992). The author writes that the "Big Lie" is that Maritimers are a hardy bunch who will endure hardship and never complain, and furthermore that we collectively give tacit approval to such a myth because it prevents us from having to deal with the problem. He says:

> It is a fact that coal mining is in the blood in parts of Nova Scotia. You can see it on the streets every day. You can see it in the faces and on the hands and arms of every miner. You can see it in their cuts and bangs and gashes that fill with coal dust as they heal and leave their telltale tattoos of bone-crushing and mind-numbing labour. It is in the blood, trying to push its way through lungs forever clogged with dust and damp. That's how mining is in the blood. (Hambling, 1992: 2)

Misconceptions are common, however, as exhibited in an article written by an academic expert who was a provincial deputy minister of development. He said that coal mining is engrained in the culture of Nova Scotia:

> There's always that thing in the back of every Nova Scotian's mind—I think they grew up with it in their mother's milk—that coal once paid for everything and maybe someday it'll do it again.... When people die in an accident like this, it just reinforces that this is the price we've got to pay and just keep pluggin' on.[9]

In another article, an academic expert attributed the acceptance of the disaster to fatalism:

> We really are a region of the country where there are horrendous disasters, whether it's people lost at sea or in a mine. You just accept it because it's there. That may be the reason we accept coal mining, because it's just part of the culture.... Yeah, coal mines are dangerous. You could lose your life doing it. But you could lose your life fishing, too. We just accept it.[10]

These explanations romanticize occupational hazards as a way of life, justifying them in the process, offering no critical insight into why the tragedy occurred and how it might have been prevented.

During 1992–93, about 700 articles were indexed under "Westray—disaster" for the Halifax *Chronicle-Herald;* they include editorials, commentaries and letters to the editor. As mentioned above, the first 50 citations were published within two days of the disaster, and during the first month, 250 articles were published. During the first week the promise to establish an inquiry was announced. The number of citations published per day quickly dropped to an average of seven at the end of the first month. Throughout June, the month following the explosion, the coverage increased slightly due to the discussion over whether or not to flood the mine. By the time safety charges were laid in October, the number of citations had dropped to an average of about one and a half per day. The Inquiry was quashed in November, and in April criminal charges were finally laid by the RCMP.

**Figure 1.3. Media Coverage of Westray by Theme**

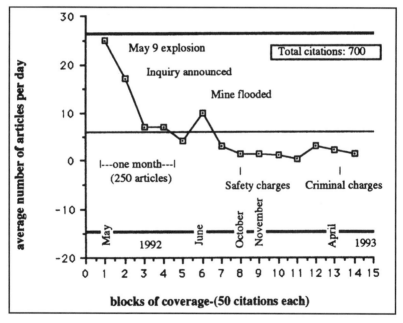

The consequence of intensive early coverage, when little was known about the tragedy, and a subsequent drop in coverage was that the amount of information published declined as the legal and criminal issues came to the fore. This means that initially, when the topic was "the Westray disaster," the coverage of human suffering and tragedy was massive and overwhelming. When the topic shifted from the human angle to the legal angle and became "the Westray case," the coverage was minimal by comparison. There are, of course, several possible reasons for this: after saturation coverage, interest in the case declined; reporters lacked the ability to understand and communicate the legal technicalities; or new topics captured public attention and the Westray story's shelf life expired. Whatever the explanations, none suffice. The consequence in terms of the textual construction of the disaster is that readers were exposed to information on tragedy but not to information which would increase their understanding of the legal, criminal, economic, and political issues involved in the case. Reporting that emphasizes the emotional side of the disaster instead of the crime and ignores or mystifies the conditions that led to the explosion in the first place, making it likely in the long run that these conditions will be reproduced. (Few and far between were the examples of media coverage that I think went a long way toward deconstructing and demystifying the disaster: Cameron et al., 1994; Starr, 1993; Campbell et al., 1993; Frank, 1994).

The tendency of reporters to cover similar stories in the same way is called convergence or "pack journalism" (Ericson et al., 1987) and has often been used to describe how different news media converge in their news content. Pack journalism results in part from the reporter's need to maximize resources and his or her reliance on the work of others to gain a sense of the newsworthiness of stories. The ideological consequence of pack journalism is a uniform, homogeneous, lowest-common-denominator type of coverage, in which orthodoxy rules. Instead of a heterodoxy of opinion, readers are exposed to a uniform world view.

The convergence in the news about Westray meant that, rather than being critical, the media seemed overwhelmed by the disaster. They struggled to put it into context but seemed unsure about the technology and terminology of mining. An estimated two hundred journalists descended on Plymouth with all of the modern communications technology at their disposal. However, they were quickly separated from the families and told that the latter did not wish to speak to them. Instead of seeing this as information control, the media focused on the rescue effort and the explosion. It was patronizing to say that "all most viewers really needed or wanted was to know whether [the miners] had survived."[11] However, despite an overwhelming presence, the media missed the story about pre-existing safety concerns at the mine. If we counterpoise the media version of why the disaster happened with that found in the testimony of miners at the Inquiry (as shown in the following quotations), we see how the extreme danger had become routine.

**Inquiry Testimony: Mr. Bonner, Day 24, Jan 24, 1996: 4762-64**[12]
Q. Did it surprise you that more people didn't refuse work in that mine?

A. It didn't really surprise me, no.

Q. Why not?

A. Well, for the simple reason that I was under the impression that if you complained too much, you were in hot water with the company, so to speak, so your job was at stake. And things went much smoother if you just kept your mouth shut and went along with the game plan, right?

And besides, management's attitude towards things like that, like if you would have something that you wanted to discuss, you would be talked to like "Well, do you have a problem with that? Maybe you'd like to pack your fucking lunch can." And this is how you would be responded to if you had a legitimate safety concern. If you went to Roger Parry, that's how you would be talked back to.

Q. I understand at one point you quit your job at Westray?

A. Yes, I did.

Q. And what brought about you deciding to quit your job?

A. The gas, the dust, management's lax attitude toward safety, the roof falls. Generally everything.

Q. Was there a particular straw that broke the camel's back?

A. Yes, there was a particular straw that broke the camel's back.

Q.. And what was it?

A. I was working in the North Mains, and I had been talking to Shaun Comish. I was in an intersection and a small rock had fallen from the roof and hit him in the hard hat. And I looked up and.... And as I observed the roof, like, I watched a dywidag bend and it turned white on the corner, like, where it was bent. And when it stretched more, it turned white. So I figured, you know, there's substantial movement going on there for me to see it move instead of taking place over a short period of—over a long period of time, rather. So I brought this to the attention of Glyn Jones, and he told me that it was nothing to worry about and shuffed it off.

So later the next day I had come in and this particular intersection had been caved in. So the

> way things were going, I kind of got fed up. I threw my water bottle against the rib, grabbed my lunch can and I started walking out of the mine.
> Q. Did that area cave in?
> A. Yes, that area was caved in that I had raised concern about.
> [Inquiry testimony conducted by Ms. Campbell, Solicitor for the Commission]

Safety regulations were not observed or were flagrantly violated, and miners were often ordered to work in unsafe conditions and were verbally abused when they protested. Day after day the danger became almost banal, as the workers anticipated they could be killed at any time. Miners even told their relatives that if there was an explosion to make sure that somebody got to the bottom of what happened.

The fact that Curragh was going to operate Westray was certainly no secret. Safety had been a concern at its Yukon mine, and the political manoeuvering to establish the mine at Plymouth had received media attention. Investment in mining is a risky business and companies are going to go where the red tape is minimal.[13]

> **Inquiry Testimony, Mr. Bonner, Day 24, Jan 24, 1996: 4772–73**
> Q. So you're both in the bucket now and you're chock blocking?
> A. Yes.
> Q. And there's nobody operating the scoop?
> A. No.
> Q. Okay.
> A. And then some lights come up. It was Roger Parry, Gerald Phillips and Arnie Smith. And I was up in the arches and Gerald Phillips said, "What's this then, a bunch of dog fuckers."
> Q. Who said that?
> A. Roger Parry [sic]. And I got quite upset because I was working quite hard and I was sweating. And, like I said, we had no operator. We shouldn't even have been up in the bucket. And for him to call me a "dog fucker," I wasn't going to stand for that. And —
> Q. Well, what did he mean when he called you that name?
> A. That we were doing nothing, we were just basi-

cally sitting there idle, doing nothing.
Q. Now who else is with Mr. Parry when he's
saying this to you?
A. Gerald Phillips.
Q. Is there anybody else there?
A. And my fire boss, Arnie Smith.
Q. So he makes that comment to you?
A. Yes, and I jumped down out of the arches and I
made a few comments to him. I threw my gloves
off and I told him for a nickel that I would gut him.
Q. For a nickel you would what?
A. I would gut him.
Q. Uh-huh. And how did Mr. Parry react to that?
A. He got quite upset.
[Inquiry testimony conducted by Ms. Campbell,
Solicitor for the Commission]

In general, the risk of being killed at work is higher than that of being murdered. The risk is greatest in the primary industries of forestry and mining. The occupational fatality rate around mines, quarries and oil wells is the second highest in Canada at 83.6 deaths per 100,000 people, surpassed only by the rate for work in forestry (Law Reform Commission, 1986). Between 1989 and 1991, the number of injuries in mining in Canada went down by 25 percent and was down 16 percent in all occupations. In Nova Scotia, however, the number of time-loss injuries in mining went up by 28 percent even though the overall provincial occupational injury rate went down 9 percent. Mining was certainly not getting safer in Nova Scotia. Injuries and fatalities are the highest in the primary occupations and, because these industries are located in certain regions, it can be argued that occupational danger is part of economic inequality in Canada. This danger is part of Maritime history whether on the water, in the woods, or in the mines. The story is all the more shocking because of its familiarity.

**Inquiry Testimony, Mr. Guptill, Day 29, Feb 8, 1996: 6275–78**
Q. Now Mr. Guptill, you stayed in touch with the
men who were on the B crew.
A. Yes, a few weeks before the ... before it happened ... at Roy's [Feltmate's] house.... They called
me up and said they were having a little gathering,
and so I went over and met with them.... It was
breakfast-ish time, nine o'clock, something around
there.

Q. Had the men just finished their ... their last shift in a set of four?

A. Yes, I believe it was. I believe they were off then. And they asked me that if something happened to them if I'd go public.

Q. Who was at this meeting?

A. Roy [Feltmate]; Mike [MacKay]; Randy House; Robbie Doyle.

Q. And what was the discussion leading up to them making that request of you? What were you discussing?

A. Safety at Westray....

Q. Do you recall anything that they told you?

A. There was more and more cave-ins and that it was just turning into a nightmare....

Q. In what terms did they talk about it, Mr. Guptill?

A. That one shift would have the entire shift lost.

Q. Were they talking about them having a 25 percent [chance] of being ... the shift that ... would be involved?

A. I think, from working on that shift, that they knew they had more than that.... They just got to a point that it was useless to talk about it. It depressed them. They didn't want to talk about it.

Q. You say that they made you promise them that you would go public?

A. Uh-huh.... That if they were the ones that were killed, that I would tell the world what was going on there.

Q. Mr. Guptill, the evidence that you've given here today, is it the truth?

A. Yes.

[Inquiry testimony conducted by Ms. Campbell, Solicitor for the Commission]

The Westray disaster is a story about political interference in the way in which grants are given to the mining business. It is also a story of laxity and ineptitude in the provincial department of labour. It certainly is a story about the political economy of death and profit. But it is also a story about how the media contributed to a climate wherein the explosion was able to occur in the first place. The media was part of the story and perhaps part of the crime in the sense that the version of risk it conveyed did not portray the reality of risk lived by the miners.

In the analysis of the "discourse of responsibility" and the attribution of blame, it is important to look at how speech involves four claims to validity: that speech is comprehensible, that there is an intention to communicate something, that it is true, and (meant to be) correct. Any "methodology that systematically neglects the interpretive schemata through which social action is itself mediated … is doomed to failure" (Habermas, 1979).

## THE AFTERMATH

The public commission of Inquiry into the tragedy at the Westray mine was established by order in council of the government of Nova Scotia on May 15, 1992. This was only a week after the initial explosion at the Westray mine in Plymouth took the lives of twenty-six coal miners. In making the announcement, Premier Donald Cameron announced that the Inquiry was to investigate, report upon and make recommendations concerning the explosion. However, it would be three and a half years before the Inquiry finally got under way.

> Webmark
> This website provides information relating to the Inquiry as well as access to the executive summary of the Inquiry's report. www.gov.ns.ca/legi/inquiry/westray/default.htm
>
> The Consolidated Findings in the Inquiry's Executive Report can be found at: http://www.gov.ns.ca/legi/inquiry/westray/findings.htm

In the legislature, the premier said that the commissioner of the Inquiry, Mr. Justice Richard, would have all the powers under the *Public Inquiries Act* and the *Coal Mines Regulation Act* to conduct a full and all-encompassing investigation. He said that it was essential that Nova Scotians know the answers to the questions surrounding and leading up to the explosion:

> Mr. Justice Richard's Inquiry will not be limited to the events of the early morning of May 9th. Nothing and no person with any light to shed on this tragedy will escape the scrutiny of this Inquiry. The answers to the many questions leading to the terrible events of May 9 can only be obtained through an independent, thorough and all-encompassing investigation."[14]

The mandate of this Inquiry was broad, as the accompanying box "Order in Council" shows. Those terms of reference encompassed all aspects of the development, financing, operation, regulation, and supervision of the Westray mine (Province of Nova Scotia, 1997, Vol. 2: 665). The Inquiry was set to start in October 1992 and was expected to be completed within two years; it was subsequently held up by a series of "legal entanglements."

Order in Council
WHEREAS it is deemed appropriate to cause inquiry to be made into and concerning the public matters hereinafter mentioned in relation to which the Legislature of Nova Scotia may make laws;

By and with the advice of the Executive Council of Nova Scotia, His Honour the Lieutenant Governor is pleased to appoint the Honourable K. Peter Richard, a Judge of the Supreme Court of Nova Scotia, to be, during pleasure, a Commissioner under the Public Inquiries Act, and a Special Examiner under the Coal Mines Regulation Act, with power to inquire into, report findings, and make recommendations to the Governor in Council and the people of Nova Scotia respecting:

(a) the occurrence, on Saturday, the 9th day of May, A.D., 1992, which resulted in the loss of life in the Westray Mine at Plymouth, in the County of Pictou;
(b) whether the occurrence was or was not preventable;
(c) whether any neglect caused or contributed to the occurrence;
(d) whether there was any defect in or about the Mine or the modes of working the Mine;
(e) whether the Mine and its operations were in keeping with the known geological structures or formations in the area;
(f) whether there was compliance with applicable statutes, regulations, orders, rules, or directions; and
(g) all other matters related to the establishment and operation of the Mine which the Commissioner considers relevant to the occurrence.

A constitutional challenge by the mining company Curragh; the managers, Phillips and Parry; and a group of Westray supervisory personnel was begun in September 1992 on the grounds that the terms of reference were beyond provincial jurisdiction in that they allowed the Inquiry to investigate criminal responsibility. While this challenge slowly worked its way through the courts, the chief justice of the Nova Scotia Supreme Court ordered a stay of the proceedings. That fall, fifty-two charges were laid against management employees of Westray under the provincial *Coal Mines Regulation Act* and the *Occupational Health and Safety Act*. The Nova Scotia Supreme Court ruled that the provisions of the Inquiry were in fact *ultra vires*, or beyond the jurisdiction of the Inquiry commission in November 1992, but this ruling was overturned by the Nova Scotia Court of Appeal in January 1993. However, because of the potential conflict between the mandate of the Inquiry and the possibility of criminal charges being laid by the RCMP, the Appeal Court ordered a temporary stay of proceedings. In the spring of 1993, more than a year after the explosion, the remaining provincial safety charges were withdrawn and the RCMP announced that they would lay charges.

In June 1993, leave to appeal to the Supreme Court of Canada (SCC) was filed by the Inquiry commissioner and the United Steelworkers of America; this was granted in December of that year. In May 1995, the SCC ruled that the Inquiry could proceed and could be carried out without doing violence to the constitutional rights of the accused in the criminal trial. The only concern expressed was about the problems that could occur if the criminal proceedings and the Inquiry were running at the same time, but in the meantime the terms of the Inquiry were amended to disallow testimony until the criminal trial was concluded.

In addition to that constitutional challenge, the Province of Nova Scotia ordered the Inquiry halted until the criminal case against Gerald Phillips, Roger Parry, and Curragh, then in process, had been completed. However, in the short time that the criminal trial ran between February and June 1995, it was plagued by allegations of non-disclosure on the part of the prosecution. This was quickly resolved with the ruling by Mr. Justice Anderson that the criminal trial be stayed. That order for a judicial stay of proceedings was appealed and had to make its way through the courts before it could be resolved finally.

Webmark
The St. F.X. Westray Collection was donated by Justice K. Peter Richard, Commissioner, Westray Mine Public Inquiry, in January 1998. The collection consists of a complete set of Westray Mine Public Inquiry Hearing transcripts totalling 77 days and Justice Richard's

resource library containing various texts and reference materials acquired by the Commissioner and Commission staff in preparation for the Inquiry's hearings and report writing.
http://iago.stfx.ca/libraries/angus/westray/welcome.htm#transcripts

The Inquiry began on November 6, 1995, and concluded on July 11, 1996, after a total of seventy-six days of testimony. Some Curragh officials, including the chief executive officer, refused to testify. The Inquiry report concluded that the disaster was "a complex mosaic of actions, omissions, mistakes, incompetence, apathy, cynicism, stupidity and neglect."[15]

In 1998, the proceedings were stayed because it did not seem that there was enough evidence to secure a conviction, and in 1999, more than seven years after the explosion, Nova Scotia's justice minister announced that no further legal action would be taken.

## It wasn't my fault

The witness at the Inquiry who is most often mentioned for the way in which he unfairly laid blame is former Nova Scotia Premier Donald Cameron. In his testimony at the Inquiry on May 28–29, 1996, he began with his version of who was to blame for the Westray explosion. His version of events was quite different from that of others, as we will see. There are two dimensions to the story Premier Cameron told: first, he sought to blame the miners working underground for their actions (which were seen by him to have caused the explosion); and second, in his testimony he sought to establish himself as truthful.

**Inquiry Testimony, Mr. Donald Cameron, Day 66, May 28, 1996: 14392ff**
Commissioner: [14392] Some months ago Mr. Cameron ... requested that he be provided with the rather unusual opportunity of making an opening address. After due consideration and consultation with Inquiry counsel, I agreed to permit Mr. Cameron to make an address. And it's not without precedent in public inquiries, but it is rather unusual. In this case, recognizing the pivotal role which ex-Premier Cameron had in the development of the Westray project and also the fact that his involvement has been subject to considerable public speculation since the disaster, I felt these were reasons

enough to give Mr. Cameron that sort of latitude.

Mr. Cameron: [14394] Thank you, Commissioner, for allowing me to make this presentation this morning, and, of course, after which I will answer all questions as long as necessary for this Inquiry.... Well, much has been written and said about this project, so much in my view that the truth has been lost in the story. Someone once said the following, I think it's just a perfect fit the kind of [sic] condition we find, and I'll quote this person:

"For the great enemy of the truth is very often not the lie, deliberate, contrived and dishonest, but the myth which is persistent, persuasive, and unrealistic. We subject all facts to a prefabricated set of interpretations. We enjoy the comfort of opinion without discomfort of thought."

[14399–14421] what I'm saying is true.... In fact ... the fact is ... the lie has been said.... Well, this was simply false, of course ... you shouldn't deal that way with anyone; you should be truthful.... They didn't tell the truth again ... in fact....

[14433] I want to go to the explosion.... [A]n RCMP map ... said there was pyrite in the coal face which is a hard rock that would cause sparking.... They said the continuous miner was in an "on" position ... of all the men operating the equipment, the gentleman on the continuous miner was the first one out....

[14435] Yeah, I did want to just run over it [the public record] again because [Mick Franks] said very clearly that the day before that he saw Arnie Smith change that methane meter on that....

[14436] I also said well, what else has happened there? What else happened in that mine that night? We had testimony from ... Mick Franks and Harvey Martin that was done by the Inquiry, and they were talking about the test buttons and they told us that the test buttons were pushed over and over and over and over again so often that they would blow the breaker switch. And all I'm asking people is that it seems to me that these would be pretty important items of why that explosion took place on that night....

[14437] "My concern is that we dealt with those things, but they're simply lost in this other story that we want to create about this whole project. I mean, if we truly want to find out why this mine blew up, I think this is pretty important evidence. It's vitally important evidence....

[14438] The fact that they would shut the vent tubes off with black plastic.... You know, I don't see why we can just—because we don't like to hear these things, that we can sweep them under the carpet.

[14439] The bottom line, that this is a very, very important issue....

[14440] And the families that have been grieving ... will never find any peace if they don't get to the truth. And that's why I'm so upset that people wouldn't own up to what they were doing. And instead of briefly speaking about it and shoving it under the table. The bottom line is that that mine blew up on that morning because of what was going on in there at that time. That's the bottom line.

[14445] I'm here to answer the questions as best I can, and I'm going to try my best.... I'll do my very best with you.

[14864] So it's easy for people to spread rumours around, but....

[14877] Well, it's not to me to pass judgment. [Inquiry testimony conducted by Mr. Justice Richard, Commissioner of the Inquiry]

In this testimony, the former premier begins by saying that he is going to counter certain myths that have arisen with regard to Westray. He then goes on to lay the blame on the driver of the continuous miner; he accuses several miners of tampering with safety equipment used for measuring methane levels in the mine and of blocking ventilation designed to expel methane before it can concentrate in dangerous amounts. He spoke of truth, evidence, and the bottom line. In trying to establish that what he is saying is the truth, he accuses others of speaking untruthfully or of trying to sweep things under the mat. He then distances himself from the responsibility of laying blame by saying that he is not trying to pass judgment.

What are we to make of this moral drama? In speech, there are certain assumptions that can be made, such as that the speaker is (interested in) telling the truth. During the above testimony the commissioner criticized Cameron for trying to shift the blame to the miners, the least powerful people in this whole play. Cameron tries to gain the moral high ground as the only person interested in getting at the truth, and he uses this perception to undermine the veracity of others who might disagree or try to dissuade him. However, in the oral submissions given on the final day, July 22, 1996, the Westray Families Group criticized Cameron, minister of industry during the opening and early operation of the mine, for failing to distance himself from the daily operation of the mine, for failing to take into account the health and safety of the miners, and for failing to accept any responsibility. However, as we can see, he is unwilling to admit any responsibility. The point is that the accusations and the denials are a significant part of the power relations which allowed the Westray disaster to happen in the first place.

I have suggested that risk is seen as pervasive in modern industrial society, yet at the same time we invest a lot in the assumption that risk can be calculated and regulated. In this schema, risk and its management is some-one's responsibility, perhaps a worker's, or a manager's, or an inspector's. Throughout this book we will consider various explanations for how the disaster happened, where the risks came in, and, ultimately, on whose shoulders the responsibility lies. That is the intention of the work: to show in as complete a manner as possible all factors surrounding what happened at Westray, from the underlying geology and working conditions to the political and legal fallout afterwards. In order to manage uncertainty in a context of risk when something disastrous happens, someone has to be blamed, a process dependent upon assembling "facts" that can convince others of the same conclusion. It is not that responsibility depends only on who can be blamed successfully, but that blaming is relative to the power that can be brought to bear in that process.

## OVERVIEW OF THE CHAPTERS

The layout of the book is meant to roughly correspond to the temporal flow of events, although the next chapter immediately breaks from this intention. In Chapter Two Shaun Comish and his wife Shirley talk about what it was like to live immediately after Westray. As a draegerman, Shaun was one of those who went into the mine in an effort to rescue/recover the miners. His book, *The Westray Tragedy* (1993), was an attempt to deal with that experience. In his contribution to this book he reflects on what it was like to go to the hearings of the Inquiry. Shirley focuses more on the personal consequences of the disaster.

I have grouped Chapters Three through Six together as "Working Condi-tions: Prefiguring Disaster." In this section a number of pre-existing factors that heightened the possibility of the disaster are discussed. In Chapter Three, Patrick Whiteway discusses some of the more technical details involved in coal mining, the technology required, and some of the difficulties encountered. As a geologist and mining engineer, he is well versed in his subject, and he tells it well. His conclusion is, of course, that the proper technology was available and that the disaster could have been avoided. In Chapter Four, Harry Glasbeek and Eric Tucker, both professors at Osgoode Hall Law School, discuss the existence of a political–economic context in which protecting workers from harm is not a major consideration in decisions made by government officials and private investors.

Chapters Five and Six build on this theme by detailing some of the occupational conditions that existed at Westray. Gerald J.S. Wilde, a psychologist at Queen's University, looks at the awareness and acceptance of risk at Westray through the use of transcripts recorded at the Inquiry. The use of the progressive production bonus scheme, in particular, is singled out for exacerbating risk acceptance. Timothy Hynes and Pushkala Prasad outline what they define as a "mock bureaucracy," characterized by the overt violation of safety rules. The collapse of safe mining practices thus becomes an antecedent to disaster.

Chapters Seven through Ten are grouped together under the title "The Aftermath: Dealing with Disaster." In Chapter Seven, Trudie Richards, a public relations professor, looks at the interaction of the mine owner, the media, and the community in the aftermath of the Westray explosion. The company's lack of cooperation with the media and the antagonistic relation that was created with the families made this a public relations crisis. Through an analysis of media coverage and interviews with professionals, she comes to the important conclusion that the event could have been handled better. In Chapter Eight, Dean Jobb, a reporter with the Halifax *Chronicle-Herald*, looks at how the justice system dealt with Westray as a "legal disaster." In his words, the justice system seemed "incapable of getting to the bottom of the disaster." The government, police, prosecutors, and courts struggled, sometimes in competition, to cope with a major disaster. John McMullan and Sherman Hinze, the former a criminology professor and the latter a (then) graduate student, analyze in Chapter Nine how the press drew upon and reproduced an ideology in its portrayal of Westray. Following an extensive analysis of newspaper coverage, they conclude that media failed to depict Westray as corporate crime and thus failed in their role as social watchdog. And in Chapter Ten, "Unsettled Accounts after Westray," Susan Dodd describes her interviews with members of the families as they suffered with tragic loss and attempted to discern which individuals were responsible for the tragedy.

This book is meant to pull together as many different facets of the Westray puzzle as possible. I hope it has succeeded. There is some overlap among the chapters as the authors each recap the event in prefiguring the story they want to tell. I have not tried to impose too heavy an editorial hand on how they want to frame up their stories—they each have a story to tell, and they each need to find their own way of doing so. We do not know as much about corporate crimes as we do about other crimes in Canada, so I hope this intensive case study approach is a contribution to criminological scholarship as well as a readable compilation for the general layperson interested in this very important event in Canadian history.

What we see here is an examination of many voices, some of which have never before been heard in the public discussion of Westray. I hope we become the wiser for hearing them.

Chris McCormick, PhD
Criminology, St. Thomas University
Fredericton, New Brunswick

## CHAPTER TWO

# THE ROAD TO RECOVERY IS LONG

*Shaun and Shirley Comish*

## SHAUN'S STORY[1]

It was a bright, sunny day in August when Lenny Bonner and I drove up to Stellarton to apply at the Westray coal mine. With a promise of fifteen years steady work, right here in Nova Scotia, everything looked good for settling down at home and not having to cross our great country just to stay employed.

Both Lenny and I were happy to get a job there because we had been laid off just three months earlier from the mine in Gays River. That mine was owned by an Australian company which had come into Canada and basically bought up a group of mines across the country. Gays River was a great place to work and you were in control of what went on in your workplace. The biggest problem encountered at Gays River was the water around the body of the mine. We had a few times when it was a bit of a problem but nothing very serious.

In early May we got word that the Gays River Mine was shutting down because the Department of Mines and Energy considered it unsafe. Later we

**Editorial Cartoon. Justice on Hold**

Reprinted with permission of the Halifax Herald Limited

40

would come to realize that perhaps this was, in reality, a well orchestrated plan by the Nova Scotia government and the infamous Mr. Frame.[2] Westray Coal needed miners, and where better to get them than to lay off 125 miners from one mine and then do some recruiting for a new ultra modern coal mine right here in Nova Scotia.

I had always disliked the idea of working in a coal mine, but it was immediate employment and, with jobs being as rare as they were at that time, a man took what he could get. The mining industry, like any other industry, has its highs and lows. In 1991 mining was nearing the lowest point it had seen for quite a few years. I had tried working at a few other jobs, but I was most comfortable when I was underground and working with the mining gear. I always felt good after a nice physical day on the job, knowing that we had advanced that tunnel another two rounds.

**Inquiry Testimony, Mr. Comish, Day 28, Feb 7, 1996: 5840–41**

Q. Were you aware of the necessity to stonedust the coal mine, Mr. Comish?

A. I was aware of it because I was told of it, yeah.

Q. Who told you about it?

A. Just the other miners, Grande Cache guys....

Q. So you learned through them. And what were they telling you? Were they telling you that there wasn't enough stone dust?

A. They were telling me that this place was the shits is what their words. [sic]

Q. And did you believe them?

A. Yeah.

Q. Well —

A. At first I thought maybe, well, they're just a couple of old miners complaining, but you know, it didn't take long to figure it out.

Q. So you figured out that it wasn't such a good place?

A. Yeah.

[Inquiry testimony conducted by Ms. Campbell, Solicitor for the Commission]

I thought that a coal mine couldn't be that much different than a hard rock mine, after all you would be performing basically the same duties. This theory is correct except for the fact that the duties were carried out differently to achieve the same result. We would find this out not too long after starting at Westray. Our first assignment was to work with a crew just inside the portal about 400 feet. We were to erect arches in the main slope to provide extra strength to the main travelway as there had already been numerous cave-ins along the section of the roadway. Before I had started working at Westray, a friend of mine was hired there, and while on his first shift he was taken on a quick tour. On the way back to the surface he and the guys on the tour were told to go out of the mine via number two road because of a cave-in in the number one roadway. My friend asked what was going on, and they told him that sixty to one hundred feet of the main tunnel had caved in. When he arrived on the surface he told the boss to remove his name from the work records and not to bother even to make up a cheque for the time he was employed with them. He left, never to return to Westray again. Some people may have thought at the time that he was being stupid, but in hindsight he definitely did the right thing.

Within a few weeks of starting work it had become abundantly clear that I did not want to spend any more time at Westray than was absolutely necessary. The four days of shifts seemed to drag on forever and a day. Cave-ins became something that were as regular as the noon cannon on Citadel Hill in Halifax. If you worked two days in a row without a cave-in it was a welcome relief, but it left you wondering when and from where the next one was coming.

**Inquiry Testimony, Mr. Comish, Day 28, Feb 7, 1996: 5813–16**

Q. But can you point me to any specific instances where you were actually intimidated by Roger Parry? ...

A. Yeah, well, he got us to do some things that normally I don't think I would have done. Like —

Q. Such as?

A. — push a 45-gallon barrel of oil up the hill to the miner when you could have just taken the miner and drove it down to the 45-gallon barrel....

Q. Uphill. And you didn't want to do that?

A. No....

Q. So he wanted you to push it to the miner instead of tramming the miner out to the —

A. Just down. Yeah. I think it was about maybe — maybe 100 feet.

Q. How long would it have taken the miner to tram 100 feet?

A. Probably less than a minute.

Q. How long did it take you and whoever helped you to push the 45-gallon drum of —

A. About five minutes.

Q. — oil? And did you have some discussion with Mr. Parry about not wanting to do that?
A. Yeah, we argued about it. I said it didn't make any sense. Why risk — for one thing, why risk hurting somebody to move a barrel to a machine that is perfectly capable of driving down to the barrel.
Q. Did he explain to you why he didn't want to drive the machine down to the barrel of oil?
A. No. He just said, "Do it."
Q. And you did it?
A. And we did it.
[Inquiry testimony conducted by Ms. Campbell, Solicitor for the Commission]

The way that the upper management treated the employees was outrageous and perhaps even illegal at some points. I don't believe any person should have to stand there and be called down to the lowest, all the time being spit upon by some loud-mouthed Neanderthal who couldn't perform the very task he was screaming at you for. The people in the higher positions at Westray were not what the average person would call professionals or, for that matter, even rank amateurs. When a person had the misfortune to be injured badly enough to have to go on worker's compensation, management would go out of their way to delay the paperwork and the sending in of necessary files required for the guy to get his money coming in. I believe this was done to force the employee back to work before he was actually ready to return to the workforce.

With all of the inadequate business practices that went on at Westray it was a wonder that the place lasted as long as it did. This again makes me wonder what kind of interference there was from the government. With the situation as bad as it was, and the reports that came in from the mine inspectors, the question is: why was nothing ever done about it?

When I received the phone call from Mike Piche on that fateful Saturday morning I was understandably upset, but I was not really surprised about what had happened. I knew that what I was about to go through would be very difficult on me and my family, but I don't think I knew just how draining it would be.

I can't even begin to try to explain to someone who was not underground at Westray after the explosion what it was like. I don't mean the actual condition of the mine but what went on in my head. Physically it was like the pictures that everyone had seen when that madman blew up that building in Oklahoma, except the conditions at Westray were in a darkened environment. Mentally it was a never-ending nightmare that intensified as the days went by. The fact that this place could explode again at any time was enough to exhaust a person's mental endurance, but as draining as it was it gave you a real rush of energy at the same time. There were times down there when I wanted nothing more than to wake up and have this all be a bad dream, but that would have been too easy.

> **Inquiry Testimony, Mr. Comish, Day 28, Feb 7, 1996: 5865–66**
> Q. And what did you and Mr. Dooley talk about?
> A. We were just sitting on the tractor, and I said, you know, "You know the methanometer is not working on that miner in the Southwest section." And, just jokingly, I said, "If we get killed, I will never speak to you again."
> Q. You said that to —
> A. — type of thing.
> Q. — Mr. Dooley?
> A. Yeah, it was just a — yeah.
> Q. You said that jokingly?
> A. Yeah.
> Q. Now as your shift wore on on May the 8th, did you start to feel in less of a joking mood?
> A. Actually, I — yeah, I felt — I didn't feel right. I didn't feel right at all.
> [Inquiry testimony conducted by Ms. Campbell, Solicitor for the Commission]

Each time you entered the mine you could see each man saying a prayer, hoping that this time we would be able to get all the bodies out and seal up this hellhole forever. It was a terrible feeling of defeat when the recovery operation was called off. Just knowing how the family members counted on you to bring their loved ones out of there, and knowing that you couldn't, was totally devastating to each member of the teams and everyone who had tried. The fact that you had put it all on the line each and every moment you were in the mine was not important to you when failure to complete the objectives of the recovery had become inevitable.

They say time heals all wounds, and I guess for the most part that is true, but time does not remove the scars that you receive from something like the Westray explosion. I thought that once the Inquiry had started and people began to hear just what went on and how we as employees were treated, there would be some sort of a venting system for what we had lived with since the time of the explosion and what we had gone through while we were employed at Westray. In the beginning of the Inquiry it was hard to trust the people of the commission, but it did not take long for me to realize that Mr. Merrick and company were there to do what had to be done to get to the bottom of things. I was impressed with Mr. Merrick's questions to those first few witnesses and with the fact that he was not willing to let questions go half-answered. Of course his greatest challenge was still to come with the questioning of the government officials, who seemed determined to either not answer the questions or answer them so obscurely that not much value was obtained from the answers anyway.

As for me, I could hardly wait to get up on the stand and tell people my side of things. I waited for what seemed like an eternity for the call to appear on the stand. I was contacted by the union's lawyers, and asked to show up in Stellarton early enough to go over the questions so as to have my story straight, which made me a little confused. I didn't think that I was going to have to protect myself at the Inquiry, but that I was there only to answer questions to enable the Inquiry to determine what had gone wrong. Little did I know how specific and precise the questions were going to be. I was now very nervous about getting on the stand and testifying. What were the different lawyers trying to accomplish with their lines of questioning?

**Inquiry Testimony, Mr. Comish, Day 28, Feb 7, 1996: 5925–26**

Q. … you overpowered that trip switch to continue to work anyway.

A. No, I —

Q. In a dangerous condition.

A. No, I overpowered the trip switch to fill the car, the shuttle car.

Q. No, but the point is the machine would be operating in order to fill the shuttle car.

A. Right.

Q. And the equipment had said no, it mustn't operate because it's unsafe for a job. You took it upon yourself to override that safety protection, which was for your benefit, and continue to do something which you shouldn't have done. Correct?

A. Perhaps.

Q. Anybody tell you to do it?

A. I was shown how to do it, yes.

Q. No, but did somebody stand there and say "I want you to do this"?

A. I don't think anybody actually stood there and said that, but it was understood.

[Inquiry testimony conducted by Mr. Endres, Solicitor for the Department of Justice]

The hardest thing about testifying was the wait to get up on the stand. Once the questions started I was quite relaxed and at times I wanted to go into more detail with some of my answers. This wasn't bad at all and before I knew it one hour had slipped into two, and then we took a break for a coffee. Back on the stand I answered and explained many things to the Inquiry. During the fourth hour of questioning things did get tense when the lawyer for the Department of Mines and Energy got his turn to question me. I was a little surprised that he was trying to accuse the workers at Westray of breaking safety regulations and saying that maybe it was the workers who were to blame for the explosion and ultimately their own deaths. I don't try to deny that rules were broken at Westray, nor would I be naive enough to think that rules aren't broken in almost every working site around, but it is crazy to think that we were responsible for the deplorable conditions that lent themselves to what happened at that mine.

A mine inspector has a duty to inspect a mine, and if he finds unfavourable conditions he is compelled to see that the conditions are made right as soon as possible. If these conditions are not corrected then it is his duty to close the mine or that section of the mine until things are corrected. The mine in Gays River was closed down for something far less critical than the condition of the mine at Westray. This leads me to believe that there was something going on at Westray that gave certain individuals the feeling that they could do whatever they saw fit. This kind of thinking always seems to bring about the same results, with someone getting badly hurt or even killed.

**Inquiry Testimony, Mr. Comish, Day 28, Feb 7, 1996: 5855–57**

Q. Now did you know who the mine's inspector was?

A. Albert McLean.

Q. Yes. And did you see Mr. McLean underground from time to time?

A. Yes.... A couple times.

Q. A couple of times? And did you ever think to talk to Mr. McLean about any of the concerns you had?

A. Not there at the time.

Q. What do you mean, "not there at the time?"

A. Well, Roger would be standing there glaring at you, so you didn't dare say anything.

Q. Why wouldn't you say anything to Mr. McLean just because Mr. Parry was there?

A. Probably out of fear for your job.

Q. Uh-huh. Now do you recall ever making any comments to Mr. McLean?

A. Yes.... I was just getting ready to leave. I had just done my shift and he was coming in. He was at the front — front booth there.

Q. So you're both aboveground?

A. Yeah.... I had just finished showering and I was leaving to the car. And I said to him, "Oh, you're in for another inspection?" I asked him if he had his blinders with him....

Q. Why would you ask Mr. McLean if he had his blinders with him?

A. Because nothing ever got done. It's like they didn't see anything....

Q. And did Mr. McLean make any reply to you?

A. He got — he said, you know, "Don't be like that." That was about it, and I just walked out.

Q. Were there any other occasions when you talked to Mr. McLean?

A. Underground.

Q. And —

A. "How's it going?" "Not bad." "Don't bullshit me." That's basically the conversation.

[Inquiry testimony conducted by Ms. Campbell, Solicitor for the Commission]

Once I had finished my testimony, all I wanted to do was leave Stellarton and never go back there again. The sooner I would be able to put this thing behind me the better off I would be. I did follow the Inquiry with interest of course. It was something I did not have the power to ignore; as much as I would have liked to, I couldn't. When Albert MacLean was testifying, I couldn't help feeling sorry for him. I don't know if he was told to act this stupid or if it just came naturally, but it was hard for me to understand how he had ever become a mines inspector. I actually had put my trust and my life in the hands of this man. If I had known then what I know now, I don't think I would have been able to work underground in Nova Scotia. A person who had one year of underground experience would have done a better job of regulating the Mines Act. I was angered to the point of feeling sick to my stomach as I listened to the bumbling of this man on the stand. As the Inquiry continued the witnesses didn't really get any better. Donald Cameron was a prime example of someone who thinks he is above the law. He was actually brazen enough to sit there in front of the family members and say that they were to blame for what had happened at Westray. His actions and his cocky attitude seem to fit him to a "T." It was interesting to hear him try to accuse Mr. Merrick of showboating and making a big production out of his questioning. I don't understand why someone would get offensive unless they had something to get offensive about.

As the Inquiry wound down to its final days, I wished that I had one more chance to get up on the stand and say a few things that I felt I should have said. This Inquiry had a purpose to find out just what had gone wrong and to make recommendations to ensure that a tragedy like this would never happen again. What happened is that a number of people got up on the stand, swore to tell the truth and either did not know the truth or elected not to tell it. Even with all of the bad information obtained, I believe that enough good information has been gathered to ensure that there is now a much clearer picture of what caused the deadly explosion on May 9, 1992 at the Westray mine.

## SHIRLEY'S STORY

Background: Shaun's brother Stephen is married to my sister Toni. They have been together since 1970. So Shaun and I have known each other for a long time. We started dating in 1985 and married on May 26, 1989. We have three children: Matthew David born May 14, 1990; Samantha Marie born March 8, 1993; and Nicholas Alexander born November 22, 1995. Shaun was working in Cassiar, BC, when I found out that we were expecting our first child. I was with him; he was mining asbestos there—six weeks out—two weeks home. At this time we decided that a job at home was what he now needed. Then Westray came up when Shaun was simply driving someone else to an interview. When he came home and told me it was four days there—then four days home—I was a little upset, but when he told me the job was guaranteed for fifteen years employment I thought perhaps it was worth a try. Shaun had worked at other mines in Nova Scotia yet they all fell through, so this was a godsend for our family to be together and to stay in our home.

> **Inquiry Testimony, Mr. Comish, Day 28, Feb 7, 1996: 5859–60**
> Q. Did you ever think about quitting?
> A. All the time.
> Q. And why didn't you?
> A. Every — every four days on I thought about quitting. And I didn't because I had to put a roof over our heads, food in our stomachs. There's no jobs out there. There's no mining jobs out there.
> Q. Were you trained in any other capacity —
> A. Not really.
> [Inquiry testimony conducted by Ms. Campbell, Solicitor for the Commission]

On Friday, May 8, 1992, Shaun arrived home early because our car needed repairs. Our son, Matthew, was almost two at the time. I was adjusting to Shaun being on his four days on—four days off shift. We were in the rec room Saturday morning (May 9, 1992) when the phone rang. It was Mike Piche. Shaun hung up the phone and cried. He told me to turn on the TV, and we watched in horror. The days seemed endless with calls coming from the mine site. Shaun was asked to return as a draegerman. That is when our lives changed forever. It seemed our TV was on for days on end. It was our only source of information. It was my only way of knowing what my husband was doing—there was no communication with the disaster site. There was much confusion about who was in the mine and who was not. The first day of the explosion I received many calls from different people at the mine site, asking if Shaun was home or working in the mine.

When Shaun left to return to the mine to help I was relieved because I knew Shaun needed to be there. However, the more I watched TV the more worried I became, thinking it was worse than I realized. Then two more calls came from the mine looking for Shaun. I felt totally unaware of what Shaun was doing or where he was, and I felt the mine staff, of all people, should know. I felt Shaun was unprotected and out of my control and here was someone from the mine calling me and scaring the hell out of me. When I became irritated and told the lady on the phone that she should know where Shaun was, as they called him back to the mine, the phone calls stopped.

At this point I really had myself convinced that the miners were all alive and nothing bad was going to happen. Maybe because I had never worked in a mine, I never really felt this could happen to us.

**Inquiry Testimony, Mr. Comish, Day 28, Feb 7, 1996: 5820–21**
Q. And we've heard that some vehicles were fuelled underground. Do you have any knowledge of the scoop ever being fuelled underground?
A. Yeah, while I was running it.... We were working the heads, so of course I was watching the guys ahead. He'd sit in the scoop, see, you sit sideways in it, and you're looking ahead. And then I just caught out of the corner of my eye, a light, down on the other side. And that's where the fuel tank is.
Q. Right.
A. And the mechanic was there fuelling it up while I was working, while it was running. So I got off and I asked him, you know, what are you doing? Because, you know, the fuel was spilling out and it was going on the ground and — he said, "This is

what we do; get used to it...."

Q. Aside from the fact that a machine was being fuelled underground, was there any other danger, to your mind?

A. I could have crushed him.... I could have crushed him against the wall very easily. That machine articulates in the middle.... If I had turned this way, he would have been crushed.

Q. Was the machine running at the time?

A. Yes.

Q. Was it commonplace for those machines to remain running underground?

A. Yes.

Q. They wouldn't be turned off?

A. No.

[Inquiry testimony conducted by Ms. Campbell, Solicitor for the Commission]

So at the time I started to remember the phone calls and conversations Shaun and I had concerning the mine safety. I remembered all the times I overheard him talking to Lenny and the other guys about the danger of the mine. So guilt started to come over me. I knew why Shaun started at the time, so he could stay home with us and provide a level of support for this family to survive. There were times when Shaun called me from New Glasgow and he would tell me what happened on his shift, for example, the roof falls or high levels of gases. We would talk because I knew he was scared; we would discuss him leaving, yet at the end of the four-day stay home he would go back. Sometimes he would tell me what management would say and I would get angry and say they can't tell people that; complain, tell mine safety. He would get depressed because I just didn't understand that life in this mine wasn't like life at my job; the chain of command theory just didn't hold water. I knew Shaun was scared because he was trapped, yet I didn't know how to help him out. He was correct; I really didn't know his world. There is one thing I do understand and to this day believe—that Shaun stayed in that mine *not out of greed,* but out of love and loyalty to his family and the need to provide his family with a level of support to survive. This was the best way he knew to fulfill his obligations to his family.

When Shaun was down there trying to save those men, I believed to the end that just keeping the faith was all we needed to do. When Shaun called the first time I could hear in his voice total and complete despair and devastation. He told me the horror of what he had seen. I only wanted him to come home alive. I watched TV and I became angry because he had to go back down there, and he could die trying to bring those miners to the surface. None of it seemed fair. Yet I knew he had to go and try to do what he could to rescue his friends. Then I started to feel guilty because I knew the families were depending on the draegerman to find their loved ones. The men were risking their lives because they knew the families were counting on them to perform a task that God knew couldn't be done. When Shaun called the last time before returning home I knew that the Shaun I had married was gone, and the mine again robbed me of a piece of my life that no one could replace or repair. I hate the mine for killing twenty-six men and destroying so many others.

> Webmark
> Since starting in 1889 in Lubeck, Germany, Dräger has been involved in the research and manufacture of breathing equipment used underwater and underground.
> http://www.draeger.net/

Shaun came home to be with Matthew for his second birthday. The absolute pain was real for me on May 10, 1992, when I was bathing Matthew. He had just become used to his father's shifts and didn't understand where he was. He looked up at me and, in his pure innocence, asked me where Daddy was and when would he be home. At that point I realized that there were children somewhere asking their moms when their dad was coming home, to find out he wasn't ever coming home. That was it. The "front" I thought I had was destroyed—I realized the pain for the children and couldn't deal with this. I then realized that if I didn't do something to help, I would lose my mind. I realized that I could now be telling my son that his daddy was never coming home, and this I could not comprehend. So I wanted everyone to know what the men were doing at the mine and that no matter what happened, they were the bravest and most heroic men and would never be failures in the eyes of others. So I started making phone calls to get medals of bravery for these men. These men were not just co-workers, they were friends and brothers. This was their job site—it could have been anyone of them. What was once their workplace was now one mass grave. I know Shaun felt that he'd let many people down, especially the families—not only because he hadn't saved the men's lives but also because he hadn't brought their bodies to the surface. At any time when the draegerman went back into that mine, they placed their own lives in danger. This did not deter them from attempting to find their friends.

I knew I had a battle before me in trying to get medals awarded to these men because normally medals are not given to a group. I wrote to the governor general, the lieutenant governor, the premier, the prime minister, and the queen of England. Each one responded. After much TV and newspaper exposure, both local and regional, we were successful; in November 1995 Shaun was awarded a medal of bravery. At that time I was the happiest woman alive.

**Oral Submissions, Day 77, July 22, 1996: 16790**
Mr. Hebert [Solicitor for the Westray Families Group]: ... Mr. Commissioner, I have not mentioned —
Mr. Commissioner: I may as well be consistent, Mr. Hebert, your time is up.
Mr. Hebert: Okay.
Mr. Commissioner: Let's wrap up.
Mr. Hebert: I had just one point, Mr. Commissioner. I guess my timing isn't as good today. I haven't mentioned the workers themselves, Mr. Commissioner.

You are to look to see whether there was any neglect. Clearly there is no evidence that the 26 men who died in the Westray mine were engaged in any activities which implied neglect on their part which resulted in this tragedy.

Indeed, Mr. Commissioner, it seems that some of the best were taken away.

At the time I became pregnant with our second child. I realized that if Shaun had died in that mine Samantha and Nicholas would never have been born. I realized how very precious and vulnerable life is. It made me feel sad and selfish, happy for my family but guilt-ridden and sad for the families who lost their loved ones. In reality this disaster made a disaster of our lives. Shaun's stress and my stress were handled in different ways. He wrapped himself around his book; I wrapped myself in the battle for the medals. Neither one of us could help the other, our grief was so intense.

My husband's entire personality changed. Even after counseling Shaun has a short fuse and no patience. The road to his recovery has been long. Shaun will never be the man I married.

The disaster cost him friendships, livelihood, respect for himself, and a piece of our relationship that will never be restored.

# WORKING CONDITIONS:
## PREFIGURING DISASTER

## CHAPTER THREE

# ENGINEERING THE WESTRAY MINING DISASTER[1]

*Patrick Whiteway*

## INTRODUCTION

The fuel that generates 40 percent of the world's electricity—coal—will become even more important in the years ahead as economic growth, especially in Asia, moves ahead. Of all the electricity generated in Canada in 1994 by burning fossil fuels (34,168 MW), 15 percent was created by coal-burning stations. Coal is even more important to Nova Scotia, where in 1997 it accounted for more than half (53 percent, or 1222 MW) of the province's total electric generating capacity of 2299 MW, according to the Canadian Electrical Association (1998).

Webmark
Coal accounted for 41 percent of the value of Nova Scotia's mineral production in 1997. Just one of the amazing facts at this Natural Resources site: www.nrcan.gc.ca/mms/efab/mmsd/facts/ns.htm

With some 1.4 billion tonnes of high- and medium-volatile bituminous coal reserves in the Inverness, Sydney and Pictou coalfields, coal is an important source of energy for the province. This coal, which lies in the Carboniferous-age Maritimes sedimentary basin, has the potential to supply the province's residents and industry with low-cost electricity for years to come. But first, the province must attract a world-class, competitive underground coal mining company to develop those reserves safely.

Coal has been mined on a small scale in Nova Scotia since as early as 1685. However, over the years, many attempts to mine coal via underground operations have ended in disaster. In the Pictou coalfield alone, twelve of the fifteen major coal seams in the field have been mined over the past 160 years, yielding about 55 million tonnes of product (see Figure 3.1).[2] During that time, 244 men have died in underground explosions. The coal resources that remain in the Pictou field are in the extensions at depths of previously-worked seams (ranging from 400 to 1200 metres deep). Although these resources are in peripheral areas where the quality of the coal deteriorates, the coal seams are thick (from 8 to 17 metres) and have a low sulphur content, therefore it remains a potentially valuable resource.

**Figure 3.1. Stratigraphic Section of the Stellarton Group**

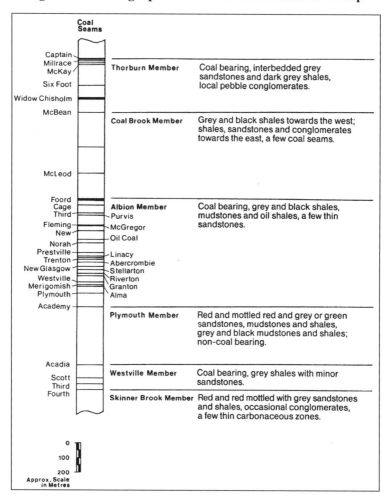

It was against this background that Curragh Incorporated of Toronto received government permission and financing in 1990 to dig 1.3 million tonnes of coal per year for 15 years from the 10-metre-thick Foord seam at the Westray mine near New Glasgow. The company would spend about $124 million to build the underground mine and heavy media wash plant that would supply low-sulphur coal to the newly-constructed Trenton power plants of Nova Scotia Power.

## FEASIBILITY

For any new mine development, many things are examined. First of all, mining companies ask if it is technically possible to mine the deposit. Then they examine, in detail, if it can be mined at a profit. To determine this they examine all the relevant economic, political, social, technological, and geological conditions that can affect a project. Millions of dollars are required to efficiently extract coal from the ground, process it into saleable products and sell it to willing buyers at prices that will earn a return on the capital invested. Any one of the many details associated with a project can make it unfeasible. If this is so, the project is shelved. However, if any of these conditions changes significantly, a project which has been "on the shelf" for years will be re-examined. The deposit could become economical to mine under new conditions.

This was the situation at Westray in 1990. At least three significant improvements to the economic and technical conditions at Westray made it possible for Curragh to prove to investors that this potentially hazardous coal seam could be mined at a profit:

- significant technological advances had been made in underground coal mining since 1951, the last time an attempt was made to mine the Foord seam;
- project financing was arranged by Curragh with the federal and provincial governments. In fact, Curragh Chairman Clifford Frame was recognized by an industry trade publication, *The Northern Miner*, for his ability to broker deals with the two levels of government; and
- a secure, long-term (15-year) contract was negotiated with Nova Scotia Power to supply about 700,000 tonnes of low-sulphur coal per year to the Trenton power station, situated five kilometres from the mine. Although the contract price was not made public, it was likely in the $50–55 per tonne range, which would have resulted in annual revenues of $35 million to $38.5 million.

## MODERN MINING METHODS[3]

Basically, there are two principal methods of modern underground coal mining practiced worldwide—room-and-pillar mining[4] and longwall mining.[5] Longwall is the least expensive method but is applicable only in uniform, flat-lying deposits where large, rectangular blocks of coal, ranging from 1500 to 2500 metres long, are situated side-by-side, such as in the Sydney area of Cape Breton. Today, the Cape Breton Development Corporation (Devco) is the only

### Editorial Cartoon. Westray Mine Engineers[6]

Reprinted with permission of Theo Moudakis of the Halifax Daily News

underground coal mine operator in Nova Scotia, producing about 3 million tonnes per year from two underground longwall mines—the Phalen and Prince mines. With subsidies from the federal government cut off, this company is struggling to become profitable.[7]

Situated within the Stellarton Graben, the Foord seam is cross-cut by a series of geological faults[8] which displace the seam. These, combined with steep grades, create a geometry that is unfavourable for longwall mining.

The high degree of variability in the dip[9] (from 0 to 18 degrees) of the Foord seam favours a more flexible and more expensive mining method, such as room-and-pillar mining, that can adjust to varying ground conditions. This method uses continuous miners, huge electric machines (see Figure 3.2), which are more mobile and flexible than longwall equipment. This allows mine planners to create several smaller, concentrated production areas. Coal from these areas can then be blended to produce a consistent final product. To

### Figure 3.2. Continuous Miner[10]

accomplish this, a well-defined, long-term mine plan is required. Otherwise there can be periods when the only coal available for production is of low quality, higher quality coal being temporarily unavailable because of a lack of planning.

Typically, it is the content of sulphur, moisture, fixed carbon, volatile matter, calorific value, and ash[11] that determines which coal is mined and when. In the case of the Westray mine, ash and moisture content were most important and therefore were the keys to designing the production schedule.

> Webmark
> The Coal Mine Safety Research Center, Hokkaido, was founded in Japan in 1938. Dedicated to the study of coal mine safety, it has contributed to the development of technology for suppressing rock dust.
> www.aist.go.jp/NIRE/nire_WWW/h-center/hokkai-e/htm

Geotechnical features are critical to the success of a mining method as well. For the seam itself, these features include the thickness of the seam, the size and shape of the reserves, the structural characteristics, the physical properties, and the quality of the reserves. In addition to these, the special characteristics of the roof rocks, floor rocks, and the stress field in the vicinity of the planned mine workings must be evaluated. The Foord seam occurs in a group of rocks known as the Stellarton Group, which consists of a series of sandstones, siltstones, shale, claystone, and coal. The seam itself is interbedded with carbonaceous shale and mudstone. Interbedded sandstone, mudstone, and shale make up the roof and floor material.

During the early days of mine development, it became evident that a phenomenon known as "cutter-type failure" would be a challenge. Common in underground coal mines in the Appalachian Belt of North America, this type of roof failure requires special measures to control. It is caused by high horizontal stresses resulting from regional tectonic forces in the Earth's crust. Under such high stresses, weak rock such as the interbedded shales and siltstones at Westray will not stand up on its own. Artificial support used at Westray included mechanical sling supports.

Unwelcome surprises and expensive mistakes in the course of mining can result from an inadequate exploration program. Of key importance are the dip of the deposit and the location of geological faults. To accurately determine these, detailed exploratory diamond drilling is required.

**Figure 3.3. Shuttle Car**

In room-and-pillar mining, access to the seam is provided by driving two tunnels called entries; at Westray, two parallel declines were driven intersecting the Foord seam at a depth of 350 metres. Then the seam is developed in individual work areas called panels,[12] each of which is individually ventilated. Each panel is mined in two steps. Between four and ten parallel rooms or entries are mined first to the full extent of the panel, then the pillars between these rooms may be extracted as men and equipment retreat in the reverse direction—allowing the roof to slowly cave as men and materials retreat to safe ground. Typically, each producing section is equipped with a continuous miner,[13] three shuttle cars[14] (Figure 3.3), one roof bolter[15] (Figure 3.4), one feeder-breaker,[16] two auxiliary ventilation fans, two trickledusters, one teletram rockduster and various service vehicles. Conveyors move the coal from the panels to the main conveyors in the main entries; the main conveyors then move the coal to surface.

This method of mining offers maximum flexibility because room mining and pillar extraction can be carried out at the same time or separately; pillars can also be left in place, depending on the geometry of the panel, ventilation requirements, and ground conditions. Room-and-pillar mining is also advantageous because work areas can be concentrated in a small area, permitting close supervision and management and relative ease in establishing and maintaining ventilation. Typically, about 37–40 percent of the coal can be successfully mined—the rest remains behind in pillars.

The room-and-pillar method does have disadvantages, and careful planning is required to avoid problems. When mining near caved areas, for example, the likelihood of a roof fall is greater as ground stresses move from the caved area to the active workings. The longer that pillar walls and the roof of the openings are exposed to air and water the greater the oxidation and deterioration of the opening. Careful planning keeps these exposure times as short as possible.

Electric-hydraulic machines designed specifically for rock bolting and screening the back (or roof) and electrically-powered, mobile, rubber-tired, machines (such as drum-type continuous miners, shuttle cars and roadheaders[17]) are readily available for mining potentially hazardous coal seams such as the Foord seam. Water spray systems are an integral part of continuous miner design. They are designed to suppress dust by wetting the coal as it is cut. Spray direction, pressure and proper ventilation are important to their successful operation.

**Figure 3.4. Roof Bolter**

## THE RISKS

For any newly constructed mine anywhere in the world, those who decide to risk hundreds of millions of shareholders' dollars on finding and developing that new mine must consider more than just geology and technology. Geology plays its most important role in the high risk, high-reward game of exploration—finding or "discovering" economic mineral deposits. Once found, the location and concentration of minerals in the deposit (i.e., its richness) determines if the deposit can be developed into an operating mine.

Since coal is one of the most common mineral resources on the planet, the general location, quality, and physical characteristics of the world's resources are fairly well-defined. The Foord seam has been known for close to one hundred years. But no one has been able to mine it profitably on a large scale. Several attempts have been made—the Allen mine being the most recent. It operated off and on for nearly fifty years between 1908 and 1954. The people of Stellarton, New Glasgow and the surrounding area are well aware of the dangers of mining this hazardous seam. Monuments have been erected to commemorate the men who lost their lives in underground fires and explosions.

There are at least two unique concerns that relate to underground coal mining: methane gas and combustible dust. Both can be lethal. To address them properly requires the allocation of significant resources by industry, unions, and government.

All coal seams contain methane.[18] The amount of methane in the coal increases with the degree to which the original organic matter in a deposit is altered by heat and pressure over geological time (something known as the rank of the coal). This, in turn, is determined by depth of burial. Methane is absorbed in the micropore structure of the coal matrix and is compressed in the fracture system of the coal seam. Under confining pressures of the overlying strata, this gas is held in equilibrium. When the confining pressures are removed by mining, methane escapes. For every unit of methane emitted, a mine operator in the US must provide, by law, at least one hundred units of air to dilute the methane to 1 percent, thus rendering it harmless. In US coal mines, work areas must have at least 3000 cubic feet per minute (cfm) of air ventilating the work area and 9000 cfm at the last open cross-cut, according to the Mine Safety and Health Administration (MSHA).

Gas outbursts are another matter. A coal seam is prone to this more violent type of release if it contains a large amount of methane, is buried to a depth greater than 400 metres, and contains numerous faults (as was the case at Westray). To safely mine this type of coal, the methane must be drained to lower gas content and pressure. Typically, this is done by drilling horizontal boreholes in advance of mining.

Inadequate ventilation, failure to test for methane, miners smoking underground and failure to remove accumulations of combustible coal dust are the most frequently cited causes of explosions in underground coal mines. But, despite strict enforcement and training, about 10 percent of underground coal mining fatalities in the US are still caused by explosions.

Preventing gas and coal dust explosions is a major concern for any underground coal mine operator. The first line of defense against such occurrences is good ventilation to dilute and sweep away methane and coal dust. The second is regular and thorough methane checks.

Methane sensing and monitoring equipment has improved significantly since the Allan mine closed in 1954. Computers were not available in the 1950s. But in the 1990s they were used for mine planning, methane monitoring, ventilation control, etc. In addition, "old" or conventional technology, such as stonedusting, could also be practised to reduce the risk of explosions.[19] Properly used, these sensing and control technologies alone could have prevented the Westray disaster.

In spring and summer, air temperature and moisture conditions can increase resistance to air flow, and mines can have a harder time maintaining the minimum quantity of ventilating air that is needed for safety. As recent as 1995, the MSHA in the US started a summer alert program to warn operators that extra attention is needed for safety when the outside air begins heating up in the spring. The Westray explosion occurred in May.

## CRITICAL KNOW-HOW

One of the challenges of ensuring the safety of miners in underground coal mines is the challenge of drawing knowledge from a number of people with a variety of experiences. People involved in underground coal mining become familiar with and learn from the experiences of others in the industry by participating in professional societies, by contributing to technical journals, and by attending conferences, symposia, and professional development workshops. So the more people involved in an industry, and the more and varied their experiences, the greater the body of knowledge that mine operators can draw from to design and operate safe underground coal mines.

Underground coal mining is not, however, a big industry in Canada. Most Canadian coal reserves are surface-mineable. In fact, the Canadian coal industry presently comprises twenty-six surface mines and just four underground mines—two in Nova Scotia, one in Alberta and one in British Columbia, according to the Coal Association of Canada (1995).

This means that about 95 percent of all coal mined in Canada is recovered either by strip mining or by open pit mining. Of the 74.9 million tonnes mined in 1995 in Canada, for example, only 3.5 million tonnes came from Nova Scotia's Phalen and Prince underground mines. With total employment of just 1950, there is not a large pool of labour nor a large pool of mine engineers and managers in Nova Scotia skilled in the use of modern underground coal mining technology, and, as noted earlier, these mines use longwall mining methods, not the room-and-pillar method used at Westray. To safely mine a potentially hazardous coal seam, such as the Foord seam, Curragh would have had to draw on expertise from outside Canada.

The situation in the United States is vastly different from that in Canada. Driving shafts and declines down into the earth and using highly mechanized and in some cases automated machinery to mechanically cut, transport, break, and convey coal to the surface is a huge industry there. The best recruiting ground for Curragh to hire its top managers for Westray would have been the US. In 1992, about 60,378 people were employed in 1415 underground coal mines in the US. In that same year, there were thirty-four fatalities in underground coal mines. This low fatality rate indicates that the industry in the US is at the forefront of mine safety (US Department of Labor [no date]). The steadily decreasing fatality rate is even more interesting when compared to the increased production of coal (see Figures 3.5 and 3.5) (US Mine and Safety, 1978–1992).

**Figure 3.5. Coal Production**

Of the 934 million tonnes mined in 1995 in the US, 360 million tonnes (or 38 percent) came from underground operations. The industry in the US, therefore, is at least 100 times as large as it is in Canada. In the US, industry associations hold meetings annually to present and discuss technical issues; there is a large community of mining equipment manufacturers who compete for business worldwide; and government dedicates significant resources to legislating and enforcing safety. So there is much to be learned from how coal is mined in the US. How safety is regulated and enforced there demands careful examination by regulators and inspectors in Nova Scotia.

In 1995, the coal industry in the US was the second largest in the world. Canada ranked a distant 12th (at 74.9 million tonnes) and the UK ranked 15th (at 52.6 million tonnes). There are twelve coal companies in the US, all of which are larger than Manalta, the largest coal producer in Canada (which produced 21.8 million tonnes in 1995, all from surface mines). The production figures listed here are for both surface and underground operations, and they illustrate that there exists a wealth of expertise south of the border from which Curragh could have acquired the necessary management to safely operate the Westray mine.[20]

Of the ten largest underground coal mines in the US,[21] seven are located in the Appalachian belt, which is in the same tectonic setting as the Westray mine. Would it not make sense for Curragh to have hired mine operators from these mines?

The coal industry in the UK is much smaller (producing about 52.6 million tonnes in 1995) but more highly concentrated in underground operations (accounting for 68 percent of total production). This is the place where two of Curragh's top managers—Roger Parry and Gerald Philips—cut their teeth in the coal industry before moving on to a small underground operation in Alberta called Smoky River Coal. In general, underground operations in the UK tend to be old, small and less efficient than the larger, more mechanized ones in the US. Unions have attributed recent increases in the number of serious accidents and deaths in underground coal mines in the UK to the privatization of government-owned British Coal Corporation in 1994. Faced with pressures to compete economically with other operations around the world, unscrupulous operators push their employees to take more safety risks for the sake of increasing production.

Against this background, Nova Scotia's 1990 underground coal mining industry was but a dot on the world's underground coal mining map, and Curragh Incorporated did not appear as a major coal producer. Unfortunately, Curragh recruited its top managers from a small operation twenty kilometres north of Grande Cache, Alberta, rather than from the larger, more experienced industry in the Appalachian region of the US. Clifford Frame's personal coal mining experience amounted to a failed attempt to develop the Quintette mine—an open pit coal operation in the mountains of northeastern British Columbia.

## US Legislation

In the much larger US industry, technology and safety standards are highly developed and enforced with violators being punished by high fines and penalties. US safety standards are more developed than they are in Canada. In fact, federal legislation to ensure the safety of miners was enacted in the US as early as 1891. It established minimum ventilation requirements in underground coal mines and prohibited operators from employing children under twelve years of age.

The US Congress then established the US Bureau of Mines in 1910, a year when there were 2821 fatalities in underground coal mines in the US. Its mandate was to conduct research to reduce accidents, and it was given authority to inspect mines in 1941. Annual inspections and limited enforcement authority was mandated by the *Federal Coal Mines Safety Act* in 1952. This legislation authorized the bureau to assess civil penalties against mine operators for noncompliance with withdrawal orders or for refusal to give inspectors access to a mine property. No provision was made for monetary penalties for noncompliance with safety provisions.

The most comprehensive and stringent US federal legislation came in the form of the *Federal Coal Mine Health and Safety Act* of 1969. It required four annual inspections of every underground coal mine and dramatically increased federal enforcement powers in coal mines. It demanded monetary penalties for all violations and established criminal penalties for knowing and willful violations. To avoid the appearance of a conflict of interest between mineral resource development and mine safety, Mining Enforcement and Safety Administration (MESA) was created in 1973 by the Department of the Interior to assume the safety and health enforcement functions formerly carried out by the Bureau of Mines.

All federal health and safety regulations applicable to coal mines in the US were then consolidated under a single statutory scheme with passage of the *Federal Mine Safety and Health Act* of 1977. It strengthened and expanded the rights of miners and enhanced the protection of miners from retaliation for exercising such rights. The responsibility for carrying out the mandates of the act was subsequently transferred from the Department of the Interior to the Department of Labor and MESA was renamed the Mine Safety and Health Administration (MSHA).

The United Mine Workers Union plays an important role in improving mine safety in the US. Created in 1890, the union has a health and safety department which is based in Washington, D.C. It represents members in the field, conducts inspections with enforcement agencies, investigates accidents and injuries, and conducts investigations when employees file a formal grievance with the company for violating safety regulations. It also ensures that federal and state laws and regulations reflect the concerns of workers.

**Figure 3.6. Underground Fatalities**

Thus, it can be seen that for a variety of reasons, underground coal mining fatalities in the US have dropped sharply to 47 in 1995 from 272 in 1977.

## CANADIAN LEGISLATION

In Canada, mineral resources are a provincial responsibility under the Canadian constitution. So Nova Scotia, Alberta, and British Columbia—the only provinces where underground coal mining presently takes place—are the only jurisdictions that regulate underground coal mines. Yet, because of a quirk of history, federal legislation governs safety at coal mines on the island of Cape Breton in Nova Scotia. So, at the time of the Westray explosion, provincial legislation applied to the Westray mine only. This is significant because it meant that provincial inspectors were new to this responsibility and had no experience enforcing the provincial regulations.

While provincial legislation to protect underground gold, base metals, and

**Editorial Cartoon. Leroy Legere**

Reprinted with permission of Theo Moudakis of the Halifax Daily News potash miners in Canada is highly advanced (because the industry is much larger and has a longer, uninterrupted history), this legislation does not deal with the hazards of coal dust and methane, unique concerns of the underground coal miner. Due to delays, Nova Scotia's *Coal Mines Regulation Act* is still being rewritten by the Nova Scotia Department of Labour, although it was supposed to have come into force in January 1997. As the federal government withdraws from its involvement in the Cape Breton Development Corporation, it is anticipated that the new provincial legislation will take effect there.

The federal legislation and regulations that apply to underground coal mines in Canada are the *Coal Mines Occupational Safety and Health Regulations* (SOR/90-97), and the *Coal Mining Safety Commission Regulations* (SOR/90-98). In Nova Scotia, coal mining is regulated under the *Coal Mines Regulation Act* (RSNS 1989) and the *Occupational Health and Safety Act* (NS Reg. 137/77). In other provinces, such as British Columbia, it is the *Mines Act* (S.B.C. 1989), the *Mines Regulation* (BC Reg. 126/94), and the *Workplace Hazardous Material Information System Regulation* (BC Reg. 257/88). And in Alberta, it is the *Occupational Health and Safety Act* (R.S.A. 1980) and the *Mines Safety Regulation* (Alta. Reg. 292/95).

A recent case in the US illustrates how seriously that country takes safety in underground coal mines. Nine MSHA-certified mine safety trainers were recently indicted by a federal grand jury for selling falsified certificates indicating that individuals had received federally-required annual refresher training when, in fact, no such training was conducted or the training session failed to provide the required safety and health training. Eight of the defendants face five to twenty years in prison and maximum fines of $1 million each. Nova Scotia's new regulations, by comparison, will impose fines of up to $250,000 or $25,000 per day and will include prison terms of up to a maximum of two years.

The US situation can also be compared with that of Russia. Since the breakup of the Soviet Union the annual accident rate has recently increased to a level forty to seventy times that of the US coal industry, according to an international trade magazine *(Coal Age*, October 1996: 7:26). Reasons cited in a recent survey include lack of reliable equipment, difficult mining conditions, low priority given to safety by management, lack of safety education, a generally low level of mechanization, the absence of or deficiencies in personal protective devices and lax enforcement of safety rules. In Russia, where 20 percent of underground coal mines are deeper than 700 metres, 94 seams are considered hazardous and another 140 are potentially hazardous due to inadequate gas-drainage systems. In 1992 there were 700 incidents of outbursts and other gas-related phenomena reported. While these mines have at their disposal most of the necessary equipment to protect against gas and dust explosions, miners are pressured to shut off methane sensors to avoid activation of control devices and to maintain production—and their wages.

## THE BOTTOM LINE

If the Westray mine had been operated under MSHA safety standards, would it have worked? I suspect it would have. But, for several reasons, it didn't.

Again, because of the size of the US industry, significant improvements in underground coal mining machinery have been made since 1951. These improved machines were purchased by Curragh. But, remember, management is more important than technology. Bad managers can wipe out the benefits of any new technologies. Curragh decided to recruit the top managers for Westray from the Smoky River coal mine, a small underground operation that uses room-and-pillar methods in a completely different geological setting.

There are inherent dangers in coal mining, especially in the Pictou coalfield. The way such dangers are mitigated is through responsible corporate initiative and government legislation, which has to be enforced and backed up by sufficient technical expertise. In the Westray case, the danger was evident and the legislation was in place, but there was a lack of enforcement and expertise.

The technology required to safely deal with the geological conditions at Westray was known and was purchased by Curragh. But what the company did not do was recruit the managers who could take full advantage of that machinery. If that had been done, Westray's managers would have taken the time to ensure that the miners were fully aware of the risks of mining the Foord seam and fully trained to guard against those risks using the best available tools and methods. As was revealed in the subsequent Inquiry, management, organized labour and government inspectors did not do their jobs. They did not enforce their own regulations to ensure the safety of the miners.

There is nothing about the geology of the deposit that would prevent an experienced, competent mining company from safely mining it. What was known about the geology of the Foord seam and the threats to safety it presented to miners (the weak ground conditions, the gassiness of the seam, and the frequency of faults) was not adequately heeded. Miners (and inspectors) were inadequately trained to mine the seam using modern room-and-pillar mining know-how, and they were not given sufficient time (because of production pressures) to adequately secure their workplace against the hazards posed by the geological conditions under which they worked. This was not a failure to understand the geology of the deposit or to purchase the latest equipment that could mine the deposit safely. It was a human failure to appreciate and guard against the risks inherent in that geological knowledge.

It is my opinion that the managers employed by Curragh should not have been in charge of an attempt to mine the Foord seam in 1992. They did not have the necessary managerial expertise. They should not have been there to begin with. Someone with the necessary experience could have mined the deposit successfully.

A company run by people having more experience in room-and-pillar coal mining in gassy coal seams as well as an ability to adequately train and prepare its workforce for the risks at hand could have succeeded. If the Westray operation had been supervised by adequately trained and experienced government mines inspectors (perhaps MSHA-trained and certified) and if it had employed miners who were represented by a responsible organized labour union, it might have succeeded. Conscious of the risks posed by the geology of the deposit, such a union could have played an important role in ensuring that the company lived up to its responsibility to operate the mine safely. Under such conditions, the Westray mining disaster of May 9, 1992, could have been avoided.

Some day, maybe fifty years from now, the economic, political, social, and technological conditions may, once again, become favourable, and someone will attempt to profitably mine the 47 million tonnes of coal remaining in the Foord seam. Hopefully, they will have more experience in underground coal mining than did Curragh.

## CHAPTER FOUR

# DEATH BY CONSENSUS AT WESTRAY?[1]

*Harry Glasbeek and Eric Tucker*

## WESTRAY STORY: INTRODUCTION

At about 5:20 on the morning of May 9, 1992, an explosion ripped through the Westray coal mine in Pictou County, Nova Scotia, killing twenty-six miners. A ten-day search and rescue operation led to the recovery of only fifteen of the miners' bodies. The horror and anxiety of the families and friends can only be imagined. Politicians and the mine owner expressed their condolences and praised the Herculean efforts of the unsuccessful rescue workers.

Mining disasters involving mass deaths are familiar events. In Pictou County, 246 miners had already been killed in a series of explosions between 1838 and 1952. Most miners killed on the job, however, die in less spectacular circumstances. Another 330 Pictou miners suffered accidental deaths from other causes (i.e., crushed by stone, crushed by coal cars, mangled by mining machinery) between 1866-1972. In addition, an unknown number of miners were killed between the time commercial mining began, 1809, and the year record keeping began, 1866. Also unknown is the number of workers who died prematurely from occupational diseases.[2] It is routine for miners to be killed, maimed or made ill by their work. Miners have the third highest fatality rate in Canada after forestry and fishing, over seven times the average (Labour Canada, 1990: Table 6).

The responses to these recurring mining catastrophes also are routine: mourning and expressions of anger followed by the setting-up of an inquiry. Westray is exceptional only in the number of inquiries it has spawned; no less than four have been initiated. Invariably, these inquiries reveal that the deaths and injuries are attributable, at least in part, to violations of existing mining regulations (Braithwaite, 1985; Hopkins, 1984; Caudill, 1977). This finding leads to statements of firm resolve that there will be no recurrences, no more violations, no more disasters. But, as the record shows, these goals are never realized.

The reason why this sequence of accidents, inquiries, and recommendations brings about little change is that, whatever practices are sought to be implemented, the broader political–economic and specific operative assumptions about occupational health and safety regulation remain unexamined, leaving the improved practices subject to the same weaknesses as the preceding standards of operation (Carson, 1989: 310–15; Carson et al., 1988: 3–8). A recent Canadian example of this approach to the investigation of occupational health and safety disasters was the Royal Commission on the Ocean Ranger Marine Disaster (Carson, 1984).

These assumptions are the focus of this chapter. We want to explore how the political–economic context creates an environment in which the protection of workers from harm is only a minor consideration in the decision-making and behaviour of government officials and private investors.

An especially important aspect of that context is the dominance of staple (natural resource) extraction in the economy. It has coloured relations between capital and the state and between labour and capital. From the beginning, the exploitation of Canada's abundant natural resources has been seen as the engine of growth. This has required the state to be more directly supportive of private capital than is the case in economies whose growth is more tied to manufacturing. Governments have had to subsidize resource extraction through huge investments in infrastructure. The hope is that the returns on the sale of resources will lead to the development of domestic industry which will supply local markets. For this strategy to succeed, much depends on the international market for the resources. Because the government cannot control those markets, it has very few tools with which to manage the economy. Its reliance on capital's willingness to invest becomes a profound dependency (Brodie, 1990). Over time, this creates an ideological climate in which governments advocate that they should do everything in their power to create a favourable climate for investment. This makes close links between elected politicians, government bureaucrats, and capitalists the norm rather than the exception. In regions where the staple-led growth strategy has failed to produce any kind of industrial development, potential employers are able to have governments create particularly attractive conditions for them. Nova Scotia is such a region. Michelin Tire, for example, was able to have the basic, well-established labour laws re-drafted so that it could avoid unionization. The government's incentive was to retain the jobs created by Michelin Tire. It succeeded. One of Michelin's factories is in Pictou County; indeed, it is the county's largest employer (Langille, 1981).

Underlying and reinforcing this political economy are a number of assumptions that we believe the events at Westray call into question: first, that risk is a natural and unavoidable consequence of productive activity in general, and staple extraction in particular; second, that private economic activity is preferable to public activity; and third, that occupational health and safety is an area in which workers and employers share a common set of interests and objectives, a consensus.

This chapter discusses both the decision to set up the mine and the operation of the mine. These events illuminate the salience of the broader political–economic context. Further, the story gives the lie to the assumptions which underpin health and safety regulation. We detail the implications of the political economy and the prevailing ideology for the enforcement of health and safety regulation. We then critically examine a component of the consensus theory which postulates that workers and capitalists share, in some roughly comparable way, the risks of production. This is done by examining the proposition that the corporate form is a neutral, facilitating device.

## THE MAKING OF A DISASTER

### The Decision to Mine

Underground coal mining in Pictou County virtually ceased by the end of the 1950s as a result of the loss of markets to fuel oil, aging facilities, and deep seams which were expensive to mine. But, the local Foord coal seam has some particularly attractive features, which made it likely that there would be someone coming forward to resume mining. The coal seam is unusually thick, varying from two to eight metres, its sulphur content is below one percent, and it is a high-energy producer, generating between 10,000 and 12,000 British Thermal Units per pound. Reserves are estimated at approximately 41 million tonnes. But, as its history has shown, the seam also presents some significant problems for profitable and safe mining. The area in which the seam is located is widely known to be gaseous, exuding significant quantities of methane, and it is highly geologically faulted, increasing the risk that the roofs of the underground rooms will collapse. Spontaneous combustion had been a problem in previous mining operations, and the ash content of the coal seam varies significantly.

Although investors are always on the lookout for new opportunities which might arise as a result of changing market conditions and new technologies, none could contemplate coal mining in the Pictou area before 1982. The federal government had set up the Cape Breton Development Corporation (Devco) as a crown corporation to mine coal in Cape Breton in 1967. When it did so, it extracted an agreement from the province not to issue new coal mining licenses on the mainland for a fifteen-year period. As the end of the ban approached, Suncor was the first resource company to express interest in resuming underground mining in the Pictou coalfield.[3] It began intensive feasibility studies in 1981, acquired coal rights and exploration licenses from the province, and purchased and optioned land above the contemplated mining site. But Suncor decided not to exploit its leases. In February 1987, Placer Development Limited took an option on Suncor's interests and conducted its own feasibility study (Placer Development Limited, 1987).

An examination of the four volumes produced by that study discloses a remarkable lack of direct and explicit concern with the health and safety of miners. To the extent that hazards are considered, they are discussed in the context of whether they would render mining technically and economically infeasible. For example, the second volume on mining operations begins by setting out the parameters which were used in developing a mine design proposal. There is no express statement to the effect that the mine should be designed to minimize the risk of harm to workers. Indeed, of the eleven parameters set out, only two or three relate to safety, and then only indirectly.[4] Existing health and safety regulations are discussed briefly in the report, but these references amount to a description of the statutory requirements regarding certified personnel and training. This lack of concern does not stem from ignorance. The report reveals an awareness of the geological faults, the dangerous roof and floor conditions to which this may lead, the potential of spontaneous combustion, and the dangerous presence of methane. These are not, however, identified as health and safety problems. Rather, they are considered primarily as problems which go to technical and economic feasibility. At best, health and safety is subsumed within these engineering and profit-maximizing calculations. A study of American mine engineers found that the mining engineers were compelled and accepted the fact that it was necessary to subordinate technical considerations that might create conflicts to overriding economic considerations (Donovan, 1988: 100).

This relegation of the value of human life to a lesser concern when engaged in planning permits the designers to feel comfortable about their belief in the capacity of modern mine technology and management to solve problems as they might arise. For example, in the first few pages of the report there is a brief discussion of mining history in the Pictou coalfield. After noting that the records "include references to fires and explosions associated with the mining industry," the report states that "technological advances in underground coal mining and more stringent regulations have decreased the frequency of such occurrences" (Placer Development Limited, 1987: Vol 1, 6). So much for the lessons of history. Later on, in the context of discussions of the potential for roof collapses, confidence is expressed that problems will be detected and that appropriate adjustments will be made.[6] Had the risk to the lives of the miners who might be killed or injured been squarely before these planners, they might have been less sanguine about their assumption that nothing would go wrong.

Placer Development merged with two other mining companies, and it chose not to proceed with the Pictou project. It was at this point that the people who were to be the Westray mine operators came forward, commissioning their own feasibility study from Kilborn Limited in November 1987 and, in December 1987, purchased Suncor's interests. Kilborn's study closely paralleled Placer's. Again, there was virtually no expression of concern over mine workers' health and safety; the criteria used to choose the most appropriate mining method made no mention of the need to protect worker safety and health (Kilborn Limited [no date]: Vol. 1, 3–5). Statutory health and safety requirements are dealt with by indicating that "[t]he mine will be managed and operated in accordance with the statutory requirements of the Coal Mines Regulation Act... [t]hese [A]cts require that the mine be safely operated by properly qualified, trained and experienced personnel" (Placer Development Limited, 1987: Vol. 1, 3-18, 3-19).

While it is not surprising that private resource companies and their mine consultants do not consider occupational health and safety to be a central question, it should be expected that governments would. After all, they have regulatory responsibility and may be held politically accountable if miners are hurt. The available record indicates that, although some federal and provincial government officials expressed concern about the issues, these were not taken seriously by those with decision-making authority.

When the federal government was asked to contribute financially to the Westray project, a study was conducted by the Canada Centre for Mineral and Energy Technology (CANMET) in 1989. It was a limited review, based on eight hours of meetings with various officials in Halifax and a ten-hour review of the Kilborn and earlier studies (Canada Centre for Mineral and Energy Technology [no date]: 1). The CANMET review raised a number of concerns, including some which were health and safety related, but they were not the focus of the study.

> The planned roof support is the minimum and will likely need upgrading in places. Whether this is included in the cost is unclear.... Room and Pillar mining forces face workers to make frequent value judgments (particularly in depillaring) that impact coal recovery, safety and the like. To initiate such mining in a new set of site specific conditions you must expect to have a lengthy learning curve even with experienced people. (CANMET 1989: 5)

While this last remark suggests a real safety concern, the predominant technical and economic focus is clarified when the author returns to this point in the general comments of the report: "The real question is whether this property can wear the cost of the learning curve to get to a routine development/ extraction practice." At best, it seems, human lives are reduced to a cost factor.

The federal government review was largely concerned with technical and economic questions because it became involved with the Westray project only when Curragh Resources was seeking federal loan guarantees and other subsidies. The direct cost of poor health and safety practices (i.e., the cost of compensating injured workers and/or their families) was a substantial concern neither to private investors nor to federal government officials reviewing the project. Moreover, the federal government did not have jurisdiction over mine safety in the province and could take the position that the safe operation of the mine was to be left to the province.

The provincial government could not pass the health and safety buck so readily since it has jurisdiction over coal mine safety. There is a requirement that notice be given where any work is about to be commenced for the purpose of opening a mine.[7] From that point on, the Department of Labour can insist that the operations be conducted in accordance with provincial health and safety law. However, the decision to mine does not have to be cleared in advance with provincial health and safety authorities.

Although there was no legally mandated reason to consider workers' health and safety when deciding as to whether or not to mine, the issue was not completely ignored during the Westray investigation. Still, the few voices that were raised attracted little attention at the time. The Development Corporation of Cape Breton was concerned about the possible development of the Westray mine because of the negative impact it might have on its operations. In a confidential submission to the federal and provincial governments, Devco pointed to the safety risks arising from the geological fault structure, gaseousness and the potential for spontaneous combustion of coal dust. However this argument appeared in a document that was much more concerned with the economic impact of the development of Pictou coal.[8] Trevor Harding, grievance chairman for United Steelworkers of America which represented the miners at Curragh Resources' lead and zinc operations in Faro in the Yukon, warned of that company's atrocious safety record there. He said there had been thirty-nine reported accidents in April 1989 and a dozen dust fires in late February and early March.[9] Apparently no one saw this as relevant to the mining to be done in Nova Scotia.

Curragh Resources' lack of experience in operating an underground mine also was raised by Derek Rance, a private mine consultant. He pointed to the gas problem and the difficulty of properly ventilating during room-and-pillar mining, especially at that depth:

> When you start getting towards the limit of the technology, it is not as safe as if you were mining comfortably inside the envelope of technology. It's like pushing something to the limit all the time. In order for that mine to be safe, everything is going to have to work right all the time.[10]

The failure to heed these warnings may be linked to certain assumptions regarding health and safety. For example, some may have assumed that, while risks are inevitable, they have been set at levels which governments, employers, and workers agree are tolerable; if particular workers want to reduce the risk further, they are free to bargain for this at their own cost. Given this assumed consensus, there is no reason for government to insist in advance that the proponents of a risk-creating enterprise should demonstrate that health and safety issues are adequately considered. An acceptable risk level has already been set and the parties can be assumed to have no interest in avoiding it.

This makes for an interesting contrast with the way in which environmental concerns are treated in the approval process. In principle, mining cannot take place before the environmental impact of that activity has been assessed. Nor can federal assistance be given until that has been done.[11] As a result, the question of environmental impact was part and parcel of every feasibility study conducted by and for the resource companies interested in mining in Pictou County. In November 1985, Environment Canada and the Nova Scotia Department of the Environment jointly prepared guidelines for an environmental impact assessment of Suncor's coal mining project. In January 1990, Acres International Limited submitted to Industry, Science and Technology Canada a detailed and lengthy environmental evaluation of the Westray coal mine development. It recommended that federal funding be contingent on the satisfaction of seventeen environmental protection conditions.

Why do we insist on such careful consideration of the external environment while no such consideration is given to the internal environment? The politics of the environment are different because there is a perception that the interests of the company in making a profit from its investment and the interests of the public in protecting the environment are not coincidental. And there is no assumption that members of the public have voluntarily accepted the risk of being harmed because of environmental degradation. In other words, once the presumptions central to consensus theory are removed, a different regime of regulation seems appropriate. Employers respond to this different political climate by making great efforts to be seen as environmentally friendly.[12] It is because of the unchallenged nature of a presumed consensus with respect to occupational conditions that governments could be involved in the development of the Westray mine without feeling the need to concern themselves too much about workers' health and safety, that is without considering whether or not there should be any mining, given the risks for workers. And this is crucial because it is exceedingly unlikely that the Westray mine would have been developed without extensive government involvement.

Placer Development's feasibility study was not premised on such government assistance, and this may have been a factor in the decision not to proceed. By contrast, the project was attractive to Curragh Resources precisely because Clifford Frame had political connections which enabled him to put together a sweetheart deal with the responsible governments. Frame convinced the Nova Scotia Power Corporation, a publicly owned utility, to commit itself to buying 700,000 tons of coal annually at about $74 a ton (production costs were estimated to be $29 a ton) for a coal-fired power plant being constructed in Trenton, Nova Scotia. The reason given by the government for agreeing to purchase from Westray was that the Foord seam coal was low in sulphur, which thereby reduced the cost of the pollution controls that would have to be installed by the government at its power plant.[13]

Even with this guaranteed sale and high price, Frame and his companies owning the leases were finding it difficult to get private financing for the operation. Further government assistance was sought and the federal government guaranteed 85 percent of a $100 million loan obtained from the Bank of Nova Scotia. In addition, the federal government provided up to $8.75 million by way of interest subsidies. Another $3.6 million was provided by the federal government by way of a development subsidy to start the mine.[14] The provincial government lent $12 million to Curragh Resources, who need not have begun repayment of the principal until 1995. To further secure the financing of the mine, the provincial government entered into a deal, the details of which it refused to disclose.[15] The agreement required the provincial government to guarantee the sale of an additional 250,000 metric tonnes of Westray coal annually. Westray had a guaranteed market for 885,000 metric tonnes of coal annually.

One question that these arrangements raise is: if various levels of government were to take virtually all of the risk of financing the mine and purchasing its output, why did they not decide to own and run the mine and reap the profits, if any, on behalf of the citizens?

Governments favour private economic activity over public enterprise as a means to create the welfare which needs to be maintained to legitimate them and to keep them in power. In this context, politicians who feel the need to demonstrate to their constituents that they are promoting economic prosperity, are willing to enter into deals with private entrepreneurs who promise to create jobs if their conditions are met. Of course, in any private enterprise economy some would-be entrepreneurs will be in a better position to influence politicians and policy-makers than others, and sometimes the political will to do a deal for instrumental reasons will be more obvious than at other times. Clifford Frame was, apparently, a person with special influence, and some federal and provincial politicians were very keen for reasons of their own to take advantage of his blandishments.

What made the Westray mine situation particularly ripe for this kind of collaboration was the fact that the mine was located in the provincial riding of Donald Cameron, then premier of Nova Scotia. While negotiations for federal support were still under way, Cameron was a provincial development minister and was campaigning to hold his seat in a fiercely contested election. Although he had hoped to announce that a deal had been reached days before the election, some details had not yet been agreed upon. This did not prevent Clifford Frame from announcing that the development of the Westray mine would go ahead.[16] Four days later, Cameron was re-elected by a slim margin of 753 votes and was subsequently appointed minister of industry, trade and technology. Although an agreement still had not been reached on the federal government's support, funds were released to Westray by Cameron's ministry to allow construction of the mine to commence in April 1989.[17] Later, when Cameron decided to run for the leadership of his party in 1990, he quickly raised $41,600 in campaign contributions in November, including $4450 from Maritime Steel and Foundry and $3500 from Satellite Equipment. Both companies had been awarded work on a $5-million contract with Westray to build a spur line to the mine. No other candidate could come close to matching Cameron in campaign contributions, the nearest being then Tourism Minister Roland Thornhill, who raised $16,600 during the same period.[18] On February 9, 1991, Cameron was elected leader of the party at its convention and became premier. On the face of it, it had been good for him to be seen as the creator of wealth and jobs.

Pictou County is located in the federal riding known as Central Nova. This is the riding in which Brian Mulroney who was elected leader of the Progressive Conservative Party in 19?? chose to run for his first federal seat in 1983. Central Nova was selected by Mulroney because it was a safe Conservative seat held by Elmer McKay, a senior Conservative Nova Scotia politician. In the next election, Brian Mulroney switched to the riding in Baie-Comeau, Quebec, and Elmer McKay re-took Central Nova and became a cabinet minister in the newly elected federal Progressive Conservative government in 19??. He was to be a main protagonist in the development of the Westray mine, fighting hard to maintain the federal government's support when it began to waver in the face of public pressure mounted by Devco; he was aided by a federal Liberal member of parliament from Nova Scotia, David Dingwall. The fact that Don Cameron has acknowledged that he spoke with Brian Mulroney to seek his support for the Westray project[19] only adds to the perception that the decision to open the Westray mine was taken because it advanced the immediate needs of that political elite.

The point being made is not that there was a conspiracy. To the contrary, the argument is that, in a political economy where government sees itself as a facilitator of private development and as dependent on its success, there is a strong tendency for this kind of decision-making to become the norm. Indeed, Frame was able to structure a similar deal with a New Democratic Party-led territorial government in order to re-open the Cyprus Anvil zinc-lead mine in Faro in the mid-1980s.[20] The dangers to political democracy posed by this tendency are so great that conflict of interest rules are continually being made and revised, without great success, precisely because government actors and private capitalists need each other.

Clifford Frame's career as a professional mining engineer and his company's non-involvement in coal mining should not have given him an advantage over a corporation such as Suncor. Perhaps his personal ingenuity made the difference, but perhaps also his contact with a former Progressive Conservative cabinet member from Nova Scotia, Robert Coates, helped him out. Frame had hired a lobbyist who was on Coates' staff. Coates has been quoted as saying that he acted as the effective marriage broker between Frame and the two levels of government.[21]

The most significant point is that occupational health and safety becomes a secondary consideration for the decision-makers. In the absence of a legal requirement to assess the health and safety consequences of this project and to develop a design which minimized risk to workers as a condition of granting it the permits and funding it required, government officials were not inclined to raise obstacles which might complicate and delay the political deal-making.

In sum, the way in which these decisions are made means that there is a bias towards a cost–benefit calculation in which the benefits of profits are given great weight while the costs of harm to occupational health and safety are discounted severely. Property owners and politicians assume that productivity, especially in coal mines, entails risk and that there is nothing unusual about that. Those risks are worth taking if profit is likely to be made. The risks can be dealt with by good monitoring and technological adjustments. Indeed, CANMET's report (Canadian Centre for Mineral and Energy Technology [do date]) was later used by the minister of energy, Jake Epp, when he was asked to defend the federal government's decision to involve itself in this kind of mining; he noted that the "memo recommended that it was feasible to open the mine.... We were all aware of the mine having high methane deposits, and that with the new technology there would have to be a learning curve."[22] Nothing could be more explicit: whatever learning had to be done was to come at the expense of workers' bodies.

## Operating the Mine: The Learning Curve in Action

Construction of the mine commenced in April 1989. With federal backing promised but not in place, construction halted at the end of July 1989. Extensive lobbying by Don Cameron and Elmer McKay was eventually successful in opening up the dam blocking the flow of federal monies. Construction resumed in January 1990, but the delay increased the difficulty of meeting the scheduled opening date of September 1991, a crucial date. It was at that point in time that the Trenton generating station, which also was under construction, was expected to need its first supply of Westray coal. Not surprisingly, this pressure to construct quickly was linked to safety problems.

On December 12, 1990, the Department of Labour issued its first order to Westray. The inspectorate found that the mine had been conducting underground blasting without qualified people being present. As was to be the case with future orders, work was not stopped and no charges were laid; rather, the company was advised that a failure to comply with the order would constitute a breach of the law which might lead to a prosecution. The violation which gave rise to the order in the first place apparently did not, in the department's view, merit a sanction.

On May 23, 1991, 24 metres of roof fell in; fortunately, no miners were injured. An independent engineering company was hired to investigate the cause of the collapse. No orders were issued with respect to this collapse, but the department did issue an order on June 24, 1991, forbidding any more electrical arcing in the mine, a highly dangerous practice in a site with so much inflammable gas. Again, no charges were laid.[23]

On July 29, 1991, there had been a report to Nova Scotia's chief mine inspector, Claude White, that the levels of coal dust on the mine floors and the methane concentration readings in the air were relatively high and presented a risk. A similar warning had been sounded by Westray's private consultant, Associated Mining Consultants, on July, 3, 1991.[24] No government action to enforce better standards seems to have been taken.

The question of the safety of the Westray mine was now beginning to attract the attention of those who had previously expressed opposition to the undertaking based on their interest in protecting the Devco mine. Bernie Boudreau, the provincial Liberal industry critic, raised the issue of the roof collapse in the legislature at the beginning of July. He argued that "[b]ecause of the fault structure and gas contained in the formation of coal seams in Pictou County, Westray mine is potentially one of the most dangerous mines in the world." He alleged that Leroy Legere, the minister of labour, was ignoring safety standards because the mine was located in the riding of Premier Don Cameron. Legere denied the charge.

The Westray mine opened on schedule in September 1991. In the two weeks leading up to October 20, there had been three more rock falls at the mine and public questioning was mounting. The ministry and Westray officials met, and the government found that there had been seven such rock falls since development began in 1989. The report of the meeting shows that the ministry officials came away satisfied with the precautionary means taken by Westray. Apparently the owners had implemented a geomechanics program and hired a geotechnical engineer to assess ground conditions on a daily basis.[26] The inspectorate's willingness to accept Westray's assurances that safety was being taken care of was to repeat itself.

On November 4, 1991, the minister of labour issued an order directing Westray to develop written rules to ensure that mine workers did not work in areas where the roof was not supported and requiring the corporation to keep records of all rock falls.[26] Clearly, there was a recognition within the ministry of the dangerous conditions created by Westray's mining activities. This alertness did not lead to precautions capable of averting further problems, however. Indeed, a miner by the name of Ryan told the press that, in February 1992, there was another cave-in.[27]

On March 28, 1992, yet another cave-in caused ministry officials to visit the mine. While there, they found that the air sample taken for testing contained 4 percent methane. The scientific assumption is that when the methane concentration reaches 5 percent, it becomes explosive if ignited. As a precaution, the law requires work to be halted and miners to be removed when the methane level reaches a level of 2.5 percent of the ambient air. When it reaches concentrations above 1.25 percent, electricity to the area is to be shut-off.[28] But, on March 28 production was not halted. Indeed, the Nova Scotia Department of Labour's safety officer, Albert McLean, indicated that he was satisfied that Westray management had the situation under control.

Throughout the period, the amount of explosive coal dust on the floors of the mine had been a constant concern. It is standard to combat this danger by putting down limestone dust to cover it. The law requires twenty bags of stonedust to be stored near every working section, and, where there is room-and-pillar mining, a "suitable amount" of stone dust must be kept nearby.[29] Between February and April of 1991, inspectors had pointed out the need for more limestone dust to be put down on at least nine occasions, and they did so again in July 1991. When the mine opened in early September, Albert McLean declared himself satisfied by the Westray's management plan to put a coal dusting plan in place by the end of the month. Apparently, no plan was implemented because on April 29, 1992, only ten days before the explosion, the ministry of labour issued formal orders to Westray to comply with the statutory requirements and design a plan for spreading the stone dust in an efficient manner. As is now known, the ministry's inspectorate had not checked again to see whether there had been compliance with these orders when, on May 10, the explosion occurred.

This officially documented record of breeches of existing safety standards and procedures shows that violations preceded the disaster. Westray remained firmly situated at the bottom of the steep learning curve which its promoters had said they would climb. And as miners have come forward to tell about their experiences, it has become increasingly clear that no steps were taken to climb the curve.

Two former employees, Evans and Taje, tell horror stories. They have spoken of the use of a cutting torch in the mine and how this led to a fire. They have said that there was no fire-fighting equipment and no rock dust nearby, although the regulations to prevent fires in mines required it. On one occasion, they said, the roof gave way and a big red flash was seen; the workers were alarmed. They also spoke of poor training and supervision. Taje claims that he reported his concerns on a number of occasions to his supervisors and once to the provincial authorities and that he had been ignored. He, Evans and one other person quit two weeks before the explosion due to the danger to health and safety. They were all experienced miners. Dwight House, Randy Roberts and Don Wentzel also quit their employment because the mine was too dangerous. In House's words, the mine was "a disaster waiting to happen," "the methane levels were so high that at times we had to stop work." He spoke of one particularly traumatic incident when he was operating his scoop with two men in the bucket. He pulled the bucket back just a minute or two before there was a cave-in. "If I hadn't moved within those two minutes, me and those other two guys probably would have been buried." Randy Roberts told the

Corner Brook *Western Star* that he left his Westray employment in February because "it was the only mine in where I never felt sleepy. I was too scared of the mine's working conditions to ever get sleepy."[30] Another miner, Wayne Gosbee, said that he and his fellow workers often talked about the mine's safety problems. In his view "as far as the company doing all they could do to make it safe … on the scale of 1 to 10, I would rate them about a 2."[31] Walter Ryan, a miner who had quit because of his anxiety about safety only to return to Westray because he needed the money, is now apparently second-guessing himself as to whether or not he ought to have spoken up more. He says that there were tractors in the mine with no jackets to prevent sparks, that there were poorly covered batteries, that oil containers and oil rags were left lying about in the mine, and that he saw an acetylene torch used underground. He recounts how experienced miners were aware of the presence of methane because they suffered from light-headedness; they commented on the staleness and the rankness of the air. The workers suffered from dizziness and headaches. In addition, Ryan claims that there were at least sixteen cave-ins, one of which caused him to quit.[32] Other miners have reported that, while work was to be stopped when levels of methane reached 2.5 percent of the air, levels of 3.5 and 3.75 percent were common. Methane monitors were said to be defective by then.[33]

As these miners' stories made the news, Westray management countered them with stout denials. Colin Benner, the executive vice-president of operations of Curragh Resources, rejected any arguments that the company allowed unsafe practices such as smoking, the use of acetylene torches or the employment of machines with electrical starters in the mine. He argued that it is unreasonably prejudicial to look for human agents as the cause of the accident, that "some people are assuming that human error is the only possible cause of such a tragedy.… Nature cannot always be predicted or controlled.…"[34]

But, the inspectors' reports support the workers' allegations, revealing that on two occasions open containers of oil were detected in working areas and that, on two other occasions, vehicles which had no devices fitted to prevent sparks were found to be in use underground.[35] And, as has been noted, the inspectorate had issued at least one order forbidding further dangerous electrical arcing in the mine.

In sum, there were many warning signals. Inasmuch as attention was paid to them, they were treated as a series of unrelated, even natural, events. There seems to have been no concerted effort to follow up on the promises to provide the best possible equipment and technology. While there was a good deal of monitoring—fifty-six inspector reports were issued—there was no vigilant enforcement. At no stage did the ministry exercise its enforcement power directly, preferring polite request and consultations to penalties. This is the norm.

### The Norm of Non-Enforcement

The roots of the norm of non-enforcement go back to the beginnings of state health and safety regulation in the mid-nineteenth century. From the time that inspectors were first appointed to enforce statutory minimum standards, they relied upon gentle persuasion rather than vigorous enforcement through prosecution to obtain compliance. The approach was premised on a number of assumptions.

The first assumption was that employers who violated the statutory requirements were, by and large, not guilty of criminal misconduct. This was true because illegalities were graded, with only some serious enough to be treated as criminal. Any other kind of violation was deemed to be quasi-criminal at worst. In Canada, the constitutional boundary between federal and provincial jurisdiction is drawn on the basis of this distinction: true crime falls within federal jurisdiction, regulatory offences fall within the provincial domain. With respect to occupational health and safety, the activity being regulated, the private production of goods and services, was socially useful. Hence it was simply not appropriate to treat the wrong-doing of the private capitalist engaged in such activity as one would the misconduct of a common criminal. Moreover, there was a deeply held belief that workers voluntarily assumed risks in the workplace and, even if the market could not be relied upon exclusively to determine the permissible level of risk, the seriousness of exposing workers to risks in excess of stipulated levels was attenuated by their apparent willingness to incur them. The fact that the illegal employment of under-age children in unhealthy conditions was viewed as a more serious wrong than the violation of existing health and safety standards reflected this perception of consent.

A second related assumption was that employers' violations were not the result of intentional wrong-doing. Rather, employers were perceived to be socially responsible citizens who, through ignorance or organizational incompetence, had failed to observe the law. Inspectors firmly believed that safety paid, that rational, profit-maximizing employers would find it was in their self-interest to comply with the law. After all, the law itself did not require uneconomic safety measures but stipulated that employers were required to take measures "reasonably required in the circumstances" to protect workers' health. Economic feasibility was always a pivotal consideration when deciding what was reasonable. Moreover, because workers were assumed to have an interest in their employers' economic viability, it could be concluded that there was a common interest between employers, workers, and the state in matters pertaining to health and safety. It followed, therefore, that health and safety were not issues of conflict. Rather, the internal self-monitoring system of the employer generally could be relied upon to achieve compliance, subject to occasional supervision, instruction, reminders, and gentle prodding by the state (Carson, 1979; Tucker, 1990; Gunningham, 1984).

Beginning in the 1970s, a second wave of occupational health and safety legislation swept through much of the English-speaking industrialized world. In part, the inspiration for this legislation was rooted in the failures of the old model of regulation, in particular the exclusion of worker participation. The architects of the new legislation were not willing to acknowledge that there was a fundamental conflict between labour and capital over health and safety. Rather, it was felt that the failure to include workers had encouraged apathy on their part, leading them to be careless at work, and had denied them the "natural right" to participate in decisions affecting their own health and safety. To some extent, the reformers were also concerned about the deficiencies of the existing external responsibility system. The aim of the reforms they offered in this respect was to rationalize and modernize the bureaucracy. The views of these influential reformers were expressed in reports of various government inquiries in comparable jurisdictions.[36]

The net effect of these changes was to create new opportunities for workers to contest health and safety issues on the shop floor and to further entrench the traditional practice of enforcement on the basis that the new and improved internal responsibility system could now be relied upon as the primary means through which compliance would be achieved. The role of the inspectorate as a support system for the internal responsibility system was emphasized. Formal sanctions were still to be used only as last resort or in the event of a fatality or serious injury. Thus, the practice of external enforcement changed little, although there were many more standards to enforce.

The opportunities created for workers to better their lot through the new internal responsibility system, however, were carefully circumscribed. Workers were given a right to know about hazards present in the workplace (including the right to have a worker-delegate conduct periodic inspections), a right to be consulted and a right to refuse unsafe work. Only the last right provided workers with the means to take direct action for their own protection, but it was carefully defined as an individual right. Health and safety strikes were not permitted (although groups of workers might refuse to work if each person felt endangered individually) and worker health and safety representatives could not shut down dangerous operations pending a state inspection. What workers could get out of such a scheme depended, to a significant degree, on their relative power resources. Clearly, the opportunity to make gains was greater for unionized workers in relatively secure industries than it was for non-unionized workers whose employers were operating at the margin. In addition, workers could make only limited use of what was potentially a very useful resource, the state inspectorate. Because inspectors were instructed to be facilitators first, workers calling upon them to back their claims were likely to be told to be reasonable in their demands and to resolve their differences with their employers through the internal responsibility system (Sass, 1989 and 1991; Walters et al., 1988; Tucker, 1992; Swinton, 1983).

Thus, the dominant assumptions regarding health and safety were not questioned at all. The view that criminal law and/or external enforcement had little if any role to play and that health and safety was a realm of consensus, not conflict, remained firmly entrenched in the health and safety bureaucracy.[37] Needless to say, the enforcement of mine safety was not significantly different from the model described here (Hopkins et al., 1984; Hopkins, 1989; Curran, 1984).

### The Case of Nova Scotia

Nova Scotia was a leader in regulating coal mine safety in the nineteenth century, largely as a result of the efforts of the Provincial Workmen's Association, the province's first colliers' union, formed in 1879. It lobbied hard to improve health and safety regulation in the mines and met with some successes, especially in the aftermath of disasters. A flood and an explosion in 1880 at the Foord seam killed sixty workers in total, leading to the enactment of legislation which strengthened the external responsibility system. It authorized the appointment of deputy inspectors, and it made special provision for gas-related inspections. The internal responsibility system was also reformed. The law empowered workers at each colliery to form two-men committees which were allowed to inspect the mine at least once a month and to file official evaluations. In 1884, legislation was enacted which established qualifications and staffing requirements. Further legislation passed in the aftermath of the Springhill mine disaster of 1891 gave miners' committees the right both to visit scenes of accidents and to begin prosecutions of management by affidavit. However, mine owners fiercely resisted their effective implementation, especially when it impinged on managerial prerogative. As a result, enforcement remained generally lax (Macleod, 1983; McKay, 1985).

Nova Scotia's position as a leader in health and safety law, at least on the books, has not been sustained. The *Coal Mines Regulation Act*, although periodically updated, has not been amended to increase workers' control rights over the operation of the mine and, although additional rules have been enacted, the maximum fine for most violations is $250. As well, the government must lay charges within six months of the occurrence of the violation.[38] In regard to occupational health and safety law generally, Nova Scotia was one of the last two provinces (the other being Prince Edward Island) to enact second-wave legislation of the kind described above affirming miners' rights.[39] The maximum fine for a violation of that Act is $10,000. This is at the medium to low end of the spectrum of maximum fines provided for in similar legislation in other provinces.[40] Evidence suggests that persuasion is still the primary strategy and that prosecutions are rare events. From 1985 to 1990, fourteen companies were charged with offences under the *Occupational Health and Safety Act* and the maximum fine imposed was $2500. No mining companies were prosecuted despite the fact that between 1987–88 and 1991–92, 1037 directives were issued to mining companies. The fact that directives never result in change does not mean there is compliance, as the Westray saga shows.[41]

Viewed in this light, the (non-)enforcement of safety at Westray was unexceptional. Sadly, then, Leroy Legere, the Nova Scotia minister of labour, was correct when, in response to charges of favouritism made prior to the disaster, he declared that "the people in the Department of Labour are not treating the Westray Mine any differently than they are treating any other mine in the province."[42] However, there is some question as to the technical capacity of the mine safety branch at the time Westray opened. It had little recent experience regulating underground coal mines, as Devco was under federal jurisdiction; the only underground coal mine it was overseeing was a small operation conducted by Evans Coal Mines Limited in Inverness County.[43] As a result of this lack of experience, the inspectors may have been reticent to take strong measures in regard to enforcement.

Curragh Resources was indebted in 1991 and needed both a good cash flow and profits from the Westray mine. Its primary business was the mining of lead and zinc concentrates. Depressed world prices for those concentrates, heavy investment in the new Stronsay lead and zinc mine in British Columbia, a failed attempt to diversify, and a ten-week strike by workers at its Faro mine in Yukon, motivated in part by health and safety concerns,[44] had caused Curragh to lose $98 million on revenues of $225 million in 1991.[45] In an attempt to raise money, Curragh Resources tried to interest institutional investors in buying convertible debentures from it. The security offered these potential institutional creditors was the Westray mine. Curragh was expecting the cash flow from the mine to repay the debt it proposed to undertake, but institutional investors were uninterested. Curragh then announced that it would put the Westray mine up for sale as a way of raising cash for its sputtering enterprises. The sale never took place.[46]

In this context there was a pressing need to get Westray going. The rock falls in October and the ensuing public pressure to do something about this kind of risk must have been a real nuisance to a company that was keen to get on with intense production. But the corporation's problems only got worse. By October 30, 1991, it was apparent that Westray could not meet its obligation to supply coal to the Trenton power plant. That plant could not use coal with ash levels exceeding 20 percent, but much of the Westray coal had a 40 percent ash level. The excess ash had to be washed out, which took time and cost a great deal of money. The Westray management was hopeful that, as the digging went deeper, the ash level would drop.[47] The investment was no longer looking so good. Westray sought to alleviate some of the pressure by obtaining rights to strip-mine at the nearby Wimpey site, but it had to continue to dig underground in order to meet its contractual commitments. The miners were offered production incentives and the opportunity to work unlimited overtime. Firms under a great deal of pressure to meet production deadlines may cut corners to do so (Grunberg, 1983; Wallace, 1987; Wright, 1986; Novek et al., 1990). The Westray case exemplifies this. The violation of regulations controlling coal dust and the frequency of rock falls suggest that production was being given priority over safety. There was at least one other major cave-in in February and conditions were highly dangerous during 1992, as the April 29, 1992, orders indicated.

Finally, Westray had a good relationship with politicians in the province. The staple model of development made the region dependent upon Westray's success to improve its economic well-being. Moreover, important politicians, led by Premier Don Cameron and federal Minister of Public Works Elmer McKay (both of whom represented the riding in which Westray was located), not only invested federal and provincial money but also their political capital in the project. The inspectors could not have been oblivious to this and may very well have understood that an especially soft approach to enforcement would be appropriate.

## CONSENSUS AT WORK—THE MYTH OF EQUIVALENT RISK-TAKING

A central pillar of consensus theory, and the regulatory approaches justified by it, is that labour and capital share a common set of goals. One aspect of this equivalence is in relation to risk-taking. Employers risk their capital, workers their lives and health. On its face, the notion that these risks are equivalent is absurd. Yet, in capitalist economic theory, all values, including the value of life and health, are monetized and, therefore, comparable (Viscusi, 1983; Moore et al., 1990).

Support for the idea of a shared ideology also derives from the belief that workers voluntarily assume the risks present in the workplac, that, if the dangers of working at Westray were so obvious, then the fact that miners continued to work and did not exhibit more resistance suggests that they were willing to incur the risk.

The idea that workers and employers voluntarily incur roughly equivalent risk not only has influenced legal doctrine in the past (Risk 1983; Tucker 1984), but it continues to serve as a rationale for not intervening to protect workers from harm. It justifies reliance on the internal responsibility system and the gentle persuasion approach to enforcement; that is, it justifies the very practices which led up to the Westray disaster.

### Workers as Risk-Takers

There is no doubt that workers at the Westray mine put their lives and health at risk, but did they do so voluntarily? Some of the miners at Westray were professional miners who moved around the country following employment opportunities; they were from Newfoundland, Alberta, Saskatchewan, Northern Ontario, and other parts of Nova Scotia. They needed jobs. They understood the dangers of mining. This is clear from the statements of the miners and their friends. They knew the risks, but an adaptive culture among them evolved, enabling them to live with the terror of it all. One journalist, Tom McDougall, after a series of interviews with miners, wrote: "There's a certain mystique about it—a soldier-like pride in sticking with a job that would scare lesser folk witless. There's also spirit of brotherhood—part old-soldier camaraderie and small-town solidarity."[48]

In addition to this complex articulation of class identity, other processes shape and constrain workers' decisions about risk. Workers develop "experience-based" standards which often depart markedly from official ones. In part, this occurs because the risk of harm is relatively remote and, in the absence of recent experience of its materialization, there is a tendency to discount its probability. Moreover, there may be immediate costs to workers if they comply with safety rules, including physical discomfort, increased workload because of poorly designed safety equipment, and loss of production bonuses. Because safety and productivity often conflict, management may endorse, implicitly or explicitly, experience-based practices if they result in increased productivity.

Also, processes of cognitive dissonance play a role here. Workers faced with objectively risky conditions may adjust their beliefs about the safety of the activity in order to avoid feelings of constant fear and uncertainty (Ackerlof et al., 1982). Thus, although miners at Westray quit because it was too dangerous, others stayed put but now say that they were always anxious and afraid. What this suggests is that when they speak bravely about the dangers they face every day, they may be making the most of necessity. In short, if going underground is the only realistic option that these workers believe they have, normal emotions like fear must be repressed, at least partially. As Alvin Jahn, an uncle of a Westray victim and a former miner himself, said about mining, "It's an eerie feeling, but it's a matter of daily bread."[49] These conditions help us to understand the behaviour of miners before the disaster. Workers are so dependent for their welfare that they seem almost oblivious to risk. They are likely to develop rationalizations for their actions, creating a culture which inures them to daily fears. In addition to the problems discussed here, it is necessary to critically evaluate the assumption economists make: that workers rationally calculate risk and behave accordingly, that thye have perfect information and that they have a proper understanding of probability relationships (Chasse et al., 1984; Felstiner et al., 1989).

A more mundane, but nonetheless important, reason for the apparent willingness to put up with bad conditions is that employers can use their powers to still resistance. This is why statutory regimes, such as Nova Scotia's *Occupational Health and Safety Act*, provide that workers should not be penalized for exercising their rights under the Act.[50] Westray management was not backwards in repressing obstreperous workers demands. Robert Chisholm, the labour critic for the provincial NDP in Nova Scotia, released copies of Westray's health and safety policy. In part this policy says that under no circumstances may information be released to any other person without the express authority of the Vice-President, General Manager of Westray Corporation. This is in violation of the *Occupational Health and Safety Act*. It helps explain why complaints made by workers got no action, and why so few workers came forward with health and safety issues.[51] One Piche, a union organizer, said that workers approached supervisors with health and safety problems but "you can only go to the sink so many times before you realize you are not going to get any water." He went on to say that if workers tried to improve safety they were told "you can go down the road and look for another job."[52] Intimidation was made all the more effective in the Westray case by the fact that the Westray operation was one of the few mines in the country which was not unionized.[53]

Under conditions such as these, the internal responsibility system, which is premised on the notion of common interests, could not, and did not, work. Randy Facette, an experienced coal miner, was an employee representative on the joint health and safety committee at Westray. In his words, "It was a joke. We never got any help at all from the company ... having actual health and safety committee meetings, having a chairman, there was nothing like that." Moreover, he said that the company seldom acted on complaints he passed on from other miners (Robb, 1992).

At the same time as Westray was being tough with its workers about health and safety complaints, it was holding out to the public that, despite the occasional glare of publicity caused by the questions raised in the legislature, it was running a safe mine. Indeed, only two weeks before the explosion Westray was awarded a John T. Ryan Safety Award. The award was granted by the Canadian Institute of Mining Metallurgy and Petroleum, which based its award on the frequency of reportable injuries in any one year. However, at least one miner stated that the company paid workers to avoid reporting injuries to the Workers' Compensation Board by giving them light duties,[54] a common tactic used by employers who are trying to minimize workers' compensation premiums.[55] A sad irony about Westray's John T. Ryan Award is that the company sent one of its workers to get it. The worker was to become one of the victims of the May 9 explosion.[56]

## Employers as Risk-Avoiders

The economic cost of poor occupational health and safety is primarily borne by workers, secondarily by the government and taxpayers, and only thirdly and, to a much lesser degree, by the employing classes. Each accident leads to direct costs, such as compensation for lost earnings and pensions for the victims and their dependants, and indirect costs, such as lost work-time, equipment replacement and upgrading, record-keeping related to the accident, and expenses incurred to accommodate returning workers and to recruit and train new people. Some of these losses are borne by employers in the first place, such as lost productivity, increased compensation, premium funds, penalty assessments, training, and accommodation, while others may be passed on. For instance, workers' compensation policies, in the end, are paid out of workers' wages; and increased costs of production can be passed on by employers. More important, perhaps, is the fact that taxpayers (mostly workers) bear many of the costs. They fund the medical care system, public pension regimes which include disability schemes, welfare, and charitable organizations which look after the victims of accidents and their dependants (Glasbeek, 1989).

As has been clearly demonstrated by the particular circumstances of the Westray case, private property owners will seek to have governments underwrite their costs. In various liberal democracies capitalists are able to pursue this goal more successfully than in others. For instance, at its Faro Mine operations in the Yukon, Curragh Resources Incorporated was able to obtain an almost identical deal to the one it got for the Westray venture. The federal government guaranteed 85 percent of its borrowings and the territorial government, run by the NDP, chipped in with an undisclosed public grant.[57]

Displacement of costs by wealth owners is acceptable because it dovetails with one of the cornerstones of working capitalism in a staple economy, namely that the state should help promote the unmediated pursuit of self-interest as much as it can. While there are occasional expressions of concern about the efficiency of public hand-outs, overall they are seen as necessary concessions to private capitalists whose willingness to take risks must be bolstered to foster general economic and social welfare (Murty et al., 1991; Trebilcock, 1985). Not only does this line of argument provide a justifying framework for the socialization of costs by employers as a class, it also serves to hide the effectiveness of another important set of risk-diluting stratagems, namely that employers, as individuals, can use the corporation to avoid personal risk.

The corporation has been given the legal standing it has to facilitate profit-making activities. It is designed to permit the pooling of small holdings of capital and human resources in one envelope to make their combined efforts more effective. For example, individuals invest some of their capital in a corporate venture by a rule which ensures that only that amount of their capital is at risk. The remainder of their assets are safe from the corporation's creditors. They are also free to take their investment out of any one corporation at any time and sell it to a willing buyer. This contrasts sharply with the position of the worker who invests in the same corporation. All of the capital she invests is at risk because she cannot safeguard some of her body from the physical dangers of the job. Moreover, the labour market rarely has as many willing buyers for her services as the capital market does for shares held in viable corporations.

The story of how C.H. (Clifford) Frame used his capacities as an individual promoter, an investor, a management consultant, and a shareholder in a number of closely related businesses to create a web of corporate connections and dealings, which seem to have left him secure and well-off, is told in the pages of Curragh Resources Incorporated's 1990 Annual Report and in those of the statement registered with the US Security and Exchange Commission on November 6, 1989, the date Curragh Resources Incorporated became a public company.

The beginning point is the incorporation of an Ontario company on April 29, 1987. It was named 715914 Ontario Incorporated and changed its name to Curragh Resources on May 20, 1987. The day it was formed the numbered company acquired all of the resource properties and other assets and liabilities of Curragh Resources. This was a firm which had been established by C.H. Frame and two partners. Because Curragh Resources was a partnership, its members were responsible for the debts and obligations of the firm. The firm had been established to acquire the Faro division and other mining properties of a company called Cyprus Anvil Mining Corporation. In order to acquire the Curragh Resources partnership's business, 715914 Ontario Incorporated had to raise $50 million. That sum allowed 715914 Ontario to acquire the assets of Curragh Resources and to undertake its liabilities. In addition, 715914 Ontario borrowed $7 million to operate the business. In short, Frame and his partners in the Curragh Resources firm were paid in full for the investments they had made.

Two years later, in December 1989, Curragh Resources bought a 90 percent interest in the mining leases and options known as the Westray Coal Property from the company 630902 Ontario Incorporated, which was a wholly-owned subsidiary of a Frame Mining Corporation. In turn, 74 percent of the shares in Frame Mining Corporation were owned by a company called the Westray Mining Corporation.[58] Seventy percent of Westray Mining Corporation's shares were owned by C.H. Frame, the man who was the promoter of the Westray coal project. As we know, it was he who had concluded the dealings which led to the very favourable conditions for extracting coal at the Westray site.

When Curragh Resources Incorporated bought 90 percent of the Westray coal project, it paid $9 million in cash to 630902 Ontario, and assumed $13 million of the liabilities which had been incurred in the promotion of the project. Once again, C.H. Frame had recouped his investment. Yet, stated in legal terms, nothing unusual had occurred: one mining development corporation had bought the interest which had been owned by another corporation. But, when Curragh Resources Incorporated entered into an agreement to buy the Westray Coal Project operations from a C.H. Frame-controlled set of corporations, the same C.H. Frame controlled Curragh Resources Incorporated.

Curragh Resources Incorporated's list of significant shareholders is now part of the public record. As of March 1, 1991, the corporation had issued 16,406,302 subordinate voting shares and 15,719,737 multiple voting shares. Each subordinate voting share gave its holder one vote, whereas each multiple voting share gave its owner ten votes. C.H. Frame beneficially owned, directly or indirectly, 100 percent of the multiple voting shares. In a company report issued in March 1991, Frame indicated that he intended to use his voting control to ensure that all of his nominees for directorships would be appointed.[59] Not only was Frame the principal engineer of the coal mining project, he was, at the same time, the very well-paid chief executive officer of Curragh Resources Incorporated. The legal ability to act in various capacities and guises obviously was exploited to the full by Mr. Frame.

There was also a company called C.H. Frame Consulting Services. Among its businesses was the supply of executive officers and personnel to Curragh Resources Incorporated. In 1987 and 1988, Curragh Resources Incorporated paid $0.9 million and $1.2 million respectively to C.H. Frame Consulting Services for this supply. C.H. Frame Consulting Services also provided management services to the Westray coal project in connection with the planning and development of the Westray coal mine. It was to get $6 million for this when the mine was in full production. Curragh Resources Incorporated, managed by a board of directors associated with C.H. Frame and with C.H. Frame as C.E.O., bought out C.H. Frame Consulting Services for $1.5 million. For this, Curragh Resources Incorporated obtained the benefits of the management services contract for the Westray coal project: a C.H. Frame-created business obtained benefits from its links with another C.H. Frame corporation.[60]

It is, of course, quite likely that many of the payments made to Frame and his associates for the projects which he had developed and sold to Curragh Resources Incorporated were made by way of shares in Curragh Resources Incorporated. In this sense, Frame, as a shareholder in Curragh Resources Incorporated, still runs some of the risks arising out of the enterprises that it operates. But his personal assets are not at risk.

Finally, Curragh Resources Incorporated is not directly responsible for the monies owed on the Westray coal project. The government of Nova Scotia's loan was secured by the assets at the Westray mine and collectable only after the loan obtained from the Bank of Nova Scotia, guaranteed by the federal government, had been satisfied. In terms of satisfaction of the debt to the bank, Curragh Resources Incorporated was required only to indemnify the bank and/or the federal government for $25 million of the $100 million borrowed. All in all, the position of Curragh Resources Incorporated shareholders is not much less secure than it was.

The story makes it clear that, inasmuch as the dominant model of occupational health and safety regulation assumes some equivalence of risk between capital investors and labour power investors, the assumption is a distortion of reality. Employers, as a class, pay relatively little towards compensating victims and are not exposed to the same kind of risk. More importantly, by clever use of the corporate form, individual investors are able to displace the economic costs of injury and death to workers and to society at large.

## CONCLUSIONS

The Westray story demonstrates that the assumptions which underlie health and safety regulation in Canada are inimical to the goal of providing adequate protection for workers. This is because, at bottom, they are wrong.

Employer–employee relationships in a capitalist economy are inherently conflictual not consensual. A truly shared ideology is an illusion; it can only be maintained by artifice and with great effort. Health and safety issues in particular are likely to undo these efforts. Only workers, not employers, get hurt at work. Because of this the notion of shared risk is unbelievable. This is why so much effort is put into creating the image of mutual concern about physical working conditions and why there are repeated assertions that responsible employers, governments, and employees enjoy a shared ideology. Another reason for denying health and safety as an industrial relations issue is that employers and state officials wish to contain any erosion of managerial prerogative resulting from the extension to workers of weak rights to participate in production decisions affecting their physical well-being. By insisting that these rights are bestowed in a sphere which falls outside "normal" industrial relations, the standard exclusion of workers from decision-making in general can be sustained (Creighton et al., 1985; Walters, 1991).

The effort to uphold this myth has been largely successful. It permits profit-oriented employers to build risks into production processes on the basis of cost–benefit calculations which suit them, subject only to whatever constraints are imposed by government or by workers through the internal responsibility system. Historically, health and safety standards have been set at levels which do not seriously infringe employer profitability or prerogative. Workers effectively participate in setting these standards principally in an historic sense: governments have reacted to previous disasters, body counts, and undeniable evidence of workers being harmed from commonly followed practices (i.e., unguarded machinery). Workers' struggles for improved health and safety are much less likely to succeed when graphic evidence of their losses is not readily available.

Now, as capital's mobility is enhanced and global competition intensifies, it becomes more difficult both for workers to mobilize and for the state to regulate on their behalf. These conditions also restrict the opportunities for worker influence through the internal responsibility system. The superior economic power of employers who may withdraw their capital if they deem conditions unfavourable, imposes clear limits on what any particular group of workers can hope to achieve. Contrary, then, to another of the assumptions which underlie health and safety regulation in Canada, particular social relations are determinative of the level of risk. At any level of productivity, different political and social structures, and the balance of forces within those structures, will produce different levels of risk. The degree of danger at work is not just simply related to natural conditions or technical capacity.

In this context, the Westray story is illuminating precisely because the particular conjuncture of unequal power and the near-total acceptance of the need to please private capital made the working of the health and safety regulatory machinery so fraught with danger. But it need not be this way. Because risks and regulatory regimes are socially constructed, a range of mediations are possible. The history of health and safety regulation attests to this. Worker struggles and changing economic, political, and ideological conditions made these developments possible.

Comparative studies provide further evidence that a range of mediations is viable. For example, in Sweden where workers' political and economic resources are highly developed, stronger worker rights and more protective standards have been legislated. At the other end of the spectrum, workers in the United States enjoy fewer participatory rights (Navarro, 1983). Moreover, even within a particular jurisdiction, the actual operation of the regulatory regime is responsive to changes in the balance of forces. Enforcement was strengthened in Ontario during the NDP-Liberal Accord in the mid-1980s. However, developments in Sweden and the United States point the other way. The retreat of the Swedish social democrats on the issue of economic democracy, the move toward integration with Europe, and the recent electoral defeat of the social democrats, all impact adversely upon the administration of health and safety and the ability of workers to make use of their legal rights (Tucker, 1992). In the United States, the election of Ronald Reagan led to a gutting of the health and safety administration without any formal change in the law whatsoever. The sensitivity of fatality rates in coal mining to the level of government spending on enforcement of strong coal mining safety laws has been demonstrated (Noble, 1986; Szasz, 1986; Perry, 1982). In sum, because a range of mediations is possible within any one set of social relations, the regulation of health and safety can be improved in Canada without waiting for transformation.

At a minimum, the political struggle must begin from the perspective that, "there is nothing subtle, refined, genteel or courtly about this struggle. This IS war. This IS life and death."[61] This war, however, can be fought only one step at a time. It may be possible to get a better level of mediated regulation, setting the stage for further struggles until the structural limits of change are reached (Wright, 1978). To this end, much more vigorous and frequent criminal prosecution, posited on the reckless disregard for human life exhibited by employers when they wilfully ignore existing standards or engineer unacceptable risks into an enterprise, would help focus attention on the fact that employers make all the important decisions on health and safety and workers take all the risks. Employers and governments may accept, or even initiate, measures which strengthen workers' participatory rights, giving them greater control over their work environment.

In the same vein, there should be a concerted effort to de-mystify the corporate form. Real flesh and blood human beings profit from the maiming and killing which goes on in the corporate-owned enterprise. This will make it more difficult for governments to hold fast to the view that there is no question but that economic welfare should be produced primarily by the private sector rather than the public one. The notion that the private sector must be supported at any cost, even at the expense of the lives of people such as the miners at Westray, may have to be addressed more explicitly than it has been to date.[62]

These tactics can be employed from within the existing scheme and its harmful assumptions. If purposefully engaged, they may yield some positive results.

## CHAPTER FIVE

# THE AWARENESS AND ACCEPTANCE OF RISK AT WESTRAY[1]

*Gerald J.S. Wilde*

## INTRODUCTION

"One thing about Westray: the money was good if you worked the overtime and that."[2] This chapter describes the results of an analysis of the public inquiry hearings held after the Westray Coal accident in May 1992. At the request of Justice K. Peter Richard, Commissioner, I investigated the content of the hearings in order to develop insight into the degree to which Westray employees perceived the risk of accident as imminent and why the miners either accepted or rejected the risk they perceived. While some miners terminated their employment with the mine because they were unwilling to accept the accident risk, others continued to work until the accident happened. Various factors that contributed to the employee perceptions of accident risk were identified, and it may be inferred that the perceived probability and expected seriousness of an accident was both high and general throughout the underground workforce. Moreover, the willingness to accept high levels of danger among those miners who did not quit may be attributed to the operation of various factors, among which economic pressures and economic incentives played a major role. Mine management, rather than putting in place a safety-incentive program of a type known to significantly improve cautious and accident-free performance, instituted instead a remuneration schedule with a progressive production bonus component that appears to have exacerbated risk acceptance and the frequency of imprudent practices among the miners. The pursuit of short-term economic gain may well have set the stage for the fatal explosion and the mine's premature demise.

Webmark
Gerald Wilde's latest book is *Target Risk: Dealing with the Danger of Death, Disease and Damage in Everyday Decisions*. It is available on the web at: http://pavlov.psyc.queensu.ca.target/

## NATURE AND LIMITATIONS OF THIS ANALYSIS

The materials available at the time were transcripts of the hearing proceedings, which were provided by Justice K. Peter Richard, commissioner of the public inquiry. Certain passages in these materials made me curious about the precise nature and potential safety impact of the production bonus system that was in operation at Westray Coal beginning March 1992. At my request, additional hearing transcripts were made available to me by Deirdre Williams-Cooper, chief administrator of the Inquiry. A total of 190 pages of transcripts and four exhibits[3] served as the raw material for the preparation of this report.[4]

The information contained in inquest/court transcripts is limited in that it offers no facial expressions, no intonation, no hesitations nor rapid periods of speeds, no trembling of the voice, no paling nor blushing nor gestures. These and other extralingual elements of behaviour are often very communicative in conveying or betraying feelings, cognitions, and motivations. As a consequence of the absence of such subtleties in verbal transcripts, several manifestations of attitudes, feelings, motivations, perceptions, accusations, allusions, insinuations, or innuendo, etc. may have escaped me. This holds both for the way questions were asked as well as for the manner in which they were answered during the hearings. Moreover, I have no systematic information regarding such factors as age, marital status, fatherhood, educational history, occupational history, seniority as a miner, coal or hard rock miner, seniority at Westray, or prospects for promotion to foreman/supervisor.

My analysis lays no claim to being the kind of quantitative and objective content analysis which is an established method of gathering data in the social sciences (C.P. Smith, 1992). Contrary to what is usual practice in content analysis, the pages of the hearings that were analyzed did not constitute a scientifically selected sample from all available pages. No effort was made to tally the frequency of occurrence of certain topics or statements of fact or opinion. I did not attempt to produce a representative account of what was said and what was felt, and how often. Instead, my approach has been qualitative and inferential in hopes of presenting the reader with a report of what seems to have been typical, characteristic of the perceptions and attitudes of the miners prior to the explosion.

In the next several sections, various perceptions, motivations and actions have been listed as they transpire from the transcripts. This is followed by an attempt to explain the miners' actions, as well as their failures to act, and a discussion of possible implications for accident prevention.

## PERCEPTIONS OF IMMINENT DANGER

There can be no question that there were various conditions that made underground personnel well aware of the potential for danger.

> You wonder how long you lived as long as you did, as simple as that.
> Like, we all knew amongst ourselves, we all knew stuff was going to
> happen but we never thought we were going to lose the whole mine
> and 26 guys.... We all risked our lives.
> Question: Rather than speak up?
> Answer: That's right. It's just the way it was there.[5]

Those who left the employ of the mine prior to the disaster commonly referred to their concerns about their safety as the reason for quitting. Typical causes for concern were the presence and accumulation of coal dust; the presence of methane; the methanometer not working or being deliberately set at a higher than prescribed level; sparks from electric equipment; torches being taken underground; poor ventilation; frequent cave-ins of the roof structure; and poor level of training of the workforce and of safety training in particular.

### Coping with Danger

There are essentially two ways of coping with stress. One can either deal with the stressful situation directly and attempt to change it so that the threat is eliminated or at least reduced, or alternatively one can deal with one's feelings about the situation.

Under conditions in which the first approach is either impossible, dangerous, or unlikely to achieve the intended effect, people may resort to the second alternative and thus attempt to make the threat less intolerable by modifying their emotional reaction to it (Mechanic, 1991).

There are several instances in the hearing transcripts where miners refer to their states of mind, which can be understood as an attempt to deal with their emotions in the face of the threat of accident. One of these is humour; another, displaced expression of anger at the mine's management; and, finally, a rather optimistic interpretation of reality and future.

**Inquiry Testimony, Mr. Facette, Day 33, Feb 20, 1996: 7264–65**

Q. Okay. Now we heard about there being a fair bit of overtime available, Mr. Facette, and it seems that you worked overtime. You've—you're indicating you worked overtime on May 7th and May 8th?

A. Not by choice; I had to.

Q. What do you mean, "not by choice?"

A. Well, we had—when we left Alberta, we moved out here and we went fairly substantially in debt to get into a home and try and set ourselves up and everything. And we borrowed $12,000 off of relatives that we had to pay back. And, plus, with the mortgage on top of that, it was—I needed the additional money. That was all there was to it.

Q. So the condition of the mine didn't stop you from working overtime?

A. Occasionally it did.

Q. What do you mean, "occasionally?"

A. I may have planned to go in for an overtime shift and changed my mind and just said, "To hell with it, I don't—I don't want to go back there."

Q. What about quitting, did you ever think about quitting?

A. It wasn't really an option to me. I know I wanted to. But, like, I say, I—there was no other work out there —

Q. Right.

A. — that I was aware of that would pay anything that would I would [sic] be able to pay my bills with and whatnot. One thing about Westray, the money was good if you worked the overtime and that.

Q. Right.

A. So I didn't consider that an option, not after having moving moved [sic] my family 3,000 miles across Canada. I wasn't prepared to quit a job and be stuck in the position with no income.

[Inquiry testimony conducted by Ms. Campbell, Solicitor for the Commission]

### Coping with the help of humour

Humour often functions as a coping mechanism and provides a method of coping with stress. To joke about a threat is to minimize that threat or to downplay it. We try to ridicule the things that scare us; and what is ridiculous cannot hurt us. Although joking about a threat fails to alter its objective features, it allows us to maintain a modicum of mental stability or peace of mind despite the undiminished presence of the threat.

We used to laugh about it, how we all had kinks in our neck from looking up [looking up continuously at the unstable roofs] … the roof would be working—Like, you'd have a stranger, a new fellow, in the mine. That's just local stuff. They called it local.… I don't know, it picked up somewhere. It started somewhere and just continued on through the whole mine.… A new fellow could see a small amount of rock that was moving, but none of the men that were there for a longer period of time expected or thought that anything more was going to develop.… But a new fellow could see that as "'Geez, I'm going to get buried." But the more experienced fellow that was there longer would say, No, you know, "That's local stuff," that there was an outlet that way.[6]

### *Displaced anger*

Another emotional defence mechanism, which like ridiculing does not affect the external threat but which does at least give a degree of relief in our feelings about it, is displacement of aggression (Freud, 1946). When we are angry at somebody, but have good reasons for not showing our anger at that person directly because expressing our frustration may lead to severe retaliation, we may find a much safer outlet for our feelings by acting out against an innocent or innocuous person or object whom we do not expect to retaliate.

> Well, if we had a fire boss coming down on your back all the time bothering you, you would probably get excited.… Well, he used to come in and rush us all the time.… And they would be rushing more and taking their frustrations out on the bolts instead of on the fire boss.[7]

### *Optimistic thoughts*

Overconfidence is more frequent than underconfidence (Wright, 1984). People are more likely to have expectations that are unrealistically optimistic than unrealistically pessimistic (Weinstein, 1984). However, it has also been observed that individuals who overestimate their perceptions of mastery and of being in control are marked by greater happiness, exhibit more persistence at tasks, and experience superior mental health; and they are ultimately more effective in their performance than their pessimistic counterparts. A degree of unrealistic optimism is characteristic of normal human thought. Not exaggerating one's mastery or chances of success is associated with low self-esteem and mental depression (Taylor et al., 1988). Self-aggrandizement is beneficial, provided it is not excessive. A healthy dose of self-overestimation is healthy, not only for the individual in question, but also for others, because it appears to promote the ability to care for others and to help them, to facilitate social bonding, and ultimately to foster a happier and more productive human condition. This optimism in the face of danger is seen in the miners as well.

Q. But you personally didn't fear for your own safety?
A. Oh, no, because I had years of experience behind me. Like, so I was more apt to recognize a, you know, something that was going wrong than a greenhorn.[8]

And once the mine got along a little ways, we would be able to get a union in there, and we'd be able to have a little bit of say and maybe change things around a little bit, you know.[9]

Dealing with the source of stress at Westray would certainly have been difficult, especially in light of the obvious dangers of working underground. When complaints addressed at the mine management and to the mine inspector seemed to be ineffective, the workers must have felt quite powerless. Making complaints and concerns public through the mass media did not seem to be an option and neither did leaving employment at Westray to try find another job elsewhere. So they found different ways to cope with the dangers psychologically.

## REASONS FOR ACCEPTING RISKY WORKING CONDITIONS

There were many reasons for accepting risky working conditions at Westray, some positive and others negative. These will be discussed in more detail in the sections to come but can be summarized here. It is obvious that for many workers the pay cheque was necessary to support their families. In the absence of alternative employment in the region, options must have seemed bleak, while at Westray there was the promise of long-term employment. They could hope that working conditions would get better with time and that they could survive by their skill/experience. For some there was the prospect of promotion and advancement through the ranks, which would certainly have been an incentive. As well, the production bonus system, discussed later in this chapter, would encourage workers to weigh risk against cash.

On the other hand, workers feared reprisals, such as not getting overtime or being fired as a consequence of complaining to management about unsafe conditions. Feeling intimidated by management and not having the necessary data to confront management or take Westray to court would have made it difficult to do anything about unsafe working conditions. The feeling of powerlessness, the feeling that government was supportive of mine management, and the feeling that the inspection department would refuse to assist miners or that complaining to the mine inspector might lead to being fired would also have worked against workers taking any action. There was a fear that (being seen to) quit work without sufficient cause would invoke unemployment insurance (UI) penalties or a delay in the arrival of a UI cheque, or that they didn't have sufficient time accumulated to be eligible for UI. Some workers also talked of being bribed into hiding a lost-time injury/accident from the Worker's Compensation Board.[10]

Finally, we can't overlook the contradictory but strong sentiments of wanting to remain loyal to colleagues who were working under dangerous conditions and of identifying with the mine. For all these reasons, and probably more, workers endured daily conditions which they knew to be potentially injurious and life-threatening.

## GENERAL INTERPRETATION

The amount of risk people are willing to accept in any given condition depends on their estimations of the advantages and disadvantages of the various risky and cautious behaviour alternatives at their disposal. When the expected benefits of risky behaviour are high and the expected costs of these actions are perceived as relatively low, the level of accepted risk will be high. Similarly, when the expected benefits of safe behaviour alternatives are low and their costs high, the level of accepted risk will be high. Thus, the amount of risk to health and safety that individuals are willing to accept is determined by four subjective utility categories of motivating factors:

a.  the expected benefits of comparatively risky behaviour alternatives;
b.  the expected costs of comparatively risky behaviour alternatives;
c.  the expected benefits of comparatively safe behaviour alternatives; and
d.  the expected costs of comparatively safe behaviour alternatives

The higher the values in categories a and d, the higher the target level of risk. The target level of risk will be lower as the values in categories b and c rise. The term "expected benefit" (or "expected cost") refers essentially to two underlying elements: the perceived likelihood that a benefit will in fact follow from a given behaviour alternative, and the size of that benefit. The expected benefit will be greater to the extent that the perceived likelihood of its occurrence is higher and to the extent that the size of the benefit is greater. Mathematically expressed, expected benefit = likelihood x size.

Rational decision-makers, i.e., rational risk-takers, will accept a level of risk for which they expect the overall (that is, net) benefit of their actions to be maximal. So, the rational risk-taker does not attempt to minimize risk, let alone maximize it, but instead chooses a behaviour that is associated with a level of risk at which the individual expects that his or her goals will be best satisfied. This level of risk may be called "the target level of risk," because the satisfaction of one's goals would be expected to suffer at levels of risk-taking that are either lower or higher than this target level.

The term "target" is meant to be synonymous with "preferred, desired, accepted, tolerated and subjectively optimal." The target level of risk differs between conditions dependent on the behaviour alternatives that are available to the individual in that situation, and the perceived or anticipated benefits and costs of these alternatives in that situation. The target level of risk is also different for different people because people differ in their perceptions of the benefits and costs of risky and prudent behaviour options. So, the target risk varies, just as the target (that is, set-point, desired) temperature on a thermostat may be altered depending on the costs and benefits associated with a given temperature.

The target level of risk should not be viewed as something that people arrive at by explicitly calculating probabilities of various outcomes and their respective positive or negative values. A person who lowers the thermostat before going to sleep or when leaving home for the weekend chooses a setting intuitively rather than on the basis of precise calculations of expected cost and benefits. This is equally true when that person resets the target temperature on the thermostat the next morning or after returning from the weekend trip.

It should also be noted that the expression "target level of risk" does not imply that people strive for a certain level of risk for its own sake. Target risk does not mean risk for the sake of risk, just as the target temperature people set on their thermostat is not necessarily the one they would choose if energy costs were less important.

As will be seen in the next sections, the hearings offer evidence of the operation of all four utility factors mentioned above which determine the extent of the accident risk that different people are willing to accept under a given condition and which the same people are willing to accept under different conditions.

## ADVANTAGES OF RISKY BEHAVIOUR

The hearing transcripts contain many indications that the expected advantages of comparatively risky behaviour (factor a above), such as remaining in the employ of Westray Coal, were viewed as high. In an area of the province with a history of high unemployment, having a job is very attractive, even if that job is a dangerous one. The underground workforce made appealing wages, which must have helped, or could reasonably have been expected to raise their socioeconomic status in a community that generally holds the miner's job in relatively low esteem (Blishen et al., 1987). Some miners were hopeful that in the long run conditions would improve in the mine and that promotion and long-term stable employment might be possible if they were willing to put up with current conditions in the short run.

> In our community ... you were down there. You were a dirty dog when you were a coal miner.... Scott Paper come in and Michelin

come in. Better paying industries, supposedly better working conditions, better working environment. When you were a miner, you were on the other end of the scale, at the end of it.[11]

Moreover, the introduction and implementation of the production bonus system held the promise of earning a level of income well above basic pay rate. As of March 1, 1992, a bonus system was instituted. Any underground employee responsible for production in excess of 500 tonnes per mine-wide machine shift per month could earn a bonus. It was explained to them, by way of an example, that a person being paid at the "Miner 1" rate of $18.64/hour could make a bonus of $536.40 per month if the average machine shift production equalled 649 tonnes and the miner worked a total of 16 shifts. Basic wage for that period would amount to 16 (shifts) times 12 (hours per shift) times $18.64 (hourly wage), which equals $3578.88. A bonus of $536.40 would thus amount to an income increase of approximately 15 percent. In fact, the employees were informed that the bonus could amount to as much as 80.3 percent of wages depending on the level of productivity.

The actual financial significance of the bonus payments for the miners becomes salient if one considers that as many as 14 of the 39 miners, who worked a minimum of 16 shifts in March 1992 and who were entitled to 100 percent of the bonus, received a productivity bonus in excess of $1000 over that month. For the same period of one month, the average bonus for employees who worked at least one shift and were no more than three days absent (i.e., 119 of 140 underground employees) amounted to $657.09.

The question of the relationship between pay for productivity on the one hand and accident likelihood on the other has a long history in the industrial safety literature. While it is generally assumed that the gradual abolition of piece rates in favour of payment per hour has greatly contributed to the reduction of the occupational accident rate in the course of this century, the case of mining has occupied a special place. As long ago as 1969 a seminal publication on risk acceptance in return for social benefits in modern society called attention to the relationship between pay and accident risk in mining. The question of whether or not "voluntary" risk is accepted by individuals as a function of income benefits is not clear, although such a relationship must exist. Of particular interest, therefore, is the special case of miners exposed to high occupational risks. The acceptance of individual risk is an exponential function of the wage (Starr, 1969). A pay increase is associated with a proportionately higher acceptance of accident risk; in popular terms, this might read as: double the pay for production and people will take eight times as much risk, or triple the pay and people will take twenty-seven times as much risk. The power function between wages and accidents may also be responsible for the fact that rewarding workers for safe behaviour by means of relatively small incentives for accident-free operation often leads to relatively large reductions in the accident rate. This is a general finding with respect to the use of safety-incentive programs as a means to prevent accidents in occupational settings (McAfee et al., 1989; Peters, 1991; Wilde, 1994, 1996, 1997, 1998a, 1998b).

With respect to mining, a remarkably strong accident-prevention effect was observed after implementation of safety-incentive programs at two mines in the US (Fox et al., 1987). Workers in a uranium mine in Wyoming and a coal mine in Arizona were given saving stamps for each month of accident-free operation. Stamps were earned on the basis of both individual performance and collective performance of the work team. They could be saved up and exchanged for merchandise. From data presented in the article it can be deduced that the total value of the stamps given to workers at the uranium mine in 1972 amounted to US $13,850 in constant-value dollars. At that time, the number of workers equalled about 288. So, the average annual value (that is, cost to the company) of the stamps was about US $83 (in constant-value dollars) per worker (accident-involved and accident-free combined). Similar calculations lead to estimation of the average annual value of the safety bonus at the coal mine at approximately US $47 per employee.

These safety bonuses would appear quite modest in comparison to the production bonuses at Westray Coal. Yet, the savings due to accident reduction were quite substantial. The costs of accidents and injuries declined at the American uranium mine from a baseline average of US $294,000 per year to an average during the incentive program of US $29,000 per year. The decline in the coal mine was from US $367,696 per year prior to the incentive program to US $38,972 per year in constant-value dollars. Both declines approximated 90 percent.

> The benefit/cost ratios, or ratios of dollars saved by the reduction of accidents and injuries to dollars spent on the [incentive programme, adjusted for hours worked and inflation] ranged from 18.1 to 27.8 at the [uranium] mine and from 12.9 to 20.7 at the [coal] mine. (Fox, Hopkins and Anger 1987)

Other studies, not detailed here, also demonstrate that comparatively modest rewards for safety can bring about comparatively large increases in safety, just as comparatively small increases in the reward for productivity can lead to comparatively large increases in the accident rate.

Although it may be difficult to determine whether these relationships also hold for Canadian coal mining in the late twentieth century, they do contain ample warning of the pernicious effect of production bonuses on employee safety. We should not be surprised by the fact that many of the Westray miners responded to the production bonus system as they did, that is by trying to increase their production while sacrificing safety by rushing, taking shortcuts, and working long hours without appropriate rest pauses.

## Figures 5.1 and 5.2. "Productivity," Bar Graph and Line Graph

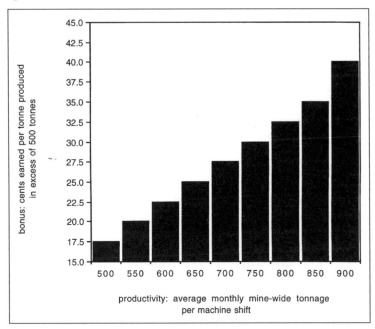

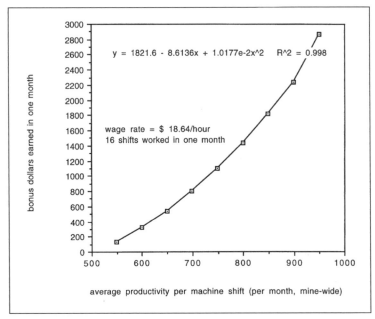

There was one particular aspect to the bonus system that makes this response especially likely and rational. The relationship between the size of the bonus and rate of overproduction (meaning production in excess of 500 tonnes) was positively accelerated. This means that the size of the bonus increased faster that the rate of overproduction or that equal increments in overproduction led to increasingly greater bonuses. For instance, an increase in production from 500 to 549 tonnes produced a wage increase of almost 4 percent, while an increase of production from 600 to 649 tonnes (i.e., the same absolute increase) yielded a wage increase of approximately 6 percent (i.e., 15 percent minus 8.9 percent).[12]

At the same time, there was a major economic penalty for missing a shift. One day lost reduced the bonus by 25 percent; two, three and four days reduced the bonus by 50 percent, 75 percent and 100 percent respectively. Clearly, there was great pressure not to miss any shifts due to sickness, injuries, or weather conditions. One miner reported that he was encouraged by the mine's management to move from Cape Breton to the Westray area, because it would reduce the chances of missing any shifts due to being snowed in and increase the opportunity for more overtime.[13]

Many miners appear to have been fully cognizant of the added danger posed by the production incentives.

> Q. Is it a good idea to have a bonus system in a coal mine?
> A. No [....], because it pushes men to a point where they'll do anything to make an extra dollar.[14]

> I wasn't too keen on that either because I figured the boys are going to start taking shortcuts.
>   ... Those fellows would still be alive today. Because everybody was intimidated. Everybody was and they played one guy against the other, one group against the other. The miners against the shuttle car drivers; the bolters against the miners; the tradesmen against the miners; these guys are holding you up, they're costing you money, you are not going to get a bonus because of this, you're not going to get a bonus because of that. If this arsehole hadn't done that, you'd got this completed, you would have had an extra four or five hours bonus money or whatever.
>   We also got 10 cables too though. Destroyed 10 cables, hitting them with the cars, the shuttle cars, miner [that is, a mining machine] running them over.
>   Some other times the shuttle car would across [sic] cables on the ground and cut them or pinch them by the wall which would create a ball of fire.[15]

They also reported that they became habituated to the dangerous conditions, that their safety consciousness eroded with the passage of time, and that they grew more and more complacent.[16] Their complacent attitude allowed an increase in their risk-taking behaviour, such as deliberately, though reluctantly, setting the methanometer higher than the required setting[17] and hiding fuel, or "jerry," cans from the inspector's eyes.

> Q.... Because not only did you know there were jerry cans there that shouldn't be there, but you now knew that you were hiding the jerry cans from an inspector which seems to make to make it twice as bad. Why did you do that?
> A. I can't honestly answer you.... I was ordered to do it and I did it.[18]

Others reported, as stated above, that they were inclined to accept the hazardous working conditions in hopes that, if they tolerated them in the short run, they would ultimately be rewarded in the long run with better working conditions,[19] promotion, and job security for a good number of years.

> If I proved a good worker—if they decided to hire me, that I could look forward to 15 years' work. And if things went alright with this seam, they might possibly go into the Cage seam and that might add another 10 years' work. So things looked pretty ... good for my future if I did indeed get hired. Work for a lifetime.
> He [i.e., Mr. Parry] said this mine is going to last 15 years. And they had another—Allan seam, I believe, and if they could get into that, it would be a 30-year project.[20]

## COSTS OF RISKY BEHAVIOUR

It is true that the expected costs of comparatively risky behaviour alternatives (factor b in the "General Interpretation" section above), and thus the perceived dangers of staying in the employ of the mine, were also high. Most miners were acutely aware of the dangers posed by the methane, coal dust, poor ventilation, unstable roofs, and lack of appropriate safety training.[21] They were also aware of the danger-enhancing effect of the production bonus system; they realized the way it influenced their own behaviour, heightening the tempo of production by increasing the rush, cutting corners, and increasing carelessness.[22]

## BENEFITS OF SAFE BEHAVIOUR

The expected benefits of comparatively safe behaviour alternatives (factor c in "General Interpretation" above) were low. There was some indication of potential risk-reducing behaviours. These included complaining to the mine's management or to the mining inspector about the dangerous working conditions and/or quitting their jobs and looking for another place of employment. In the opinion of the miners, the expected safety gain of all these options for action, with the exception of quitting, was very small.

They felt that complaining to the Westray Coal management about the hazardous working conditions was unlikely to have the desired effect on safety.[23] Conversely, it was seen as a sure way of getting fired or losing the privilege of working overtime.[24]

> Q. So, you were prepared to work in what you thought were unsafe conditions instead of going to the inspector notwithstanding that?
> A. Well, there was no other place to acquire a job at the time.[25]

Workers also said they felt intimidated, and they feared not having the necessary proof or data to substantiate their concerns about safety.[26] The possibility of complaining to the provincial mining inspector about the hazardous conditions prevailing in the mine was also viewed as hampered by management[27] and useless.

> [Wayne Cheverie]:
> At the time—I remember very clearly Roy saying; "I'm not going in there. You're fucking going to kill somebody there and you don't care." And Roger's answer to that was: "Roy, either you go in there and bolt that fucking heading or you can go fucking take your lunch can and go up the drift; you're fired."
>
> Shortly after he went on his own, there was an incident where the burning torches were brought underground during his shift. He left the mine. He wouldn't stay underground while there was a burning process going on underground. When he went to surface— and I'm not sure of the time frame except that I talked to Steve about it afterwards, and he told me that he was suspended for leaving the mine and told not to do that again, to think about his job. And if he was going to do that sort of thing again that he would be suspended or fired.

> [David Matthews]:
> Q. And what happened to Mr. Pasemko as a result of the complaints he made?
> A. Roger told him one day: "If you don't like it here, pick up your lunch can and go back to Alberta."[28]
>
> I don't care what anybody says, when a man's pushed he's going to do stuff. I don't care, even it's you or anybody. You fellows will say now, oh no, I wouldn't work in there. But if you was in our situation, you would do it. And I don't care what they say. Or anybody says.

When you've got a job and you've got a family to feed, you keep your mouth shut.

I don't really know that they ever fired anybody, but intimidation was always there because this mine was—and they knew this when they started the mine down here, that it was in an area where they had a high instance of unemployment.

It was intimidation, intimidation from day one.[29]

[Aaron Conklin]:
I come in that morning and there had been a roof fall, and the crew had attempted to start to arch it. And it started to come in again, and they had run out of the way. But the boom truck had got caught under the fall. And I had only been working there maybe two or three months at the time, and I was a little nervous. So I jokingly asked Mr. Phillips if there was any danger pay, hoping that he would tell me to stay on surface. And he said there was no danger there. And I said: "You wouldn't lie to a fellow?" And he said: "If you're scared, go the f'ing home."

[Jonathan Knock]:
The mannerism of the place was "do your job. Don't complain, and get it done as fast as possible."[30]

Some miners even expressed the feeling that the mine management was being supported by the mine inspector and that productivity was given priority over safety.[31] The mine inspector was reported to have said, when asked if he could put a stop to the bonus system, that "his hands were tied and there was a lot of pressure to make this mine a success."[32] Furthermore, employment at a different and better mine might be refused because of an understanding or agreement between other mines and Westray Coal.[33]

## COSTS OF SAFE BEHAVIOUR

The expected costs of relatively safe behaviour alternatives (factor d in "General Interpretation above) were high. Among these alternatives was the possibility of complaining to the mine's management about the work hazards, looking for another job, or going on unemployment insurance. Some miners expressed the feeling that going to the mine inspector could also lead to the loss of one's job because the mine inspector might communicate the name of the complainant to the mine's management.

I don't think it would have made any difference, because I would have been out the door and it would have been covered up and I would not have been there.

If I had submitted something to one of the inspectors, I honestly believe in my—this is my own way of thinking, that if I complained to Albert or any other mines inspector, that it would have got back to Roger. I know the point would have been made to Roger ..., but my name would have been brought up. And I know very well that I would have been gone.

Q. Well, what would Roger's presence have to do with you raising a concern, as a mine examiner, with the mines inspector?
A. Well, like I said, I don't think I would have been there too long if had made too many waves.[34]

Apparently, there was a case in which a miner did indeed complain to the inspector with the result that the miner was fired.[35]

Fear of retaliation for complaining in an attempt to reduce accident risk appears to have been a major factor in discouraging miners from this course of action. They felt that, while their complaint would be ignored, they themselves would be fired and readily replaced by another person who was looking for work in an area that was marked by a large proportion of unemployed people.[36] It was also for this reason, i.e., fear of losing his job, that one miner decided to refrain from going to the mass media and bringing the dangerous conditions out into the open.[37]

Q. What about quitting, did you ever think about quitting?
A. It wasn't really an option to me. I know I wanted to, but, like, I say, I—there was no other work out there.

There was no other place to acquire a job at the time.

I just said I'm not going back. He—I don't think they were too worried about it because there was lots of people coming and going. Lots of people had applications in, I mean, easy to fill one spot ....[38]

Moreover, there was concern about being turned down for unemployment insurance benefits due to either having left Westray voluntarily, which might be viewed as frivolous and unwarranted[39] or having accumulated an insufficient duration of employment to qualify for UI benefits.[40]

Finally, some miners mentioned reasons for not quitting the mine that transcended the predominant economic motives and practicalities that we have seen so far. These miners felt that discontinuing their presence in the mine would constitute a breach of the moral obligation of solidarity with one's endangered colleagues[41] or of devotion to the mine which deserved to be looked after, no matter the discord between workers and management.[42]

## RECAPITULATION

The picture that emerges from the above considerations is one of a workforce knowingly taking the risk of an extreme occupational accident. This comes as the result of three major factors working together: the behaviour of management, the general economic conditions, and the motivations of the miners themselves. Mine management was perceived by the employees to be emphatically focused on production at the expense of safety. General economic conditions in the region were characterized by a high rate of unemployment, meaning that voluntarily quitting one's job at the mine implied a high risk of lasting unemployment. The miners were also motivated to enhance their income and status in the community as well as pursue their search for job permanency. Under these conditions, there were essentially two options in the face of accident risk: either stay with the mine or resign. Many stayed, many resigned. As one miner put it quite eloquently: "You have got to evaluate how much risk they considered it was and how much risk it was losing the job. Any man has to weigh that in the balance."[43] Few could have said it better. This statement differs little from what one may read in textbooks on human decision making in the face of uncertainty and what decisions under these conditions are rational (Yates, 1992). But, why were there only two options for workers who wanted to reduce their exposure to accident risk? Why were there no other options?

> **Inquiry Testimony, Mr. Dooley, Day 36, Mar 20, 1996: 8041–42**
>
> There was a complaint made to the Department of Labour, and Roger Parry came in to deployment this—you know, in one of his crazy moods, just hollering and screaming and belittling everybody on the crew. He brought all—he brought the crews together, the two crews, like, the one that was coming up and the one that was coming down. And I mean, he said to every man there, like, the supervisors were there, all the working men were there, and he was there. "One of you blankety-blankers went to the Department of Labour, and if I ever find out who, I will fire you." And, I mean, like, he's screaming; the slobber is coming out of him. Like, he's just irate. Like, he's not sitting here like I am just saying this to you people. He is just going crazy; he's ranting, he's raving, he's kicking the garbage can, he's kicking the door, he's kicking the wall. Like, he's going—he's going crazy. "And if I

ever find out who, you will be fired."
[Inquiry testimony conducted by Mr. Merrick, Solicitor for the Commission]

It is obvious from the hearing transcripts that the miners felt that attempting to alter the attitudes and actions of mine management were not only useless
but hazardous, because of the risk of getting fired. Expressing safety concerns
to the provincial mine inspector was also not considered helpful as a way to
reduce danger, and in fact it was potentially dangerous to job security. In other
words, any attempt to reduce the dangerousness of the job was felt to be
ineffectual in reducing danger, as well as counterproductive in terms of employment. Thus, the expected benefits of taking safe behaviour alternatives
were perceived as small and their costs as high. This, of course, is a condition
that would be expected to lead to increased risk acceptance.

On the other hand, despite the expected high costs of taking the dangerous
decision of staying in the employ of Westray Coal considering the potential for
an accident, and probably quite a serious one, the expected benefits of staying
with the mine were also considerable. These expected advantages were largely
economic in nature: good pay, the possibility of advancement through the
ranks, long-term employment, and thus a potentially major improvement in
prosperity and socio-economic status as well. The prospect of good wages was
greatly expanded by the introduction of the productivity bonus scheme. Because of its nature, this scheme, which extended more than equal increases in
income for equal increments in productivity, also led to an extraordinarily high
level of accident risk acceptance.

## IMPLICATIONS

In the last several years, a number of studies have dealt with the comparative
safety effects of various accident prevention measures in occupational settings. In some of these studies comparisons were made among the safety
benefits that have been achieved by interventions such as safety education and
training, poster and other mass media campaigns, personnel selection, engineering improvements, disciplinary action, exercise and stress reduction programs, and, finally, safety incentive schemes. In general, the safety incentive
schemes have been found to be the most effective, or at least among the most
effective, means of intervention (Guastello, 1991). Reductions in the accident
rate per employee-year by 50 percent or even 80 percent are not uncommon in
manufacturing, construction, and other industry. The transportation division of
a German food processing plant saw a reduction in direct accident costs by
more than two-thirds in the first year of implementing an incentive program,
and the reduction remained at that level for over three decades (Wilde, 1996).
The results are better still, as in the case of two American mining companies

where the burden of lost days dropped by 89 percent and 98 percent respectively (Fox et al., 1987). Sometimes the results are more modest.

The ratios between benefits (savings on accidents prevented) and program costs are usually greater than two to one, meaning that industrial companies can make money on such accident prevention efforts—largely due to the reduction in both fees to workers' compensation boards and other insurance following an improvement in a company's safety record. The favourable effects continue to last over time. Incentive plans in two American mines were studied over periods of eleven and twelve years. In one mine the number of days lost due to accidents was reduced by about 89 percent of baseline, and in the other by as much as about 98 percent. Benefit/cost ratios varied from year to year between eighteen and twenty-eight at one mine and between thirteen and twenty-one at the other. There was no sign that the effectiveness of the incentive plans diminished over time at either mine. Another program was implemented in a construction company at a cost of about US $30,000 a year and produced savings in workers' compensation insurance premiums of about US $400,000 a year, which amounts to a benefit/cost ratio of approximately thirteen to one (Synnett, 1992).

Only one negative side effect of safety incentive programs has been noticed so far, namely, the tendency of people to under-report accidents when incentive programs are in effect. Fortunately, however, such under-reporting has been found to occur with respect to minor accidents only (McAfee et al., 1989; Peters, 1991). Past experience with incentive programs shows that some programs have had much greater effect than others. It is, therefore, important to identify the distinctive features of the more successful incentive schemes. An effort has been made to cull the ingredients of the most effective incentive plans from the separate published reports (Wilde, 1994). Of special importance in the present context is that (1) the incentive scheme should be developed in cooperation with the employees to whom it will be addressed; (2) both group safety performance and individual safety performance should be rewarded; and (3) all workers should be included, that is, not only shop floor workers, but also foremen, supervisors, and middle managers. This leads to a more cohesive and pervasive safety orientation, producing a "safety climate" or "safety culture" in a company.

Against this background it is easy to see why incentive programs are able to bring about major improvements in safety records, just as production bonuses may enhance productivity. The latter, however, are likely to have a detrimental effect upon safety as we have seen above (especially when they take the form that they did in the Westray case), while no productivity loss has ever been reported in association with the operation of a safety incentive scheme. On the contrary, safety incentive schemes have been shown to have remarkably high benefit/cost ratios.

For the purpose of future accident prevention, it would, therefore, seem entirely appropriate to consider more extensive implementation of safety incentive systems in mining operations and to seriously question the appropriateness of production bonus schemes in such operations that have comparatively high accident involvement rates (National Safety Council).

## CHAPTER SIX

# THE NORMAL VIOLATION OF SAFETY RULES[1]

*Timothy Hynes and Pushkala Prasad*

## INTRODUCTION

Recent studies on the antecedents of industrial crises have tended to focus on disasters in high risk systems involving complex technologies and tightly knit processes. This chapter examines events leading up to mining disasters which past research has characterized as being typically more foreseeable and avoidable. We discuss how many mining disasters are likely to be the result of "mock bureaucracies" or situations characterized by overt violation of safety rules at the workplace. Using the Westray mine explosion as an illustrative case, the chapter traces the development and institutionalization of a mock bureaucracy in an organization. Implications for further research and understanding of industrial crises are drawn.[2]

In recent years, the vivid images left by the Challenger crash, the Bhopal leak, the Chernobyl melt-down, the Exxon-*Valdez* oil spill, and various other disasters have stimulated considerable scholarly research on understanding and managing organizational crises. Moreover, there is a growing sense that industrial crises are significant events because of their increased frequency, the vast damage they cause, and their overwhelming cost to organizations and society (Shristava et al., 1988). In general, the organizational crises literature looks at four major issues. These include the antecedents of crises (Milburn et al., 1983; Pauchant et al., 1992; Perrow, 1984; Shrivastava, 1987); organizational responses to crises or what has been labeled "crash management" (Dunbar et al., 1978; Trotter et al., 1989); consequences of organizational crises (Marcus et al., 1987); and organizational sense-making during and after crisis situations (Gephart, 1993, 1987; Vaught et al., 1991).

The phrase "organizational crisis" denotes a wide range of disasters and crisis situations. The roots of the term "crisis" itself can be found in medicine, where it refers to phases of an illness and injury in which the body's self-healing powers virtually collapse, making recovery either extraordinarily difficult or impossible. Crises in social systems, including organizations, refer to situations that threaten the existing form and structure of the system. As a result, the notion of organizational crisis can include a wide variety of events or situations, ranging from financial collapse and ecological damage, to product tampering and industrial accidents (Kuklan, 1988; Newman, [no date]; Mitroff et al., 1984; Bowman et al., 1988).

This chapter's focus is exclusively on the antecedents of industrial crises, a subset of organizational crises, which is defined as a situation in which organized industrial activity causes major damage to human life, or to natural and social environments. We use the term "antecedents" to refer to the entire series of intra- and interorganizational patterns, processes, and events that culminate in industrial disasters. We argue in the chapter that current theorizing on industrial crises does not fully explain the antecedents of mining disasters, which take place in more linear and loosely coupled systems. We employ our analysis of the Westray coal mine explosion of 1992 to provide new theoretical insights into this phenomenon. This chapter is best understood as an essay employing both empirical illustrations and theoretical interpretations in order to enhance our understanding of crises in linear and loosely coupled organizations. We focus explicitly on the emergence of a "mock bureaucracy" to explain the collapse of rules in organizations, how these disasters come about, and the way in which a mock bureaucracy becomes institutionalized in the everyday operations of an organization (Gouldner, 1954).

## THEORIES OF THE CAUSES OF INDUSTRIAL CRISES

While industrial disasters have stimulated considerable interest among organizational researchers over the last three decades (Hale et al., 1970; Lawrence, 1974; Turner, 1976), more recent work has tended to focus on disasters taking place in highly complex systems. This is a result of the publicity drawn by spectacular events such as the NASA Space Shuttle disaster and the Chernobyl meltdown, generating a vast body of literature focusing on the connections between complex organizational processes and the triggering of industrial disasters. Overall, this body of literature recognizes the vast multitude of factors potentially responsible for provoking industrial crises and stresses the role of internal and external players in triggering these crises.

Over a decade ago, research identified the sources of industrial crises within elements of the external and internal environments of organizations, suggesting that the internal environment of the organization is likely to be the culprit in triggering crisis situations. In particular, it pinpointed executive characteristics, organizational demographics, and organizational history as key internal variables likely to be responsible for industrial crises. Much research identifies several probable sources of organizational crises but ultimately fails to develop any systematic connection between these different organizational elements.

Based on their analysis of three different industrial crises, other analysts conclude that crises are caused by two interacting sets of failures. One set of failures takes place within the organization on account of a complex combination of human, organizational, and technological (HOT) errors. These in turn, interact with regulatory, infrastructural, and preparedness (RIP) failures in the organization's environment to produce a crisis. Linkages between elements in the internal and external environments of an organization may lead to crisis events. Within this framework, however, many theoretical relationships remain unexplored. For instance, are there any specific conditions under which organizations are likely to experience the interaction between HOT errors and RIP failures? Are some organizations/industries more prone to experience such interactions? Do these interactions become manifested in specific patterns which may be visible in the everyday processes of an organization?

The theory of "normal accidents" takes us several steps closer towards addressing some of these questions, with a typology of organizational processes constructed along two dimensions. The first is the level of systemic complexity, and the second is the nature of organizational coupling. On the one hand, organizational processes can be understood in terms of their systemic complexity. Some processes are straightforwardly sequential or linear, while others are made up of more complicated and less predictable interconnections and can be described as having "interactive complexity." An assembly-line operation best illustrates a simple linear process used to manufacture a product. Products and services offered by contemporary organizations, however, are rarely the result of such straightforward and linear processes. Nuclear power, education, television news reports, and innumerable other products and services are produced out of disjointed, fragmented, and complicated processes within different organizations. Simultaneously, organizational processes can be coupled or tied together differently. Loosely coupled systems, whether they are linear or complex, have built-in slack in terms of responding to problems. Tightly coupled systems, on the other hand, are made up of rapidly occurring processes which cannot easily be stalled, disconnected, or isolated from each other. These organizational processes are both highly complex and tightly coupled and have maximum built-in catastrophic potential. In other words, such a combination of systems characteristics will inevitably produce, at some point, an accident of considerable magnitude. Given this systemic inevitability, this kind of accident or crisis is a "normal accident."

In the most indepth examination yet of the "phenomenon of crises," hundreds of organizations were examined to better understand how and why modern industrial crises happen and what lessons can be derived from them. Just as some individuals are accident prone, so are some organizations. Other organizations have taken sufficient care to both prevent and prepare for various crisis situations. The latter organizations are considered "crisis prepared" while the former are labeled "crisis prone."

The "diagnostic model of crisis management" enables managers and researchers to determine whether an organization is crisis prone, "at the bad end of the spectrum," or crisis prepared, "at the good end." To make such a diagnosis, or to determine an organization's vulnerability to crisis, one must examine an organization at four different levels: its organizational strategies; its organizational structure; its culture; and finally, the subjective experiences of the individuals that make up the organization.

Crises are events triggered by both the complexities of the organizational systems and the individuals in charge of these systems. However, much of the research has focused on organizations which are labeled complex or tightly coupled. Indeed, both Perrow's (1987) theory of normal accidents and Shrivastava's analysis of the Bhopal gas leak, while enormously influential, have resulted in students of industrial crises focusing almost exclusively on accidents in these "high risk systems." Yet, there is a potential for crises in more linear and/or loosely coupled systems. And, given key differences in systems characteristics, industrial accidents in less complex and more loosely coupled systems might require a different kind of framework than that offered by this literature on high risk systems.

In this chapter, we turn our attention to mining disasters, a part of a subset of crises occurring outside of high risk systems, which Perrow (1984) labels "earthbound disasters." Earthbound disasters take place within systems whose processes are closely connected to the "earth," such as mines, dams, oil wells, logging, and the construction and maintenance of bridges. While all earthbound systems are not identical in terms of their levels of complexity and degrees of coupling, most industrial accidents occurring within them are both foreseeable and avoidable (Perrow, 1984; Sethi, 1987); yet earthbound disasters continue to occur with relative frequency. In terms of assessing their complexity and coupling levels, an analysis would suggest that mines are characterized by relatively linear processes and loose coupling. Hence, many of the insights offered by studies of crises in complex systems are not entirely relevant to understanding mining disasters. In other words, since mines have neither the highly sophisticated technology nor the tightly coupled processes common to nuclear power plants and space shuttle launches, we may need alternate explanations for the frequency and severity of the crises that take place within them.

## MOCK BUREAUCRACIES IN MINING DISASTERS

Since mining disasters do not usually possess a fatal combination of complexity and tight coupling, accidents within them tend to be the result of simpler malfunctions. Given that the technologies used are relatively simple (especially in comparison with nuclear reactors and most chemical processing plants), disasters are more often caused by organizational rather than technological failures. Furthermore, relatively straightforward operator errors and the disregarding of expert warnings and safety rules appear to be the leading causes behind mining and other earthbound disasters. What this suggests is that in studying this type of industrial crisis, organizational culture and character issues may hold the key to understanding why these types of tragedies happen in the first place and what can be done to prevent them.

In the field of organizational crises, mining disasters remain a significantly under-researched phenomenon. Yet, mining itself has long been recognized as a hazardous activity (Fitzpatrick, 1974; Wardell et al., 1985). In a 1992 census of fatal occupational injuries by the US Bureau of Labor Statistics, occupational fatalities in the mining industry were estimated at 27 per 100,000 employed. This fatality rate is well above the national average of 5 fatalities per 100,000 workers (Toscano et al., 1993). Even with significant improvements in coal mining health and safety regulations over the past three decades, mining still has the dubious distinction of containing the highest death rate per 100,000 workers in any occupation in the 1980s (Stowers Carr, 1991). Though the vast majority of mining accidents are caused by roof cave-ins and result in single person deaths, methane or coal dust explosions claiming a large number of human casualties are also relatively common. Since 1968, more than one hundred coal mine explosions have occurred in North America. However, scholars looking at the antecedents of industrial disasters have paid scant attention to mine explosions.

In part, this lack of attention may be the result of a general perception that the causes of mine accidents are readily discernible. And, at a superficial level, that may well be the case since most mine accidents occur from the simplest of causes and are frequently attributable to individual actions and failures of enforcement of safety policies. Yet, at another level, this in itself raises an interesting question: why are so many mining and other earthbound disasters the result of operator carelessness and/or system non-compliance with safety measures? Indeed, given the frequency of mining disasters in our society and the fact that the most powerful motivational tool prompting organizations to improve proactive crisis management is the repeated direct experience of major crises, one would think that, by now, mining would be one of the safest occupations.

Earlier studies on similarly foreseeable and preventable disasters have also stressed the key role of systematic non-compliance to safety regulations in industrial crises but have neglected to explain why carelessness and non-compliance to safety is such an endemic part of many organizational systems. This chapter suggests that the notion of mock bureaucracy may offer a useful framework for understanding some of the antecedents to mining disasters. The development and enactment of mock bureaucracies can have serious consequences for organizations and can easily precipitate industrial crises. Using the Westray coal mine explosion as an illustrative case, we show how antecedents of mining disasters can be located within patterns of mock bureaucracy.

In an important work, *Patterns of Industrial Bureaucracy* (1954), Alvin

Gouldner studied the mining and milling operations of a gypsum plant with the intention of sifting out the variant bureaucratic patterns. While the study itself involved a comprehensive examination of various facets of organizational bureaucracy, this chapter focuses on his discussion of internal compliance to organizational rules. Basing his analysis on the "no-smoking" regulations within the gypsum plant, Gouldner depicts a situation in which a number of "bureaucratic cues" (e.g., rules, posters, inspections, etc.) calling for the enforcement of these regulations were present. Yet, in the everyday working life of the plant, these rules were predominantly looked at as mere "bureau-cratic paraphernalia" and were consequently disregarded by most employees. The name that Gouldner gives to this pattern of overt organizational non-compliance is mock bureaucracy. It describes a scenario in which both manag-ers and workers are aware of certain rules but make few attempts to adhere to them. Within this particular type of bureaucratic pattern, although various rules are in place they are not enforced by either managers or workers because they do not hold any legitimacy for either group. According to this analysis, a rule legitimated in terms of the group's values will be more readily accepted if it is seen as furthering their own ends.

Thus, Gouldner sees mock bureaucracies developing due to the complete lack of legitimacy attached to certain rules. First, the rule is perceived to have little intrinsic value in and of itself, and second, any violation of the rule is perceived to result in few negative consequences. As a result, key groups in the organization fail to buy into these rules. Thus, a mock bureaucracy is charac-terized by rules and regulations that are not enforced by management nor obeyed by workers. In fact, management's decision not to actively enforce regulations can even promote a sense of harmony and cooperation between the two groups.

In direct contrast to mock bureaucracy are patterns of "representative bureaucracy." Using the example of the safety program at the gypsum plant, the safety rules were enforced by managers and obeyed by workers because the rules had legitimacy for both groups based on their own key values. For instance, the safety program had legitimation for management because it was tied to production and because it was linked to an explicit recognition that accidents could increase insurance premiums. Workers, on the other hand, could buy into the safety program because of their very real concerns with personal injuries and their awareness of the inadequacy of the current workers' compensation plans. At any given moment within an organization, clusters of rules will be characterized either by patterns of mock or representative bu-reaucracy.

More recently, these notions of mock bureaucracy as an organizational facade have been explored in a study of a police bureaucracy (Jermier et al., 1991). Official/formal organizational missions and rules are frequently sub-verted by multiple organizational sub-cultures, which formulate and enact contrary sets of norms, goals, and values. Needless to say, the subversion of formal rules and goals has enormous consequences for the everyday processes of the organization. This chapter shows how these internal patterns of bureaucracy can significantly influence organizational actions and result in serious consequences. In essence, this chapter seeks to answer two questions: (1) to what extent was a mock bureaucracy responsible for the Westray explosion; and (2) how did a mock bureaucracy around safety develop in the everyday interactions of the mine. In trying to answer these questions, the chapter also provides an analysis of the many interrelated factors (both external and internal) that combine to create a mock bureaucracy within an organization. These include the role and interests of various external stakeholders, economic conditions, managerial ideologies, occupational sub-cultures, and notions of masculinity. With the help of a political sense-making framework, we show how diverse factors intersected in the Westray mine to create conditions whereby safety was overlooked on a regular basis (Gephart, 1984).

## THE WESTRAY MINE EXPLOSION: A BRIEF DESCRIPTION

The Westray mine, located in Pictou County, Nova Scotia, had its mining lease transferred to Curragh Resources Incorporated, a Toronto based firm, in 1988. The mine was noted for its "compliance coal," a "clean" burning fuel that burns with the highest efficiency on account of an unusually low sulphur content. The mine, under the management of Curragh Resources, received considerable financial support from both the provincial and federal governments: a $12 million loan from the Province of Nova Scotia and $85 million in loan guarantees from the Canadian federal government (Cameron, 1992a). The company also obtained a fifteen-year contract with the Nova Scotia Power Corporation to supply over 700,000 tonnes of coal per year.

Production at Westray began in the spring of 1991, and the mine employed approximately 225 people during peak times. However, concerns regarding the safety of the mine were voiced as early as 1989. A number of reports, including one released in April 1992, warned of problems involving coal dust (a potentially explosive substance), cave-ins, and dangerous levels of methane gas (Ward 1992). Despite the incidence of "minor" accidents, including a cave-in on March 28, 1992, it was only on April 29, 1992 that the provincial labour department issued a formal order to the company, requiring it to "apply some stone dust to prevent explosions of coal dust occurring, and to comply with the [mining] regulations (Cox, 1992b, 1992c). The company was given until May 15, 1992, to comply with this order. Six days before the deadline, however, a deadly explosion ripped through the Southwest section of the mine, killing all twenty-six men underground.

The fallout from the Westray disaster had an enormous impact on more than just the families and friends of the miners killed in the blast. The local communities, painfully familiar with the "costs" of underground coal mining, were once again faced with the need to assess these costs against the alternatives of fewer jobs and the disappearance of the communities themselves. In addition, the explosion called into serious question the roles played in the disaster by mine management and individuals at various levels of government. As a result, six days after the explosion the provincial government established a wide-ranging public inquiry into the mine disaster, headed by Nova Scotia Supreme Court Justice Peter Richard, initially postponed by a successful legal challenge to the Inquiry's mandate by seven Westray managers. Hearings did not begin until the fall of 1995, some three and a half years after the explosion.

In October 1992, the provincial labour department laid fifty-two charges under the *Occupational Health and Safety Act* against Curragh Resources Incorporated and four members of the company's management. The charges of safety violations dealt with fifteen separate facets of the mine's operations and ranged from forcing miners to work in unsafe conditions to allowing empty fuel cans to litter underground mine facilities (Jobb, 1992). Although these charges contained serious allegations of mine and safety code violations, all fifty-two were subsequently dropped so as not to prejudice the rights to a fair trial of anyone later charged with criminal offences by the RCMP (Moon, 1993).

Finally, as a result of a criminal investigation that examined the Westray disaster, the RCMP, on July 23, 1993, laid charges of criminal negligence and manslaughter against Curragh Resources Incorporated and two of its senior managers. These charges included thirteen specific offences, most of which were identical to those originally alleged by the provincial labour department. Although these charges were stayed by the Nova Scotia Supreme Court in the spring of 1995, that decision was subsequently overturned by the Nova Scotia Court of Appeal. The Appeal Court's ruling was upheld by the Supreme Court of Canada, the result being that the mine managers face a second trial.

The Westray explosion can clearly be categorized as an industrial crisis when we take into account its ramifications for the firm and the local community. As a result of the explosion and its aftermath, Curragh Resources Incorporated sought protection from creditors, arguing that it did not have the cash to pay interest on its debt.[3] In addition, the Bank of Nova Scotia recalled its loans to the company, which was unable to pay them. As a result of its earlier loan guarantee, the federal government was required to pay $80.75 million. Overall, the Westray mine disaster resulted in heavy economic, social, and political prices being paid by the corporation and local communities as well as by the provincial and federal governments.

The remainder of this chapter traces and analyzes the antecedents of the Westray explosion based on an examination of relevant documents. Retrospective analysis of archival data can offer insightful accounts of industrial crises (Gephart et al., 1993). Accordingly, in the course of our study, we looked at a variety of archival sources, including transcripts of testimony from the provincial public inquiry, newspaper reports, and publicly available government documents such as mine inspector reports, Occupational Health and Safety records, and the *Nova Scotia Mining Code*. Additional sources included secondhand interviews with former workers at the Westray mine contained in published materials subsequent to the disaster.

Our study of the Westray mine explosion is best characterized as an instrumental case study, in which insights from an individual case can offer a broader theoretical understanding of similar or parallel situations (Stake, 1993; Hartley, 1994). This study does not claim to look at every aspect of the organizational situation but only at how a mock bureaucracy came to be established within the Westray mine. Most investigations following industrial disasters seek to identify specific individuals or groups who can be held either partially or wholly responsible for the crisis. The objective of this chapter is not to assign blame to specific individuals, nor to pinpoint a set of narrow immediate causes for the event, but rather to examine some internal and external conditions that influence the workplace and have serious consequences for system malfunctioning.

## PATTERNS OF MOCK BUREAUCRACY AT THE WESTRAY COAL MINE

Early investigations into the Westray mine disaster clearly indicate the prevalence of patterns of mock bureaucracy at the workplace. These patterns manifested themselves in the rampant violations of mine safety regulations which appear to be the principal cause of the disaster. Records of the mine inspectors show that Westray was continually cited for violations of sections of the *Coal Mines Regulation Act*. Most of these safety violations centred around the accumulation of excessive coal dust. According to workers at the mine, the company's way of handling the coal dust problem was to look for volunteers who would be willing to stay after their shift and earn overtime pay by sprinkling or "dusting" some neutralizing limestone on the explosive coal dust. In the words of one of the miners, "If nobody volunteered, it was something that was forgotten about and no one said anything. It wasn't something that was pushed" (Tibbets, 1992) It appears that rock dusting, allegedly a part of everyday work at most coal mines, was seldom carried out at Westray. Not surprisingly, the records reveal that nobody volunteered to dust at the end of the day shift on May 8, 1992.

The *Coal Mines Regulation Act* also requires that a minimum of twenty bags of stone dust must be stored in every section of the mine and within reasonable distance of the working face. According to workers, this rule was completely ignored. Other safety problems that came to light included the underground use of acetylene torches with open flames and the casual discarding of flammable oil cans and oily rags inside the mine. Additionally, diesel fuel that was spilled in the course of refuelling machines was often allowed to remain, sometimes on top of matches and cigarette butts, on the mine floor. One miner described it in the following words: "It was just like Irving Oil down there. It was just a horror show" (Tibbets, 1992).

It is tempting to greet these alleged gross violations of safety regulations at the workplace with moral outrage, public anger, and a search for individuals responsible. What is more important is an understanding of how such a systematic pattern of mock bureaucracy becomes embedded within enclaves of an organization. Furthermore, given the record of the mining industry, it appears that the conditions at Westray were far from unique to that organization. Jim Cameron argues that despite technological innovations, the situation underground remains as dangerous and unpredictable as it was during the early 1700s (Picard, 1992). Therefore, we need to ask how and why patterns of mock bureaucracy come to be so firmly entrenched around safety rules in mines and perhaps even within other earthbound systems.

In the analysis of the gypsum plant mentioned earlier, relatively few insights are offered into this process. The no-smoking rule at the gypsum plant displayed all the characteristics of a mock bureaucracy because it held no legitimacy for either workers or managers. In the Westray example, the lack of compliance with safety regulations is obviously not the same as the situation involving the no-smoking regulations in the gypsum plant, because it would be hard to argue that managers and workers at Westray did not understand the ramifications of the safety rules. These were not trivial rules, and they had obvious and far-reaching consequences if violated. Yet, non-compliance was the prevalent norm in the mine. The safety program in the gypsum plant exemplified a "representative bureaucracy" because of the obvious significance of its intent. Yet, conditions at the Westray mine indicate that the safety rules themselves showed all of the characteristics of a mock bureaucracy.

A more meaningful analysis of the conditions conducive to a mock bureaucracy is possible with the help of a political sense-making framework, which combines a social constructionist view of organizations with an understanding of the political forces that shape organizational actions. The sense-making approach to understanding industrial crises has been used to focus on the connections between organizational actors' interpretations of events and the enactment of industrial crises, yet we don't want to suggest that organizational crises are due only to errors in perception and judgment.

Sense-making approaches tend to ignore macrostructural contexts of power and politics, yet industrial accidents are microsituational events embedded in macrolevel industrial and technological development (Gephart et al., 1993: 239). To grasp organizational actors' sense-making, we have to also understand the intricate web of economic, cultural and social influences on them. The subjective experiences of the individuals within the organization and the unwritten and unspoken rules, rationalizations, and unique belief systems of organizational culture are connected in the remainder of the chapter. Based on our document analysis, we show how a mock bureaucracy around safety rules was produced through the enactments of managers and workers operating within a complex context of economic pressures and specific cultural rationalities.

## MANAGERIAL NON-COMPLIANCE WITH SAFETY

It is actually relatively easy to understand the gross neglect of safety from a managerial perspective. The dominant driving concern at the time was coal production. Although no one would suggest that management would have been as negligent had they anticipated the tragedy of May 9, in their daily struggle to meet production requirements managers began to downplay and eventually to neglect safety concerns. To begin with, mine managers were constantly under pressure to pay attention to production goals over and above other imperatives, including safety.

From the start of its operations, Westray had a problem meeting its commitment to Nova Scotia Power. This meant financial problems for Curragh Resources Incorporated An internal memo dated December 6, 1991 indicated the extent of this problem, for it stated that: "Production during initial development to the end of 1991 not sufficient to finance development operations" (Moon, 1993). Other memos obtained from court records also indicate that the company was under tremendous pressure to keep up with production schedules. Another memo, this time from Westray to Nova Scotia Power in April 1992, announced the company's inability to meet its contract for April and May.

> Box One: Safety Violations
> "All they were into in that mine was production. After a while, they didn't even want you going five minutes away to get fuel. You'd be sitting there with the motor running and the mechanic would be pouring the fuel in. It was just like the Indianapolis 500." *Globe and Mail,* June 20, 1992: B2

Several safety violations at the mine can be linked to the need to "keep production rolling." For instance, it has been alleged that adjustments were made to the methanometers in order to keep the equipment working when it would have shut off due to high concentrations of methane (Jobb, 1992). A former miner described situations in which the bolter (a piece of mining machinery) would be refuelled by a mechanic who kept the machine's motor running, while spilling fuel from the spoutless gas cans directly on to the floor.

Other documents also indicate that as the financial problems worsened, shortcuts were used and safety regulations became less and less of a priority. Protests to management about safety conditions in the mine repeatedly fell on deaf ears. Miners who came forward with such complaints were informed that they could quit if they were not satisfied with the safety conditions. Furthermore, Westray had a health and safety policy that was explicitly designed to prevent workers from talking to outsiders about problems in the mine. In fact, the policy also imposed a gag order that decreed that "under no circumstances may information [about safety] be released to any other person without the expressed authority of the vice-president or general manager of Westray Coal" (Jobb, 1994). In effect, this policy was in direct contradiction of the *Occupational Health and Safety Act*, which granted employees the right to complain directly to mine inspectors who were responsible for enforcing safety laws.

Managers in the Westray coal mine soon began disregarding safety regulations because systematic adherence to them potentially jeopardized production rates and consequently impacted the company's relationship with leading customers and lending institutions. Moreover, given some of the financial pressures on the company, management inevitably saw production goals as having more immediate legitimacy than safety goals. One way to understand this situation is to see management as having to choose between investing time and energy in two clusters of goals. One cluster of goals ensured high production rates and another ensured high safety rates. One problem was that the rules around production goals and safety goals were not always complementary to each other. Not surprisingly, perhaps, managers invested over and above in achieving production goals.

Understanding managers' collective concern for production over safety also requires an appreciation of the managerial ideologies and cultural rationalities shaping their views of organizational reality (Alvesson, 1987; Gephart et al., 1990; Jackall, 1988). Managerial decisions privileging production over safety are not really questions of individual managers' ethics, but they point to the pervasiveness of "bureaucratic consciousness," a mode of thinking which places a premium on a functionally rational and pragmatic habit of mind that values economic goals above all others.

In a similar vein, in contemporary industrial societies, capital accumulation is a primary justification for taking all manner of decisions. "Capital is organizationally based and mobilized as an interpretive scheme; agents of corporations act as agents of capital offering the needs of capital as explanations of organizational action" (Gephart, 1984: 213). From this perspective, managers, as agents of capital, are likely to interpret production imperatives as being more important than any others, leading to a devaluation of safety imperatives.

Finally, managerial attitudes towards safety have to be understood against a backdrop of organizational constructions of risk. Bureaucracies, in general, rarely engage in comprehensive calculations of the risks they face. The operational rule in industrial organizations is actually to avoid learning about the magnitude of immediate safety risks (Douglas et al., 1982). While financial risks are often directly addressed, physical risks facing organizational members tend to be ignored. Thus, even though managers are committed to playing by the rules, the underlying logic of capital allows them to cut corners on the grounds that some rules may interfere with productivity, which is the driving imperative of bureaucratic consciousness. Given these ideological and cultural notions of risk, it becomes even easier to appreciate why managers at Westray repeatedly attended to production goals at the expense of safety.

## WORKER NON-COMPLIANCE WITH SAFETY

Our findings show that the underground miners were as much engaged in the non-compliance of safety rules as management. While it may seem harder to understand why the safety regulations had so little legitimacy for workers, closer analysis offers several possible explanations.

First, at a simpler level, the miners were not unionized and therefore lacked a formal and collective voice through which they might have articulated safety concerns. It was far easier for individual miners to go along with management's disregard for safety regulations than to oppose it.

Second, many of the miners at Westray were relatively inexperienced and were less familiar with the more common precautions adopted in coal mining. Many of them had received very little training in safety regulations and were consequently less aware of some of the hazards resulting from safety violations. Not surprisingly, the less experienced miners treated many of the safety rules as mere bureaucratic paraphernalia which were not to be taken seriously. However, the issue of miners' attitudes towards their own safety is a highly complex one, extending well beyond discussions of adequate versus inadequate training. Even miners with many years of experience are often the victims of careless accidents, suggesting that experienced miners become so accustomed to hazards in the environment that they also become more careless than novice miners (Stowers Carr, 1991).

Other more enduring explanations can be found by adopting a "cultural theory of risk perception," which examines how different groups in organizations and societies pay attention to different risks and, in fact, frame different phenomena as being risky, dangerous, or otherwise (Douglas et al., 1982).

Within this framework, miners' orientations towards hazardous working conditions can best be understood by looking at the cultural traditions designated as an "occupational sub-culture of danger," found frequently in underground mines (Vaught et al. 1991). Studies examining social interactions within coal mines indicate that the shared sense of danger substantially influences the development of sub-cultural values and expectations among miners (Fitzpatrick, 1974; Vaught et al., 1980). Miners develop cultural mechanisms for coping with imminent disasters which paradoxically may blunt their own responses to risky situations. In learning to live with potential hazards, miners also learn to be less cautious and therefore become more habituated to disregarding safety procedures.

As an occupational culture, mining is woven around legends of tragic heroism, with a history of black lung disease, mine fires and explosions, roof cave-ins, and near escapes from innumerable disasters (Wardell et al., 1985). The miner emerges as a tragic hero, and often mining communities across Canada and the US have prominent memorials dedicated to miners who have lost their lives in tragic circumstances, much like cenotaphs erected in many towns to honour those killed in war. The miner as tragic hero thus becomes an integral part of the occupational identity of coal miners. This in turn generates some degree of fatalism, which can in part contribute to patterns of non-compliance to safety exhibited by miners themselves.

Underground miners' cultural rationalities are also likely to be substantially influenced by notions of masculinity at the workplace. In recent years, a number of writers have underscored the ideological role of masculinity in a wide variety of organizational situations, ranging from professional sports and NASA to mining and offshore drilling and in making decisions about physical injury and danger (Messner, 1990; Young, 1993; Mater, 1994; Schwartz, 1990; Carson, [no date]; Fitzpatrick, 1974). Broadly, these researchers present a "culture of masculinism" in traditionally male occupations that often equates violence and danger with "appropriate manly performance" and eventually facilitates workers' own participation in potentially hazardous actions. Miners' collective constructions of masculinity might well culturally reinforce the value of non-compliance to safety rules.

Perhaps the most striking conditions influencing worker non-compliance of safety rules could be found in the poor economic conditions in the Pictou County region. Work in the region was extremely scarce. Indeed, the mine had secured political backing partly because it provided sustained employment in a depressed area. As an indication of the scarcity of job opportunities in the region, a 6000-name petition signed by Westray employees was presented to the Nova Scotia government in July 1992 after the explosion had taken place, requesting that the mine be reopened. Recent revelations in the public hearings held to look at the Westray explosion indicate that most miners were convinced that complaints about safety violations would cost them their jobs and were therefore more likely to contribute to the mock bureaucracy around safety.

What may be most intriguing here is the miners' apparent inclinations to regard prospective unemployment risks as more threatening than safety risks. But again cultural theories of risk suggest that any group's or community's sense of future time will mediate their perceptions of risk (Douglas et al., 1982). Conditions of poverty often foreshorten the future, making individuals more prone to worrying about economic risks than physical hazards, which are seen to lie in the more distant future (Lewis, 1966). Given the chronic and intensive unemployment in the Pictou County region, we can hypothesize that many miners were far more sensitized to the risks of unemployment than they were to the risks of physical danger. These anxieties about unemployment may also have made many miners reluctant to quit solely on account of safety concerns.

Additionally, certain external institutional forces were also shaping miners' cultural rationalities. Miners knew from experience that the unemployment insurance office often penalized workers who quit their jobs because of allegedly unsafe work conditions. This lesson was all the more sharply driven home by the case of Michael Wrice, a miner with ten years' experience who quit working at the Westray mine in October 1991 as a result of his concerns with safety. Wrice had repeatedly complained to provincial inspectors about safety problems at the mine. After leaving Westray, he applied for unemployment insurance (UI) benefits and was told that he had "no justifiable reason for leaving." He was therefore disqualified from receiving benefits for nine weeks and was considered eligible for only 50 percent of his former wages instead of the customary 60 percent (Zataman, 1992). Wrice made a subsequent appeal of the ruling, which was denied when officials from the labour department told the hearing that the mine was perfectly safe. Even after the Westray explosion, the Department of Employment and Immigration, in addressing another of Michael Wrice's claims, indicated that he would have to prove that events subsequent to his leaving justified his reason to quit. What can be seen here is a pattern of negligence, also on the part of external institutions, which further legitimated the non-compliance with safety procedures.

Overall, what is evident is that worker non-compliance with safety rules, while also resulting in a mock bureaucracy, took place for reasons which were strikingly different from those driving managerial non-compliance. First of all, workers took their cues from managers' disregard for safety regulations. Second, workers lacked a collective voice with which they could confront managers with the flagrant violations of safety codes. Third, some workers lacked the appropriate training required to recognize key safety issues, while, simultaneously, the occupational culture of mining blunted more experienced miners' awareness of hazardous situations. And finally, regional unemployment conditions ensured that safety rules were perceived as less legitimate than continued opportunities for employment. While external institutions such as the Unemployment Insurance Commission and the labour department also delegitimized the importance of safety by not taking workers' concerns seriously, workers had few options but to resort to the same flagrant violations of safety rules that were the operating norm at Westray.

## DISCUSSION

The character in the Chinese script denoting crisis combines the characters representing both danger and opportunity (Brantlinger, 1990). Our analysis of the Westray mine disaster, while focusing on the hazardous conditions of the mine, also provides an opportunity for understanding some of the processes behind the emergence of a mock bureaucracy, which can precipitate serious accidents and disasters. Primarily, we have pinpointed some of the conditions conducive to a flourishing mock bureaucracy.

What we are suggesting is that institutional and economic pressures combined with varying cultural traditions and ideologies to promote a local organizational climate in which non-compliance with safety rules became a norm or informal rule. At Westray, while managers and workers engaged in non-compliance for somewhat different reasons, this non-compliance soon became an issue on which there was considerable shared understanding. Managers were stirred to non-compliance mainly by performance pressures, while workers were motivated by livelihood pressures. Both were substantially driven by specific cultural rationalities as well. We suggest that in many similar situations, managers and workers may collude with each other in creating a culture of non-compliance, thereby creating a mock bureaucracy around safety at the workplace.

It is not our intention to claim here that mock bureaucracies are behind all or most industrial crises. However, we cannot ignore the fact that, in case after case of earthbound disasters, investigations reveal a systematic pattern of failure to adhere to safety regulations. Thus, understanding the phenomenon of mock bureaucracy can provide vital insights into some of the processes triggering these earthbound disasters. Furthermore, the stakeholder and institutional pressures identified at Westray are similar to those in other mines and other earthbound systems as well. Logging companies, for instance, also frequently face similar financial pressures and the need to meet urgent customer demands. Loggers, like miners, are confronted with harsh economic conditions, they often lack a collective voice and are influenced by an occupational culture of danger. Reports on safety in the logging industry are rife with instances of safety neglect by relevant external bodies. Thus, the logging industry may be situated in circumstances conducive to non-compliance with safety regulations. At the same time, the logging industry is also somewhat different in structure and practice from the mining industry. For instance, loggers are often employed by contractors who are subject to different goals and imperatives than mine managers. Future research in this area should employ comparative case studies set in different earthbound systems such as logging, mining, dam maintenance, etc. in order to provide meaningful analysis of similarities and contrasts in an understanding of the emergence of mock bureaucracies.

This study suggests that antecedents of industrial crises in mining and other earthbound disasters are perhaps best understood through appreciating the social context in which they are situated and the political sense-making that informs local organization-level decision-making. Unless these phenomena are understood, reforms designed to eradicate industrial crises can have only limited impact (Tucker, 1995). For instance, public inquiries following many industrial crises often recommend tighter safety regulations and more safety rules. Our chapter questions this systemic over-reliance on rules. What we suggest is that more and better rules may not be the way to prevent industrial crises. The Westray case indicates that formal rules are clearly subordinate to workplace norms and ideologies. However, changing norms around safety compliance or non-compliance is not an easy task. This is made more difficult because these norms are not exclusively the product of local interactions between managers and workers but are substantially shaped by external institutional demands and pressures. Workplace safety in itself has little value for some external stakeholders, such as customers and banks. In order to dislodge the mock bureaucracies around safety, we may have to link safety goals more tightly to production goals and lending criteria. It is important to remember, however, that in such situations it is not a lack of adequate rules but rather compliance that is the problem. For scholars of organizational crises, the current challenge is to develop strategies for converting mock bureaucracies around safety procedures into representative ones.

This chapter suggests that normal accidents are not likely to take place only in complex and tightly coupled systems. Rather, any organization that is a site for mock bureaucracies around safety regulations can be characterized as a crisis prone or high risk system (Pauchant et al., 1992; Perrow, 1984). In other words, even linear organizations operating with relatively simple technologies can have a high built-in catastrophic potential given a particular configuration of institutional features, notably strong pressures on production, specific cultural attitudes towards risk, and a systematic failure on the part of regulatory institutions to uphold safety standards. Once we recognize that "normal accidents" can occur as easily in linear and loosely coupled systems, scholars of industrial crises may focus their attention on a whole group of industries that have hitherto been largely neglected.

And finally, the chapter raises some issues concerning organizational legitimacy that may be worth discussing. Innumerable scholars have underscored the importance of legitimacy for understanding organizational action (Ashforth et al., 1990; Dowling et al., 1975; Elsbach et al., 1992; Prasad, 1995). And in discussing the emergence of a mock bureaucracy, it has been proposed that legitimacy itself is sufficient to ensure compliance. However, the legitimacy of rules in themselves may not be sufficient to ensure internal compliance owing to a whole web of complex institutional pressures. Additionally, the role of social legitimacy in ensuring safe workplace practices has to be examined. Few would question the fact that workplace safety is a socially legitimate issue, and legitimacy can strongly influence organizational actions. Yet, in the coal mining industry, the legitimacy of workplace safety has not prevented organizations from engaging in flagrant violations of safety rules and regulations. We suggest that one reason that the social legitimacy of workplace safety is an ineffective deterrent to unsafe working conditions is that workplace safety issues are largely invisible and hidden from the gaze of the general public. This is entirely in keeping with the theoretical argument that organizations and organizational processes that are less visible are also less likely to be affected by questions arising out of social legitimacy.

By contrast, an organization's financial operations are invariably open to constant public scrutiny and therefore are regularly impacted by questions of legitimacy. In the case of Westray as well, the balance sheets of Curragh Resources could be easily scanned by relevant stakeholders, who could then exert pressure to influence actions considered to be socially illegitimate. However, the everyday safety practices of most organizations are rarely exposed to the public except in the case of an accident or disaster, at which time the entire organization may come under public scrutiny. Perhaps safety practices in organizations need to receive the same kind of constant public attention given to their financial statements for social legitimacy to have an impact on them.

These issues of legitimacy can contribute to current theories of crisis-prone organizations. Most organizational crisis arguments focus more heavily on variables, such as organizational structure, technological choice, leadership, culture, etc., to explain the emergence of high risk organizations. However, this chapter suggests that rule legitimacy both within and outside organizations plays a vital role in shaping the extent to which these organizations become disaster prone. This legitimacy is the product of complex cultural, ideological and political forces. To understand when accidents might become "normal," therefore, we would suggest that researchers do not confine their analysis to technology, leadership, and structure, but that they focus on certain moments when a particular constellation of stakeholder interests becomes incompatible with the goals of workplace safety.

# THE AFTERMATH:
## DEALING WITH DISASTER

## CHAPTER SEVEN

# PUBLIC RELATIONS AND THE WESTRAY MINE EXPLOSION[1]

*Trudie Richards*

## INTRODUCTION

The Westray mine in Pictou County, Nova Scotia, exploded on May 9, 1992, killing the twenty-six miners who were trapped underground. The interaction between the mine owner and the media, and how the behaviour of each affected the families of the trapped miners in the days after the explosion, form the basis of this study of relationships between corporate communicators and journalists in time of crisis. This analysis shows that Curragh Incorporated demonstrated an unwillingness to cooperate with the media and an insensitivity toward the families of the trapped miners. It also shows that journalists relied on human interest to tell their stories and, consequently, decontextualized their coverage (Wilkins, 1989). And finally, the study suggests that although corporations are advised to have a crisis communications plan in advance of a predictable event if they have something to hide, as is alleged in this case, the presence or absence of a plan per se is unlikely to affect the eventual outcome (Blythe, 1992; White, 1991).

Research for this article was conducted in the year following the explosion. Journalists, communications specialists, and members of the community of Pictou County were interviewed, including families of the deceased miners. A literature review was also conducted and CBC Television news coverage was surveyed from May 9 through May 19. Print coverage from the *Globe and Mail,* the Halifax *Chronicle-Herald* and the Halifax *Daily News* was examined from September 1988 through to the end of 1994. Coverage of the explosion in the New Glasgow *Evening News* was also examined. Senior officials of Curragh were advised by their lawyers not to participate in view of a pending criminal trial and public inquiry, although one senior executive read the document and, on condition of anonymity, endorsed the accuracy of its content. Public relations advisors to Curragh were available, however, and were very helpful.

The Westray mine was owned by Curragh Incorporated, a Toronto-based company with mining operations in British Columbia and the Yukon. Although technological crises are both predictable and inevitable, and mining is considered a high risk industry (Pinsdorf, 1987), most mining companies have no communications plan in the event of a crisis.[2] Curragh was no exception.[3] The literature recommends that corporations be open with and accessible to the media before crisis strikes and during the event itself, to the extent that is reasonable (Charron, 1989; Grunig et al., 1984). They are also encouraged to have a crisis communications plan so that their strategy in times of upheaval can be more proactive than reactive (Murray et al., 1992), and particularly so in an era when the incidence of corporate crises is increasing (Drabek et al., 1991). In the case of Curragh, the absence of a "what-to-do-when-the-unthinkable-happens" guide meant that the company was dealing with two crises: the event and how to handle the event.

As this study reveals, Curragh ultimately alienated two of its key publics—the media and the families—partly because it was not prepared, and also because officials were unable to refute allegations of unsafe working conditions at the mine. If an organization does not perform well during a crisis it may have difficulty recovering, and it is estimated that 43 percent of organizations hit by "severe" crises never recover (Blythe, 1992). Curragh is now bankrupt, and the Westray tragedy played a significant role in the company's demise.

## A BRIEF LITERATURE REVIEW

The relationship between public relations practitioners and journalists often appears to be one of conflict. Public relations practitioners complain their work is misunderstood, and the media complain about the degree to which PR people try to manage and influence them. Repeatedly, surveys suggest that journalists hold negative perceptions of public relations people (Aranoff, 1975; Kopenhaver et al., 1984; Stegall et al., 1986). In a 1984 survey in Florida, for example, journalists ranked themselves first out of sixteen professions in terms of status, and they ranked PR professionals second last, just ahead of politicians. In that same survey, public relations people ranked themselves fourth, and journalists ninth (Kopenhaver et al., 1984: 863).

In reality, however, journalists and public relations practitioners are interdependent. Both professions are engaged in information dissemination, the former as information source and the latter as information processor. Although journalists say they prefer to keep their distance and they operate either competitively or even by practicing avoidance, surveys suggest that resistance has met with limited success. In a survey of 1146 stories in the *Washington Post* and the *New York Times* over a two-week period in each of five different years, it was found that the stories which originated with routine sources, such as official documents, news releases, and news conferences, outnumbered reporter-initiated stories by more than two to one. When background briefings, meetings, and leaks were factored in, the number climbed by an additional 16 percent (Sigal, 1973). More than a decade later, researchers found that journalists still relied on source-generated news. "Most reporting relies on routine channels such as press conferences and press releases" (Brown et al., 1987: 53).

In 1989, the sources of news in a smaller American paper (circulation 17,000), owned by a large newspaper chain, were analyzed, and it was observed that the newspaper concentrated its beat coverage on "institutions that [were] most visible to readers," such as municipal governments, police, the courts, and education. In a survey of 632 locally-produced, by-lined stories over a one-year period, they were analyzed according to their "news channels": routine, such as news releases, news conferences, and official meetings; informal, such as stories arising from backgrounders, leaks, and personal contacts; and enterprise, such as stories based on a reporter's original research or analysis. "[It was found that] 337 or 53.3 percent of the stories ... came from routine channels, 120 or 19 percent from informal channels and 175 or 27.7 percent from enterprise channels" (Soloski, 1989: 862).

In its March/April 1980 issue, the *Columbia Journalism Review* published an analysis of one day's edition of the *Wall Street Journal*. The *CJR* contacted each of the 111 companies that appeared in the October 4, 1979 edition, to see which stories were based on news releases. Seventy companies responded.

> In 53 cases—72 percent of our responses—news stories were based solely on press releases; in 32 of these examples, the releases were reprinted almost verbatim or in paraphrase, while in 21 other cases only the most perfunctory additional reporting had been done. Perhaps most troublesome, 20 of these stories carried the slug "By a *Wall Street Journal* Staff Reporter." (35)

Scott M. Cutlip, retired dean of the Henry W. Grady School of Journalism and Mass Communications at the University of Georgia, does not put the number quite so high. Nevertheless, he argues, "It is a safe generalization to say that 40 percent of the news content in a typical newspaper originated with public relations press releases, story memos, or suggestions" (Blyskal et al., 1985: 50).

There is a more recent Canadian illustration of the degree to which journalists appear to rely on official, or "institutional," news and official sources. John Miller of the Ryerson School of Journalism surveyed the *Toronto Star*, the *Globe and Mail* and the *Toronto Sun* for a week in May, 1990. He found that "institutional news made up 93.2 percent of the content of the *Sun*, 84.5 percent of the *Star*, and 80.2 percent of the *Globe*. In other words, they used most of their resources to react to planned events" (Miller, 1990: 24). He also found that "the most popular source of news in the three papers was press conferences, press releases or public non-governmental meetings or speeches—between 33 and 37 percent of the total content" (Milleer, 1990: 24).

Furthermore, "only 6.8 percent of the news content in the *Sun*, 15.6 percent in the *Star,* and 19.8 percent in the *Globe* could be classified as "unofficial," meaning it demonstrated the reporter's own initiative" (Miller 1990: 24). That survey considered only the quantity of stories, not length or positioning in the papers, and the week was not compared to any other period of time. Nevertheless, while it might not be "scientific," it does indicate that reporters tend to react to official agendas rather than to initiate news themselves.

## THE CHALLENGE FOR CORPORATE PUBLIC RELATIONS PEOPLE

The public relations profession has devised ways of establishing relationships with the media to address negative perceptions. Public relations scholar James Grunig recommends what he describes as the "two-way symmetric" model, in which practitioners seek to keep lines of communication open between an organization and its publics to build good relationships between them. There is a greater degree of risk in this model because there is less source control; however, "the more open you can make your organization, the greater is the likelihood of fair and accurate media coverage" (Grunig et al., 1984). Unfortunately, the approach has not been endorsed by a majority of public relations professionals.

The corporate sector has a variety of publics it must address. Journalists are not only one of them, they are also a conduit to many others: investors, consumers, and the community, to name several. Organizations cannot ignore the role of the media in this process without serious risk. Media attention, intense competitiveness, and government regulation, ensure the corporate sector is carefully scrutinized (Chajet et al., 1991).

A corporate priority, then, is to establish a positive image and maintain public confidence. However, since the corporate image reflects the corporate reality, one cannot be changed unless the other changes as well. Furthermore, a company shares an image with the industry in which it is involved. Unless it goes some distance to separate itself from the common image, or to refine it, the company acquires the negative as well as the positive industrywide associations.

The mining industry, in Canada and elsewhere, has historically had a problem with its image (O'Keefe, 1984). The legacies of child labour, harsh living and working conditions, and high risk of accidental injury or death have contributed to a negative perception of the industry. For example, the May 1993 edition of *Liaison*, a Labour Canada bulletin about occupational safety and health, includes the following paragraph about accidents in mines under federal jurisdiction: "In 1991, the mining industry recorded the highest disabling injury incidence rate at 27.1 [injuries] per 100 workers, followed by longshoring at 15.7, road transport at 9.26 and air transport at 8" (1993:20).

Another publication from the same department, entitled *Employment*

*Injuries and Occupational Illnesses, 1985–87* suggests that "for the period 1983–1987, approximately 42 percent of deaths from occupational illnesses occurred in mining" (Labour Canada, 1990:20).

Furthermore, "the public has a morbid fear about underground places which may be impossible to dispel," and every mining accident further entrenches the negative perceptions of the industry (O'Keefe, 1984: 81). The challenge for a contemporary mining company, then, is to create a corporate reality that will justify an improved image.

The disenchantment attached to the corporation also applies to its leader. A Harris poll measuring public confidence in corporate executives shows the percentage dropped to just 18 percent in 1984, from 55 percent in the mid-1960s (Gray, 1986). One way to improve the image of the corporation and that of its chief executive officer is to design a media strategy that incorporates proven methodology. For example, corporate spokespersons, from the chief executive officer down, should receive media training, be consistent, and be accessible.

## THE RELATIONSHIP IN TIME OF CRISIS

The incidence of corporate crises is increasing. In the introduction to an emergency management manual for American government officials, the increase in technological crises such as chemical explosions is attributed to the fact that there are so many new substances created every year, "giving rise to that many more opportunities for human error" (Drabek et al., 1991:5). According to Bruce Blythe of Crisis Management International, an Atlanta-based firm which specializes in crisis readiness programs, more than half of the major industrial disasters that occurred in this century occurred in the eight years prior to 1993. And, as if the devastating effects needed to be underscored, "forty-three percent of companies hit by severe crises never reopen, and 29 percent close within two years" (Blythe, 1992: 14).

The Institute for Crisis Management, based in Louisville, Kentucky, defines crisis in the business sector as "a significant disruption in the organization's normal activities that generates media coverage and public attention." The biggest single growth area in corporate crises today is in human resources—discrimination, sexual harassment, and the like.[4]

There is a tendency to use the word "disaster" for what is more accurately called a "crisis." Although the definitions of both are evolving, they are distinct terms by virtue of degree. Not all crises are disasters. The latter are defined as accidental or uncontrollable events

> concentrated in time and space, in which a society, or a relatively self-sufficient subdivision of a society, undergoes severe danger, and incurs such losses to its members and physical appurtenances that the

social structure is disrupted and the fulfilment of all or some of the essential functions of the society is prevented. (Fritz, 1961: 655)

Although the Westray tragedy has been labelled a disaster by many public relations practitioners and reporters, the context of "crisis" is more appropriate because the incident did not incur such losses that the social structure was disrupted. Instances will arise, however, where references to disaster literature are unavoidable.

There is perhaps no time when the relationship between public relations practitioners and the media is more severely tested than during crisis. Public relations people argue that preparation for such an event must begin long before the event itself. Jon White (1991), a public relations expert based in the United Kingdom, says corporations must work at trying to establish a positive, open relationship with the media well in advance of a crisis so that, if and when a crisis occurs, there is a history that will help both sides deal with the event. When preparation hasn't been made, the organization will find itself having to deal with the situation and with learning how to work with journalists at the same time. White cites the example of Air Canada, an organization which, he says, actively cultivates a relationship with the media by encouraging and training its line managers to deal directly with press requests. During one emergency, when an Air Canada jet ran out of fuel in transit, the company was able to rely on its reputation and credibility with journalists and survive the event with no lasting damage to its image (White 1991: 32–33). This illustration suggests a successful two-way symmetrical strategy, as described earlier, in which a previous relationship of openness meant the journalists told the story much as the PR adviser would wish (although not perhaps in such a way that would fully inform the media consumer).

An organization's behaviour during a crisis can affect its treatment in the aftermath. People will remember how it behaved, which may affect the outcome of a subsequent inquiry, for instance. After the crisis is over, the organization may have to try to regain credibility. Sometimes this is impossible if, for example, the organization behaved poorly during the crisis or if the damage is so great that public confidence is lost.

Business leaders know if they are involved in a high risk operation. Mining is high risk, and corporate officials are advised to have an emergency plan and to test it, revising it if necessary. An organization in crisis is under public scrutiny. The event is significant and will be remembered. The high level of stress during a crisis can be reduced if people know what to do (White, 1991; Pinsdorf, 1987).

Advance crisis planning means considering the worst-case scenario and devising a plan to deal with it. A crisis plan provides the corporation with a model for behaviour when the event occurs. It identifies the crisis team. The chief executive officer is most often the corporate spokesperson. He or she is considered the one who is best able to both be in control and show concern. The plan also identifies risk areas and how to respond in each case to key publics: employees, media, and the community at large (Murray et al., 1992: 14).

It is difficult to make disaster planning a priority. People's daily demands are such that it is often all too easy to postpone the planning process, even when they know that being prepared will reduce the damaging effects. But if there is no plan, the crisis may unfold at two levels. The first is the crisis itself. If the company is unprepared, that in effect precipitates a second crisis. "The company is reactive rather than proactive and the result is a crisis in public perception."[5]

Michael Regester (1989), a British public relations practitioner with expertise in crisis management, recommends that corporate officials establish several rooms during a crisis: one for decision-makers (such as the chief executive officer), one for advisers (such as public relations people and lawyers), and one for the media. Each of these groups needs to be able to work alone. Each also needs to be in frequent contact with the others. Information should also be made available to the media as soon as possible. Journalists will have something to report, and officials will demonstrate "a willingness to communicate" (Regester, 1989: 116–17).

Public relations professionals often recommend the following cliché: "tell it all and tell it fast"; giving out information in stages only guarantees a longer lifespan for the story (Pinsdorf, 1987: 45; Regester, 1989: 123). This advice is not always easy to follow. Often information is known only in stages, and often it takes time to establish rumour as fact. Furthermore, corporate decision-makers may be reluctant to divulge information they know may be damaging, such as legal liability and responsibility to employees and shareholders. Ideally, the more accurate the information and the more openly and honestly it is shared, the better the image. However, spokespersons should watch what they say, be sure the information is complete and honest, and consider as many ramifications as time and deadline pressure permit.

Not to underscore the obvious, corporations with something to hide are at serious risk. If that is the case, the best advice is to tell the truth up front. Concealing information only heightens media coverage and scepticism. Robin Cohn, who has his own crisis management firm in New York, puts it this way: "The cardinal rule: never hide the facts. If the media don't get information from the company, they'll get it from other sources, usually unfriendly" (1991: 19z).

## The Westray Story Prior to the Explosion

The Westray mine had been politically controversial in Nova Scotia, and to a lesser degree in Ottawa, since 1988. Journalists tended to cover the story from a political perspective. They acknowledged former Premier Donald Cameron's commitment to Westray and the location of the mine in former Conservative MP Elmer MacKay's riding (a seat held briefly by former Prime Minister Brian Mulroney). They also covered the bickering over competition for limited markets between coal from Cape Breton, which was heavily government-subsidized, and coal from Pictou County, which would receive government loan guarantees of over $100 million.[6]

Media coverage of the Westray story in Nova Scotia prior to the explosion reflected what is perceived by some observers as a curious attitude among journalists based there. Most journalists in Nova Scotia share with Nova Scotians in general a desire for positive development in their province. Linden MacIntyre, a host of CBC Television's *The Fifth Estate*, describes it as "a symbiotic relationship between the Nova Scotia population and the news media" (Starr 1992: 11). MacIntyre, who is from Cape Breton, argues that many Nova Scotians believed then-premier Donald Cameron's claim that Westray was a good idea because they wanted to believe it. He adds that the local media followed suit because they seem to be in sync with the mental state of the province (Starr, 1992: 12). That general desire may have diminished journalistic zeal to be critical of the Westray project prior to the explosion. Furthermore, it is argued that there is a bias against Cape Breton among much of the Nova Scotia population in general, which is reflected by many of the province's mainland journalists at the two biggest mainland newspapers, the *Chronicle-Herald* (Halifax) and the *Daily News* (Halifax).[7]

On the morning of May 9, as journalists learned of the explosion of the Westray mine, an awareness dawned that there had been another Westray story they had not much told. The mine was located in a volatile and dangerous coal seam. For example, from 1809, when coal mining began, to the 1950s, the number of mining-related deaths in Pictou County alone is estimated to be more than 600 men. Of those, 246 are known to have died from mine explosions (Cameron, 1974: 9). There had been warnings about the dangers of extracting the coal. For example, in a report prepared by the Cape Breton Development Corporation (Devco), which was obtained by the media, Derek Rance, a former head of Devco, warned that "in order for [Westray] to be safe, everything is going to have to work right all of the time" (Devco report, December 8, 1987). The report received considerable media attention, but a survey of coverage suggests that this particular reference appeared only once. Furthermore, there had been complaints from miners at Westray about safety. With very rare exceptions, reporters ignored those issues. Journalists missed the safety angle in the Westray story at least in part because they perceived the complaints from Cape Breton as sour grapes and because they wanted another part of the province to be the beneficiary of the financial largesse that had previously been directed to Cape Breton.

It is also possible that reporters believed Westray's assurances that the mine was high-tech and state-of-the-art; that kind of faith can lull journalists into a false sense of security because of the "technology bias." It is tempting to think that such mining accidents as rock falls, fires, and explosions wouldn't happen anymore because modern technology would prevent them.

Reporters cannot be chastised for dwelling on the political dimensions of the Westray mine. What is regrettable is the virtual exclusivity of that focus, and that is a regret with which, a year later, journalists still struggled.[8]

## The Explosion of May 9, 1992

At 5:18 Saturday morning, May 9, 1992, an explosion erupted at the Westray coal mine in the village of Plymouth, Nova Scotia. The explosion was so strong it blew the top off the mine entrance, more than a mile above, and shattered steel roof supports throughout the mine, trapping twenty-six men below. In the nearby towns, windows shattered and houses shook. Kathy Dobbs, a mental health worker at the Aberdeen General Hospital in New Glasgow, lived close to the mine, and the force of the explosion woke her: "It was this incredible thud like I'd never heard before. The house shook. It was like a noise that filled the atmosphere," she said. "I felt this fear and dread. I remember thinking, 'Oh my God, the vastness of this.'" Within minutes, the phone rang, and she was instructed to stand by. She would spend the next week with the families of the trapped miners.[9]

In the early hours after the explosion, three distinct groups positioned themselves for their roles in this tragic incident. The families of the trapped miners, supported by a community of friends and neighbours, gathered to seek and provide comfort and to await news. The media converged on Plymouth to collect news. And Curragh's senior managers were installed at the mine site, to manage the incident and to disseminate news.

The draegermen, miners trained in rescue work, spent the next week slowly working their way through the wreckage, looking for survivors, knowing that the chances of finding anyone alive were slim. On the second day, they discovered eleven bodies. Three days later, four more. As each day passed, hope faded that anyone would be found alive.

George Muise, a Cape Breton miner who has been a draegerman for fourteen years, was captain of one of the mine rescue teams at Westray. It is believed the first eleven men they found died of poisoning from carbon monoxide, produced by combustion. There were signs of high heat, as the hair was singed, and the hands were closed into fists. The four bodies the draegermen found on Wednesday were in much worse condition, badly burnt, and their clothes were burnt off. One man's body was intact, but it appeared as if someone had put him through a trash compacter. But before the draegermen could recover that body, the search was called off. On Thursday, May 14, Colin Benner, president of operations for Curragh, told the reporters that there were no survivors and that the risks to the draegermen were too great to continue the search for bodies. That was a difficult decision to make because there is a strong commitment to retrieving the dead in mining communities.

By the next day, Friday, the event was over, at least for the rest of the world. Most of the media had left. And the community of Pictou County began the process of adjusting to terrible loss.

Twenty-six miners died. The remains of eleven bodies are buried in the sealed mine.

It is believed the tragedy was caused by an explosion of methane gas, which is a natural by-product of coal. When it is mixed with oxygen, it is combustible, which is why proper ventilation underground is so critical. The presence of coal dust makes mining even more dangerous because a single spark can ignite the dust and travel through it as if it were gunpowder. As the flames lick up the dust, they strike pockets of methane and air, and the explosion intensifies. It is therefore crucial to treat the coal dust with rock dust or ground limestone. Rock dust is heavier than coal dust, so it pushes the coal dust down to the mine floor and covers it so that it won't explode.

## The Relationship between Curragh and the Media

Curragh installed the trapped miners' families in the fire hall not far from the mine and placed the journalists in the community centre, directly across the street. The RCMP patrolled the road separating the two buildings and prevented the media from speaking to family members. The journalists had no direct access to the company offices or the mine site, except at the company's initiative. Restrictions were similar for the families.

### Figure 7.1. Curragh and the Media

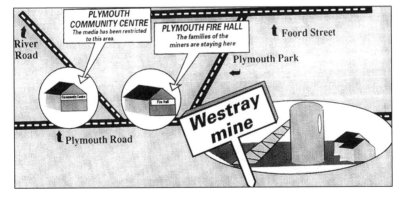

The positioning of the media and the families in such close proximity guaranteed animosity. The fact that the police blocked media access to the families heightened the tension. *Globe and Mail* journalist André Picard, who was at the site to provide support to Halifax-based bureau chief Kevin Cox, wrote that there was a "strange tension between local people and journalists" (1992:

A4). The journalists felt they had been wrapped in "a virtual cocoon," he wrote, and the families and the press were kept apart by the RCMP, "with strict orders to keep the media in their place" (Picard, 1992: A4).

Curragh was not prepared for this event. It had no crisis communications plan. If it had, the company might have been able to reduce media antagonism, at least to a degree. The plan would have forced Curragh to think in advance about media needs; to try to schedule news conferences at convenient times; to use understandable language; to ensure that a mining expert with knowledge of Westray was available to answer questions about the technology; to provide first-hand updates of the search for survivors; and to encourage the families to speak to the media on their own terms. Curragh did none of that.

Crisis management specialists recommend that information be made available to the media as soon as possible. Tom Reid of Reid Management in Toronto, who had worked with Curragh's Chief Executive Officer Clifford Frame for many years, handled communications initially from his office. He provided journalists with "whatever facts they needed, diagrams, maps. I had the background. The employees at Westray didn't."[10] Although Kevin Cox, a Halifax *Chronicle-Herald* reporter, was sceptical about having to rely on a Toronto-based source for information about a Nova Scotia story, he was amazed at Reid's grasp of what was happening. "He knew everything."[11] Reid also advised on the tone of voice Curragh spokesmen should use and suggested the following priorities of what should be said to the media: that the explosion was a terrible tragedy which could not have been foreseen; that the mine owners ran a safe mine; that the families and the rescue workers were showing great courage; and that the company would participate fully in any investigation. But that arrangement was only satisfactory in the immediate aftermath, on May 9 and 10 and perhaps May 11.[12] In fact, Reid recalls it was about that time that he started to notice something about the way Curragh was treating the media.

> They were devising strategies that they weren't asking me about. I'm sure there was a good reason, but they never bothered to explain it to me. And that was they'd make a statement, they'd answer two or three questions, and then they'd get out.... I thought that was not a positive, constructive strategy, and I tried to advise them against it. I said, 'Once you're in the room, you stay there until you're satisfied you've answered all the questions. Then excuse yourself and get back to your operations.' But they maintained this 'in, quick hit, couple of answers, and then out.' I didn't understand that strategy.[13]

Rather than responding to journalists' needs by providing background briefings or scheduling news conferences at convenient times (Fishman, 1980), perhaps unavoidably but regrettably nevertheless, Curragh did the opposite and often held news conferences at inconvenient times—2:00 a.m., 6:00 a.m., and midnight. Dean Jobb, the on-location editor in charge of coverage for the *Chronicle-Herald* (Halifax), recalled that the news conferences would invariably occur right on his deadline, so he barely had time to file a story and hardly ever had time to get reactions. The hosts of the CBC supper-hour television news program for Nova Scotia, *First Edition*, referred to "information by news conference, when mine officials are ready to share it with us," and later, to "broken deadlines, 'about to have' news" (CBC-TV, May 12, 1992). On one edition of the program, the news conference had barely ended as the program began; on another, the news conference began while the program was on the air.

Company officials made only a limited effort to help the media understand what was happening, and although advisers explained Curragh wanted to be accurate above all else, even that wasn't always the case.[14] The following observation was made on the air by the host of *First Edition:*

> At one point we reported rescuers were 100 metres from the trapped men. Then they [Curragh] said they were 300–500 metres from the trapped men. Then there was an indication today that they had moved back, uh, to a less deep position in the mine, to a new fresh air base. It is very difficult for us to tell you what is going on in the mine. It is very difficult for us to know what is going on in the mine" (CBC-TV, May 12, 1992).

Curragh officials used unfamiliar language and made insufficient effort to explain the technology of the Westray mine to reporters. Bob Allison, a senior producer with *First Edition*, recalls that the journalists were trying to learn "what were so many 'parts per' of methane. We were trying to find out whether those numbers were high or low. They were not forthcoming in describing how high or how low."[15] Kevin Cox was also having problems following the jargon. When officials first started talking about "crosscuts," he says, "we didn't even know what a crosscut was. We gradually understood, but they would make no effort to tell us."[16] That behaviour was not necessary, but it is not unusual.[17] Curragh did not provide scientific expertise about the mine. Access to such an expert would not excuse the media from seeking out another, more detached perspective. But if Curragh wanted to encourage a relationship of trust and openness, providing such a person would have helped.

Curragh told the media they could not speak to the draegermen.[18] It is true that the rescue operation was their first priority, and de-briefing and rest shifts were also important. But an opportunity could have been found on a regular basis to give the media access to firsthand accounts of the rescue effort. Draegermen are miners, who work for mine owners. They are not likely to disparage their employers, although they might inadvertently have said something that would be damaging to Curragh. The media wanted that firsthand accounting; it should have been made available to them.

Curragh could also have suggested that the families choose representatives to talk to the media, rather than insisting that journalists leave the families alone. In his internal post-event assessment, emergency measures coordinator Daryn Smith recommends just that. Even family member Isabel Gillis, whose husband died in the explosion, says if the restrictions on the media had not been so severe, "they wouldn't have had to hound the families to death."[19]

Joseph Scanlon, a Carleton University disaster specialist, maintains that there usually are victims who want to talk (Scanlon., 1993). He cites the following example of when an American military aircraft crashed near Gander airport in Newfoundland in December 1985, and relatives gathered in Fort Campbell, Kentucky, to await word. Reporters gathered there, too. The army's chief information officer told the media he was not prepared to allow reporters to talk to the families of the soldiers unless the families asked. They asked. A lot of families want to speak to reporters:

> If you've just had a horrific experience, letting yourself go to somebody who's sympathetic is very positive.... So the journalist does not need to cause emotional damage. He may well be cathartic if he's empathetic. (Scanlon., 1993)

Public relations specialists recommend that the media have some sort of access to decision-makers; however Curragh denied access of any kind to journalists. They could not even approach Curragh, with a question, for example, on their own initiative.

Chief Executive Officer Clifford Frame appeared only twice before the media, on Tuesday (when he was able to return from a working holiday in Japan) and Friday, the last day of the major news coverage of the explosion, although specialists recommend the CEO be the designated spokesperson, particularly in severe crises. Public relations advisor Tom Reid recommended that Clifford Frame play a greater public role:

> I advised them to actually put Cliff in that community and that he should be there until he was satisfied that he'd done everything he could do for the families, emotionally or financially, or whatever it took to help them. And they just saw that as too much of a investment.[20]

Usually the president of operations, Colin Benner, spoke. Benner is photogenic, telegenic, and he comes from a family of miners. Benner knows mining, but he was new to the Westray operation, his first priority being Curragh's Yukon operation.

In short, Curragh did not treat reporters well, and that treatment contributed to a growing sense of frustration and suspicion among the journalists, which gelled around one key theme: the issue of safety.

### The issue of safety

The safety of the Westray mine became an immediate concern for journalists. They recognized it as a key element to the Westray story that they had not adequately covered prior to the explosion, and that haunted them.[21] But Curragh deflected the safety issue from the outset. Often questions from the media during news conferences were not allowed, especially questions about safety. Reporters would rotate responsibility for asking "the safety question," to make sure someone always asked. On the Tuesday, Benner used this phrase to deflect the safety issue: "Mother Nature cannot always be predicted or controlled," and reporters were offended.[22]

Public relations adviser Tom Reid raised the safety issue with Curragh very early. He recalls that the media started asking him questions about it almost immediately. "I would say that every third question was a safety issue." Reid was not pleased with the way the issue was being addressed and made sure Curragh officials were aware of his concerns. In hindsight, he says,

> It was probably a wise thing on their part to say, "you stay in Toronto and give us the perspective," because they know I have certain standards, shall we say. And I would just fight them, [when] they had something that was of concern that they'd made up their minds they didn't want anybody else to know about. I kept harping on it, because that's my style.... They either address it or they find somebody else to represent them.[23]

The following canvass of media coverage suggests that the safety issue became an increasingly significant component of journalists' coverage, even though Curragh continued to avoid addressing it. The Halifax *Daily News* is the only Nova Scotia paper which publishes on Sunday, although the local Thomson-owned New Glasgow *Evening News* put out a special edition on May 10. The *Daily News* carried five stories the day after the explosion, one of which raised safety concerns. The *Evening News* published a four-page special edition, with fourteen stories and a full page of photographs. There was no mention at all of the safety issue. Television coverage was much more critical, however. *The National*, on CBC-TV, devoted thirty-one minutes to the Westray explosion. There were four reporter-stories, two feature interviews, and a re-broadcast of a portion of a documentary broadcast on *The Fifth Estate* on December 11, 1990, which focused on the politics of Westray and mentioned safety only in passing. Safety was addressed in the first news report, in which a former Westray miner said he was fired because he complained about safety.

And it reappeared later in a background report by Keith Boag, who referred to documents from the Department of Labour that showed there had been seven different roof falls between 1989 and the fall of 1991.

By Monday, the safety angle was evident throughout media coverage. A headline in the *Toronto Star* ran "Why did safety system fail? Sad questions grow louder" (Boyle, 1992). CBC Television's *The National* ran a separate story on safety concerns at Westray, as did *CBC Newsworld*. Kevin Cox painted a sensitive portrait of a community in mourning in the *Globe and Mail*, describing Colin Benner as "shaken," "his voice choking with emotion" as he gave the news that the bodies of eleven men had been discovered. Cox also mentioned safety, but only once, in paragraph thirteen of a twenty-seven paragraph story.[24]

The Halifax *Chronicle-Herald* devoted all of its front and second pages, plus a special four-page report, to the explosion. Although the safety angle was not explored on page one, it was peppered throughout the rest of Monday's coverage, which included two stories suggesting the mine was not safe. CBC-TV's *First Edition* devoted the first twenty-two minutes of its Monday program to the explosion. There were five reporter-stories, and the third dealt with safety concerns.

The advice that communicators "tell it all and tell it fast" in a crisis warrants examination. There were legal charges of criminal negligence and manslaughter outstanding against Curragh and two of its mine managers in July 1997, and furthermore, the report resulting from a public inquiry had not yet been released, but it is now evident that the mine owner most definitely did not "tell it all and tell it fast." There are allegations of such things as poor ventilation in the mine, dangerous accumulations of coal dust, and the discovery of oil-soaked rags underground, all of which could have contributed to the intensity of the explosion (Comish, 1993).[25]

The media were not a top priority for Curragh. The company had other key publics very much in mind—shareholders and lenders, and ultimately a judge and jury:

> A lawyer always gets precedence. We know that from our experience with other clients. They [Curragh] didn't want the media in there. [They were preoccupied.] If they'd made some horrible screw-up, then who was liable and how much liability was there, was it the end of Curragh—they didn't know. "We're all going to jail." These are serious questions that came long before the media.[26]

Other research analyzing the communication behaviours of thirty-nine organizations charged with sexual harassment, observed that "legal strategy dominated [the] organizational decision-making process" in almost two-thirds of the situations (Fitzpatrick et al., 1995: 30). It is not surprising, then, that

Curragh did not address safety as an issue and deflected and ignored it when reporters asked. That does not make the behaviour acceptable, however, and efforts at concealment were to no avail. Ironically, Curragh's decision to prevent media access to predictable sources for human interest, and the company's unwillingness to confront the safety issue, may have resulted in more journalistic investigation, more quickly than might otherwise have been the case.

### The Local Media Perspective

As is often the case with disaster coverage, the local media provided basic information. The local cable company broadcast information about which facilities were open and when, about church services and candlelight vigils, and about where people could pick up the black ribbons everyone had decided to wear.[27] The New Glasgow *Evening News* had a firm editorial policy that had to be followed at risk of dismissal. Reporters would cover the news conferences and write on the tradition of mining in the area, but they were to stay away from the families. According to editor Doug MacNeil, the national media have a lot to answer for: "The entire community was invaded. Reporters parked on people's doorsteps. Every time a family member turned around there was a camera or a microphone stuck in his face.[28]

The relationship between Westray officials and local reporters changed dramatically on May 9. Previously, mine managers had been accessible and news releases were issued frequently. But after the explosion, there was no communication except in controlled news conferences, and releases virtually stopped. Local reporters observed that the change was particularly noticeable because the community is so small, and many of these people were personal acquaintances.[29]

### The "Come-From-Away" Press

"Come-from-away" is a term Atlantic Canadians often use to describe people who are from somewhere else, and to the people of Pictou County, most of the journalists who covered this story were considered "come-from-away" people. It is estimated that one hundred journalists and support staff converged on the scene.[30] The media often contribute in a negative way to convergence. They arrive in great numbers and make tremendous demands on limited facilities, and Westray was no exception. There were very few available phone lines, for example, and residents in nearby homes agreed to temporarily give up their lines to accommodate the media's needs.

Sometimes the media can help to mitigate convergence. If they are regularly informed, for example, they can help control the volume of inquiries by passing on information to worried friends and relatives, and they can even make requests for certain types of aid. But at Westray, there was very little information forthcoming from the company, so the media remained part of the convergence problem and did not contribute at all to its resolution. Curragh released only two written statements to reporters. The first was issued at 12:01 a.m. on Sunday, May 10 (the night after the explosion), and the other at the end of the day on Friday, May 15 (the last day of the major news event). There were only about four journalists still in the media centre at midnight that first night.[31] The release was very confusing, and contained no less than twenty-one references to statistical data, in both percentages and parts per million. It disclosed that carbon dioxide levels taken in the mine earlier that evening, more than twelve hours after the explosion, registered 100 and 200 parts per million. The release said that methane levels were also still high, at 1.25 percent. Government standards dictate that a mine must stop production if carbon monoxide levels reach 50 parts per million, and if methane levels reach 1.25 percent.[32] The reporters learned from local miners that even if anyone survived the intensity of the explosion, they would be unable to survive the lack of oxygen. But Curragh was searching for survivors, and the media were unwilling to say the search was futile. Kevin Cox's first story was headlined "Holding on to hope," and he wrote that there seemed little hope that anyone would emerge alive. And for those discouraging words, the families were angry at Cox.[33]

Michael Lightstone of the Halifax *Daily News* described the relationship between Curragh and the media as follows:

> We were feeding off each other.... We were holed up there, waiting for these briefings, even though they were sometimes completely useless. There was no real news, they just felt that they had to come, and we felt that we had to write or broadcast something.[34]

On Thursday, May 14, Curragh spokesman Colin Benner announced that the search was being suspended, that there was no hope of finding survivors. That evening, CBC Television's *First Edition* ran a story that was more thorough and more critical than any other that appeared that week in the television or print coverage surveyed. Reporter Rob Gordon prepared a four-minute piece which charged that ten hours before the mine blew up, methane levels exceeded 3.5 percent. Gordon reported he had spoken to draegermen who were too upset to go on camera, but they told him that high methane levels were so common it wasn't unusual for miners to pass out at their work station, that miners saw one or two cave-ins "almost on a daily basis," and that "it was push, push, push. They were behind in their production. Management was pushing everybody to the limits" (CBC-TV, May 14, 1992).

## The Relationship between Curragh and the Families

Initially, the relationship between Curragh and the families was one of trust, and that is understandable. Both were victims, and both had much to lose. In some crises, a bond not unlike the Stockholm Syndrome emerges wherein "the hostage is usually dependent on the hostage-taker for life and death, food and sustenance, over an extended period of time" (Mitroff et al., 1984: 59). They also shared an antagonism toward the media, reinforced by occasional media transgressions, discussed below.

But Curragh officials seemed insensitive to the families' needs. Isabel Gillis, whose husband's body was among the first eleven found on Sunday, says she will never forget how she heard the news her husband Myles was dead:

> He [mine manager Gerald Phillips] walked in the fire hall and got his coffee first. He put his hand through his hair, and walked down to the front, dry-eyed as can be. I passed out when I heard, just for a moment, but I came to, and they [Curragh officials] didn't even come to see if I was okay. And I was not that far away from them.[35]

As the days wore on, the trusting relationship between Curragh and the families was severely tested. People in the fire hall were receiving even less information than the media. They were initially informed by an accountant, who was unable to answer the most basic questions. According to two family members, Curragh officials would not only tell the media first, they wouldn't tell the families and the media the same thing:

> I'd leave the fire hall and go to a hotel for the night, and watch television. [Colin] Benner and [Gerald] Phillips [the mine manager] would appear before the media. It'd be a totally different story from what they told us. It was a more complete story. I'd rather myself know than the country.[36]

The Emergency Measures coordinator wrote in his report after the event that by Monday evening, the situation in the fire hall was becoming critical, in part because Curragh was not giving enough information to the families:

> Constant delays in information and the fact that accountants were often giving the briefings were leading to this tense atmosphere. At the 1 a.m. briefing, which reported nothing of substance to the families, people's emotions were running very high and the mood worsened. By 4 a.m., the situation continued to deteriorate, so I called Westray officials and informed them of the gravity of the situation and the need for substantive briefings. I was informed by mine officials that someone would be down at 5 a.m. to present a technical report. When [information about that planned briefing was] relayed to the families, the tension became almost unbearable. (Smith, [no date]: 3)

Many of these people had not slept since Saturday morning. Because they were exhausted and frustrated at the lack of information from mine managers, they'd begun arguing with each other. "It was at this point I spoke to the families to try and bring them together and not confront each other," Emergency Measures Organization coordinator Daryn Smith ([no date]: 3) wrote. At his encouragement, the families agreed to present "a unified front" and decided on a list of questions, which they phoned in to Westray officials—questions about conditions underground, and about why they had not been getting "information of substance" at previous briefings. Finally, at 5:15 that Tuesday morning, Colin Benner arrived at the fire hall with two other Curragh officials.

> The concerns [about the way they'd been treated] were relayed to these men and when these were addressed, families began to feel better, as they felt they were finally being treated appropriately by the mine officials. (Smith, [no date]: 3)

But Curragh made another mistake that made officials appear insensitive. On Thursday, the families decided they wanted to issue a news release to thank everyone who had been so supportive. According to Smith's report, they were about to release it when Colin Benner arrived to say the rescue operation was being discontinued. Unfortunately, we had received no advance warning of this announcement, and we were caught off guard and had to try and comfort all the families with our existing staff (Smith, [no date]: 3).

Daryn Smith and grief counsellor Dr. John Service tried to comfort the families and presented their announcement to the media after Benner's statement.

## The Relationship Between the Media and the Families

Relations between the media and the families were tense from the outset. Curragh told the families not to trust anything the media said.[37] Reporters, photographers, and television cameras had virtually surrounded the fire hall. There were no televisions or radios in the fire hall and no newspapers until Wednesday. In those early days, many families remained in the fire hall, so they were not aware of media reports of the rescue effort or the speculation about safety concerns.[38] They heard only what Curragh officials wanted them to hear. Curragh also told the media that the families didn't want to speak to them, and although that was generally true, it was never suggested that providing a family member to speak on everyone's behalf might have made the journalists less intrusive.

Kevin Cox recalls one of several low points during that long week. On the Sunday afternoon, May 10, Colin Benner came into the community centre and began his remarks by saying:

Ladies and gentlemen, this is the report that we all hoped we would not have to give. Rescue teams have reported that they have located the bodies of 11 men in the southwest area of the Westray coal mine. These bodies will be brought to the surface for identification by the RCMP as soon as possible. It would appear that these men died instantly.[39]

As Cox says:

We'd been up all night. People were in pretty rough shape.... And then we think, well obviously, you have to go out and get reaction. Well, your heart just falls to your feet. I mean, you don't like doing this job. This is the worst part of journalism.[40]

Michael Lightstone of the Halifax*Daily News* recalled covering one of the funerals:

I have three small kids and all I could think of was, Oh God, these guys were all my age, and they all had small kids, and how sad that was. Plus they all didn't want you there and hated your guts.[41]

Lightstone was standing beside his photographer as the hearse pulled up and the pallbearers came out to take the coffin.

As one of the pallbearers came out of his own car to go towards the hearse, he was smoking a cigarette, and he came and flicked it at us, or toward us, and said something like "fucking bastards." I probably would have done the same thing.[42]

On the other hand, Rob Gordon of CBC-TV News was angry about the way the media treated this story right from the beginning. He says journalists were not looking for information. They were looking for feelings.

The coverage centred around this press conference-driven thing. You know, the draegermen have moved four feet. We have established a fresh air base. We have discovered 11 bodies. And then there was a mad scramble to find the relatives of the 11 bodies. How do *you* feel about this?[43]

Gordon was frustrated that so little of the coverage concentrated on what caused the explosion. He says he had that story by Monday. Rather than staying at the community centre and waiting for news briefings, Gordon went looking for original sources. He found draegermen who were staying at one of the motels, and convinced them to talk to him. They spoke of alleged high methane levels before the explosion, about alleged oil-soaked rags in the tunnels, and about rock falls and roof cave-ins that should have been warning signs. Gordon's story wasn't broadcast until Thursday because he'd been trying to convince the draegermen to go on camera. But no one else had even come close to getting the information he'd been sitting on for four days. Gordon believes print reporters, who were not slaves to pictures, should have had it. Dean Jobb, a print reporter, tends to agree:

> Rob was one of the few people who got out there and did some digging. But, there's a real shift in the media these days. It's the trivial now, it's the fluff, it's the feelies, it's the people angles, human interest. I mean, there's nothing wrong with any of this, but is that all there is to this mine disaster?[44]

Family members were experiencing severe stress by the very nature of the event. The placement of the media directly across the road aggravated their condition. And it was further exacerbated as families learned that the media knew more than they did about what was going on.

## The Search for Human Interest

Journalists tend to rely on human interest to tell their stories (Gans, 1980; Conrad Smith, 1992). In the case of Westray, the search for emotional detail was difficult because the families and the draegermen were off limits. Newsgathering behaviour was therefore occasionally inclined to excess. Very early in the event, a television crew, from Radio France but based in St. Pierre and Miquelon, tried to cross the so-called White Line separating the media from the families. They were forced back by the police and by the rocks angry family members pelted at them.[45]

One national television reporter went to a draegerman's home. There was no one there but, this being New Glasgow, the door was unlocked. The reporter went into the house and walked through the kitchen and hall to the living room where she left a note on a coffee table, requesting an interview. When Rob Gordon spoke to the draegerman that night, he was hostile, "he felt invaded."[46]

Family member Genesta Halloran recalls being approached by one woman who was crying. She asked, "What family are you related to?"

> And she said, "I'm not a family member, I'm just concerned." And I said, "Well who are you?" And she said, "I'm so and so from the*Montreal Gazette*." And I literally chased her down the field. To put on false tears![47]

These incidents suggest that the more detached reporters are from the event, the more aggressive they are prepared to be to get their story. But their willingness to go to such extremes made their relationship with the families only that much more strained. In fact, in one particular case, the families chose to believe an example of media excess which the media say is untrue. A local minister, in the fire hall to console the families for a good part of the week, said the media had installed sophisticated scanners to eavesdrop on private conversations, based on equipment the RCMP said they saw in the media centre.[48] The mayor of a nearby community said the RCMP wanted the families to know the media had this gear, but the reporters denied this categorically.[49] They say no one had scanners, and no one eavesdropped on private conversations. The RCMP's incident commander denied any knowledge of scanners and was not aware his officers had given the families this information.[50]

Bob Allison recalls that the CBC finally found out the name of one of the men trapped below. They knew he was from Antigonish, a town about half an hour's drive from the mine. They called every person in the phone book with that surname who lived in Antigonish. According to Allison, one of the people the CBC called was so angry, he drove to the community centre, stormed over to the CBC contingent and said that if anyone called the family in Antigonish again, he'd be back with a gun.[51]

Rob Gordon believes the families had reason to direct their anger at the media. They were constantly under a camera's gaze. Camera lenses were set on the family centre. Gordon says, "What you'd see on TV is people with tears streaming down their faces, hugging each other. What you didn't see is two seconds later, they were giving the camera the finger."[52]

But Gordon also says people unfairly blamed the media for telling the truth. Because Curragh held out hope, the families held on. They did not want to hear the media say no one survived. As Gordon says, they were mad at the media, but "the media didn't blow the mine up. The media didn't allow a build-up of coal dust. The media didn't practice unsafe practices. Curragh did. But we were the bad guys. And the company was the good guy."[53] The families had a point. As Genesta Halloran said, hope was all they had:

> How do you think the families were able to last 6 days in the fire hall? That's what they were going on. You heard about Springhill [two mine explosions in 1956 and 1958, where some of the trapped miners were brought out alive]. You knew they could be trapped down there. And the company was saying the air they were breathing down there was cleaner than what it was up here.[54]

On Thursday, May 14, the New Glasgow *Evening News* ran an editorial entitled "Sensitivity required," which referred to the indescribable sadness of events so far, but also expressed some of the community's concerns. It concludes:

> Sadder still is the lack of consideration for the families' privacy shown by some visiting journalists.... Maybe the bottom line is some of the visitors won't be here after this terrible tragedy is all over. They will move on to another story. But in the meantime they should be professional enough to respect the deep sensitivity of the people of this community, or leave us alone.[55]

As often happens in crisis coverage, there were examples of reporters making mistakes (Kreps, 1980; Smith, [no date]; Scanlon et al., 1985). The chances of getting it wrong are enhanced, however, when the source provides so little solid information. For example, Curragh was slow to reveal the names of the trapped miners and even those of the dead miners. That's why Bob Allison's CBC-TV team did what they did. But mining company officials were not altogether sure who was down there (Wells, 1992). Eugene Johnson's wife, Donna, says she got a call from Curragh minutes after the explosion asking if her husband was on shift. Joyce Fraser says the first two times Curragh tried to provide the families with a list of the trapped men, they left off her husband's name. She had to keep telling them, "My Robbie's there too" (Mayor Mary Daley, Westville, N.S., personal communication Feb. 26, 1993).

For Dean Jobb of the *Chronicle-Herald* it was a journalist's worst nightmare. One of his reporters filed a story on the Monday which incorrectly identified Mike MacKay as being one of the first eleven miners whose body was found the previous day. But MacKay's body had not been recovered. A correction appeared on page one of Tuesday's edition, with the following addendum: "The *Chronicle-Herald* regrets the anguish this mistake has caused Mr. MacKay's family." Jobb also personally apologized to the miner's brother. Jobb said that man couldn't look him in the eye, he was so enraged. The man said his mother had been getting condolence calls all day. Jobb felt like saying to him, "Go ahead, hit me. I wouldn't blame you."[56]

One of the most common mistakes journalists made, almost without exception, was reporting that the Westray mine was located in then-Premier Donald Cameron's riding. It wasn't at the time, although the redefinition of constituency boundaries for the 1993 election put Westray where most journalists thought it had been all along.

## The Decontextualization of the Westray Tragedy

Disaster scholars have lamented the way in which the media turn their microscopes on disaster events for as long as the ghoulish details sustain interest, only to turn their attention to the next assignment once those details are exposed. They tend to interpret each disaster as a unique, rather than as a "normal," predictable occurrence. To a degree, this was true at Westray. Because the mine had been treated as a political story before the explosion occurred, journalists were caught in the position of trying to explain an event that they did not understand. The effort required to do so meant that the crisis was compartmentalized, as if separate from the wider context of technology and Canada's reliance on coal as a resource, which make such events both predictable and inevitable. Decontextualized reporting is not at all unusual, and this makes debate over genuine solutions difficult. An illustration of this type of context appears in *Death by Consensus: The Westray Story* (Glasbeek et al., 1992: 43), in which the authors point out:

> From 1985 to 1990, a total of fourteen companies was charged with offenses under the [Nova Scotia] *Occupational Health and Safety Act*, and the maximum fine imposed appears to have been $2,500. No mining companies were prosecuted, however, despite the fact that, according to another tabulation, between fiscal years 1987–88 and 1991–92, 1,037 directives were issued to mining companies. The fact that directives never result in change [means there is not] much compliance.

A survey of the content of each *First Edition* program from May 11 to May 15 reveals not a single mention of that kind of context, in spite of the fact that the program often devoted almost half of its 60-minute time slot to the tragedy.

There were exceptions in the print media, but they were rare. On May 11, two days after the explosion, a background report appeared in the *Globe and Mail*, headlined "Perilous Industry Vital to Province" (Vieira, 1992: A4). The story concentrated on the history of mining accidents in Nova Scotia and throughout Canada, but it also quoted the president of Nova Scotia's mining association, John Amirault, as saying that for each of the 5500 people employed in the mining industry, four ancillary jobs are created. That report was almost 500 words long, and the description of economic interdependence ran about 125 words.

*Globe and Mail* writer David Olive (1992) wrote "a discourse on events" one week after the explosion. It provided the context other reportage missed. It began, "Lest we forget" and proceeded to remind readers of how "the promise of economic prosperity can overpower even the strongest doubts."

> That even before disaster strikes, even the most obviously risky of propositions can be sugar-coated as an alarmist hypothesis when placed against the sirenic lure of ready wages and profits. This is the principle underlying Exxon's decision not to use tankers with costly double-lined hulls in Alaska's Prince William Sound; Union Car-

bide's willingness to operate a pesticide plant at Bhopal, India, whose casual management standards would never make the grade at Carbide's US facilities.... That for all our heartfelt concern about workplace safety, somehow little progress has been made (Olive, 1992: D4)

The only other striking exception to decontextualization came from New Brunswick historian David Frank (1992), whose analysis appeared in the May 19 edition of the *Globe and Mail*. Frank documents in about 1100 words the tradition of lives lost in mining accidents in Nova Scotia, the miners' "remarkable historical achievements ... to enforce rules and regulations to improve the safety of the workplace," their respect for coal as a people's resource which made them "strong supporters of public ownership," and their stubborn refusal to enter the mine when conditions were unacceptable. He argued that most believed the mines are much safer now, "or so it seemed."

Then there is an explosion in a modern coal mine in a province with more than two centuries of mining experience and a large volume of legislation and regulation. Twenty-six men, most in their 20s and 30s, are lost. Tragedy. In the months ahead the question will be asked, what went wrong? In looking for answers, we can also look to the past. We need to know whether, somehow here in the work world of the 1990s, we have been cut off from the history of achievement and improvement in coal mining. For all the accumulation of experience and knowledge in the industry, the price of coal is still paid in blood. (Frank, 1992: A15)

## The Week's End

Bob Allison was at the site from Saturday afternoon until Friday. He makes no apology for the media's behaviour under the circumstances. He says the last time he experienced restrictions to parallel those at Westray was during a prison riot, when the RCMP and prison administrators initially refused to let reporters on the property and finally permitted them inside only the administration building, which was outside the prison wall.[57]

The *Globe and Mail's* Kevin Cox says he has "never" seen anything like it. He covered the CN train accident near Hinton, Alberta, in 1987, where twenty-three people died and another seventy-one were injured. Reporters were allowed to walk to the site of the collision, with CN police escorts, view the mangled trains, even look at the bodies inside. He also covered the 1987 Edmonton tornado, where reporters were not only allowed to explore the devastated suburban trailer park, but the police also provided them with bus transportation to and from the site.[58]

On Friday, May 15, one week after the explosion, and one day after

Curragh announced rescue operations were being discontinued, the company held one more news conference. The news was that Curragh would not "reactivate the search." Clifford Frame appeared before the media, for the second time that week, to read a statement. It was 5:30 p.m. (just 30 minutes before *First Edition* goes on the air), and almost all the media had already left. Frame said:

> I would like to state that any coal produced for sale from the open pit mine at Stellarton ... up to a certain sum, will be contributed to a fund ... for the benefit of the families and children left behind (Curragh Incorporated, statement to the press, 1992, May 15).

Frame had been trying to get permission to take coal from an open pit mine in nearby Stellarton, without a lengthy environmental assessment. Bob Allison was busy rewinding a tape when he heard Frame make that comment. He said to himself, "That's a bribe."[59] Frame must have anticipated that. He said, "I acknowledge that I may be criticized in the media for making these announcements today."[60] But it was too late to do much about the so-called bribe. There was barely time to get an item ready for the 6 o'clock news or a story written for the next day's early edition. Because news programming is reduced on the weekend, it is standard practice in most newsrooms to reduce staff. News that breaks late in the day on Friday often dies during that two-day lull. In the public relations industry, it is known that late Friday is a good time to release controversial information to the media, because it is more difficult for journalists to get reaction and points of view so late in the day and news editors like to start the next week with a fresh slate. Saturday coverage concentrated on the other elements of Frame's statement, the provincial government's announcement of a public inquiry, and reaction from family members.

## CONCLUSION

When a tragedy such as the Westray mine explosion occurs, the flow and focus of information is highly charged for those involved and highly sought after by many, including the general public. Curragh officials were not sensitive to the understandable need for thorough and accurate information by the media, the community, and media consumers.

Organizations are encouraged to have a crisis communications plan, but any plan presumes corporate integrity. If allegations of unsafe conditions at the mine are true, a communications plan and its basic tenet of honest, accurate, prompt information delivery would have been very difficult for Curragh to follow. At the very least, such a plan would have warned Curragh about the implications of its alleged operational practices.

While corporations are encouraged to have crisis communications plans, less attention has been paid to the media's need for parallel plans. Journalists should be prepared for inevitable events, such as disasters. A competent media plan ensures that news outlets know what to do when disaster strikes. The plan would prepare journalists for the need to be sensitive about such issues as invasion of privacy and the impact of seemingly small mistakes. Journalists who covered the Westray explosion pursued human interest angles at the expense of the context of the technology. A plan would encourage news gatherers to familiarize themselves with the context in which disasters occur, in advance of an event, so that they do not find themselves in the position of trying to explain an event they do not understand, and so that they are able to broaden their coverage beyond the immediate drama to include an examination of the system that produced the event in the first place.

## CHAPTER EIGHT

# LEGAL DISASTER:
## WESTRAY AND THE JUSTICE SYSTEM[1]

*Dean Jobb*

## INTRODUCTION

The image neatly summed up the Nova Scotia justice system's ponderous search for causes and culprits after Canada's worst mining disaster in almost thirty-five years. The editorial cartoon in the Halifax *Daily News* portrayed an upended tortoise bearing the words WESTRAY JUSTICE on its shell, wiggling its legs in a futile bid to right itself. In terms of lives lost, Westray stands as the worst coal mining disaster since the Springhill tragedies of the late 1950s. On November 1, 1956, a methane explosion at a mine in the northern Nova Scotia town killed thirty-nine miners. Less than two years later, on October 23, 1958 a bump—a sudden settling of the earth—left seventy-four dead at another colliery. There was one other major mining incident in Nova Scotia before Westray: twelve miners died on February 24, 1979 in an explosion at the Cape Breton Development Corporation's No. 26 mine in Glace Bay (McKay, 1987: 162–85; *Report of Commission of Inquiry, Explosion in No. 26 Colliery Glace Bay, Nova Scotia on February 24, 1979*).

The cartoon appeared on May 9, 1995, the third anniversary of the underground explosion at the Westray coal mine that killed twenty-six men. By then, the trial of Westray's operators on criminal charges was in its death throes. Exactly one month later, on June 9, Justice Robert Anderson of the Nova Scotia Supreme Court stayed charges of manslaughter and criminal negligence causing death against two mine officials and Curragh Incorporated, the Toronto company that owned the colliery. Curragh Mine Manager Gerald Phillips and the Underground Manager Roger Parry were accused of failing to fulfill their legal duty to ensure the safety of the men in the pit. Justice Anderson tossed out the charges, ruling Crown prosecutors had failed to fulfill *their* legal duty to provide defence lawyers with all documentation relevant to the case.[2]

The abrupt end of the trial created a furore. "There's no justice system in Canada. Not a bit," Robert Bell, whose son Larry was among the victims, bitterly told reporters as he emerged from the courtroom in Pictou.[3] "The government and the system of justice in Nova Scotia have disgraced themselves and the people of this province," the *Chronicle-Herald*, Nova Scotia's largest daily newspaper, agreed in a blunt editorial. "Justice has showed itself to be 'an ass' and, we might add, a complete ass, in the Westray case."[4]

The bitterness and harsh words were a reflection of public frustration with a justice system seemingly incapable of getting to the bottom of the disaster. The road to Supreme Court Justice Anderson's ruling was littered with delays, roadblocks, and false starts. The courts intervened in the fall of 1992 to delay a public inquiry headed by Supreme Court Justice Peter Richard.[5] In October 1992 Nova Scotia's Department of Labour filed fifty-two charges against Curragh, Phillips, Parry, and two other mine officials, alleging violations of the provincial *Occupational Health and Safety Act*. By the spring of 1993, however, all had been dropped in favour of criminal charges. Then a judge tossed out the initial manslaughter and criminal negligence charges, ruling them too vaguely worded.[6] By the time Justice Anderson stopped the prosecution in its tracks, the word "Westray" was becoming a synonym for colossal failure.

> Webmark
> In 1990, Nova Scotia became the first Canadian province to create an independent public prosecution service, based on a recommendation made by the Royal Commission on the Donald Marshall, Jr., Prosecution. *The Interim Report of the Review of Nova Scotia's Public Prosecution Service* can be viewed at: www.gov.ns.ca/just/pps.htm

How did a mine disaster come to be perceived as a legal disaster? Competing jurisdictions and conflicting precedents played a role, creating confusion and uncertainty as investigators, lawyers, and courts picked through the evidence. The *Canadian Charter of Rights and Freedoms* erected roadblocks to ensure the rights of individuals were not trampled in the rush to find answers, justice, or scapegoats. But one factor was unique to a justice system still coming to grips with the wrongful conviction of Donald Marshall Jr. two decades earlier. A royal commission reported in 1989 that racism and political favouritism tainted not only Marshall's case, but Nova Scotia's justice system as a whole. The Marshall commission's recommendations included new rules for disclosing Crown evidence to defendants and led to the creation of Canada's first independent office of public prosecutions.[7] That miscarriage of justice prompted the creation, in 1990, of Canada's first Crown's office to operate independently of government. The Westray case, with its political overtones and allegations of government duplicity, was the first major test of Nova Scotia's fledgling Public Prosecution Service.

## Editorial Cartoon. John Pearson

Reprinted with permission of Theo Moudakis of the Halifax Daily News

The aftermath of the Westray disaster revealed the problems that can arise as government, police, prosecutors, and courts struggle, sometimes in competition, to cope with a major disaster in an increasingly complex society. It points to the pitfalls and suggests ways of preventing investigations of future tragedies from collapsing under the weight of their own legal baggage.

## ESTABLISHING RESPONSIBILITY

At 5:18 on the morning of May 9, 1992, a massive explosion rocked the Westray colliery in the village of Plymouth, near New Glasgow. Experts who studied the blast agree a spark from a piece of machinery ignited methane, a gas that seeps into the mine air as coal is gouged from the earth. The methane fire, in turn, may have touched off a powerful explosion of coal dust that tore through the maze of tunnels in seconds. Clouds of poisonous carbon monoxide, cave-ins and the searing heat left no survivors.[8]

Westray had long been the subject of political controversy. Nova Scotia's Progressive Conservative government gave Curragh a $12 million loan. Premier Donald Cameron, a Pictou-area MLA and former industry minister, was the leading advocate of a new mine to provide thermal coal and create up to 250 jobs. After intense lobbying from Cameron and Curragh officials, the federal government guaranteed Curragh's bank loan—to a maximum of $85 million—and provided a grant of up to $8.75 million to subsidize the interest rate. The largesse drew criticism from opposition parties and from Devco, the federal Crown corporation that operates two Cape Breton collieries (Glasbeek et al., 1993: 14–41; Starr, 1993: 5–9).

With the mine in ruins and twenty-six men dead, the Nova Scotia government moved quickly to determine the causes and, in the process, head off the inevitable political storm. A public inquiry was promised within a day of the blast; on May 15, after rescue efforts had been suspended, Cameron appointed a judge of the Nova Scotia Supreme Court to investigate. Justice Richard was given a wide mandate under the *Public Inquiries Act* and the *Coal Mines Regulation Act*. "It is essential that Nova Scotians know all the answers to the questions surrounding and leading to this tragic event," Cameron told the legislature in Halifax. "Nothing and no person with any light to shed on this tragedy will escape the scrutiny of this inquiry."[9]

Webmark
The Order in Council setting out the terms of reference for the Inquiry are available at:
www.gov.ns.ca/legi/inquiry/westray/terms.htm

The Inquiry's terms of reference gave Justice Richard the power to call evidence and make recommendations on all "matters related to the establishment and operation of the mine which the Commissioner considers relevant to the occurrence." The Inquiry's wide terms of reference posed specific questions. Justice Richard was to examine whether "any neglect caused or contributed" to the explosion and to determine whether it could have been prevented. On a technical level, the Inquiry was asked to find any defects in the way the mine was built and the mining methods used, and to assess whether these were in keeping with the geological structure of the explosion-prone Foord seam. There was certainly reason for suspicion. Before Westray, 576 men and boys had died in Pictou County's collieries since coal mining began in the early 1800s. Of that number, 246 perished in methane and coal-dust explosions. Most died in mines tapping the Foord seam, where explosions in 1880, 1914, 1918, 1924, and 1935, left a total of 145 dead. The 1918 blast, which killed 88, stands as the worst disaster in the history of the Pictou coalfield (Jobb, 1994:

90, 95–97; Cameron, 1974). The judge was asked as well to determine "whether there was compliance with applicable statutes, regulations, orders, rules, or directions."[10]

Webmark
The Nova Scotia government publishes its regulations on the web, including, for example, occupational health regulations at:
www.gov.ns.ca/just/regulations/regs/cmr13777.htm

The latter provision clearly overlapped with the mandate of another provincial agency. Nova Scotia's Department of Labour was responsible for prosecuting any violations of the *Coal Mines Regulation Act* or the statute governing workplace safety, the *Occupational Health and Safety Act*. But the presence of gas and dust in quantities sufficient to fuel such a massive explosion cast suspicion on the department's mine inspectors as well as Westray's operators. Levels of methane and coal dust are regulated under the *Coal Mines Regulation Act*, an antiquated statute that was being revised when the explosion occurred. Methane, produced as coal is exposed, is explosive at concentrations of between 5 and 15 percent in the closed atmosphere of a mine. The Act stipulates that electrical equipment must be shut down when methane in the surrounding air reaches 1.25 percent; workers must be withdrawn from any area where the level of the gas "in the general body of air" reaches 2.5 percent; coal dust must not comprise more than 35 percent of the dust coating the floor, roof, and walls of underground tunnels.[11]

The department's mine inspection branch had been monitoring the project since development began in 1988.[12] By May 9, 1992, inspectors Albert McLean (safety) and John Smith (mechanical/electrical) and the director of mine safety, Claude White, had visited the site more than fifty times. Reports of their inspections show that Mine Manager Gerald Phillips was badgered for nine months to draw up a plan for spreading limestone dust on a regular basis to neutralize coal dust. It never materialized.[13]

Questions about the department's vigilance intensified after Labour Minister Leroy Legere's disclosure, on May 20, that McLean had issued written orders to Roger Parry, the underground manager, on April 29—ten days before the disaster—threatening prosecution unless immediate steps were taken to clean up coal dust and spread stone dust to prevent an explosion. McLean gave Westray fifteen days to file the long-overdue plan for spreading stone dust.[14] He never conducted a follow-up inspection to ensure the orders were carried out—a tragic example of the non-confrontational approach that characterized the department's dealings with Westray.[15]

**Inquiry Testimony, Mr. McLean, Day 56, May 8, 1996: 12364–70**

Q. Did you ever issue a directive or an order instructing Westray to put a stone dusting sampling procedure in place?

A. I can't recall....

Q. Under the *Coal Mines Regulation Act* you have the authority to request that the coal company or the manager put a procedure in place and have samples sent to you. Did you ever do that?

A. Yes.

Q. You did?

A. I believe I issued orders for that....—my orders on the 29th —...

Q. In order to have the coal dust at 15 percent incombustible, would there need to be a lot of stone dust stored in the mine to comply with that on a regular basis?

A. Stone dust, the minimum required for stone dust is 65 percent, 35 percent combustible and 65 incomplete combustible....

Q. Did you ever see a large quantity be stored on the surface?

A. Did I ever see large quantities?

Q. Yeah.

A. Where at?

Q. On the surface?

A. At where?

Q. At Westray, Mr. McLean.

A. No.

[Inquiry testimony conducted by Mr. Burchell, representing the United Mine Workers]

The RCMP's involvement began within minutes of the explosion. Officers were responsible for identifying victims brought to the surface, and they helped local police forces control traffic near the mine. On May 21, prompted by allegations that documents were being shredded at the mine's offices, the force launched a criminal investigation.[16] The RCMP took control of the mine site and named Staff Sergeant Ches MacDonald as lead investigator. The force announced the probe would encompass all aspects of the disaster.[17]

When the smoke cleared at the end of May, three separate investigations were under way. In addition, Curragh hired five of the top mining experts in the world to conduct an internal investigation.[18] There was almost a fifth probe; in Ottawa, opposition critics pressed the Mulroney government to hold parliamentary hearings or launch a federal inquiry into a disaster that would cost the federal treasury some $70 million once the loan guarantee was honoured. The federal response was to leave the matter in the hands of the provincial inquiry.[19] As it was, the field was crowded with investigators competing to assemble documents and interview witnesses. A battle for precedence was inevitable; it was a recipe for legal chaos.

## The Inquiry

Justice Richard's plan to open public hearings in Stellarton in the fall of 1992 was the first casualty. All summer the Mounties quietly built a case for charging Curragh and as many as three Westray officials with criminal negligence causing the twenty-six deaths. The scale of alleged wrong-doing was unprecedented in a Canadian mine disaster. The RCMP hoped to prove conditions were so bad, and condoned by management for so long, that it amounted to a breach of the criminal law. The *Criminal Code of Canada* defines criminal negligence as conduct—including the failure to fulfill a legal duty—that shows "wanton and reckless disregard for the lives or safety of others."[20] In search warrants, the Mounties claimed that the company had failed to properly train miners, that the ventilation system and measures to combat coal dust were inadequate, and that methane detectors had been illegally altered to keep mining machines operating. To gather evidence to support the allegations, the RCMP seized the idle mine site in mid-September and sent officers underground to photograph equipment and collect dust samples.[21]

> *Canadian Criminal Code*
> Criminal Negligence
> 219(1) Criminal negligence
> 219. (1) Every one is criminally negligent who
> (a) in doing anything, or
> (b) in omitting to do anything that it is his duty to do, shows wanton or reckless disregard for the lives or safety of other persons.
>
> 219(2) Definition of "duty"
> (2) For the purposes of this section, "duty" means a duty imposed by law. R.S., c. C-34, s. 202.
>
> 220. Every one who by criminal negligence causes death to another person is guilty of an indictable offence and liable to imprisonment for life. R.S., c. C-34, s. 203.

> 221. Every one who by criminal negligence causes bodily harm to another person is guilty of an indictable offence and liable to imprisonment for a term not exceeding ten years.
> R.S., c. C-34, s. 204.

During the search seven of Westray's top officials, including Phillips and Parry, launched a legal challenge to the Inquiry. They asked the Nova Scotia Supreme Court to strike down the commission as unconstitutional or at least delay its hearings until any criminal or mine-safety charges cleared the courts. Lawyers advanced two arguments, the first based on the division of powers in the constitution. The Inquiry was a provincial creation but its terms of reference spilled into the realm of criminal law, a federal jurisdiction. Justice Richard had been asked to look for breaches of the law and determine whether neglect led to the explosion. Furthermore, the *Coal Mines Regulation Act* obliged the Inquiry to report any evidence or suspicion of "culpable neglect" in the mine's operation.[22] Culpable neglect, lawyers for the mine officials argued, was synonymous with criminal negligence. A similar argument had been used in Ontario to shut down an inquiry into the actions of political fund-raiser Patricia Starr and to limit the right of another commission to assign blame to individuals. Courts have been quick to strike down provincial inquiries into the conduct of individuals that take on the trappings of police investigations or the preliminary hearing in a criminal case.[23]

A second argument was advanced under the *Charter*. The Inquiry's hearings promised to be front-page news in Nova Scotia for months, creating an avalanche of publicity that would prejudice the mine officials' right to a fair trial if charged. Those facing prosecution could also be forced under subpoena to testify at the Inquiry, violating their right to remain silent. Finally, incriminating evidence uncovered by the Inquiry could be unfairly used in subsequent prosecutions.[24] On September 30 Chief Justice Constance Glube of the Supreme Court issued a temporary injunction halting the Inquiry.[25]

The challenge arose as new proposals were being put forward to ensure that provincial inquiries operate in accordance with *Charter* principles and do not infringe on federal jurisdiction.[26] In March 1992, the Law Reform Commission of Ontario released a report in response to what it termed the "scepticism, even cynicism, about the utility of public inquiries."[27] Mounting costs, delays, and concerns about the rights of individuals who are the targets of such inquiries have raised doubts about their benefits as an investigative and policy-making tool. Among the commission's recommendations was a provision to grant immunity from prosecution to those testifying at inquiries, creating a balance between the rights of individuals and the public's need for answers. In light of the *Charter* and the *Starr* ruling, "as a policy matter … governments will in some cases have to choose between conducting a public inquiry and pursuing subsequent prosecutions."[28]

But the *Charter* rights being invoked by the managers could tie the hands of any inquiry into any matter that could lead to charges under the *Criminal Code* or other statute. Since inquiries were invariably set up in response to disasters or other controversial events, there was always the possibility some-one involved could face prosecution. In Britain, the practice has been to let inquiries do their work and forego prosecution of those to blame, no matter how strong the evidence against them.[29] The Westray case would force Canadian courts to decide whether a public inquiry and a prosecution could co-exist and on what terms.

Within a week of Chief Justice Glube's injunction, the spectre of charges became real. On October 5 the Department of Labour filed fifty-two charges under the *Occupational Health and Safety Act* and *Coal Mines Regulation Act*. Accused were Curragh and four of the seven officials challenging the In-quiry—Phillips, Parry, Head Mechanic Robert Parry, and Assistant Superin-tendent Glyn Jones, who was one rung below the underground manager. The allegations included forcing men to work in unsafe conditions, particularly in excess amounts of methane; failing to take steps to prevent a coal-dust explo-sion; using machinery not certified for underground use; failing to train workers; and improperly using acetylene torches in the mine. Each offence was punishable upon conviction by a maximum $10,000 fine for the company, while the managers faced a similar fine and up to a year in jail.[30]

Methane and coal dust are well-known hazards; controlling them is sim-ply a matter of common sense in the coal industry. At Westray, however, management refused to let such basic safety practices get in the way of producing coal and profits.[31] Yet the allegations said as much about the Department of Labour as it did about Westray management. The sheer volume of charges begged a question—how could mine inspectors allow such wrong-doing to flourish under their noses?

The inspectors, Justice Richard's Inquiry would eventually conclude, had been "derelict" in their duty to enforce safety laws. At every turn, they deferred to Westray officials or gave them repeated opportunities to conform with the law. Under-staffing, lack of training, and bureaucratic indifference were factors in the lax approach. Interference from politicians or other superi-ors has never been proven, and may not have been necessary. The Nova Scotia government's financial and political support of Westray was no secret; the mine was a pet project of the ruling Progressive Conservatives. In the face of such pressures, *Chronicle-Herald* columnist Ralph Surette argued, McLean "would have had to be a hero merely to do his job." No one, Surette wrote, had to tell inspectors to go easy on Westray.[32]

## MORE WRANGLING

With Labour charges filed and criminal charges likely, lawyers for the management group had little difficulty convincing the courts that their concerns were real. In hearings before Chief Justice Glube in November 1992, the Inquiry promised to walk the fine line between uncovering the truth and naming names. But its creators were not so sure. The Nova Scotia government undercut the Inquiry by supporting a ban on hearings until all Westray-related prosecutions were complete. With a provincial election in the offing and the Inquiry vowing to take a hard look at the government's financing and monitoring of the project, the position smacked of political expediency and damage control.[33] It also revealed the dilemmas and conflicting interests that arise when politicians use inquiries to examine the actions of their own government.

The courts at first ignored, then endorsed, the government's position. In a November 13 ruling, Chief Justice Glube struck down the Inquiry as *ultra vires* the province's powers. She followed the *Starr* precedent, ruling Justice Richard's terms of reference were "so specific to the occurrence, and overlap so deeply into the field of criminal law, that as they are presently written, they cannot stand."[34] While she invited the province to draft new terms of reference, the government opted to appeal.

Three judges of the Court of Appeal issued a judgment on January 19, 1993, reinstating the Inquiry as within the province's powers. But the court was troubled by the *Charter* implications of having an inquiry, a labour prosecution and an RCMP investigation proceed simultaneously. "There is a great deal of merit in a regime which requires a government to either lay charges or conduct a public inquiry, but not to do both except with the safeguards proposed by the Ontario Law Reform Commission," Justice Doane Hallett noted in the unanimous judgment. With the government unwilling to intervene, the court stepped in. Justice Hallett ordered the Inquiry to delay its hearings until all trials arising from the disaster were complete.[35]

The Westray Inquiry has the dubious distinction of being the only public inquiry in Canada halted in its tracks out of deference to the rights of individuals. The ruling's impact went beyond the province's borders. The New Brunswick government followed the precedent when it set the terms of reference for an inquiry into sexual abuse at a youth correctional facility. The military investigation into the beating death of a Somalia prisoner was delayed until Canadian peacekeepers stood trial on murder charges. British Columbia's justice department has suggested that nine public inquiries set up between 1985 and 1992 would have been vulnerable to the same *Charter* challenge (Jobb, 1994: 292).

How long the Inquiry would remain in limbo was unclear; the labour charges were expected to clear the courts by the summer of 1993. But if criminal charges were laid, it would be two years or more before Justice Richard heard his first witness. The Inquiry's future lay in the hands of prosecutors and the RCMP.

## GOOD REASONS

To understand the tangled history of the Westray criminal prosecution, it is necessary to revisit a notorious case that reshaped Nova Scotia's legal landscape. Before Guy Paul Morin, before David Milgaard, there was a native teenager named Donald Marshall Jr. In the early 1970s, Marshall was convicted of murder in the stabbing death of another youth in Sydney. He served eleven years in prison before new evidence surfaced to exonerate him, leading to the conviction of another man (Harris, 1986).

A royal commission made up of three out-of-province judges investigated in the late 1980s. They produced a damning report showing how police and prosecutors used flimsy evidence to railroad Marshall while ignoring eyewitness testimony absolving him of the crime. But the case pointed to deeper problems within the Nova Scotia attorney-general's department (it was merged with the solicitor-general's department to create the justice department in 1993).[36] The commission discovered that politicians had intervened to prevent the RCMP from laying criminal charges against a provincial cabinet minister in the early 1980s. To prevent such abuses, the commission recommended the prosecution of crimes be conducted at arm's length from government. In 1990, the Nova Scotia government set up Canada's first independent office of public prosecutions. Its director could be removed from office only by a majority vote of the legislature; directives from the attorney general on policy, or laying or withdrawing charges in specific cases, would have to be made—and defended—in public.[37]

The Westray explosion thrust the service and its first director, John Pearson—a career prosecutor from Ontario—into the spotlight. Despite the magnitude and complexity of the case, Pearson did not assign staff to the file full-time until September 1992. Chris Morris, who had about eight years' experience, and rookie prosecutor Stephanie Cleary were appointed just in time to vet the labour charges and advise the RCMP on drafting the warrant for the underground search. They set up shop in a spare office while Pearson lobbied the government for extra funding for proper offices and support staff (Cameron et al., 1994: 54–60, 83–84; Jobb, 1994: 260–65).

The labour prosecution was short-lived. In December 1992 Pearson stayed thirty-four of the labour charges, among them serious allegations such as tampering with methane detectors and failing to prevent the build up of coal dust. Four months later he stayed the remaining charges which, once withdrawn, could not be reinstated. The motive was to ensure the survival of the imminent criminal charges, which would be based on the same evidence of wrong-doing as the labour charges. If Curragh and its managers were convicted under the *Occupational Health and Safety Act*, a court was likely to quash any criminal charges on the principle of double jeopardy.

Meanwhile, Morris and Cleary faced indifference. They peppered their superiors with memos pleading for the resources needed to ensure that the

RCMP received "the best advice possible" and that "appropriate charges are laid, or not laid, as the circumstances require." By early 1993, they believed they were no longer in a position to offer that advice. "We have been maintaining responsibility for the largest criminal prosecution in the history of the province without offices, desks, telephones or full-time support staff for the last five-and-one-half months," they complained in a February 22, 1993 memo to criminal trials director Martin Herschorn. "If we cannot do the job properly, we cannot do it at all." They asked to be taken off the case.

Morris and Cleary used the memo to put their concerns on record. The Nova Scotia government, they said, was a "suspect" in the Westray case—a reference to the government's responsibility for worker safety and mine inspection. Yet the prosecution service was forced to go "cap in hand" to the same government for money. "This case may become a watershed for the Public Prosecution Service in terms of its relationship with government," they predicted. "It is a prime example of what can happen when we do not control our own budget."[38]

Their concerns were echoed by others in the service. Robert Hagell, a senior prosecutor in the appeals branch, weighed in with his own letter to Pearson. "The Premier, Cabinet and many Government officials had a direct interest in this file ... the failure to provide proper legal and support staff to this file is, in my opinion, a disgrace," he wrote in June 1993. The failure to provide proper staff and funding, he warned, had "fatally flawed" the prosecution (Jobb, 1994: 282).

Government control of the purse-strings was, and remains, a serious threat to the service's independence. Months later, after the memo was leaked to the *Chronicle-Herald*, Pearson acknowledged that the government had been slow to approve his request for an additional $600,000 to conduct the Westray prosecution. But he argued the service, like any other publicly funded agency, had to be fiscally responsible.[39] He also rejected the notion the service's independence had been compromised.[40]

The funding delay and resignations had an impact, leaving the RCMP without "the best advice possible." The result was a slip-up. Under the *Criminal Code*, police can keep items seized under a search warrant for only three months without laying charges. A court order is required to retain evidence for a longer period,[41] but this was not done. On March 26, Curragh lawyers went to court demanding the return of dust samples, a methane sensor, and other items removed from the mine; the company wanted its experts to analyze the evidence. A judge gave the Mounties one month to lay charges or hand over the crucial evidence.[42] The timing could not have been worse. "We were getting a case together and we had a (prosecution) team in place. And then we didn't have a team and I wasn't very happy," the lead investigator, Staff Sergeant MacDonald, later told *Saturday Night* magazine. "It was such a setback.... We had to bring a whole new team up to speed."[43]

The Mounties called a press conference on April 20, 1993, to announce the laying of charges.[44] Curragh, Gerald Phillips, and Roger Parry were charged with manslaughter and criminal negligence causing death. Treating the disaster as a criminal act increased the stakes for the defendants. A conviction for either offence can bring a life sentence in prison for an individual, while a convicted corporation would face a fine, with no limit on the amount a judge can impose.[45]

Cases of companies and employees charged with crimes arising from workplace fatalities in Canada are few. Convictions are fewer still. Syncrude Canada Limited was charged with criminal negligence causing death after a 1981 nitrogen gas leak killed two workmen at the oil sands project in northern Alberta; the company was acquitted. An employee at an Inco mine in Ontario was acquitted of the same offence in 1988 after an ore spill killed four workers. Inco was spared criminal charges but was convicted under Ontario's *Occupational Health and Safety Act* and fined $60,000.[46]

At least two other Canadian coal mining companies have faced homicide charges. In 1898 a coal train running on the Union Colliery Company's line near Nanaimo, British Columbia, plunged thirty metres through a trestle bridge, killing seven passengers and crew. The bridge's timbers were rotten and the company was charged with putting lives at risk by failing to keep the structure in a safe condition—an offence that evolved into today's criminal negligence provision. Union Colliery was convicted after a jury trial and fined $5000.[47]

The other is Brazeau Collieries Limited, which operated a mine in the village of Nordegg in the Alberta Rockies. Brazeau was charged after twenty-nine men died in an October 1941 methane explosion. The charge was failure to take safety precautions over a three-month period leading up to the explosion. In January 1943, after a two-week trial before a judge of the Alberta Supreme Court, the company was convicted. The sentence was a slap on the wrist, even by Second World War standards—a $5000 fine, which works out to roughly $172 for each man who died.[48]

The corporation and top officials responsible for safety at Westray were facing the music but not their watchdogs. RCMP Superintendent Robert Tramley announced the investigation had found "no evidence of criminality" on the part of government officials. Staff Sergeant MacDonald later defended the decision. "We haven't, in my view, found any evidence to support the laying of any criminal charges against anyone in the Department of Labour, or the Department of Labour itself" (Jobb, 1994: 266-67).

## THE CHARGES

The day charges were laid, Pearson announced that a new team of four prosecutors had been assembled and that a budget for the case was in place. The lead prosecutor was Herman Felderhof, who boasted twelve years' courtroom experience and a geology degree.[49] But the prosecution never fully recovered from its halting start. In July 1993, Provincial Court Judge Patrick Curran quashed the criminal charges, deeming them "fundamentally deficient" and so vaguely worded the defendants could not defend themselves.[50] Within seventy-two hours the RCMP and prosecutors drafted a new, more detailed set of charges. The manslaughter count alleged that Curragh, Phillips, and Parry caused the deaths by failing to keep coal dust in check. The second charge alleged that all three had been criminally negligent in more than a dozen aspects of the mine's operation, including inadequate training, use of unsafe equipment, lack of stonedusting, failure to deal with the buildup of methane, and straying from government-approved mine plans.

The new charges withstood a second challenge.[51] Pearson, however, remained under the cloud of a planned review of his four-year tenure as director. The review had been a campaign promise of the new Liberal administration of Premier John Savage, elected in 1993. Pearson resigned, effective July 1994, to take a prosecuting job with his former employer, the Ontario attorney general's department.[52] The government promptly appointed former Prince Edward Island premier Joe Ghiz, the dean of Dalhousie Law School, and Halifax law professor Bruce Archibald to examine the operation of the Crown's office. The report, delivered in the fall of 1994, identified a host of problems. Among the most serious were lack of computers for Crown offices; outdated filing systems to keep track of cases and court dates; and low morale, fueled by some of the lowest salaries for Canadian prosecutors. While the review uncovered no evidence of political interference, it recommended that an independent mechanism be established for setting prosecutors' salaries and that the service's budget be controlled by an all-party committee of the legislature, not the justice department. The government, however, refused to relinquish control over the purse-strings.[53]

## THE TRIAL[54]

The Westray trial opened in February 1995 in Pictou. Phillips and Parry were the only defendants; Curragh, now bankrupt, was prosecuted in name only and had no lawyer present. Evidence about safety lapses and the causes of the disaster took a backseat to a running battle over disclosure of Crown evidence. Testimony was repeatedly disrupted as defence lawyers fought for access to Crown and RCMP files. Only twenty-three witnesses made it to the stand over the course of forty-four hearing days.

Webmark
In the Supreme Court decision *R*. v. *Stinchcombe*, May 2, 1991, it was ruled that the Crown has a legal duty to disclose all relevant information to the

defence, in order to ensure that justice is done. The complete text is located at: www.droit.umontreal.ca/doc/csc-scc/en/pub/1991/vol3/html/1991scr3_0326.html

The case came off the rails on March 2 when the presiding judge, Justice Robert Anderson, secretly phoned the service's head office in Halifax. He reached Pearson's replacement, Acting Director Martin Herschorn, and demanded Felderhof's removal as lead prosecutor. Justice Anderson blamed him for the disclosure problems paralyzing the trial. When prosecutors revealed the incident in court and sought a mistrial, Justice Anderson refused. The Crown secured an emergency hearing before the Supreme Court of Canada on April 5, but the court said it had no jurisdiction to intervene in the midst of trial.[55] The trial resumed with Felderhof in charge, and it limped along until June 9, when Justice Anderson granted a defence motion to stay the charges as an abuse of process, based on the failure to disclose evidence about methane sensors and coal dust samples that he considered essential to a fair trial.[56]

### Editorial Cartoon. Justice Is Slow

Reprinted with permission of the Halifax Herald Limited

The Crown appealed and won a sympathetic hearing from the Nova Scotia Court of Appeal. In a terse judgment delivered in December 1995, the court overlooked any shortcomings in disclosure and granted a new trial based on the appearance that Justice Anderson had been biased against the Crown. Justice Doane Hallett ruled that the phone call "incurably infects" the judge's subsequent decision to grant a stay. A new trial was ordered.[57]

The prosecution service welcomed a second crack at the case. A newly hired director of public prosecutions, Jerry Pitzul, committed six prosecutors to the file. The budget for Westray grew to about $0.5 million a year, a hefty chunk of the $8 million budget for all prosecutions. This time around the government—a Liberal administration with no Westray baggage—was more forthcoming. Pitzul has described the government as "very responsible in responding to requests" for additional funding for Westray and other cases (Jobb, 1998b: 18–21). Much of the money was devoted to systematically cataloguing more than a million pages of documents to prevent future disclosure problems. Ironically, such an inventory had been recommended years earlier by the two prosecutors originally assigned to the case.[58] It was more proof that fiscal constraints had compromised the prosecution from the outset.

## THE INQUIRY REVISITED

As the prosecution sank, the Supreme Court of Canada revived the Inquiry. On May 4, 1995, the high court granted an appeal by the United Steelworkers of America, the union representing Westray miners, and lifted the ban on hearings. The decision was influenced by the fact that Phillips and Parry had chosen trial without a jury; fear that publicity surrounding the Inquiry's work would prejudice the case had evaporated. But the court also said it is the responsibility of government to choose whether to proceed with an inquiry in such circumstances, weighing the risks of compromising any parallel criminal case.[59]

At hearings in 1995 and 1996 the long-delayed Inquiry heard from seventy-one witnesses, including mining consultants, miners, inspectors and other government officials, and the politicians who promoted the project. Most mine managers boycotted when they failed to work out an arrangement to cover their legal fees; Phillips and Parry declined to attend with the criminal charges hanging over their heads. The Inquiry lacked the power to subpoena witnesses living outside Nova Scotia and several key players living in other provinces refused invitations to appear. Inquiry lawyers took legal action in the Nova Scotia and Ontario courts to force two former Curragh executives—Clifford Frame, the chairman and founder, and Marvin Pelley—to testify. The case was unresolved by the time Justice Richard released his report in late 1997, however, Justice Richard concluded that he had sufficient evidence to assess mine management's actions without their testimony.

As Justice Richard was finalizing his report, the Supreme Court of Canada again clarified the powers of inquiries. In a September 1997 ruling arising from the work of the Krever Inquiry into Canada's tainted blood scandal, the court decreed that inquiries could assess the actions of individuals and point fingers of blame, if the wording used did not amount to a finding of criminal or civil liability.[60] While Justice Horace Krever shied away from using the new power to assign blame, Justice Richard ran with it.[61] His report, released December 1, 1997, spared few adjectives in criticizing those responsible for a disaster he concluded was both predictable and preventable.

"The *Westray Story*," he wrote, "is a complex mosaic of actions, omissions, mistakes, incompetence, apathy, cynicism, stupidity, and neglect." The formula for the disaster, he concluded, was tragically simple: "management failed, the inspectorate failed, and the mine blew up."[62]

Primary responsibility for the unsafe conditions that led to the disaster rested with mine management, the judge said. Westray's bosses, from Curragh chairman Clifford Frame on down, had utterly failed in their duty to ensure that miners were properly trained and that they worked in a safe environment. Next came the regulatory agencies. Labour inspectors were "derelict" in their enforcement duties; engineers at the Department of Natural Resources were "wilfully blind" to unauthorized changes made to the layout of underground tunnels. Finally, he rapped former premier Donald Cameron for letting the Westray project cloud his judgment at the expense of the public interest.

The report contained seventy-four recommendations. All were accepted by the Nova Scotia government, which promised full implementation by mid-1999.[63] They included overhauls of the safety inspectorate at the Department of Labour and the mineral resources division of the Department of Natural Resources; guidelines for cabinet ministers to reign in overzealous politicians; a raft of detailed regulations governing underground mining, workplace safety, and enforcement; and a review, in conjunction with the federal government, to ensure that corporate officials and directors are accountable for workplace safety under the criminal law.[64]

Meanwhile, the criminal case against the mine's operators remained on shaky ground. On March 2, 1997, the Supreme Court of Canada again passed judgment on Westray. In a seven-to-two decision, the court upheld the Court of Appeal's order for a new trial. The majority ruled it need look no further than the bias exhibited in Justice Anderson's "unfortunate if not ill advised" phone call. One judge, Justice John Sopinka, sided with the majority even though he viewed the Crown's breach of its obligation to disclose evidence as "egregious." The dissenting judges, Justices Beverley McLachlin and John Major, would have reimposed a stay of proceedings. In language rarely heard from the court, they condemned the Crown's handling of the 1995 trial. Non-disclosure of evidence was only the beginning of a litany of Crown abuses, they said— prosecutors had misled the court, ignored court orders, and broken rules and then attempted to cover up when caught. "This case is about the appearance of justice.... The entire proceedings were tainted by prosecutors who were playing to an enraged public, and playing to win...."[65]

While the majority withheld comment on Crown conduct, the court made its feelings known through an unprecedented order of costs to the accused. Phillips and Parry were entitled to recover their legal costs for the first trial, since its failure was the result of what the court saw as "systemic" failures on the part of the judge and prosecutors, with emphasis on the judge's actions. The Crown was also ordered to pay the defendants' "reasonable legal costs" for the upcoming trial, a tab estimated to reach into the millions of dollars.

A second trial was never held. In the wake of the Supreme Court ruling, Pitzul ordered a series of internal reports assessing the strength of the Crown's case and the likelihood of securing convictions. Among the new prosecutors assigned to Westray after a new trial was ordered in December 1995 was Robert Hagell, the early critic of the lack of resources devoted to the case. He filed reports in October 1997—just as Justice Richard was about to release his findings—recommending the criminal charges be withdrawn. It was "fundamentally unfair" to prosecute only Phillips and Parry when many others, including miners, foremen, and government inspectors, shared responsibility for safety. The RCMP investigation was flawed, important evidence had been lost, and charges had been laid in 1993 before making a "thorough assessment" of the legal responsibility of all parties. That assessment, he said, should have been made in concert with prosecutors and mining experts. Left unstated in his reports, which were made public in late 1998, was the Public Prosecution Service's failure to contribute sufficient resources to ensure that the evidence and the law were weighed properly before charges were laid.[66]

Hagell quit the case. His colleagues soldiered on, only to agree by mid-1998 that the case was a lost cause. On June 30, the service announced that charges against Phillips and Parry had been stayed and would not be revived. Conflicting evidence and disagreement among mining experts on the cause and spread of the explosion, Crown attorneys said, made it unlikely that either man could be convicted. A critical factor was growing doubts about whether coal dust fueled the blast.[67] The announcement ensured that no one, despite the abundant evidence of wrong-doing at Westray, would ever be convicted of a crime or breach of safety laws. The 1993 decision to pursue criminal charges and forego the many allegations of mine-safety violations was, in hindsight, a tragic mistake.[68]

## WEIGHING THE COST

What are the lessons to be drawn from the legal morass created by the Westray disaster? In some ways the problems and roadblocks encountered in the search for answers and justice should be expected in a complex, modern justice system which values the rights of individuals. Much of the fallout from this disaster, however, lies firmly rooted in the way in which Nova Scotia's government and justice system operate.

First, there was the charade of a regulatory body, the Department of Labour, scrambling to investigate a major industrial tragedy that could have been prevented if inspectors had simply done their jobs and enforced the law. Westray was a low point, too, for the Public Prosecution Service. Poor decision-making and lack of budgetary control compromised the prosecution of criminal charges from the start. The service's response was to beef up its special prosecutions branch to handle violations of workplace safety laws and other specialized regulations.[69]

A swat-team of prosecutors has been proposed, ready to head for the scene of any future disaster, legal pads in hand, to advise investigators on the seizure of evidence and possible charges.The larger question remains of whether the service's operational independence is compatible with budget control by government. The Nova Scotia government steadfastly refuses to relinquish its control over the purse-strings, citing the need to be accountable to taxpayers.[70] Independence, however, gives the government a convenient rationale for ignoring problems plaguing the service and a means of ducking political responsibility for solving them.[71] In part due to controversy generated by the abrupt end to the Westray prosecution, retired Quebec judge Fred Kaufman was appointed in July 1998 to conduct a second review of the service. His mandate included an examination of the service's relationship with government and of whether or not prosecutors are accountable to the public. As part of the review, Kaufman retained two prominent Halifax criminal lawyers to study whether the Westray prosecution was properly handled. His findings were expected in early 1999.[72]

The legal tug of war between inquiries and prosecutions has been settled, after a fashion. There is now a Supreme Court of Canada precedent that puts the onus on the executive branch of government to decide which should proceed, and live with the consequences. But what happens when the government of the day is so deeply involved in the disaster that it cannot make such decisions without inviting charges of political self-interest? Justice Peter Cory envisioned such a situation in the Supreme Court of Canada's 1995 decision on the Westray Inquiry. A government attempt to delay an inquiry, he wrote, "involves the inevitable risk that the public will lose faith in the government's ability and willingness to get to the truth, and in the political system as a whole."[73] The government causes the conflict in the first place by appointing a commission. Not to denigrate the fact-finding benefits of inquiries, but they have long been known as an effective tool for defusing controversy and avoiding tough issues. Examples of the situations alluded to by Justice Cory are not hard to envision: a disaster at sea caused by government cutbacks to coast guard services or the number of navigational aids; a plane crash at a small airport no longer manned by air-traffic controllers or emergency crews because a government department decided they cost too much.

In any event, politicians may lack the power to favour an inquiry over a prosecution. The government has the right to appoint an inquiry and to tell its regulatory agencies, such as the Department of Labour, to look no further. Government departments and their political masters have sole discretion to decide to investigate or lay charges of violating safety regulations, anti-pollution laws, and an array of other non-criminal statutes. Among them, in Nova Scotia, is a revised and tougher *Occupational Health and Safety Act*, introduced in 1997 in response to the Westray tragedy.[74]

Neither the Nova Scotia government nor its prosecutors, however, has the right to tell the RCMP or any other police force whom to investigate, when to investigate, or whether to lay charges (MacKenzie, 1993: 6–5). Likewise, the Nova Scotia government may find it impractical, if not impossible, to order its independent prosecution service when to prosecute and when to drop charges. While the minister of justice retains that prerogative, it has yet to be exercised in the service's eight years of existence. It is unlikely a government facing a political firestorm after a major disaster would have the courage or credibility to take that power for a test drive, no matter how compelling its reasons or how noble its motives. So, in Nova Scotia at least, the government's only option appears to be delaying an inquiry, or foregoing one entirely, while other prosecutions play out. As the Westray prosecution shows, that process can take years, precluding a timely examination of the causes of a disaster and blocking testimony from key players who face charges. In the meantime there's a risk that the same mistakes and problems, left undetected and unchecked, will lead to a future tragedy.

Was Westray a legal disaster? The answer is yes and no. Yes, in terms of the delays and missed opportunities and the system's paralysis when it came to holding individuals and institutions accountable for the loss of twenty-six lives. At the same time, the law surrounding the powers and parameters of inquiries has been clarified. Justice Richard's Inquiry, once freed to do its work, made solid findings of blame and far-reaching recommendations for change. There have been demands in Parliament for amendments to the *Criminal Code* to ensure that corporate officials can be held accountable for unsafe workplaces like Westray; the federal government has responded with a review of existing provisions.[75]

Will this be enough to help avert future disasters? And when such tragedies occur, will officialdom's response be swifter and more decisive? Sadly, as the dust continues to settle in the wake of the Westray mine explosion, those questions remain unanswered.

CHAPTER NINE

# WESTRAY:
## THE PRESS, IDEOLOGY,
## AND CORPORATE CRIME[1]

*John McMullan and Sherman Hinze*

## INTRODUCTION

On May 9, 1992, Canadians witnessed a mining disaster of enormous proportions. An explosion ripped through an underground mine in Pictou County, Nova Scotia, claiming the lives of twenty-six miners, eleven of whom remain buried underground. This paper analyzes how the newspaper media reported on the Westray situation and how that reporting activity constituted a representational reality about Westray (Surrette, 1992: 14; Bonner, [no date]: 36). As the disaster and the aftermath unfolded, did the media reflect or create public perceptions? What images were portrayed to the public? Did they change over time? What stories were told and which ones were not? What does the media discourse reveal about corporate ideology? To what degree was the media itself part of the story and part of the disaster (Barak, 1994; Evans et al., 1987; Box, 1983: 17; Sumner, 1990; Sumner et al., 1990).

Typically, lower-class crime becomes news. It is a regular staple of newspaper accounts, prime-time television, radio talk shows, and movie dramas (McCormick, 1995: 2; Murdock, 1982; Roshier, 1973; Graber, 1980; Chibnall, 1977; Sparks, 1990; Ericson et al., 1991). As (Kappeler et al., 1993: 102) says:

> In the popular imagination, a crime is an act committed against an innocent victim by an uncaring perpetrator. A crime occurs when someone breaks into your house and steals your television set and stereo. A crime occurs when an anonymous mugger knocks you to the ground and steals your wallet and watch. A crime occurs when a serial killer goes on a rampage and slaughters innocent victims.

By comparison, corporate lawbreaking is rarely described as criminality. It is usually underplayed by the media and reported as "accidents," "tragedies," or "unforeseen incidents" (Lichter et al., 1981; Evans et al., 1983; Coleman, 1989; Barak, 1994: 98). With corporate malfeasance there is a different condensation of organizational images at play. Corporations invest in the "symbolic politics of news and advertising because sophistication in defending bad news and trafficking in good news is seen as an essential part of achieving capital gains" (Ericson et al., 1991: 14). Corporations often deploy "experts" who cater to a journalist's need for quick news—background briefings, schedules and deadlines, press conferences, press releases, etc.—and who simultaneously seek to shape, make, and manipulate a story (Awad, 1985: 6). Their sources filter narratives, explanations, and legitimations through the media, often transforming or neutralizing their harmful, dangerous, and violent deeds into seemingly normal business practices or ethics (Simon et al., 1990: 296; Clinard, 1990). Journalists and corporate sources "form a hermeneutic circle for rationalizing business practices and articulating business interests" (Ericson et al., 1989: 260).

In this chapter we explore, in a preliminary way, the ideological character of news coverage concerning the Westray explosion from May 1992 to December 1995. Our central thesis is that the press coverage of the Westray event, while investigative and insightful in places, nevertheless, was very similar in content, tone, and form to that often articulated by corporations about their own misconduct and violence. What the media told was a disaster story, not a story about state crime or the political economy of reckless death. This does not mean that there was a straightforward corporatist ideology embedded in the media discourse about Westray, or that the media, the company, and the state conspired to control what was seen or read; but it does suggest that reporters were ideological actors, reflecting and articulating not only generalized economic and political relations, but also the "structure of feeling," or the general mood or predisposition of a society at a particular point in time (Williams, 1977: 128).

This, of course, makes reading the news difficult. Two caveats are called for. First, ideologies in complex societies are highly situated, pseudo-descriptive accounts that conceal their fundamental premises. Amid an often complex articulation and overlapping of different social themes and divisions, media discourse will reflect and reproduce ironic, paradoxical, and contradictory mixtures of ideology in both individual stories and in institutional practices. As Counihan observes, "a theory of content as discourses and texts is a partial but necessary precondition for an analysis of how dominant political and aesthetic ideologies are at work within the texts, dictating their silences as well as their statements" (1975: 36).

Second, we want to emphasize the dialectic between the text and the reader. Our concern is with the rhetorical means whereby news texts worked towards the reader, promoting certain responses over others, in effect, demarcating the life-world of their audience (Eco, 1979; Gitlin, 1979: 253; Ricoeur, 1981). We have moved in our research through a series of approximations, from first impressions to what we hope are more adequate accounts of the relationship between media discourse and its generative social practices

(Sumner, 1979). This means that we have not only interrogated or decoded news texts, we have also placed them in a critical interpretative framework so that we may investigate how their ordering of events; their imagery of social order; their sources of blame, ofpraise and scorn, and of appropriate response were connected to dominant cultural values. Our aim is to explore the varieties of stories, characters, and moralities surrounding reporting on Westray and to ask how far the conventions, presuppositions, and regularities of news writing circumscribed the ways in which the conduct of corporations, governments, the judiciary, the miners, and their families were made to make sense. To paraphrase Raymond Williams (1974), questions about media reporting are ultimately questions about "form and meaning," and about institutions and the organization of social relationships.

## METHODOLOGICAL CONSIDERATIONS

Hours after the 5:18 a.m. explosion of May 9, 1992, journalists descended on Plymouth, Nova Scotia, "like a plague of high tech locusts, weighed down with portable computers, cellular telephones, cameras, microphones and truck-loads of electronic gadgetry."[2] Within a week, over one hundred stories were published by the Halifax-based *Chronicle-Herald* and *Mail-Star* newspapers, and by January, 1996, 1765 articles about Westray appeared in these two papers. Eight hundred and thirty stories were written in 1992; 415 appeared in 1993; 151 in 1994; and 369 in 1995. We did not, however, analyze the entire sample. Instead we divided the three and one half years of coverage into five discernible periods. The total number of articles for each period was calculated and then a sample was drawn for each time-frame. In order to be as comprehensive as possible, every fourth article within the total sample of each period was analyzed. The reporting times were as follows: May/June, 1992; October/November/December, 1992; May/June, 1993; October/November, 1994 and October/November, 1995.

The spring of 1992 was selected because Westray was very much in the public mind. This was a time of intense media coverage, which set the theme for subsequent reporting. In all, 365 articles, or an average of seven per day, were published in this two-month period. The fall 1992 period was chosen because of new developments regarding legal culpability, law enforcement, and public accountability. Charges were being considered in the Westray case and a possible public inquiry was being debated. Five months after the explosion, Westray, its parent company Curragh Resources, and the local state were still dominating newspaper reporting. One hundred and sixty-six articles, an average of about two per day, were published in this three-month period. The spring 1993 period was selected because it was the anniversary of the explosion. Intense reflection about the event was occurring, as was a growing interest in government involvement in Westray. A provincial election was looming and Westray was front-and-centre in the election campaign. Seventy articles, about 20 percent of the total coverage for 1993, were published in this two-month period. The fall 1994 period was chosen because it reflected developments in legal and criminal justice fields. Trials were being arranged and legal arguments and manoeuver were almost a daily staple of reporting. A veritable litany of accusations and excuses were being proffered in the media, and this allowed for some coverage on who was thought to be responsible for the deaths and injuries and for what reasons. Thirty-one articles, about 30 percent of the total coverage for 1994, were published in this time-frame. Finally, we concentrated on the fall of 1995 because there was now considerable media coverage of a new public inquiry into the "Westray disaster." The expectation was that new voices would be heard, new facts would be presented, and new causes would be ascertained. Not surprisingly, the total coverage for 1995 picked up from the previous year to total 369 articles, 47 of which appeared in this time-frame.

We focused exclusively on the *Chronicle-Herald* and the *Mail-Star* newspapers for a number of reasons. First, the *Chronicle-Herald* and the *Mail-Star* are Nova Scotia's largest dailies, employing 116 full-time reporters and editors and 20 part-time employees within 9 regional bureaus. These two newspapers share the same owners, staff, resources, and stories and have a combined metropolitan circulation of approximately 73,769 readers and a combined provincial circulation of approximately 73,966 readers. These newspapers were "on the spot," and so their reporters did not rely on wire services or secondhand informants to get the story. They reported continually from the front lines and produced by far the most exhaustive coverage of the Westray situation. Second, the *Chronicle-Herald* and the *Mail-Star* newspapers have a long history of covering mining disasters. They have expertise in handling local and regional news and in writing about mining matters and mining communities. Wilkie Taylor, for example, wrote about the Springhill Explosions of 1956 and 1958, as well as about the Westray disaster of 1992. Third, phases and longevity of coverage are important in newspaper reporting. In a world of instant news and numerous stories, events can easily lose their newsworthiness. For international, national, and other regional carriers, Westray had a short shelf life. Not so for the *Chronicle-Herald* and the *Mail-Star*. They stayed with the story continuously, although it must be said that the amount of information declined as the legal and political issues came to replace family and emotional themes (McCormick, 1995: 202). The *Chronicle-Herald* and the *Mail-Star* have published over 2000 articles, and they have the most comprehensive archive from which to sample and understand media discourse surrounding Westray.

Of course, different sampling techniques, different time periods, and larger sample sizes might uncover fresh content and different significations. Certainly an exhaustive sampling of everything that the national press published on Westray in a given time period, or about particular issues like regulatory enforcement, might reveal interesting findings and different clusters of connotations. But we want to emphasize that we familiarized ourselves with the total press coverage available from the *Chronicle-Herald* and the *Mail-Star* [N=1763] before we identified our periods and drew our sample size [N=183]. We are convinced that our analysis identifies many of the basic themes that make up a complex, composite discourse of media reporting about Westray. This essay represents an early step in moving the research boundaries beyond first impressions. As Sumner and Sandberg observe, the critique of ideology and the press media "is never-ending and open, although never unprincipled and shapeless ... as theory and history move on, findings deepen, take on a new shape and acquire sharper/fresher tones" (1990: 166).

## THE PRESS COVERAGE OF WESTRAY FROM 1992–1995

The tone for early reporting was set by Donald Cameron, premier of Nova Scotia, in a television interview the day after the explosion, as well as by Colin Benner, a Curragh mining executive, and Gerald Phillips, the Westray mine manager, during press conferences on the night of the explosion. Cameron declared his grief for the families, the children and the parents and hoped that a rescue effort would find some survivors. Asked about safety and the government's role in bringing the mine into production, he said "The reality is that we have a major disaster today, but I'm not sure that we're going to help these people that are grieving, and all other people that feel so badly about this, getting into a political argument about things." There have been so many "lies told about this Pictou mine," he insisted, that "it's hard to separate them from fact." "Clearly, we have a major disaster," he conceded. "Something was wrong." Phillips, who was coordinating the rescue effort, was quick to dismiss any corporate wrong-doing or responsibility. Westray was "as safe a mine as there is," he said. Operations, he told the public, were conducted within government guidelines. Benner, who was the designated corporate spokesperson, acknowledged the terrible human tragedy, praised the victims, the families, the miners, and the communities for their courage, but stressed that safety had always been a priority at the mine. "An instantaneous buildup of methane gas," he claimed, seemed to have caused the explosion. The Westray explosion was apparently an accident in an all-too-dangerous industry (McManus, 1992: 9–13, 60; Jobb, 1994: 57, 59, 63; Cameron et al., 1994: 55–84).

## PERIOD ONE: THE IDEOLOGICAL FORMATION OF TRAGEDY

In the months that followed, the press pursued the disaster angle rather vigorously, while giving only limited coverage to safety, legal, and political concerns. In the first period of reporting [May/June, 1992] we analyzed ninety-seven cuttings: forty-six of them emphasized human tragedy, eighteen focused on political concerns, seventeen raised the issue of occupational safety, ten reported about a possible public investigation, and six were miscellaneous in content. Most stories concerning Westray appeared in Section A of both newspapers, although human disaster stories were far more prevalent on the front page [52 percent of the time] than were political ones [11 percent of the time].

The most frequent cluster of connotations was the ideological formation of tragedy. In numerous stories, tragic loss and hope were reported on in a manner so as to evince a powerful set of signifiers.

The press focused on the sorrow, sacrifice, and suffering inherent in expecting or managing death. They evoked strong emotive terms, images, and symbols, while simultaneously downplaying the context for these feelings. The actual explosion—its causes and agents—were neglected or displaced in the coverage, and a mining disaster was reworked as a "family disaster." Following from this was a multitude of stories exploring how families, friends, and rescuers coped with the despair and the discovery of dead bodies. "I told them [families] never to give up hope, even if one person comes out alive," said Norma Ruddick, whose husband, Maurice, spent nine days trapped underground before he was rescued in Springhill in 1958. The first eleven miners pulled from the rubble of the Westray Mine died a quick and painless death, says Nova Scotia's Chief Medical Examiner. "Exhausted dragger men cried ... as they told of ravaged Westray Coal Mine ... the dragger men hauled out 16 bodies, over smoldering coal and twisted steel ... they returned to their motel emotionally wrung out...."[3]

**Box One: Newspaper Coverage of the Tragedy**
PLYMOUTH—Families of 15 miners still trapped in Westray Mine held tight to a slim thread of hope Monday as they watched and waited near the disaster site. "I think that there has to be hope at this point in time, or these people cannot continue this vigil," said Bruce Stephen, brother-in-law of one of the men still not found. But he said while hope now is "very slim," it won't be extinguished as long as they continue to wait for news for Westray officials.... Mr. Stephen who crossed the street from where families are waiting ... said the families feel no anger toward the mining company. "They don't feel anything except a desire to get this over with." "Families Hold Tight to Hope," Halifax *Mail-Star*, May 12, 1992: A15

Even as friends and mourners paid their last respects at the graveside to seven of 11 men killed in last weekend's Westray mine explosion, there was more tragic news from the village of Plymouth on Wednesday. Yesterday afternoon, rescuers burrowing through rubble to reach 15 men still trapped in the shattered mine discovered the bodies of three more miners.... [T]hat mournful discovery made still another claim on the strength of a community whose reserves of strength seem to run deeper than its famous coal.... Pictou County's mining communities have borne their burden day after day with dignity, fortitude and grace.... Above all else, though, Pictou County showed us what it is to hope, to have faith....

"Community Bears Its Tragedy," Halifax *Mail-Star*, May 14, 1992: C1

The general impression conveyed was that the harm, injury, violence, death, and suffering were the result of capricious causes. "Underground coal mining ... has been a story of great human courage pitted against great natural hazards," wrote one journalist, "it is still brave men toiling in the face of unseen danger in the dark" ("Tragedy at Westray," editorial, Halifax *Chronicle-Herald,* May 11, 1992: C1). A certain mystique about coal mining was advanced. Experts were cited to the effect that coal was in the blood and miners knew and accepted their lot in life, even if it meant dying hard. A regional culture, we were told, mixed courage, hope, fortitude, and fatalism into an ideology of self-reliance. Dying underground was a brave but necessary choice. The effect of much of the early reporting was to distance the company from the event by dwelling on the emotional effects of the explosion. For example, one account reported that a miner in the pit enjoyed "the work and will go back despite the tragedy.... Westray followed safety guidelines; if they hadn't, he would have complained." Another noted how the explosion left miners confused and divided.[4]

**Box Two: Newspaper Coverage of the Tragedy**
Some Westray miners lost their brothers, others lost their friends. And now they are torn: should they return to the same mine that exploded three weeks ago, look for another job or quit mining forever.

"Miners Torn Over Prospects," Halifax *Mail-Star*, May 30, 1992: A2

According to these reports, the mine was a safe place to work. The explosion was a normal event with understandable, if deplorable side effects.

Of course, not all coverage in this period was so incurious. Questions about safety were reported from the beginning. But what is interesting is the focus of the coverage. Many of the stories emphasized the dangerous physical properties of hard rock mining. Scientists, engineers, mine consultants, medical doctors, coroners, and other technical experts were consulted and quoted, but the overall impression was to reinforce the anonymity and the unpredictability of the causes of the explosion. Inanimate chemicals or hazardous by-products were to blame, not human judgments or organizational decisions. There was little coverage on how the methane gas went undetected, or why it was there in the first place. Nor was it revealed how combustible coal dust remained on the mine floor, although there was a hint of possible corporate and regulatory impropriety, in that it was noted that there was an accumulation of "up to 20 centimetres." As one miner put it:

> The company was very good at deception.... I knew something was going on as soon as I saw the pretty boy they [Curragh] had brought in from Toronto to do all the TV reports.... He did an excellent job of making the public feel sorry for the company, but it was all done that way with one goal in mind: public pity. (Comish 1993: 47)

Only one article from our sample for this period discussed safety from a worker's viewpoint. It appeared in print on May 23, two weeks after the explosion and is reprinted in Box Four.

**Box Three: Newspaper Coverage of the Tragedy**
Methane, either as a toxic or an explosive gas, has always posed a lethal threat to coal miners working in underground tunnels. The gas is blamed for the explosion which rocked the Westray mine Saturday morning and claimed the lives of at least 11 miners.... If methane's explosive properties are not the cause of death, then its qualities as a toxic gas can kill a miner trapped in a damaged mine shaft, says a specialist at the Victoria General Hospital....
"Methane A Lethal Threat To Miners," Halifax *Mail-Star*, May 11, 1992: A2

An Alberta mine expert blames the Westray disaster on a buildup of coal dust—a combustible substance that workers say was up to 20 centimeters deep on the mine floor the week before the explosion....

"Westray Miners Anxious to Testify at Disaster Probe," Halifax *Mail-Star*, May 22, 1992: A1

**Box Four: Newspaper Coverage of the Tragedy**
STELLARTON:—The provincial NDP caucus heard a three-and-one-half hour "nightmare" account of working conditions at the Westray mine from about 50 miners Thursday night. "It really was a nightmare account of the absence of health and safety provisions, procedures and protection that is intended under our provisions, procedures and protection that is intended under our health and safety, legislation," NDP leader, Alexa McDonough told reporters after the meeting....
"Politics of Disaster," Halifax *Mail-Star*, May 23, 1992: A2

What followed from this coverage, however, was not an actual reporting on safety complaints. The conditions underground and their connection to the explosion were not examined in any detail, although it must be said that a few stories reported on suspiciously high methane gas levels and unsafe underground equipment. Rather, safety was mobilized to construct a different type of story—one in which the voices of the workers underground were overshadowed by the voices of politicians and experts. The overall effect of this reporting was to suggest wayward conduct but to enshroud it in ambiguity and uncertainty. Instead of developing a crime focus, the almost uniform journalism of this period stressed an homogenous type of coverage that swamped readers with grim details of tragedy but left them wondering about the messy and troubling legal, corporate, and economic issues involved in the making of the explosion (McCormick, 1995: 212; Ericson et al., 1987: 232, 267–70; Ericson et al., 1989). The first direct coverage of political involvement in our sample appeared in print on May 23, and it linked the premier's office to the Westray site.

**Box Five: Newspaper Coverage of the Tragedy**
His somber expression told the story of good intentions gone horribly wrong. A day after a huge explosion shattered his dream of reviving underground coal mining in his native Pictou County, a downcast Premier Donald Cameron went on national television to promise a full inquiry into the disaster that killed 26 miners.... Nothing it appeared, could stand between Westray and Pictou County coal. Rival mine promoters were sent packing, repeated

> warnings of unsafe conditions in the mine were
> dismissed as political opportunism, fears of lost
> mining jobs in Cape Breton were ignored, and fed-
> eral bureaucrats who felt Ottawa was offering too
> much financial backing were attacked in the press....
> Westray was a creature of politics. In the mid-
> 1980s the government of Cameron's predecessor,
> John Buchanan, was looking for a firm to develop a
> mine to exploit Pictou County's low-sulfur coal....
> From a political standpoint, the timing was perfect.
> Cameron—whose riding borders the Westray site—
> and two other Tories in the Pictou area were re-
> elected, helping the Buchanan government cling to
> a four-seat majority.... Westray remained the gov-
> ernment's favourite son after Cameron reached the
> Premier's Office in early 1991....
> "Miners Recount 'Nightmare' Conditions," Hali-
> fax *Mail-Star*, May 23, 1992: C1

Westray, as a "creature of politics," appeared on line 92 of the article, which itself was featured in the third section of the newspaper on page C1. While this story made reference to earlier political revelations, there were in fact very few political reports printed in this time-frame; in an analysis of multiple news stories for 1992–93 it is noted that "the facts on the politics of the disaster received little attention in the press" (McCormick, 1995: 208). Political content stories tended to be buried and contextualized in benign terms: "A sombre expression that told the story of good intentions gone wrong." If he could have predicted what happened, Cameron is quoted as saying, "I'm sure we would have made different judgments" (Halifax *Mail-Star*, May 23, 1992: C1). The portrayal is that the explosion was unforeseen and that politicians were uninvolved in the making of the disaster. If much reporting was hesitant about assigning responsibility to the premier, there were some stories that actively probed other government officials involved in the explosion.

This reporting, like other stories of the period, and indeed like the cover-age in 1993 and 1994, identified the need to offer explanations but focused on individual incompetence. Inspectors from the provincial department of labour and the minister responsible for their enforcement mandate were especially denounced for their failure to act in light of known violations such as cave-ins, high methane gas levels, use of unauthorized and unsafe equipment, and improper storage of dangerous materials underground. The news narratives emphasized surprise and shock at what they frequently portrayed as a "bun-gling state of affairs."

**Box Six: Newspaper Coverage of the Tragedy**
Senior officials from Premier Don Cameron's offices worked almost around-the-clock this weekend, going over files from the Westray mine.... The Tories were hammered in the house last week as the opposition leveled charges that miners continued to work underground in potentially lethal conditions.... Labour Minister Leroy Legere—who was poorly briefed on mine inspections carried out prior to the explosion and couldn't answer most questions about safety concerns at the mine—was the focus of the opposition attack last week....
"PCs Move to Contain Damage: Cameron's Aides Scour Files from Westray Mine," Halifax *Mail-Star*, May 25, 1992: A1

The last topic to emerge in our sample from the early reporting period was centred around the establishment of the public investigation. Immediately after the explosion, the premier ordered an inquiry, promising that "no person would escape scrutiny." The terms of reference were broad, and the tasks assigned to the commissioner, Mr. Justice Richard, were wide-ranging and included an examination of the event; whether it was preventable; whether neglect caused or was a contributing factor in the explosion; whether there were defects in or about the mine or its mode of operation; whether applicable statutes, regulations orders, rules, or directions were followed; as well as investigation into anything else related to or deemed relevant to the establishment and functioning of the mine.[5] What was interesting about the ten cuttings we surveyed was how ubiquitous they were in content. Many of the reports wrestled with legal and technical terms and seemed unsure as to the differences between administrative and criminal procedures. Others seemed to lack definite focus and narrative structure. Some of the story-writing promised more than a fact-finding mission to determine causes. They misled the public into thinking that persons would be charged and that remedial action of a sort would be taken after the Inquiry.

**Box Seven: Newspaper Coverage of the Tragedy**
At least 70 Westray employees want to testify at the inquiry into the mine disaster and have asked the province to cover their costs, a miner said Wednesday.
"As far as I can tell, from anybody I've talked to, there's not one person who doesn't want to tell their side of the story," said miner Gordon Walsh, Co-

> chairman of an employees' committee formed in
> the wake of the May 9 explosion....
> "As employees, we feel we have a lot to offer the
> inquiry.... I really think the only fair way is to take
> every man who worked there and have him testify
> under oath...."
> "Details of Westray Inquiry to be set in Couple of
> Weeks," Halifax *Mail-Star*, May 21, 1992: A1

Nevertheless, some of the reporting was developing a critical edge. Stories were pointing to a construction of events which differed from that offered by state and corporate officials. Perhaps there was another representation of events than the methane theory of causation? Perhaps there was a different news discourse emerging that would tell a story about the political economy of a criminal offence?

## PERIOD TWO: THE INDIVIDUALIZATION OF RESPONSIBILITY

In the second reporting frame [October/November/December, 1992], there were 166 articles published, of which 44 articles were analyzed for content. Two topics were predominant: government involvement in the Westray mine and explosion [44 percent of the coverage], and legal decisions and actions pending against Curragh Resources Incorporated [32 percent of the coverage]. Family disaster stories, along with new reports about Devco coal benefiting from the closure of the Westray site, accounted equally for all remaining coverage. Eighty percent of reports mentioning state involvement were published in Section A of the newspapers. Seventy-eight percent of all legal stories were in Section A of the newspapers, as were all stories related to Devco. Family tragedy stories were not only less plentiful, they were moving to the back pages, appearing in Section A only 40 percent of the time. Interestingly, however, articles reporting on the government's role in Westray were front-page news only 20 percent of the time, while no reports on legal matters from our sample had front-page status.

> **Box Eight: Newspaper Coverage of the Tragedy**
> The Liberals are calling for a parliamentary investigation into the role Prime Minister Brian Mulroney and other top Tories played in winning federal financial backing for the ill-fated Westray coal mine. Evidence is mounting daily that the prime minister and his cabinet overruled federal officials who had warned the government against the project on safety and economic grounds....

> Mr. Dingwall has formally asked the Commons
> standing committee on industry and regional devel-
> opment to call a special inquiry into Ottawa's in-
> volvement in establishing the mine....
> "PM's Role in Westray Questioned," Halifax *Mail-
> Star*, October 9, 1992: A4

In analyzing both the number of news items and the placement of stories, it is clear that Westray as a news-making event was declining in interest and significance. As noted by another analyst, when "the Westray disaster" became "the Westray case," the coverage dropped considerably from an average of about twenty-five articles a day to about two a day (McCormick, 1995: 210–11). Yet Westray was still continuing to evoke moderate interest, even after initial, enormous saturation coverage. What also changed was the narrative focus and the typification of the public idiom. The news narratives, while less voluminous and vociferous overall, were now working towards framing the political and the legal as an audience event.

Press coverage was increasingly suspicious of government claims. There was doubt, even cynicism, in the reporting of their motivations and activities. But instead of sketching a context for government conduct, most news narratives tended to individualize politics. The coverage tried to establish a cause and effect relationship that was easy to trace and name.

> **Box Nine: Newspaper Coverage of the Tragedy**
> More personnel changes are in the works at the
> beleaguered Labour Department, the new minister
> said Wednesday.... The department's safety enforce-
> ment record and problems in the occupational health
> and safety division have been questioned since the
> May 9 explosion at the Westray coal mine which
> killed 26 men.... The house cleaning in the Labour
> Department began three weeks ago when then-min-
> ister Leroy Legere was sacked and Mr. McInnis
> was brought in to oversee an independent review.
>
> A week later, deputy minister Hugh MacDonald
> retired to make way for Innis Christie.... The latest
> change involves Jack Noonan, who was dismissed
> from his job as executive director of the occupa-
> tional health and safety division late last week....
> "Further Changes in Works at Labour Department,"
> Halifax *Mail-Star*, December 10, 1992: A3

Once again, the Department of Labour was identified as the source of problems. But the reporting mirrored the language of the press conferences. It was a faithful catalogue of shamed individuals. The impression conveyed was that Westray would not have happened if the Department of Labour had competent officials in positions of authority. Middle-level bureaucrats, not elected politicians, were at fault. Indeed in this one cutting (Box Ten) the federal government is presented as a concerned agency desperately seeking the truth.

> **Box Ten: Newspaper Coverage of the Tragedy**
> The federal government has budgeted up to $393,328 in the current fiscal year to explain and document its involvement in the ill-fated Westray mining venture, documents show.... Most of the money spent so far has been for the massive task of assembling and making public, thousands of pages of documents connected with Westray.
> "Ottawa sets $400,000 to Explain Westray Role," Halifax *Mail-Star*, December 8, 1992: A2

This reporting denied a larger institutional role in the event. While the "social" was inserted into the reporting discourse alongside the "natural" as a possible cause of events, the focus was almost exclusively on personal impropriety and "bad apples" in an otherwise good barrel. Westray soon became a story about wayward individuals, not wayward corporate/state behaviours.

> **Box Eleven: Newspaper Coverage of the Tragedy**
> Charges of safety violations ranging from forcing miners to work in unsafe conditions to allowing empty fuel cans to litter underground workings have been laid against the owners and top officials of the Westray mine.... Charged are Curragh Incorporated, Westray Coal's Toronto-based parent company, and four of Westray's most senior employees, including Gerald Phillips, who was mine manager during the mine's troubled nine months of production.
> The others are underground manager Roger Parry; his brother Robert Parry, maintenance superintendent; and assistant superintendent Glenn Jones.... Curragh, Mr. Phillips, Mr. Jones and Roger Parry are charged with failing to withdraw miners from that area when levels of methane exceeded

> 2.5 percent of the air in the mine....
> "Action Very Gratifying, Says Westray Families
> Spokesman," Halifax *Mail-Star*, October 7, 1992:
> A2

On September 17, four months after the explosion, the RCMP finally secured the mine site and seized documents and equipment pertinent to a possible criminal case. In the interim, there had been no police presence and no continuity at the scene. Thousands of documents had been removed by Westray's managers and hundreds of others at the site had been shredded. The prosecution was similarly bogged down in an orrery of errors, delays, financial problems, and personality conflicts. In October 1992, five months after the explosion, Curragh Incorporated and four of its managers were eventually charged with fifty-two violations of the provincial *Occupational Health and Safety Act* (Cameron et al., 1994: 59, 60, 83).

News coverage of the legal charges followed that of politics. The press focused on specific actors. In focusing on the charges against Mr. Phillips, Mr. Jones and Roger Parry, which alleged that they did not take steps to prevent an explosion, corporations were represented as persons, not economic enterprises with business goals, systems of authority, and ideologies (McMullan, 1992; Snider, 1993). They were endowed with remarkably reactive personalities and presented without a history of harm or reckless behaviour. Thus the individualization paradigm worked to simplify and convert complex organizational dynamics and memories into atomized legal actors. A sense of cumulative, collective action and collective responsibility, linking owners and managers in a production plan that may have contributed to the explosion, was only rarely suggested. Instead of exploring whether this was a case of corporate crime, a law and order story, the bulk of the news coverage focused on the obstacles to prosecution and on the conflicts between the company and the legal system.

> **Box Twelve: Newspaper Coverage of the Tragedy**
> The owners of the Westray coal mine will be in court today in a bid to keep about 120 documents out of the hands of investigators probing last May's fatal explosion.
> Westray coal and its parent company, Curragh, Incorporated of Toronto, contend the documents are privileged correspondence between the firms and their lawyers, and must remain confidential....The RCMP, which is conducting a criminal investigation of the disaster, used a search warrant last month to take possession of those

> records.... Bruce Macintosh, who acts for the mine's owners, says a lawyer from his firm reviewed the sealed material last week and decided not to claim privilege on the bulk of the material....
> "Westray Owners in Court Today," Halifax *Mail-Star*, October 15, 1992: A4

While the cluster of connotations signifying "legal battle" was insightful and informative, the language was altogether rational and tempered. Everything was sensible, good-mannered, and polite. This polemical style stands in marked contrast to the early evocative terminology of disaster, heartbreak, pain, sacrifice, courage, etc. The imagery of the "Westray case" worked to suppress the violent effects of the explosion, to sanitize its meaning, and to distance the company from the consequences of the event. Consider the following:

> Curragh Incorporated has replaced Westray general manager, Gerald Phillips, who was mine manager for Westray coal when the May 9 explosion occurred.... Mr. Phillips is one of four Westray officials charged with infractions of provincial occupational health and safety laws following the disaster. He left his post as mine manager following the explosion....[6]

Interestingly, Curragh Incorporated was not even mentioned as a plaintiff. "Four Westray officials" were charged with infractions, but one of them had "left his post." The corporation, as a social entity, was moved back further to the discursive background, while middle-level managers were moved forward. Journalists were by now almost entirely events-oriented. They rarely reported anything beyond the latest happening, seemingly captured by the anticipation of the next individual revelation (Walters et al., 1989: 73). What followed from this rather narrow reporting lens was a remarkably banal and benign signification of corporate culpability that inhibited critical reflection on the motives and effects of the powerful. As observed by another analyst, it is in the nature of the "news effect" to "homogenize or mainstream," and to present diverse groups with a set of common symbols, vocabularies, and shared experiences (Gerbner et al., 1980; Gerbner et al., 1984).

It is worth noting, however, that a minority of stories followed up on legal issues and placed them in a more critical perspective. Some reporters investigated, as well as merely recorded, the day-to-day legal developments. They disclosed information about the political and financial deals that set the mine up in the first place. They disputed company accounts of events and revealed misinformation. They pressured the police and the courts to discover the truth and not to forget the death of twenty-six miners. It seems clear that there was a measure of pluralism in press coverage concerning political and legal matters. While there was a range of opinion presented, nevertheless, it must be said that reporting merged more than it diverged (Murdock, 1980; Hall et al., 1978; Chibnall, 1977; Sumner, 1982).

The representation of tragedy declined in the coverage from the late spring to the autumn of 1992; nevertheless, the form and sentiments of the narratives remained similar. Stories told of grief, painful remembrances, awesome courage, and a stubborn resolve to carry on despite the personal and community losses. This "selective sampling" tactic (C. Smith, 1992), played on the eagerness of Westray families to provide information about their tragic experiences and then linked these representations to other mining communities and experiences, as in the following:

> ... More than 3,000 people are expected to pack a memorial service for the dead men this morning in the Yellowknife community Arena. Among those will be five people whose family members died in the Westray Mine disaster in May.
>
> Kenton Teasdale of Stellarton, NS, had a son and a son-in-law die in the Westray disaster. He says Yellowknifers were among the first to call and offer help to the Westray families and now it's their turn.... [7]

While initial articles in the first reporting period compared the explosion to other mining disasters, such as Springhill in 1958, the textual construction in the later reporting was on wider community impacts. Much of the reporting retold, updated, or expanded the emotional overtones of the tragedy discourse: resetting the explosion, applauding the rescue work, exploring the structure of family feeling, and drawing out community values. Westray's disaster was Yellowknife's and vice versa. First we suffered and were comforted, "now it's their turn." Indeed the media fascination with the spectacle of family and community pain led them to event-chase. An explosion elsewhere was a reason to revive pictures and memories of Westray.

Of course, the sentiment behind the human interest story was understandable, even necessary. The public was concerned to know who survived and how people were coping in the aftermath. But the depictions were unremitting and overwhelming. Stories in the later sample periods added some new information but, for the most part, about 200 reporters managed to share resources and ideas in such a way as to produce a remarkably singular symbolic world that cut across both print and electronic modes of information. Stories seldom deviated from the frequent association of limited signifiers, amounting to a persistent paradigm of "disaster without a cause." Just as in the modern televised police story, the appropriate response to misfortune and victimization was a resigned pity rather than a cause-finding critique. The very prevalence and staging of concern through the language of a kind of morality tale amounted to what Knight calls a "disavowal of knowledge of human causes" (1980: 179). It seems to us particularly apposite to view this news coverage as constituting "a projection of a world" onto a societal moral order—one whose essential features remained relatively unchanged from month to month (Ricoeur, 1981).

> **Box Thirteen: Newspaper Coverage of the Tragedy**
> For the past several days, Joyce Fraser's thoughts have often been 2,000 kilometres away.
>     She has been thinking about the families of the eight miners found dead Wednesday after an explosion at a coal mine in Virginia on Monday.... "When I first heard about it Monday ... everything just kept coming back," the Westville woman said Thursday. "When something like this happens you keep up-to-date because you know what they're going through."
> "Virginia Mine Blast Generates Sympathy of Westville Families," Halifax *Mail-Star*, December 11, 1992: A4.

Finally, in this time-frame, a number of articles in our sample reported on the unintended consequences of the explosion for other communities and corporations, as in the following:

> The closure of the Westray coal mine has translated into a new coal order for the Cape Breton Development Corp.... Nova Scotia Power Incorporated announced Wednesday it will buy an additional 300,000 tonnes of coal from Devco over the next six months to feed its generating plants at Trenton, NS.[8]

These sorts of economic spinoffs were alluded to in earlier reporting, especially in the proposed new Westray-backed strip mine venture in nearby Stellarton which, it was said, would provide jobs for laid-off miners. What followed from this type of coverage was a different reading of community. Instead of the iconography of devastation and moral altruism, these reports highlighted the fact that a mining tragedy in one place could be another community's boon.

## PERIOD THREE: REMEMBERING FORGETFULLY

In the third reporting period [May/June, 1993], there were seventy articles printed of which we analyzed eighteen for content. Two topics predominated: stories pursuant to politics and government involvement at Westray comprised about two-thirds of the coverage, while reports about family suffering and tragedy accounted for the remainder of the coverage. Eighty percent of the political reports were located in Section A of the papers, half of them on the front page. Sixty percent of human disaster stories were published in Section A, only 14 percent of them made the front page.

In the autumn sample of 1992, the reporting of Westray had become critical of the role that individuals in government had played in the explosion. Five months later, the news narratives were reworking the point of contact between the "life-world" of the reader and the surrounding economic and political environments (Giddens, 1987). Questions about compensation for corporate losses were displacing questions about human losses and state culpability.

> **Box Fourteen: Newspaper Coverage of the Tragedy**
>
> Curragh Incorporated, the owner of the Westray mine, wants another pound of flesh out of the tax-payer's hide, and it has gone to court seeking it. In an application filed in Ontario Court earlier this month, Curragh argues it is entitled to a $2.4 million from a $16 million insurance settlement negotiated in the wake of the May 1992 mine explosion.
>
> The company will also seek an unspecified amount of "compensation from the federal government with respect to a portion of certain other maintenance and improvement costs" incurred after the Westray tragedy.
>
> "Westray Jobless Confront Savage on Campaign Trail," Halifax *Mail-Star*, May 22, 1993: A1

Governments, instead of being questioned and probed as active subjects in the explosion, are now presented as passive objects. The state/corporate connection is reported on so as to evoke sympathy for the former—"another pound of flesh out of the taxpayer's hide." There is no coverage of why governments gave loan guarantees in the first place, or why they were on the hook for further insurance-related costs. The state is depicted as a rather reactive complex of institutions, just doing its job, sometimes receiving grief for its troubles. This is evident in the following report, which covers the provincial election at the end of May, 1993.

> **Box Fifteen: Newspaper Coverage of the Tragedy**
> It is Donald Cameron's judgment, and it might be history's as well, that no government in this province would dare undo some of the reforms he put in place in two busy years in office.
> And the outgoing premier's record was indeed impressive, if less than perfect.
> Judges are no longer appointed (solely) for their political leanings. All major contracts are let by tender, and administered by neutral civil servants. The Civil Service Commission now interviews and hires new employees, without fear that a cabinet minister will push forward a party hack as a favourite candidate.
> And the list goes on....
> His critics (this paper included) also pointed out the premier's failings: the government never really came to grips with the Westray tragedy.
> "... And 'Bye, 'Bye Don," Halifax *Mail-Star*, May 27, 1993: B1.

By this account, Premier Cameron was a man for the people. Eleven positive developments were cited as his true legacy. In fifty-eight lines of narrative, Cameron and his government's involvement in the Westray explosion received but one line of typescript. The overall effect was to suggest an image of Cameron as a builder, a "true patriot" of Nova Scotia, who inexplicably "never really came to grips with the Westray tragedy." This type and tone of coverage worked to radically decontextualize the event and to depoliticize the role of government. It denied the possible preventable features of causation and implied once again that the explosion was essentially a capricious act. Such coverage restored the Westray story to a narrowly specified conventional range. At the level of narrative structure, plot function subsumed the explanation of the event, contributing to a convenient form of remembering forgetfully.

> **Box Sixteen: Newspaper Coverage of the Tragedy**
> WESTVILLE—Westray's jobless—frustrated, angry and just days away from the welfare line—stopped John Savage's campaign machine dead in its tracks Friday night.
> "We want some jobs, you bastard," shouted one from a cursing, picket-waving job which blocked the leader's path to a Liberal rally at the

local Legion Hall.... "We've got a resource, we've got a place to sell it and we've got people that want to work," said union head Randy Facette.... Standing nose-to-nose with workers who support Curragh's bid to resume mining, Mr. Savage said he'll never allow the same company back in.... "You've as much as convicted Curragh ... already," replied an angry Facette. You're the judge, jury and executioner....

"Blast Blamed on Coal Dust," Halifax *Mail-Star*, May 22, 1993: A1

There are many more things that could be said about ideology in the news stories of Westray. For example, generally, Curragh was denounced for their repeated efforts at corporate welfarism, while simultaneously they were lauded as an economic saviour. Corporate capital was frequently depicted as having the difficult job of revitalizing the local economy. Curragh was portrayed as able and willing to resume production, and politicians were cast in the unhappy role of preventing the "start-up." Union anger and solidarity seem to be saying, "Jobs at any cost"! There were no dead miners, only resources, markets, and people who wanted to work. The news narratives carried an approach to business that was profoundly ambivalent and ambiguous. On the one hand, there was an implication that Curragh did something wrong. On the other, there was a perception created that they were being discriminated against. Curragh was the victim of an unfair judge, jury and execution.

No such uncertainty characterized the coverage of family remembrance on the anniversary of the explosion. Personal and emotional suffering were once again connected to dramatic representations of intractable collective grief, as seen in Box Seventeen.

**Box Seventeen: Newspaper Coverage of the Tragedy**

SUNDAY: On the first anniversary of the Westray mine disaster, friends and relatives will gather around the permanent memorial to the 26 men who died so tragically and so violently a year ago.

The black granite memorial, with 26 beams of light commemorating the victims, will replace a wooden cross erected in a field near the mine. The cross had been the only site where loved ones of the 11 men still buried underground, could go to mourn.... It is difficult for family members to cope with this tragedy.... If you've got somebody dead,

> you want to go and mourn with him," Joe MacKay told The Canadian Press....
>
> "Where are you going to mourn?" Mr. MacKay said. "The bodies are still underground, you cannot get down to them."
>
> "Flowers Fade, Questions Remain, Private Service to Mark Anniversary of Westray Tragedy," Halifax *Mail-Star*, May 8, 1993: A4

Techniques of extra-locality were deployed to set a sombre mood and to draw the distant reader back to the event and on to the ceremony of group remembering. The public was addressed authoritatively and indiscriminately from a single source. Journalists wanted us as readers "to feel" the narrative of remembering and to be constituted by it (Hackett et al., 1992; Taras, 1992). As noted by another analyst, the media punctuates the daily rhythms of people in the most intimate, domestic settings (Kellner, 1990). News not only informs, but it permeates, organizes, and defines interaction within the life-world of the reader.

> **Box Eighteen: Newspaper Coverage of the Tragedy**
>
> Beneath a simple wooden cross on the outskirts of New Glasgow lies a jumble of wreaths and flowers, the once bright ribbons faded after the rigors of a harsh winter.
>
> For the families of the 26 men who died in the Westray mine explosion a year ago Sunday, this is hallowed ground.
>
> About 350 metres directly below, in the rubble of the tunnels they helped dig, are entombed the remains of 11 men who eluded the grasp of mine rescue teams last May.
>
> At this windswept spot, sandwiched between a ball diamond and a race-track, they and the 15 other Westray victims are remembered. More than a kilometre to the south, partly obscured by the bare branches of trees, two coal storage towers mark the Westray mine in the village of Plymouth.
>
> "Westray, A Year Later," Halifax *Mail-Star*, May 8, 1993: A1

The reporting recreated the memorial in vivid terms. The textual reconstruction of events emphasized the tragic, the sentimental, and the stoic. Indeed the very prevalence and the sequelling of coverage surrounding these themes were the sources of a "blindness," of an "invisibility" of coverage. The distant "coal storage towers," for example, were not only mute sentinels on the Plymouth skyline, they signified in the news coverage how far removed corporate capital was from the cause and consequences of the Westray explosion. The next cutting had the same distancing effect.

> **Box Nineteen: Newspaper Coverage of the Tragedy**
> Draegermen participating in this weekend's provincial mine rescue competition—the first since the Westray disaster—didn't need any reminders of how important their skills are: the real thing was still in their minds.
>
> Many of the draegermen who took part in the competition at Lingan mine went through the ultimate test of their skills and courage last year when an explosion ripped apart the coal mine in Plymouth, killing 26 people.
>
> Nova Scotians gained a new found respect for the teams of draegermen who doggedly entered the mine over and over again in search of survivors or bodies. "You couldn't help but be affected by what the draegermen went through at Westray."
> "Mine Rescue Competition Grim Reminder," Halifax *Mail-Star*, May 31, 1993: A3

Again the connotations were ones of bravery, loyalty, fortitude, and sacrifice. Such narratives, notable for their routineness and seriality, certainly sustained a sense of familiarity and continuity for the reading public, but they did not tell us that these noble traits were honed by necessity not choice, that rescue skills were required because occupational safety standards were lax, or that draegermen and miners alike had little choice about working and dying in unsafe conditions; in short they offered no explanation for Westray. One year after the event, the "Westray tragedy" has been orderly, predictably, and repetitively packaged as the "Westray mystery." The "senders of the news" had reduced plurality to a minimum, promoting in the process a preferred universe of shared dramatic meaning around redundant horror (Eco, 1979). Forgotten in all this remembering was Mr. Frame in the boardroom with the time bomb waiting to go off.

## PERIODS FOUR AND FIVE:

## FORMALISM, TECHNO-TRAGEDY, AND THE DENIAL OF THE SOCIAL

In the two remaining time periods [October/November, 1994], thirty-one articles were published, ten of which were analyzed for content and in [October/November, 1995], forty-seven stories were printed, fourteen of which we analyzed for content. Two themes were predominant: legal action and the public inquiry. All of the eleven cuttings regarding legal issues were placed in Section A, two of them making front-page news. Seven of the ten public inquiry stories were also located in Section A, with one report making the front page. The three remaining stories dealt with a controversial book published on Westray and with a commemorative ceremony honouring the dead miners.

In our previous discussions of legal coverage we noted that fifty-two charges were pending against Curragh Incorporated and four of its managers. In December 1992, thirty-four of the charges were dropped and then, in March 1993, the remaining eighteen charges were also stayed. It was not until April 1993, almost a year after the explosion, that criminal charges were finally laid. These new charges were that Curragh Incorporated and two mine managers had committed criminal negligence causing death and manslaughter. Those charges were immediately contested by Curragh Incorporated and eventually refiled, amidst allegations that the Crown investigation and prosecution teams were woefully understaffed and underfunded. The trial of Curragh Incorporated and the mine managers began in earnest only in February, 1995. Not surprisingly, by the fall of 1994, both prosecution and defence attorneys were locked in a war of words and legal manoeuvers as evinced by the following stories from our sample.

> **Box Twenty: Newspaper Coverage of the Tragedy**
> Prosecutors and the RCMP were mum Wednesday on the fate of their bid to view documents seized last month in connection with the Westray mine explosion. "All I can say is, until the thing is completed and a (judge's) order is in place, I cannot discuss the proceedings," said Herman Felderhof, who heads the Westray prosecution team. On October 12, the RCMP seized a lawyer's notes of an interview conducted with Roger Parry, one of two former Westray managers facing criminal charges in the May 1992 explosion deaths of 26 coal miners. The notes were placed in a sealed envelope pending a court hearing to determine whether solicitor-client privilege protected them from disclosure.

> "Methane, Coal Dust Dominate Testimony at Westray Inquiry," Halifax *Mail-Star*, November 10, 1994: A3

The coverage documented, in some detail, the adversarial information-control techniques employed whereby legal norms and precedents were used to deny access to company records, reports, memoranda, legal notes, etc. and the managerial information-control techniques employed whereby incriminating evidence and documents were withheld and government agencies dissuaded from obtaining access to them (McMullan, 1992: 92). Mr. Parry and Mr. Phillips certainly took their share of knocks in the press. Criminal charges were a lightning rod for criticism of a sort. Yet much of the coverage dwelled on the formal and the technical, not the substantive character of the case, as in the sample from November 10, 1995 (Box Twenty).

Typically, lawyers' conduct, client privileges, legal rules and proceedings, and not who actually caused the explosion, constituted the primary focus of the stories. This carried through to the fall of 1995 when four articles reported on judicial matters; a section of one, from October 25, 1995, is reprinted in Box Twenty-One.

> **Box Twenty-One: Newspaper Coverage of the Tragedy**
> Prosecutors are still trying to downplay the seriousness of the disclosure problems that halted the Westray trial, says the lawyer for the coal mine's manager. In a legal brief made public this week, Gordon Kelly asks Nova Scotia's Court of Appeal to uphold a stay on criminal charges arising from a 1992 mine explosion that killed 26 men.... During a Supreme Court trial earlier this year, Justice Robert Anderson stayed manslaughter and criminal charges against Mr. Kelly's client, Gerald Phillips and another former Westray official, Roger Parry.
> "Disclosure woes downplayed says defense in Westray Case," Halifax *Mail-Star*, October 25, 1995: A7.

The "paraphernalia of the big case" was usually the plot line of most press narratives. Typically, the legal matters were separated from the site of the production of the event and then rhetorically presented as autonomous. Characters, scenes, actions, and events were arranged to exhibit a rather narrow, narrative plot function, the effect of which was to balance law against order (Murdoch, 1982).

We do not say, however, that the media did not expose irregularities or question the integrity of the criminal justice system. Dean Jobb, a journalist for the Halifax *Chronicle-Herald* and *Mail-Star,* and Stevie Cameron, in her book *On the Take* (1995), emphasized the connections between greed, politics, the absence of law, and the Westray mining explosion. They reported on the event and the aftermath in critical and systemic terms. Clearly coverage was not *ipso facto* individualistic, homogeneous, or romantic. But their method of reconstructing events was in the minority. For the most part, the narrative iconography of press accounts signified remarkably conventional images and interpretations. They reaffirmed the deviant actors as clever, misguided, or mistaken and discussed the legal system in a language of sensible and familiar calculation. Meanwhile, if we turn to examine the coverage of the long-awaited public inquiry, we learn that it was to be a "fact-finding mission" … not a trial. "The ultimate goal of this inquiry is not to name names or punish people or to focus blame on an individual. It is to resolve what happened."[9]

The public inquiry, it must be remembered, was from its inception also entangled in a web of constitutional and *Charter* challenges. On September 30, 1992, Chief Justice Glube of the Nova Scotia Supreme Court's trial division temporarily ordered the Inquiry to hold off public hearings; and on November 13, 1992, she struck down the Inquiry as beyond the scope of the Nova Scotia government's powers. The Steelworkers Union appealed the decision and, on January 19, 1993, the Nova Scotia Supreme Court's appeal division overturned the Glube decision and reinstated the public inquiry. But the Supreme Court imposed a ban on public hearings until all other trials arising from the explosion were completed. The ban lasted for almost three years as police, prosecutors, defence lawyers, and judges wrangled tirelessly with criminal charges, pre-trial motions, motions to stay proceedings, and financial considerations. Finally, the Supreme Court of Canada lifted the ban in May 1995 because the accused chose trial by judge alone, making a decision regarding their right to a fair trial moot (Tucker, 1995). The Inquiry was back on track. Here is how one reporter characterized its promise and its problems.

**Box Twenty-Two: Newspaper Coverage of the Tragedy**

It's the last chance to uncover the whole truth about the Westray disaster. The months ahead should provide the definite word on the causes of one of the worst tragedies in recent Canadian history. Evidence presented at the inquiry should answer questions hanging over the Westray disaster, once and for all.… Some key players are boycotting the hearings, and others may be beyond the inquiry's grasp.… The explosion set off a political storm.

> Premier Donald Cameron and his Tory government were attacked for promoting Westray. In Ottawa, Brian Mulroney's government scrambled to justify risking $80 million in taxpayers' money on the project.... Mine Inspectors at Nova Scotia's Department of Labour were censured for turning a blind eye to dangerous conditions. Miners complained of working in illegally high levels of methane and coal dust-explosive substances that fueled the explosion. Safety took a back seat as the eight-month-old mine struggled to produce coal.... John Merrick admits grappling with the estimated 750,000 pages of material collected from the company and government departments has not been easy.... The result is some 70 volumes of evidence, many the size of a thick phone book.
>
> "Will We Know the Truth," Halifax *Mail-Star*, November 4, 1995: B1–2

Interestingly, the story acknowledges the complicated history of Westray and its aftermath. It insinuates that much more needs to be known and accounted for by the Inquiry. The story holds out the hope that the Inquiry will provide the "whole truth," the "definite word on the causes," while simultaneously noting that key players will boycott the hearings and others will escape testifying. But despite the bringing of criminal charges against the company and its managers, and despite the impressive catalogue of moral wrong-doing and harm, this report, like most others, excludes the language of criminal behaviour from its typification of the public event. While Westray may be legal news, it is not a law and order narrative. The incursion of criminal images into the reporters' visions of Westray was relatively limited and peripheral. The explosion, while encircled in a thicket of complaints about illegality, was still basically a tragic accident waiting for a cause to happen. Consider the following excerpts from November 1995.

> **Box Twenty-Three: Newspaper Coverage of the Tragedy**
>
> Methane and coal dust—a deadly combination that fueled the Westray explosion 3 years ago—dominated testimony Tuesday at the provincial inquiry into the tragedy. Tom Smales of Victoria, a retired mining engineer retained by the inquiry as a consultant, told of what could have gone wrong ... methane and coal dust have to be considered.... Mr.

Smales said numerous cavities in the mine's roof—left after earth had fallen—could have trapped higher concentrations of methane.... Methane is lighter than air and explosive in concentrations between five and fifteen percent.... The mining expert believed Westray had such equipment to circulate methane.... Ignited methane produces a bluish flame....
"Explosion Wrecked Mine in 20 Seconds—Expert," Halifax *Mail-Star*, November 8, 1995: A3

The two stage Westray explosion that killed 26 miners could have been over in just 20 seconds, suggests evidence presented Thursday at the provincial inquiry. The ignition of methane in the Southwest Two area gave some workers 10 or more seconds to react, said Reg Brookes, a mine explosion expert from England.... Westray was the 11th mine explosion investigated by Mr. Brookes, who said he has probed more of the blasts than anyone else in the world. He went underground about a month after the blast and based his opinions on that visit, documents and other evidence.
"Explosion wrecked mine in 20 seconds—expert" Halifax *Mail-Star*, November 24, 1995: A8

In this coverage, the focus is on reporting Westray as a "techno-tragedy." The emphasis is back to natural explanations. The "science" or "expertise" of Westray is reported on in such a way so as to make invisible the socially constituted and mediated features of the physical world. The news narratives imply that the physical world caused the disaster independent of the social world. There was little mention of human negligence, recklessness, or willful wrong-doing, and when these matters were raised, they were usually contained within a discourse of personal decision-making and conduct.

Like the public inquiry about which they wrote, those providing the news coverage seldom considered inequality and conflict between workers and employers to be causally relevant. Journalists rarely raised questions about the culture of risk-taking that pervaded mining at Westray and led to the collusion of management and workers in the violation of health and safety rules. They did not inquire into the public inquiry proper. Who are the commissioners? What values and assumptions do they hold and how similar are they to those held by corporate and government officials? To what degree will pragmatic politics promote self-censorship in the hope of pleasing the government of the day with "acceptable recommendations"? How just can this process be to the dead miners and to their living relatives and friends? At bottom, the news coverage vastly overplayed the themes of natural disaster, human tragedy, and family suffering and grossly underplayed power and politics in the making and the management of the explosion. As another analyst notes, part of what constitutes media representations as "political" is precisely the "denial of the social" in the circulation and consumption of symbols and images (Bourdieu, 1980). In turn, this refusal to see the social creates the invisibility of what stands directly in front of us.

## IDEOLOGY AND THE PRESS' DISAVOWAL OF CORPORATE CRIME

We have argued that the news coverage of Westray reveals a composite ideology with definite, quite predictable formulations: a discourse of disaster, a typification of "techno-tragedy," an imagery of individualization, a disavowal of social organizational causality, and a denial of the event as crime news. Of course, we recognize that this news coverage did not apply equally across time and space, and we do not contend that all news reporting was the same. Nevertheless, we do say that there was a limited number of underlying axioms or propositions which "framed" most reporting of Westray and which constituted the news in terms of similarities and repeated patterns rather than differences or diversity. Westray stories were circumscribed narratives which typically invited readers to share received opinions and customary reactions to dying hard in the mines. They addressed certain social anxieties in their reading audience. Like television dramas, these news stories achieved prevalence and popularity by offering courage as a kind of consolation in the face of a world which, they also asserted, was dangerous, unpredictable, and difficult to comprehend. These "tragedy" accounts permeated our lives so persistently and so intimately that the institutional and ideological sites of their production were often lost or forgotten (Kellner, 1990).

The sociologically interesting questions are: how and why did the news get constructed the way it did? Why did Westray not get constituted as crime and social control news, especially since this genre of coverage in Canada accounts for about 15 percent of all news space (Royal Commission of Newspapers, 1981). Indeed, as others have observed, newspapers and television are "particularly noted for their emphasis on sensational crime, violence, sexual aberrations, major fires, disasters, and other tales of the unexpected that titillate and entertain" (Ericson et al., 1987: 48). All the more reason, then, to expect journalists to provide criminally oriented coverage of corporate crime involving multiple deaths.

Yet this did not occur. The media missed the story about safety at the mine *before* the explosion happened. Danger brought about by production goals, market demands, corporate profits, and work shortcuts were routine. Curragh's "safety record" was known from its previous production site in the Yukon, and workers were constantly complaining of the cave-ins, the unsafe methane and dust levels, the dangerous equipment, and the uncaring mine management at the Westray site. Nor were the politics behind the establishment of the mine site a secret. Federal and provincial government investments were considerable and the "politics of speed" imposed by corporate and state actors had led to known violations of the law and to the norm of non-enforcement by safety inspectors (Glasbeek et al., 1992; Comish, 1993; McCormick, 1995). Indeed, coverage amounted to a "nihilation" strategy, which delegitimated the business nature of the explosion and then accounted for it in a language of fate, moral altruism, and consensual order (Berger et al., 1967: 159–60). Corporate capital was able to restrict access to important information about activities while simultaneously enforcing enormous control over the flow of images that they sent to the public at large (Schiller, 1986).

To start, Curragh Incorporated imposed its own "intelligence system" on the community of journalists. They hired the services of a public relations firm, Reid Management, to immediately manufacture and manage impressions surrounding the explosion. Reid faxed instructions to Curragh's operations director and spokesperson, Colin Brenner, telling him to advise the media of the following:

> This is a terrible human tragedy that could not be foreseen. The company has done everything physically and humanly possible to guard against dangerous conditions.... There have been no dangerous or suspicious conditions or methane gas readings; dust kept under strict control. There were no warnings of any kind. Safety always the first consideration. Dangers acknowledged daily.... Mines designed for safety and emergencies.... Procedures carefully monitored.... The families, rescue teams and other employees have demonstrated extraordinary courage.... The company will encourage a comprehensive examination of the causes of the accident to ensure against similar tragedies in the future. (Cameron et al., 1994: 56)

Reid Management manipulated the early image-making politics surrounding Westray. They controlled the information sources and flows and circulated the view that the explosion was an exceptional and random event. The belief advanced was that the corporation was a fair, just, and concerned moral actor and that employees were brave victims of a natural disaster. Information was distributed to the press on a timely and strategic basis so as to proactively engender publicity that created overall confidence in corporate behaviour. Most obviously, Curragh "tied in" reporters to their perspective by doing their jobs for them: providing good materials, photographs, press conferences, interview exclusives, and so on (White, 1991). They converted the reporters' lack of time, material resources, and organizational needs into a source tactic and created a "good-news story" in the context of a "bad-news crisis."

Not only did Curragh hire information experts and set out storylines, they also limited who could access information. Aside from authorizing designated spokespersons to deal with the press, they managed and monitored the territorial site for the production of the news. The media were placed in the local community centre, and the families of the trapped miners were installed across the street in the local firehall. Journalists were denied entry to the company offices and to the mine site, and employees and their families were instructed to stay away from the press, because "the media lied" (Jobb, 1994: 59). Curragh officials, in turn, informed the press that waiting and worried families did not want to speak to them (Cameron et al. 1994: 58). Finally, the police were asked to patrol the street that separated the media from the miners and their families. On the outside of the information barricade, the press waited and reacted to the information flow and to the deadlines set up by Curragh. They "picked up" on the packaged materials, rarely following up or obtaining other reactions to corporate news sources. They were encouraged to see newsworthiness in sensational terms, to frame Westray as a "human interest story," but not to question the role of private capital nor to develop a crime angle on the explosion. News, it seems, was "primarily a communication between journalists and their preferred corporate sources, with the remainder of the public left in the position of spectator" (Ericson et al., 1989: 260). Or as one miner put it:

> I have never seen so much snow in May. The media was snowed and so was everyone else. The company controlled every bit of information given out to the public and the families. The company knew for hours what was going on underground before they decided to send someone over to the firehall to let the families know. Westray did an excellent job of turning everyone against the media. (Comish, 1993: 48)

Yet more than information control was at play in the news coverage. After all, the ideology of tragedy was continuous through most reporting periods. The media stayed with the emotional and the tragic because it also made good theatre that was popular, commercial, and easy to stage and because this type of storyline fit well with the organizational beliefs and practices of news workers (Chibnall, 1977: 31–33; Fishman, 1980; Clarke, 1981; Rock, 1973).

One of the historic obligations of the press is to entertain in order to increase audience markets and expand revenues from advertising (Young, 1981; Sumner, 1982; Graber, 1980). Commentators on Westray have noted that the explosion was an audience maximizer. In the first six days of reporting, more than 100 stories were published by the *Chronicle-Herald* alone and at its peak about 200 journalists were reporting to local, national, and international audiences (Jobb, 1994: 52):

> The community centre had been transformed into a jumble of electrical cables snaking their way to cameras and microphones, monitors and tape decks ... the Westray explosion was the lead item on radio newscasts across the country; CBC Newsworld and local television stations were installing satellite dishes... so they could go live with updates.... Reporters for newspapers with Sunday editions were already tapping stories into portable computers. The American networks, including CNN in Atlanta, were beaming the story to the world.

Furthermore, the popular aspects of Westray news were very much in concert with the activities of corporate sources who controlled the flow of knowledge through carefully staged news displays and briefings. These settings allowed Curragh to circulate their perspective through ritual and rhetoric. They wrote the scripts, provided the stage, and trained their actors for a public-culture drama, while journalists were left to write about the performance. News of Westray functioned as a morality play, a conflict between good people and evil forces. Like other disaster coverage, it engaged the audience by being sensational and titillating, but also by being reassuring insofar as the natural world was condemned as fickle and fatalistic and the conflict resolved by appeals to moral courage and conviction (Walters et al., 1989: 23).

Finally, from the viewpoint of writing and editing the news, Westray was a reflection of the dynamics of the social organization of reporting proper. It accorded with the preferred focus of the news as an important departure from the normal course of conduct (Chibnall, 1977: 115–16; Fishman, 1980: 135). Westray was replete with narratives about the activities, procedures, and controls that corporate and government bureaucracies were supposed to effect, but especially about the personalization of events: the recollections of the victims' families and friends; the impact on community life; and the sometimes benevolent, as well as blameworthy, behaviour of authoritative officials. These stories were simple to process and to move quickly into news copy. Standard leads about family suffering, natural disasters, and mining experts, for example, were easily uncovered and written up. Deadlines were conveniently set and met, and stories were routinely followed up over time, making it seem as if reporters were systematic, objective, and fair-minded (Lester, 1980; Walters et al., 1989: 173; Sumner, 1979; Clarke, 1981). Indeed, the frequent use of single, credible official sources, and the deployment of a "two sides to a problem with a point/counterpoint format," enabled reporters to construct an image of themselves as concerned public engineers cleansing and restoring civic life while simultaneously speaking to, and on behalf of, a general public interest. The legitimacy of the media, like that of the law, is based on a disavowal of the partial and the particular and on fostering the belief that reporters are neutral arbiters of difference and disaster (Hartley, 1982: 55).

If corporate information and image-making strategies, entertainment value and theatricality, and the organization of news writing and news work conspired to set the tone and character of Westray coverage, it must be remembered that this coverage took place within the context of a dominant ideology. We do not live in a society which simply grafts news on to it; rather, the media prescribes a set of central cultural practices. News reporting is carried on by companies who "must adapt to their environment or die" (Garnham, 1973; Williams, 1974a; Barak, 1994). The external context includes the world of economic ownership, and politics in the public sphere on the one hand, and the world of readership on the other hand.

In the context of Westray, the cry for jobs has much appeal to local residents. In Nova Scotia, the exploration of coal has been a prevalent and historic avenue of economic development for over a century. From the very beginning the state has played a directly supportive role for private capital (Casey, 1992: 22–36; Goff et al., 1980; Francis, 1986; McMullan, 1992; Snider, 1993; Gordon et al., 1991). To attract Curragh, the state guaranteed loans, subsidized operations, provided markets, and acted as a general economic catalyst. Political capital and corporate capital were tied together. Over $100 million of taxpayers' money was invested in the mine site. Not surprisingly, the local provincial state went to great lengths to cast the Westray mine scheme in a positive light. Reporters seem to have shared the beliefs of their political elite, rarely reporting critically about the overall mining project or its political dimensions before the explosion; and they seem to have had little desire to examine corporate misconduct and political malfeasance after the explosion.

The press "bought into" a technicist belief that modern science and engineering could overcome any safety problems and that, in any event, workers at Westray voluntarily assumed risks on the job. Their "authorized knowers" were businesspeople, mine experts, managers, and government officials, not workers or critics (Hatty, 1991: 171–91; McManus, 1992; Jobb, 1994). Furthermore, the media got tired of complaint stories about Westray (Starr, 1992). They did not think that Bernie Boudreau (a Liberal MLA and an outspoken critic of Westray) had any credibility. The press would "roll their eyes when Boudreau got up on his favourite sawhorse [i.e., safety at the minesite] again." After the explosion, journalists were reluctant to pick up the story they had previously minimized as unimportant. The die was cast to look away from the political–economic context and to focus instead on unforeseen physical risks rather than preventable human wrong-doings. From a press perspective, there was a symbiotic relationship between governments, corporate capital, and reporters and their public. Curragh was not only "good at deception" (Comish, 1993: 48), the public wanted to believe the political and business claims that Westray was a good idea, and the local press followed suit because they reflected and articulated "the mental state of the province" (Starr, 1992: 12). It was as if there was an underlying complicity in the news coverage, an "unthought element" which could not or would not admit the criminality of the powerful, and a "thought element" which operated to confirm existing frames of propriety and to maintain conventional sensibilities (Bourdieu, 1977: 169).

In fairness to the press, coverage in the fall of 1992 did investigate and evaluate the role of corporate capital and government in the explosion. However, the reporting lacked the moral certainty and the obvious social disapproval of major conventional criminal-law enforcement stories. Some reporters struggled to comprehend the administrative law-compliance system and to place it in a wider framework. But there was no "quick fix" of crime, capture, and punishment, as officially provided by cases of street crime, which could then be galvanized into news production. Instead, newsworthiness was constructed out of moral ambivalence, private contexts, invisible enforcement, interpersonal bargaining and in the absence of obvious victims and final and dramatic actions (Ericson et al., 1989: 284–85; McMullan, 1992; Snider, 1993). There was no formal, easily accessible authoritative context in which to produce news stories routinely and safely. The organizational complexity and secrecy surrounding private and state decisions made it more difficult for reporters to visualize deviance in collective terms, and it allowed the reckless and harmful decisions of executives, bureaucrats, and politicians to be reported at a distance from the actual deadly event. Writing about the "corporate conscience" is hard because the boundary between legal and illegal is deliberately made to blur and shift (Croall, 1992). Instead, reporters found it more convenient to identify negligent individuals and to construct the "bad apple in the barrel" discourse. Much like the way corporate executives account for their own deviance, journalists neutralized the responsibility, harm, and consequences of corporate harm by reporting about Curragh and Westray in a language of ethical numbness. Westray was an accident. There was no criminal intent. The explosion was the risk of doing business (Box, 1983: 54–55; Clinard et al., 1980: 69–73; Reasons et al., 1981; Coleman, 1989: 211–17; Hills, 1988: 90–198; McMullan, 1992: 67–71).

When due diligence was found to be lacking, the press, like the courts, focused on those actors who could not exercise "the right not to know" what was happening in their production sites or offices. Rather than reporting about the process of executive distancing and the evasion of criminal stigma at the top, the coverage became preoccupied with middle-level, designated "fall guys." Sadly, we read little about how and why unethical, dangerous and illegal practices seem to have been "built into" the way Curragh did business at the Westray mine site. Notwithstanding the responsibility of individuals, the press avoided the thorny but crucial question: to what degree were the multiple deaths the result of structured abdications of moral and legal authority and the direct consequence of organizational imperatives arising from within Curragh headquarters and from within the federal and provincial state systems.

Perhaps the press was reluctant to report the Westray deaths as law and order news because they identify crime rather narrowly (Graber, 1980; Sheley et al., 1981; Fishman, 1981). The media in general are relatively silent on the crimes of the powerful and the trusted (Friedrichs, 1996: 19). They do not usually visualize people as victims of crime unless the perpetrators have already been labeled as criminals by authoritative sources (Elias, 1986: 33; Hatty, 1991: 171). But the voices of the experts and official data and statistics present a misleading picture of crime. These sources overestimate the criminality of the "groups most vulnerable to sanctions [lower-class or ethnic people] and underestimate the numbers of crime and the amount of damage done by more powerful segments of the population" (Snider, 1993: 30). Reporters and jour- nalists, rather like corporate executives, seem to see their own virtue reflected in the guilt of those beneath them. They are not only confused as to corporate crime, they are misdirected as to the distribution of crime in general. "Newspa- pers protect corporate reputations by failing to provide frequent, prominent, and criminally oriented coverage of common corporate crimes" (Evans et al., 1983: 539). In the case of Westray, both mystification and misdirection pre- served the appearance of corporate respectability and helped keep invisible to others the underlying ugly reality behind the explosion. In this sense, the media were part of the story and very likely part of the "disaster" in that what and how they covered the news may have contributed to the ideological background that enabled the explosion to occur in the first place (McCormick, 1995). Indeed, they continue to contribute to the "tragic cycle of disasters" whereby explosions are followed "by public inquiries, recommendations and more disasters" (Tucker 1995: 117). In failing to imagine the Westray story as law and order news, the press not only were duped and side-tracked by "spin doctors" (Jobb, 1994: 57), they expressed an ideological position: an articula- tion of presuppositions, perspectives, and practices which "silenced" the mean- ing and significance of corporate homicide and exaggerated the merits of the powerful. In short, the bulk of news stories seemed to carry an approach to Westray and corporate crime strikingly correspondent to that of the corporate elite and their leading ideologues.

## CHAPTER TEN

# UNSETTLED ACCOUNTS AFTER WESTRAY[1]

*Susan Dodd*

> Mother: I talked to an old miner from Westville and he had scars. He put his arms around me. He said: "They murdered your son." And that stuck with me. That's exactly what they did.

## INTRODUCTION

In February 1997, almost five years after the deaths of twenty-six workers in the Westray mine, I interviewed members of the men's families.[2] This was an unsettled time for family members. They anxiously anticipated the release of the report of Nova Scotia's public inquiry into the causes of the explosion and deaths. The criminal trials of Mine Managers Roger Parry and Gerald Phillips for negligence and manslaughter were in procedural limbo. And flamboyant Westray CEO, Clifford Frame, had just hit the media again; claiming that the explosion was a "simple accident" and hoping, to get on with his life as a mining entrepreneur.

Family members talked about their loss with a horror that was remarkably raw given that five years had passed since their men's deaths.[3] They were preoccupied, even obsessed, with their demand for accountability and their growing fear that they were betrayed in this demand. Their fear and preoccupation were so infectious that thinking about what has happened to these families since the Westray explosion became, for me, a disturbing exercise in thinking about fundamental aspects of our economic, political, and legal systems.[4]

In this chapter I present family members' reflections and begin a sociological analysis of the unsettled nature of the Westray story. In the first section, I introduce the social context of these February 1997 interviews, and, in the second section, I present family members' reflections on Westray's aftermath as a journey into a critical perspective. As family members became increasingly concerned that their demand for accountability was being betrayed, they came to rethink their relationships with our legal, economic, and political systems. This critique is articulated from four main, interrelated claims: first, family members demand the retrieval of the eleven remaining bodies from the mine. This is a claim of the sacredness of the body and of the families' fundamental right to bury their dead. Second, family members still seek an acceptable causal explanation of the deaths: how did this happen? This is a claim for truth against strategic or interested versions of events. A trustworthy causal explanation should make the third claim possible: that responsible people be identified and punished and that appropriate legal changes be made to improve workplace safety, to protect workers who "blow the whistle" on unsafe workplaces, and to prosecute those who profit from flaunting safety regulations. Finally, family members reflect on the resistance they have met in pursuing these claims in the five years since the explosion, and they extend their critique from individuals to economic, political, and legal systems.[5]

In an appendix entitled "Why the Family Members' Version? Accounting Problems as Resistance to Rationalization," I will speculate about the significance of the unsettled character of social accounts even after the report of the Westray Inquiry. Though aspects of the families' demand for accountability have been met through the public inquiry and insurance payments, no full social settlement has been reached. Instead, family members have been subjected to processes of rationalization, which reduced their demands to monetary terms and deferred the most fundamental aspects of their demands indefinitely. Such "settlements" are typical and Westray's aftermath is structurally very similar to both *Ocean Ranger* and Bhopal gas leak aftermaths (Dodd, 1995). Aspects of the family members' demand for accountability that are not accommodated by the public inquiry or legal avenues or insurance settlements have been ostracized from official recognition and memory. They do not disappear, though, and will haunt public discourse so long as family members have voices to speak and members of the public have ears to hear.

## ONE: ACCOUNTING FOR WESTRAY

Since the Westray explosion family members have fought to protect the memory of their men. They want to ensure that their men are remembered as good men who were killed by greed and government inattention. In this, family members run up against a very powerful view called possessive individualism, a line of thinking that sees human beings as free from dependence on the wills of others except in those relations entered voluntarily (i.e., contracts) and as "proprietors of [their] own persons and capacities, for which [they] owe nothing to society" (MacPherson, 1962). Family members represent a collective, embodied understanding that challenges the interpretation of economic risk as something that is shouldered by entrepreneurs who extend the benefits of their initiatives to workers through fair labour contracts.

> Wife: "Somebody's got to take responsibility for it. But who? Who?"

Donald Cameron exemplifies the possessive individualist perspective, particularly in his testimony at the Westray public inquiry. Cameron was Nova Scotia's minister of industry during the mine project's development, as well as the elected provincial representative for many of the men who were killed in the mine. Shortly after the Westray deaths, Cameron, who was by then premier of Nova Scotia, appointed Justice Peter Richard to inquire into the causes of the Westray explosion. Testifying at the Inquiry, Cameron did his best to cast the dead men in the role of imprudent workers: "The bottom line is that that mine blew up on that morning because of what was going on in there at that time" (Testimony at the Inquiry, May 28, 1996: 14432). In this version, Westray workers were rational actors who took bad "risks" in exchange for money: they gambled for wages with their lives … and they lost. In this line of thinking, the dead are seen to have consented to unsafe work conditions and thus contributed as equal partners in perpetuating Westray's deadly work conditions. By authoritatively casting the dead men in the role of imprudent workers, they might be remembered as responsible for their own deaths and the loss of government money that had been poured into Westray. "Imprudent workers," so the story goes, lack appropriate regard for their own safety, the property of others, and the welfare of their co-workers. This attribution of responsibility for workplace accidents came about when customary master-servant relations were transformed into more "contractual" forms (Tucker, 1990: 45).

At the time of these interviews, the unsettled nature of public memory left open the possibility that Cameron's interpretation of the causes of the explosion would triumph and that Canadians would remember the Westray deaths as simply the consequence of the dead men's own imprudence. Disgusted by Cameron's line of argument, family members and miners walked out of the Inquiry during his testimony. Not only had Cameron offended traditions of ministerial responsibility by not confessing his government's failure to regulate workplace safety, he had tried to protect his own reputation at the expense of the dead. Months later, this offence remained fresh in the minds of family members, and they were determined to counter Cameron's individualist line.

> Mother: And Donald Cameron sat down there and said it was all their own fault.
> Brother: 26 guys committed suicide.
> Interviewer: If they can prove to you that someone, and they named one of the 26, had been tampering with the methanometers, what would that mean to you?
> Sister-in-law: Every one of them were scared. None of them were miners. They were just hired there 'cause they didn't know anything about it. These

> guys were just herded like sheep....
>
> Brother: They changed them from shift to shift regularly so that they wouldn't get to know each other, and they couldn't form a group and do something.
>
> Father: I used to work in a pit, and there was always old people and young people there, and the old hands that had been there, they would always watch the young constantly, that they didn't do anything that they shouldn't do, and if they did something, they told them and see there was nobody in that mine that ever told any of these young fellas—like my son was never in a mine in his life before, and there was nobody that ever told him what to do.
>
> He was telling me about it, and of course he didn't know anything about mining to begin with so he couldn't explain, he couldn't answer my questions really. But I'd have never left him work there if I'd known the conditions and the fact.... I didn't *believe* that in 1990, that anything would be allowed to be like that. In the mine I worked, if that place blew up, it would be a real accident. It would have to be an accident, because everybody in there knew what to do, and they wouldn't allow anything to go wrong.

Here family members are drawing on terms that reach back through the common history of those who *spend* their lives working *for* others. This exchange contains tensions, long present in working-class histories, between concepts of workers as "sheep"—passive victims sacrificed to capital by managerial brutality—and workers as craftspeople—bearers of experiential knowledge that is either not held by bosses or ignored by them (Thompson, 1963). In coal mining such know-how seems to cluster around safety practices: gas and dust levels, wall and roof conditions, and so on (Comish, 1993). In the excerpt above, the deaths are explained as the result of communication failures; hiring practices interrupted the transmission of safety know-how from one generation to the next. Shuffled shifts rendered solidarity less likely. And the workers at Westray were tragically unable to get their descriptions of work conditions to register as unacceptable risks in the minds of those above ground.

> Brother: Nobody knew that this stuff was going on and nobody knew what to think if they knew.

Raising such communications issues draws us away from individualist accounts towards more systemic considerations, locating the causes of the Westray deaths deep in our social, economic, and political practices rather than in flawed contracts between free and equal parties. Such systemic considerations threaten to open widening circles of guilt and responsibility and thus to multiply and broaden avenues for attributing blame. The larger the number of actors sharing responsibility, the more difficult it is to determine who, precisely, needs to be held accountable. Guilt could spiral out to include everyone who, for instance, depends on the news media for information. Since many of us, like the father in the excerpt above, didn't believe that in the 1990s a workplace as terrible as Westray could exist just down the road, we, as fellow citizens, could be somehow guilty because we failed to demand news media that could hear the Westray miners' complaints and convey them effectively in public debate. The men who did try to blow the whistle on the conditions in the Westray mine were unheard by the regulatory systems that were in place, ostensibly to protect them. Perhaps Nova Scotians believed in the efficacy of the regulatory system so unreflectively that we could not entertain the truth even on those rare occasions that it was presented to us.[6] If Westray was in some sense a *systemic* failure, is there any scope for identifying individual culprits? And, perhaps more importantly, is there any good reason to try to hold individuals accountable as well as to pursue systemic change?

Family members certainly think so. They stand their ground against interminable diffusions of accountability, drawing an effective distinction between actors who failed to stop the explosion for complex social reasons (the men, their co-workers, the family members themselves, the news media) and those they deem actively culpable and hold to have been integral in the positive causal chain that led to the deaths (owners, mines inspectors, shareholders, politicians, middle-management).

> Interviewer: What would you like to see come out of [the ruling on the trials]?
> Brother: Criminal charges. Put them back to trial.
> Sister-in-law: Back to trial and convicted of course.
> Interviewer: What kind of sentence?
> Brother: Guillotine! [laughs]
> Sister-in-law: I don't know, I can't be that harsh about it, but....
> Mother: *I can!*
> Father: They got to do some time. They got to do some time.
> Mother: They murdered 26 people.
> Father: Sure they did.

The emphasis here on criminal convictions is a demand that the men's deaths be recognized as a crime against Canadian society and not simply a stroke of misfortune suffered by the families of imprudent risk-takers. One of the shocks of Shaun Comish's "miner's story" is delivered through his descriptions of the daily denigration of workers by Westray management—and by the Yorkshire-born foreman Roger Parry in particular (1993: 54):

> The morale at Westray was low at the best of times, mainly because of the way we were treated by management. It is pretty pathetic when the mine superintendent, the second highest man at the mine site, grabs himself by the crotch and starts yelling at you to suck his cock and calling you a brain-dead fucker. This was his usual way of getting his point across to you.

Another shock, this time from the Inquiry testimony of miners, is the extent to which workers broke with the safety practices of mining culture. Since the explosion, miners have admitted that they smoked in the mine and knew that supervisors tampered with equipment that had been installed to keep explosive gas at "acceptable" levels. They also reported that they worked in sections of the mine that they felt had unstable roofs and walls. At the same time, as family members are quick to point out, Curragh Resources used tractors that weren't modified for coal mine use; installed safety equipment strategically so it wouldn't read gas levels in the most likely danger spots; used conventional welding equipment in the mine; reproached managers for shutting down production when safety was in question; and failed in what is perhaps the most basic safety practice in coal mines, spreading limestone dust to keep coal dust from becoming airborne, and thus explosive.

> Wife: "They blame the guys for having a smoke down there when there were welders using a six-inch flame!"

Even without questions of worker participation in the re/production of an unsafe workplace, we can't help but ask, why did they keep going back when they waded daily through dangerous levels of coal dust? This raises systemic questions, not only about social pressures to "keep a job" and "pay the bills" but also about perceptions and definitions of "acceptable" risks.

> Wife: You wonder why they did it? Why did they keep going under? Like I said it was the job. If they lost their job then they had nothing.

An individualist account like Donald Cameron's considers the danger of the workplace to be a trade-off for a "good paying job" in times of low employment. In this view, "risk" is simply a worker's private concern, and a "prudent" worker must evaluate workplace danger relative to the hazards of unemployment. Risk management, in this view is the moral responsibilty of the worker rather than a political and social issue (O'Malley, 1996: 197).

Comish's account of the daily intimidation of Westray workers by Curragh's agents suggests power-based considerations of "cause" or, at least, of how the deadly chain of events was left uninterrupted by worker intervention. Altering workplace conditions, either through union activism or more strenuous attempts to bring Westray work conditions to public light, are not frequently considered by families as ways in which the deaths might have been prevented. Quitting or actively "getting fired" are the options most recalled, though the families are positive about trade unionism and some mention that the Westray miners failed to organize "in time." Most often, the men are described as constrained by the social brutality of mine management and disoriented by lack of adequate information about the risks associated with the substandard safety practices at Westray. Family members point also to unemployment levels in the region and often repeat stories of Curragh officials "managing" safety concerns by pulling workers into an office, gesturing at a stack of resumes, and forcing the worker to acknowledge that if he quit, hundreds were waiting to take his place.

> Wife: "They *were* scared of them. I know they're grown men ... but work is scarce."

Cameron's reduction of the men's work and death in the unsafe mine to a fairly entered contract, and their assumptions of the risks at Westray as simply voluntary, is perceived by families as a gravely injurious lie. Possessive individualist calculations can explain neither the men's daily return to the deadly mine nor the corporate persons' and governments' systemic power over the men and their families. Such calculative thinking denies a fine web of social relations, both in the positive sense of affirming family relations and collective productive activity and in the negative sense of systemic coercion, at home and at work. In the families' memories, their men are owned by past and future generations, particularly by their mothers and their children (with their wives as executors). For instance, one mother refers to her lost son with a possessive pronoun: i.e., "*my* Joey." Family members embody the claim that the men's lives weren't simply their own to gamble away.

> Wife: And if you could turn the clock back, I always said, *I wish*, but there's always *but ... if only ... if I had of...* You see, he wanted me to call in sick for him that night, and I picked the phone up and I dialed half the number, then he sighed and said, "Never mind, I may as well go in, it's my last

> shift anyway." And I said, "Well if you don't want
> to go in, don't."

Family members review their own roles in the material and social demands that contributed to their man's risking the Westray pit shift after shift. They tell "I wish" stories, revisiting conversations about risk at the mine and regretting not having been clearer about their man's "freedom" to quit if things were unsafe. Wives assert that they wouldn't have minded if they lost the house, parents wouldn't have minded an unemployed man dependent, once again, to some extent on them.

Family members are clear also that they couldn't release their man from familial–social expectations with a word or two as one might, in theory, dissolve a formal consensual contract.

> Wife: He didn't tell me too much. I know he told
> my father quite a bit.
> Interviewer: Why?
> Wife: Because he knew I worried enough. [mimicking father] "You'd better get that man from underground." I tried to talk him into quitting, but he kept saying, "I can't, how can I afford to quit? I've got a wife and two kids...." He was looking for something else.

A crucial aspect of the aftermath of death-by-industry is the implication of family members in monetary exchanges as "compensation" for the death of their man. Workers' compensation "replacement of lost earnings," private insurance payments, tort or government-guilt settlements ... all are necessary to the families' survival after the loss of their man. More than this, however, the reception of money in exchange for their man's life diminishes the family members' public moral authority. The money is rightfully theirs and much needed indeed, but it is seen to work against the fullness of family members' demand for accountability.

> Brother: There was one politician's sister that we sat with one day and off to the side she said, "How much do you fellas want?" We said, "We don't want no money." And she asked twice again before that session ended: "How much do you fellas want?"

Even after monetary exchanges, however, a supplement remains. When appearing in public as the "Westray Families," family members bring all the symbolic and factual collectivism that inheres in the family to belie possessive individualist fictions. Their presence disrupts a settling of the Westray account in possessive individualist terms. In other words, Westray family members disrupt the (re)assertion of an evaluation of their men's lives in economic terms. The impropriety of financial "compensation" for death-by-industry is thrown into relief by the family members' diligent pursuit of accountability, and thus the exchange of human time for money in the day-to-day employment contract is exposed as problematic. Rationalization processes transform the loss of life into an account that can be settled with monetary payments: without retribution, without holding particular individuals responsible, and without substantive systemic reform. Financial settlements, which cannot (and I think should not) be refused, are powerful tools of rationalization. Family members recognize the receipt of money as a threat to their overall struggle to keep their full demand for accountability accessible to public debate. They pursue financial settlements only when they come to see that taking money from governments and corporations may be the only form of accountability they can achieve. But monetary payments are not the only rationalization tools at work here.

For rationalization to be complete, grief over the loss of the men must be pressed back into the familial home, its reality as a public loss dismantled: privatized, sentimentalized, commodified. At least two other types of rationalizing accounts conspire with possessive individualism towards such a reduction of the family members' demand for accountability. A bureaucratic "impotent individual" account closes around government and business functionaries who claim, Eichmann style,[7] that they were just following the instructions of rightful authority holders (even when this meant they were actively *not* doing their jobs). Meanwhile, a therapeutic account works on the family members themselves, casting them in the role of "unhealthy grievers" of whom it is increasingly acceptable to wonder "why don't they just get on with their lives?" Of course, "healthy" here means to forget the premature, preventable deaths of their men; accepting the impotency of bureaucrats means to "get over" the utter inability of our society's justice system to trace responsibility through corporate veils and bureaucratic hierarchies to power-holders.

## TWO: THINGS THAT WE NEVER DREAMED

At this point, I want to describe the development of the family members' critical perspective. The confusion caused by the blast gave way to the family members' realization that they were in an antagonistic relationship with Curragh and its agents. For many, this realization occurred when family members came to believe that Curragh's agents were lying about the possibility of finding survivors. Such lies were terrible because they provided false hope and because they prolonged the torture of radical confusion of fundamental distinctions: the men may be living, or they may be dead. Not knowing which is excruciating, even maddening. The discovery that someone has manipulated this fundamental knowledge is devastating, particularly as it reveals the willingness of Curragh's agents to utterly abandon truth in the interest of the corporation. A widening estrangement of family members from economic, legal, and governmental institutions and their agents follows from this initial breach in family members' unreflective expectation of truth-telling from Curragh's agents. These institutions come to seem arbitrary and violent, and the very processes that once seemed to guarantee at least a broad cultural commitment to seek the truth come to be viewed with deep suspicion. (Some family members make this leap immediately and others take time.[8]) From this estrangement comes the family members' increasing ability to articulate their demands for accountability and corresponding criticism of the social institutions that permitted the deaths of their men. Finally, family members recognize that they must communicate with other citizens to defend their full understanding of accountability from powerful forces, which press to rationalize family members' claims by translating their demands for justice into dollar terms, their demands for legislative changes into endless deferrals, and their demands for recognition into symptoms of psychological pathology.

## From Rescue–Recovery to the Demand for Accountability: Estrangement becomes Critique

For family members, news of the explosion brings the first moments of the excruciating estrangement that marks the "rescue–recovery" period. During this time, teams of miners entered Westray in search of survivors and bodies. Mine searches must be some of the most heroic ventures of our society, as miners are transformed into draegermen and re-enter their former workplace, which is now blasted beyond recognition. In search of co-workers, they hope to find survivors, dread to find corpses (Jobb, 1994: 71; Comish, 1993).

For Curragh Resources Incorporated, Westray's corporate owner and operator, one of the first urgencies seems to have been to determine who was underground. Curragh's agents telephoned men's homes, piecing together the shift's roster; they needed to be sure which men they were looking for and which families they needed to inform about "the accident." As family members and friends learned of the explosion through phone calls from Curragh or cautious calls from relatives or friends, they experienced a horrible coincidence of confusion and clarity. Here a brother recalls how his faith in the most basic truth-telling expectation from Mine Manager Gerald Phillips was destroyed soon after the explosion. The disgust in this speaker's tone is lost in transcription; it bore the bewildered fury of realizing that even what seemed to be the most essential fact imaginable—knowing who was dead and who might yet live—was subject to strategic manipulation by Curragh's interested agents.

> Brother: I think the first indication [that it was a cover-up] was how long it took them to release the press releases to the press and to the general public.

One night the press release—Gerald did the press release—and Gerald was up at the fire hall and Gerald said, "They found the boom truck and they found a 'dozer, but they didn't find anybody," which was a good sign that they got to these safe areas. And my friend was working underground, and he said, "There's no such thing as these safe areas underground." And then I knew that they found the ones they would have found. After Gerald left, Gerald's wife was outside there and she was telling me that you gotta hold out hope that they're going to find them, everything was going to be alright. And I said, "No, they're all dead, I said." "Oh, no," she said, "They're gonna find them. They're gonna be alright." I turned around and looked at her, I said, "I was there, I was working that night. I saw the explosion and the fire that came out of that mine." And all she did was gasp and ran away from me with her head in her hands crying because then she realized that I knew the truth about what happened and this charade that they were doing to try to fool the public and the press was eventually going to blow up in their face. And it did. Curragh, Gerald, the premier of the day and the rest of them were all in bed together.

Family members recall that during the rescue–recovery period, while Curragh Resources' agents protected the corporation with public relations strategies, the families waited and waited.

The rescue–recovery period lasted from the explosion at 5:18 am on May 9, through the recovery of fifteen men's bodies, until 129 hours after the explosion when the search was called off at 1 pm on May 14. Eleven men remained in the mine (Jobb, 1994: 79). In this intensely uncertain period, hope for the rescue of survivors turned to grim commitment to recover the eleven remaining bodies. Precisely during this time, the families' critical perspective began to take articulate form. Believing now that Curragh Resources' agents, some of whom were close neighbours, even friends, would lie to protect the corporate person, family members began to define themselves as a collectivity in contradistinction from Curragh Resources. Family members began to suspect that anything said by Curragh's agents was strategically formed. For some, estrangement from social institutions is remembered to have occurred at the very moment of the news of the explosion.

Father: See the Company went down underground and they made the first people who went down [the rescue team] sit and not go anywhere. They made them stay there. They went in for how many hours? How many hours were they in? It was a long time. Obviously, the dead guys were laying around. They must have been in looking for things—what they were going to cover up.

Brother: Sure, yeah.

Father: They said, "Oh, we're waiting on word to see if anyone's alive. We're waiting on word." That was all Hollywood....

Interviewer: So they were telling you that they thought they were safe?

Brother: Yeah, they were there for two days.

Brother: They were letting on there might be hope yet.

Mother: I went down when they were tapping that morning. I seen this fella with the white hard hat, and I said, "Oh my God, get [my son] out, will ya?" And he said, "We're gonna do everything we can," And I said, "Well get him out, if you can." I went to the hall, I didn't see anyone. Then [my daughter] took me home. All the time they came in with the speeches they kept saying, "We didn't come to anyone yet."

Father: We went home and sat by the TV keeping our hopes up. The bodies were down there, and they were still saying, "We're gonna find them." I talked to that cop and he said, "There's no bodies." But there was bodies. They lied to us.

This initial moment of estrangement coincides with terrible uncertainty. Unsure if their men still lived and, if they did, in what underground trap with what injuries and which companions, family members began revisiting conversations with their men about Westray and coal mining in general. The estrangement of the rescue–recovery period casts new light on the past. Family members re-think things previously taken for granted, particularly around responsibility for risk-taking. The moral character of the dead men, their personal prudence, commitment to the care of their co-workers, and their tight familial integration become noteworthy.

Father-in-law: Just a quick thought on philosophy ... one that sticks in my mind the most, not just after the disaster, but even before, was his strapping the children in with their seatbelts: safety, safety, safety. And he was a fireman, he took the mine safety, mine search and rescue and I guess that's why we had such hope in the beginning.

> Interviewer: When did it first strike you that they were, that there was something potentially criminal going on at the mine?
> Brother: Well, when it blew up! [all laugh] Uh you know like a lot of guys before it blew you'd talk to them and you knew damn well there was things going on, like there was too much gas, like the roof wasn't really safe, like my brother got hauled off the damn thing [the bolter] few times ... and the foreman was trying to push him back in. You know like right at this time, I told [my brother], I likely blatted at him a few times, "You shouldn't be the hell over there." But where the hell are you going to make that money for their families? And [my brother] would say, "Shut your goddamn mouth." You know, I kept telling him, "You could get another job somewhere else." He was working on construction before, but things got slack and he said, "I've gotta feed my family." You knew from talking to the miners that nothing was right there, and then some of those old miners would go in for a day and they'd come out and say, "I'm not working in that hellhole," and away they'd go. And then, after it blew, everything just kind of pieced together.

The symbolic importance of the bodies, both the fifteen that were recovered from the mine and the eleven that remain below, is paramount. Some families who did recover a body spent hours waiting to identify their man after they had been informed that the bodies had been brought up. Family members recall an intensifying suspicion that the delays were related to the strategic manipulation of evidence. They also seem to have had ample time to begin sharing these suspicions.

> Father-in-law:...[our son in law's] body was one of the first recovered and, uh, me and [his brother], we decided ... and we talked with [our daughter] about this, but anyway ... uh we [crying] we almost immediately wanted a ... we decided almost immediately that we wanted a complete autopsy. My wife and I went up Sunday night,

May 10, Sunday evening, May 10...
Mother-in-law: Seven o'clock we were supposed to be up there.
Father-in-law: To recover the body....
Mother-in-law: ...to view the body....
Father-in-law: ...to identify the body and so on, and we went up and we waited and waited....
Mother-in-law: ...and waited....
Father-in-law: ...and waited....
Mother-in-law: All night long.
Father-in-law: And this was after knowing that the body had been recovered and that we were asked to identify and so on and uh this bothered.... [crying]
Interviewer: The two of you went up?
Father-in-law: We went up and waited first at the basement of St. Gregory's Church and about seven o'clock in the evening ... and....
Mother-in-law: [our daughter] at that point was in no....
Interviewer: Yeah
Father-in-law: So we ... during that time uh we spoke ... I shouldn't say we spoke, we listened.... We were involved in discussions with other people waiting, and they raised more concerns and uh anyway, it bothered me that the uhm officials, if you will, were taking this long to prepare a body before we would see it and, uh things like that uh and....
Mother-in-law: We were told that we would be able to see his body at seven o'clock in the evening. We left the fire hall at what about two in the afternoon? When we got word that ... and uh they told us to be at the basement of the church at seven o'clock in the evening. We were there at seven but we didn't see his body until, what six the next morning?
Father-in-law: About five o'clock the next morning.
Interviewer: So they kept you there? Waiting?
Father-in-law: Oh, yes....

Five years after the explosion, the sustained intensity of all family members around the importance of retrieving the eleven remaining bodies from the mine is truly astonishing, whether they recovered their man's body or not.

Mother: If [my son] hadn't come out, I'da probably been over there with a spoon or something, digging my way in. That's the way I woulda been.

The difference between families who recovered their body and those who did not has been a point of tension among Westray families. It has also been a point of great solidarity. For some families, particularly families of "the eleven" who remain in the mine, the political struggle has concentrated on the unwillingness of the provincial and federal governments to make body retrieval a priority. Concentrating on body retrieval may have provided a respite from being immediately cast into rationalizing haggling over the price of lives. Focused on the sanctity of the bodies and protected at least subjectively by this focusing, families developed their critical perspective. With some family members the demand for accountability concentrates at least as much on the obscenity of the public facades that have been constructed in Curragh's and governments' avoidance of spending the money necessary to retrieve the bodies as on the original loss of their men.

> Brother: ...they'd stopped the search for bodies, the politicians come down and they were up at the museum and some of them were over at the community college and one of the families had asked them, "Alright now what are you going to do about body retrieval?" And Old Golden Voice there turned around and said, "We're here to make money not spend money, and if you want to get your bodies back, go see your politicians." And that came right from old Benner himself and after that he was Old Golden Voice in all their media....
>
> The Silver Tongued Devil some of us called him, 'cause he'd sit there and put on the sympathetic thing and he looked real. He looked real real. But that one day he showed his true face to us and that was when we went in and asked, "What about the body retrieval?" And that was his remark, "We're here to make money not spend it. Go see your politicians."

This story was told to me in a couple of versions during these interviews; in all, the basics were the same: Curragh's Colin Benner, that handsome, empathetic face most of us remember from television, was asked by a family member what was to be done about body retrieval. In all versions, Benner's response referred to Curragh's single aim: *we're here to make money not spend it.*

The theme of the villainy of Curragh's agents surged forward whenever issues of body recovery arose.

> Brother: They were taking bodies out and the underground guy was pissing against the side of a wall talking to them about the strip mine. Having a piss there! You can't think that mankind's that bad.

During the rescue–recovery, as "Old Golden Voice" Benner was spinning the story of the "simple accident" to the tightly controlled media and family members gathered in the Plymouth fire hall, one wife asserts: "Clifford Frame went to the mayor of Stellarton on the day of or the day after the explosion to ask about getting the strip mine. He sent lobster back to Ontario, went to Truro and bought three bulls for his farm in Ontario."

The continued presence of men's bodies politicizes the mine site and makes it a sacred place well beyond it being a simple site of factual evidence. The bodies that have not been returned to the families continue to lay a claim on all of the Westray family members.

> Wife: Nobody ever noticed that mine before. That's the funny thing. But now, every time you drive through New Glasgow, there it is. Everywhere I went, I went to the mall, and what I see, I see the mine, everywhere you drove.... Just take me back to the house.... Then we'd come back from Halifax and go over the hill and there it was all lit up.... You don't notice it. You just didn't notice it all the time ... but now it just, more or less draws you to it, you just get this cold feeling, surely to God they're not going to reopen it. There's still men from the last time it blew up in 1958.

> Interviewer: In terms of the way you look at the world, the way you look at other people, do you think there's been a change in that?
> Mother: Definitely! Profound. Definitely more tolerable to people around us, and more intolerable, I guess, to the systems—how they work and don't work. You realize now that things can change in a minute and you're that little extra more tolerant and you don't let the little things bother you any more 'cause you know damn well there's things a lot more....
> Father: ... things that we never dreamed before, and now that it hit us we know it's there.
> Sister-in-law: My kids never thought they'd see their grandmother out with a picket sign.
> [Father laughs]
> Brother: That was a big shock. "There's Grammy! On the news! Picketing the mine site!"

The aftermath is an odyssey for the families, a voyage that began in estrangement and is fueled by the desire to go home ... but home can never be as it was. Through struggles over the bodies and the men's reputations, family members have traveled into realms of knowledge usually left to "experts": criminal, tort, regulatory law; mining and safety technology; policing investigation methods; forensic pathology; psychological and in some instances psychiatric treatment. Even truth has become contentious as family members have been confronted with what is for them a mind-boggling reconstruction of "truths" out of increasingly suspect "evidence."

### Accountability Resists Rationalization

From the moment of the explosion, through the rescue–recovery to the end of hope for survivors, family members moved from bewildered estrangement to a complex social critique, articulated in terms of their demand for accountability. The family members' determination to protect the integrity of their dead made them aware of their antagonistic relations with Curragh and eventually with governments and legal forums. The term "rationalization" describes how the full terms of the family members' demand for accountability are cut up and managed, rather than engaged.

> Interviewer: What is it that you want?
> Wife: First of all, my husband's body back. I hope it'll be brought back. Second of all, I want the answers. Nobody yet has told us what happened, you know, no expert has said, no government official, no mining expert, has come out publicly, or you know the company, to say what caused the explosion. The company has hidden; the provincial government is certainly doing everything to hide under every rock possible. The big word would be accountability, to make them more accessible to what's going on at Westray.

She goes on, finally, to demand change, so that "*this will never happen again.*"

This summarizes a four-term demand being made by politicized Westray families. The first term, demanding the return of the body, is a demand for recognition of the sacredness of the dead and a corresponding claim that "ownership" of each body is rightfully the family's rather than the mine owners' or the states'. The Westray aftermath is a violent denial of the embodied claims of family life; the political crime of Westray is, in part, made possible by the instrumental use of traditional separations of family (private) matters from political (public) matters to justify and perpetuate oppressive and violent economic relations. The second term is a demand for a comprehensible explanation of what happened, and this includes how this could be permitted and, more specifically, at what points and by whom this could have been prevented. This second term implies that an acceptable explanation will shed light on responsibility and thus on appropriate avenues of blame. For if we can know what happened, then we can surely know who should have intervened to prevent the deaths. The third term is a collection of the first two into an undefined demand for the accountability of individuals. And the fourth term is the extension of accountability from individual culprits to social systems: that changes must be made to ensure that this never happens again. These four aspects are tangled together in the families' reflections, so excerpts rarely illustrate one aspect without pulling others in. The families' demand for accountability, then, is a complex social critique, not simply a call for retribution nor some "primitive" lust for revenge and retribution.

At the time of these February 1997 interviews, family members were anticipating the Inquiry report with great anxiety. As a result, family members articulate their thoughts in tension with the possibility of a possessive individualist, blame-the-dead narrative from the public inquiry report. Not knowing what Richard's report might bring, family members had begun to develop a critique of the "disinterested" or "arms length" character of the Inquiry itself.

> Sister-in-law: Here in Stellarton ... that service at the stadium—the big service. Who was down? Donald Cameron, Mulroney and Hynathsyn....
> Brother: ...Clifford Frame, and they all sat together.
> Sister-in-law: And the impartial judge! Richard sat with them!
> Interviewer: When was that?
> Brother: At the time of the explosion.
> Sister-in-law: A community service, about a couple of weeks after.
> Interviewer: And Richard was the one doing the Inquiry?
> Brother: Yeah.
> Sister-in-Law: Clifford Frame and Richards and Donald Cameron and Mulroney.
> Brother: Yeah, they all sat together.
> Interviewer: Wow.
> Brother: Nice independent thing, you know?

Furthermore, family members talked about becoming suspicious of various forms of "evidence." Beyond the banality that people in trouble will lie to protect themselves and their reputations, family members expressed surprise that some people, particularly people in power, are able and willing to construct whole alternate realities. They were surprised besides that some people will not participate in such willful reconstructions of the past, that some yearn still at least to try to "tell the truth."

Interviewer: Who did you believe in terms of the [Inquiry] testimony?

All: The miners.

Sister-in-law: And some of the experts.

Interviewer: Why did you believe the miners?

Brother: No, I don't believe any of the experts. I've had a lot to do with a whole lot of experts over the last of these years, and it's whoever pays them gets the answer they want.

Father: Exactly.

Brother: If we had the expert, he told us what we wanted to hear. If it was the government, or the company, tribunal or whatever, he told them what they wanted to hear.

Father: Whoever pays....

Sister-in-law: ...But one expert volunteered to come back here at his own expense to help us with the trial, so that's why I say some of the experts are good.

Mother: The miners, because they were in the mine. They knew what was happening. They saw it. They were there.

Brother: And a lot of them said, "I complained about that! I went to Albert McLean. I went to so and so." And when Albert McLean got up there and said, "I don't know that guy, he never told me nothin'."

Father: "I didn't see him."

Brother: You got forty-nine saying, "I told him," and you got six or seven trying to say, "Oh no, they didn't." Well, who's right?

Interviewer: Were you surprised by that?

Father: Surprised?! God, yes, there must be some....

Brother: ... in the system, that can override this sort of thing, make these....

Father: ... make these guys answer the question....

Brother: ... if you don't answer and answer properly, give them 30 days. Hell, when they drag them out in 30 days time, are you ready to talk now? No? 30 more!

Father: Off he goes.

Brother: And after a while you get sick of the 30-day bit, and you'll start telling the truth.

Father: After a while when he loses his house and his car and his wife divorces him, he'll talk then. But here they just.... [shakes his head]

Family members are clear about the vulnerability of the "truth" as it is recollected under liberal law. Expertise rules, and it can be bought. They argue also that a more truthful version of events might be extracted from power-holders if only the political will was stronger.

Here family members discuss what it might mean to make Donald Cameron more accessible. The fury of this exchange is indescribable. The brothers moved around restlessly while talking, the mother spoke clearly, crying, and the father who doesn't speak here, rocked quickly in a softly squeaking chair.

> Mother: I wanted to go after Donald Cameron when they put him on there [the stand at the Inquiry]. I was going to take a taxi to Stellarton. I had the phone up, I dialed the number, and I hung up. I just wanted to go up to his face and ask him. Because he knew who [my son] was, too. That's why he never came here.[9]... He knew he was guilty or he would have come and he woulda said he was sorry....
>
> Brother A: Mom, if you knew the dirty deals that were going on, you'd puke. I never even thought about law ... and now I'm really seeing how our justice system works. It's terrible, frustrating; it'll make you pull your hair out. You want to kill somebody. Every other day I'm freaking. I know it's just freaking. I wouldn't trust myself. If nothing is done ... one of them dies in the parking lot, I'm ... that's the way I feel about it. Every little battle. The bullshit. The red tape bullshit.
>
> Mother: All these papers, documents ... my God, they got papers! There's millions of papers. They have enough evidence without even thinking.... Stupid paperwork.
>
> Brother A: You know, Mom, ten days of shredding, you can get rid of a lot of loose ends. They were covering their tracks, they knew they were doing wrong....[10]
>
> Brother B: Roger Parry, Gerald Phillips, and Donald Cameron was all on the phone, telling these fellas down here 'cause they weren't at the mine when it blowed. Donald Cameron and them was shredding evidence, anything with their name on it, they were getting rid of it. They're coming down. If the law don't do it, they're coming down. Some way. There's all kinds of ways.
>
> Brother A: You can see how revolutions start. They start screwing so many different people. We're pulling together with other people. Maybe you get things done. You got support.
>
> Mother: How can they let this go? Twenty-six miners. And they flooded that ... without ever getting [the last of] the remains up. And they're in that bloody old mine down there. I think that's a very sad situation.

What is at stake here for this family is the effacement of their particular man, and their particular loss, behind what they see as Cameron's self-serving testimony. While family members' social critiques may have been articulated during conflicts over the bodies, their most focused fury is inflamed with each menace to the memory of their dead.

Some family members focused on the responsibility of Nova Scotia mines inspectors, Claude White and Albert McLean. At the time of these interviews, both men were still employed despite their central role in the failure of Nova Scotia's occupational health and safety regime.[11]

> Father: They wanted an inquiry so they had an inquiry. For some reason, they didn't do anything with the Department of Labour. The same people are doing the same jobs that they were doing when this all happened. There's been nobody fired or disciplined for their actions. They're still there. So how can you go and put these rules in, and these same people wouldn't enforce the rules that they had back then? What are they going to do with these new—if they go out and have new legislation and new rules, what have they got? They never enforced them then, why the hell, why do you expect that they're gonna enforce them now?
> Brother: Well, they wouldn't fire anyone, too. They had to have a reason and that reason was because they didn't perform their job right, and that would be an admission of guilt, so the thing is to keep on and ride out the storm.
> Father: How much longer are we gonna be?

In the next excerpt, the speaker makes the complicity between law and political will perfectly clear. Clifford Frame is protected, in this brother's view, by the corporate veil of limited liability. Law's protection of corporate murderers makes the death of the Westray worker a political issue. In this sense then, the Westray worker's death is an injustice, whereas the loss of other family members are sad, but natural.

> Interviewer: Can you say something about why you can't let it go?
> Brother 1: Well, [sigh] it's been rough, like, we, uh we lost [another brother] first, then [another brother] died right after that and then the mine blew up and then Mom died of cancer the year after, it was just.... So, it's just, those bastards did this and they're walking away from this and the one thing that pisses me off the most is that you can't touch Frame. Even once we were going through all the rules and regulations, we had one of the [lawyers].... When he was going through it, all the way through it, he kept saying that responsibility goes to the top. Even though this guy did this, this guy did this; it goes to the top and he's ultimately responsible. So I threw the question at

him, I said, "If that's the case, then why the hell is Frame exempt?" "Well," he said, "I really don't want to get into that." And I said, "Yeah, same as the rest of the goddam politicians and lawyers and everybody else around. They don't want to mention nothing about Frame 'cause they can't touch him. And yet you're here telling me that it starts at the top?" He's the ultimate. There's where the blame lays. This man came down here even before he dug a hole, he went and got extra money because he knew he had roof conditions bad, he knew he had gas conditions bad, he knew he had faults there. And he said, "I need this extra money so I can hire the best to run this mine." And then he goes out and hires people who don't know shit-all about mining and puts them in there so he don't have to pay them big bucks and he's pocketing the rest, but yet they can't touch him. And this is the law system that's supposed to be saying the guy at the top, he's responsible. And yet we can't even get at the goddam managers that were there! So I'm trying to see where this friggin' justice system fits. It doesn't fit nowhere. Unless you happen to be a nobody, then they'll nail your ass right to the wall. It's odd. I just can't let it go that these people were able to kill twenty-six people and just walk away. Walk away.

Interviewer: Are you going to be involved in civil suits?

Brother 1: No, no. Uh [my brother's wife] doesn't want to be there. She turned around and said, "It's just going to open up a whole big bag of worms that I really don't want." And I myself don't want to get into it. I'd rather see something happen towards these guys period. Where the criminal charges go. But to start civil, I really don't want it.

Interviewer: Does it have to do with money?

Brother 1: No, I don't want any money out of them. All I want to see is something done justice-wise. And it don't seem to be going that way. It just doesn't seem to want to happen. It's cruel. Because there's guys down there. The money that was supposed to be left, the 13.8, 16, million, they gave 2.2 back to Frame so he could take that with him, and took 13.8 into their fund to draw up their loss. And they kept saying, "Don't worry that money's going to be there for body retrieval."

Interviewer: "They" being...?

Brother 1: The government. Period. And then the feds found out that they could reclaim some of their losses—it's gone. NOOoo you'll never get enough money to do it, to recover the bodies ... the eleven aren't all in the same section...

Brother 2: [Almost inaudibly] They could see one in the North mains....

The demands raised in this passage are hardly the ranting of bloodthirsty grief. Again, the demand for accountability is linked directly to governments' refusal to retrieve the bodies. And again, the family member is clear about his disinterest in any possible money from civil suits.

In most interviews people reflected on the fundamental importance of having the major players come to the Inquiry, even though they expected them to come and lie. In this, family members assert an aspect of accountability that is often articulated in terms of the need for recognition.

> Wife: Gerald Phillips and Roger Parry never got on one stand yet, in front of a microphone like I am right now and saying anything about Westray. Never yet. The people responsible for it, and they never ever got in front of a microphone yet and this is five years later. We've done more outbursts on Westray than they have. They've done everything to hide it. So that's what we're fighting for, to get them to say anything. Not that I'd believe what they say, but I want them to come out and say something.

In the following, another wife reflects more critically on the importance of keeping the Westray story alive in business media, particularly with regard to Clifford Frame's reputation. Since Frame refused to face the families of the dead Westray workers at the public inquiry, this wife explains that they decided to find him where he lives.

> Wife: Everything was Gerald Phillips, Roger Parry and Westray. But where's Ontario people? Where's the Curragh Resources? This is their biggest baby. And I want Curragh Resources to become accountable and tell me what's going on.... Clifford Frame loves ... he describes himself as a mining mogul. He came down, and you know what he said, he even used his dead brother. "You know I lost my brother in a mine...." His brother didn't die by an accident caused by other people....[12] [The Curragh Resources] Annual Report in 1991 talks about Westray. He brags about it and brags about it.... Every businessman reads the *Globe and Mail*, every politician reads the *Globe and Mail*. This [article critical of Frame's role at Westray] is to rub it in their face.... I wanted to bring Clifford Frame down. In the media they're still saying he's doing well, he's doing well. He just walked away.... I want him to answer me, but he says, "Look I can't. I've got important business to do." He couldn't answer us. That brought him to his knees. Because I want his buddies to know, look that accident was preventable.... Because he was still getting investors, he was still having his board meetings....

Frame is inhuman in the eyes of family members, more so even than is Cameron. This is perhaps because Frame is "from away" and, worse still, directs his affairs from Toronto. Frame's self-conception as a mining entrepreneur is a central target in some family members' demand for accountability. Since he refuses to take part in the public inquiry, he should at *least* be prevented from running any other mine.

> Interviewer: Do you think about justice in all this?
> Wife: Umhm. There's no justice in all this. Like Clifford Frame said in the paper the other day, "It was a simple accident." Well come on. You're sitting up there in Toronto with a cigar in your mouth, you know. Let it be one of your sons and say, "Oh it was just a simple accident." Oh that really hurts.
> Interviewer: Why do you think he's saying that?
> Wife: I don't think he has a heart. I don't think he has a heart, to tell you the truth. I don't think he has any feelings whatsoever. And now they're going to let him open another mine. I don't think he should be allowed to open anything. I believe that the reason they don't want to come down and testify is that they're guilty. If I had to go to court and I had nothing to be guilty about, I'd be there ... you're as much as saying you're guilty if you won't come down.

Workers at Westray encountered a stark discontinuity between what they experienced below ground in their subterranean workplace, and the above-ground assumptions of the non-mining people on the one hand and of mining people on the other. Many non-mining people don't believe that in the 1990s Westray-type work conditions are possible, while for mining people a coal mine represents a whole culture of safety practices. This discontinuity between the men's daily work experiences and the presuppositions of everyone around them cut the men off from common terms of reference. Pictou and Antigonish counties have long coal-mining histories, and in fact some of the families I interviewed had grown up working bootleg pits in their back yards. Among parents, at least, there seems to be some culturally transmitted knowledge of coal mining, so many family members (parents of both genders in particular) are astonished by what they now see as anachronistic conditions at Westray. They are dazed by modern failures to sustain even the most technologically primitive, commonsensical practices of coal mine safety.

Mother: [There was] no safety. Years ago they had better protection.

Some of them were burnt, but they had a chance to live, to get out. They had no chance. Not a chance in the world. That explosion down there, nobody needs to tell me that my [son's name] and the rest of them didn't know what happened. You're damn right they knew what happened, and it was torture, and they suffered down there while they died, and nobody'll ever make me think any ... because you can't have explosions like that without knowing.

Father: ... takes three minutes or something to die.... that's what the coroner said. Three minutes is a goddamn long time ... *three minutes!*

Mother: A miner told me this himself.... Here we are. This is the part ... what about them? There was 26 of them. You know, [my son] didn't want to die down there. So why? Why should they be doing what they're doing to us? And why isn't this solved? And why don't they punish the ones that did this? It was bad. A real bad situation. I knew before it exploded 'cause [my son] would come home ... I'd say, "How come your boots are so full?" And he'd say, "'Cause it's real bad down there now, Mom. It gets up to your knees." Yet the people know this. The government knows this. Donald Cameron knew it. And there he is, having a good time, not worried about anything.

Interviewer: Do you think he really believes he did something wrong?

Mother: He has to know!

Father: He thinks he's God. He's guilty. He blames it on the dead miners.

Ironically, one of the effects of our belief in welfare-state health and safety regulations may be to institute a communication problem for workers in dangerous workplaces, particularly when occupational health and safety agencies are favouring businesses. Perceptions of risk (and repressions of such perceptions) are communicatively achieved. They are fundamentally social and integral to moral judgment—particularly, to our understandings of what it is to be prudent.

Father: Life don't mean nothin'. In the olden days, when the horses were in the mine, they said, "Never mind the men, but for Christ's sake don't kill the horses." They'd look after the horses. But at least the men understood things. They had the canaries, they understood that.... Now, you may as well put a goddamn sign on the mine: enter at your own risk if you're going to work because you ain't gonna get compensation. Of all these people, we gotta hope that there's somebody that's good. And I'm sure

> there is good people. If we could get a coloured
> judge or something, a coloured woman judge, then
> I'll have a little faith in her. She wouldn't be biased.

In this father's understanding, the communicative achievement of risk perception was altered radically by technology. The bosses weren't any better in the "olden days" but at least the men understood things. Now, in contrast, a worker is seen to work at his own risk, that is, at a remove from collectively held experiential knowledge of the hazards of his/her trade. "Now" we really need judges who aren't of the boss and owner class to help us draw undeniable causal and intentional lines between workplace injury and the actions of owners and bosses.

### Three: I Wonder Sometimes If He's at Rest...You Know?

At the end of my time among Westray family members in February 1997, I had an inkling of what it is like to be haunted: such eyes and voices of suffering, of long-term preoccupation with injustice.... The Westray story was far from a settled account.[13] One mother describes the aftermath as ongoing punishment at the hands of those who have impeded the settling of accounts by evading the truth-telling forums of the Inquiry (i.e., Marvin Pelley and Clifford Frame) and the criminal trials (i.e., Gerald Phillips and Roger Parry).

> Mother: ... This is not over. I think it's very bad for them to punish us anymore, because they're punishing us—that's all they're doing—by doing this. It's not helping. They're still hurting us. And this is what I think. These big guys, they don't need this slapped into their faces, for them to come to reality, to think of what they're doing. And that's the way it is.

Family members have lost their men and much of their faith in legal fairness, political integrity, and economic freedom. One woman, whose husband's body remains in the mine says, "I wonder sometimes if he's at rest... you know?"[14]

The prices paid by family members who remain active in the struggle for accountability are clear: phone bills; missed work time; abandoned retirement projects; missed time with the living; local public fascination with "Westray widows'" romantic–sexual lives and scrutiny of their spending habits; terrible psychological suffering, including nightmares, sleep disruptions, on-going post-traumatic stress, etc. As one wife says, "It's always on the news, and I love that, don't get me wrong, but it doesn't take much to throw you back to day one, and if I'm upset about a court decision, am I going to take it out on my kids?" Staying active around Westray is an endurance test.

> Father: I was on the [Westray Families Group] executive first, then I couldn't hack it anymore, and then the younger fella, he took it and he done it for a couple of years or more till he found himself sitting in the corner at work crying. He had to go and get his head straightened out, and he had to give that up. So did [a member from another family]. The only tough one is Teasdale.[15] He don't flinch!

Promises to the dead are invoked against therapeutic pressures to "get on with life" for sanity's sake. One wife recalls a promise to give her man a proper burial, another recalls agreeing to pursue the truth: "If I ever die in that place, Isabel, promise me you'll have a full investigation into my death."[16] Such promises work like debts the living owe to the dead, and they weigh heavily on family members. At the same time, these promises fortify family members against myriad pressures to let Westray quietly settle back out of public view.

> Brother: This Inquiry thing. I used to go to a lot of that, and I really did get interested, into it, you know? I'd hear all the miners telling their stories, and these other guys. Clifford Frame and that Pelley. I mean, if they're not trying to hide nothing why couldn't they come down, do their thing, get it all over with now, you know? Let us get on with our lives. Lord Jesus we'll be dead before it's over. I get all these things all balled up into me that I just couldn't, I just—my nerves go on me and I get so stressed I just feel that everything's falling down on me. And this is what happens. And even the doctor, when I explained to her, I said, look, I lost my best friend there, and I said, I promised her, his wife and the kids, that I'd be with them 'till the end. And I just can't go back on my word. I'm gonna keep it as long as I can.

## APPENDIX: WHY THE FAMILY MEMBERS' VERSION?

## ACCOUNTING PROBLEMS AS RESISTANCE TO RATIONALIZATION

In February 1997, a possessive individualist account beckoned, inviting a public re-writing of the lives of the dead as though they were abstract workers, each responsible for weighing the risks of his workplace against the risks of unemployment. Donald Cameron's testimony was so odious to family members because it represented this very real threat to the memory of their men. The family members' struggle to articulate and sustain their version of accountability against possessive individualist as well as therapeutic and bureaucratic rationalizations reveals much about the ways we, as a public, remember (and forget) the actions of fellow agents. It throws our market-determined evaluations of one another's lives into relief against embodied community webs of mutual responsibility. This conflict is represented by family members each time they appear in public as Westray Families. If money is an offensive medium with which to evaluate the life of a dead man, isn't it also inappropriate to evaluate the lives of the living in monetary terms? Family members' power to put this question into play in public discourse marks what I am calling the accounting problem of Westray's aftermath.

My reasons for privileging the family members' version of accountability relate to the idea that, in unsettling the possessive individualist version of events, in preventing it from hardening into place "naturally" as it were, family members keep open a space for social critique. Such critique depends on a public consideration of the relations between liberal ideals of truth-telling and promise-honouring as they clash with capitalism over the lives, deaths, bodies, and memories of the Westray workers. With this in mind, I focus on the families' version of accountability for the following reasons.

First, the family members emphasize the incommensurability between the economic "risks" assumed by government and the corporation in developing the Westray mine project and the (very real) risks run by workers. Curragh Resources Incorporated has dissolved in bankruptcy—it dismantled itself only to have its various elements join other corporate configurations: its managers work for other mining corporations,[17] its former CEO, Clifford Frame, finds new investors and attempts to continue his version of economic development.[18] The twenty-six men who were at work when the mine exploded are dead: families and friends have buried fifteen, eleven remain in the now flooded mine. The men's families remain forever bereft.

Second, family members' beliefs about how the deaths happened and what should be done about them do not take the form of "official" documents. Trials, inquiries, and internal bureaucratic or business reviews create official documents to preserve their versions of the events leading to the disaster; they also produce plans for reform and versions of what it would be for their agency to achieve internal accountability. Such formal, "rationalized" institutions produce documents that justify their existence as part of their day-to-day being. Families do not. So, I'm contributing here to a history of marginalized voices. Furthermore, although the families' version is vulnerable to re-writings and exclusions, it has great rhetorical strength. Family members who have suffered a grave injustice have symbolic potency; "Westray Family" members have unique power to resist the settlement of the Westray story into a manageable format. *You cannot put a price on human life*, the families say. *How much do you fellas want?* comes the reply.[19] The resilience of the families' version derives in part from its ability to awaken empathetic imagination: most people have some sense of how they would feel if someone in their family died in a place like Westray. The rawness of the families' version has a power to startle the reader from complacent forgetfulness; and the capacity to startle us indicates the family members' ability to communicate with citizens outside of the rationalizing terms of systems.

Hence, since Westray, a number of questions that usually remain unarticulated have animated public debate: Is it possible for workers to contract away their own lives through tacitly consenting to unsafe work conditions? What is an acceptable level of risk at work? Who decides? Who should decide? Is it possible to track responsibility back to particular persons? To punish them? To break the social conditions that made the deaths possible, thus to make sure this never happens again? Describing the struggle of the families to keep their full version of accountability accessible to public debate also describes something of the mysterious way in which such fundamental questions coagulate in public discourse after an event like Westray, only to dissipate again into occasional quiet, sideline musings. In part, what I'm describing through these interviews is the almost revolutionary aspiration of family members who want to be sure that "this will never happen again."

Beyond this, I am describing the absorption of that almost revolutionary aspiration into the rationalization processes of liberal capitalism. The symbolic importance of the families' version of accountability is that, once public attention is called to their suffering, family members articulate aspects of accountability that resonate deeply with many non-family members.[20]

So, a third reason to focus on the families' demand for accountability is that following the history of the families' estrangement, critique, and consequent demands for accountability provides an unusually clear opportunity for ideology critique.[21] The rationalization of family members' demands reveals something about the way that the violence inherent in possessive individualist myths can be reflected on publicly, only to recede into the "private" sufferings of family homes. This coincides with a turning away of public attention and a marginalization of some of the richest moral claims that nourish family members' working understanding of what "accountability" means.

A fourth reason to focus on the family members' versions is that the interview texts reveal the interlocutive nature of the family members' understandings of accountability. The families' version is articulated as a defence of the "memory of the dead" against what they come to fear is the vulnerability of public memory to strategic manipulation. The families' version emerges also, then, out of an increasing suspicion of all truth claims but their own (and those of surviving Westray workers). In these senses, the families' version develops into critique as a defence against rationalizing accounts. Rationalizing forces take narrative form, and their sense-making mechanisms stand ready, at the moment of the explosion, to counter familial claims. Rationalizing narratives gather the pieces of the past into explanations of "what happened" in such a way that some rich moral claims embodied by the families are trivialized and thus forced out of public debate. For family members articulating and sustaining a demand for accountability that cannot be satisfied from within rationalizing plot lines, Westray's aftermath is a disturbing re-thinking of social relations—particularly the powerful ways that human life is evaluated in market terms. More positively, the families' version of accountability develops in the course of articulating two moral claims: that families should possess the corpses (and that society should recognize the imperative of this claim) and that truth-telling must be held sacred especially around the memory of the dead men.

The powerful, well-established rationalizing plots stand ready to lead collective memory into more comfortable pathways, away from the discon-certing, disruptive fullness of the families' demands for accountability. The "possessive individualist" plot line casts the dead men in the role of impru-dent workers, as individuals who bet their lives on wages and lost. During the interviews of February 1997, with Justice Peter Richard's report still unformed, family members were uncertain as to how this highly symbolic report would present the role of the men in the fatal explosion. And so, family members were stating their version of events with this possibility in mind: they emphasize their memories of their men as "good" men, men who supported one another, loved their families, and would not willingly contrib-ute to an unsafe work environment. In fact, as Kenton Teasdale, chairman for the Westray Families Group, suggests, the unwavering blame-the-miners line taken by Donald Cameron during his notorious Inquiry testimony may have so shocked the sensibilities of Justice Peter Richard that he refused to hint at worker responsibility in his report. Nonetheless, the possibility that the dead might be deemed responsible for their own deaths is one version of "ac-countability" that stood ready, threatening to overwhelm the families' ver-sion.

In the possessive individualist version that framed Donald Cameron's position, the dead men are cast in the time-worn role of imprudent workers. Such ready-made narratives vie to make sense of the terrible events by gathering them into a comprehensible narrative version of "what happened." Each narrative is organized around a plot that works with pre-existing expec-tations about how the deaths occurred. These expectations include character types, and each narrative casts actors retroactively into character roles that flesh out its plot line.[22] Donald Cameron's claim that workers themselves were responsible for their deaths works only if the people hearing his version of events share the same pre-suppositions about the men as social beings.

My fifth reason for privileging the families' version of accountability is that it exemplifies the optimism of critique. While rationalization threatens to dominate public memory, a supplement remains. Not only does the desire for vengeance remain, but so too does a complex suspicion of everything from common honesty to "expert" claims to knowledge. These are directly linked to what the families take to be sacred, that is, the particularity of their men, their suffering, their unnecessarily premature deaths and their identities as held in memory after their passing.[23] The memory of each family member becomes the repository of the sacred, the particularity of each human that can never be commodified. The continued presence of family members in public debate is a lingering reminder both of the sacredness of human life and the violent attempt to commodify all of human time.

A sixth and final reason that the families' version is privileged is to focus on the way in which their role in unsettling possessive individualist accounts raises the problem of account*ability,* that is, the question of the relation between justice and knowledge. In other words, the problem of accountability lies at the very core of the relationship between an interested and coercive shaping of the past and the possibility of an understanding that recollects events without serving the purpose of some will. Interview texts reveal the intermingling of versions of how to keep social accounts. Even within this preliminary analysis, the interviews demonstrate that we give accounts in (at least) three ways: a) we "balance" accounts, as in balancing the books, keeping an accurate and authoritative record of exchanges according to a commonly understood value scheme; b) we give an account of our behaviour; we appear as actors before our peers to present explanations of our motivations and the effects of our actions on the lives of others; and c) we compare and evaluate competing accounts of causality: possible ways of interpreting what has happened in terms of cause and effect are weighed against one another where only one can become authoritative. The Westray families' call for accountability evokes all of these aspects.[24] Thus, "account*ability*" refers to the quality of the forums in which we come together to reconstruct the past in comprehensible terms—in terms that orient us in the present and make bearable the thought of the contingent future. This indicates how crucial accounting is for democratic thinking: there must be a "place" of congregation where "accounts" can be settled.

In this chapter I have begun to describe a particular instance of liberal-capital's rationalizing violence. Capitalism achieves its seeming naturalness at the expense of the particularity, the sociality, the familiarity of the living as well as the dead. Like the politician's sister above, rationalization processes read monetary motives into and over the families' call for accountability, thus reducing debates about responsibility and justice to negotiations over money: *How much do you want?* To reduce families' legitimate demands to monetary terms is to dominate embodied collective, familial self with market instrumentality. This means that families have to accept that both the lives and deaths of the men will be turned into a function of market exchange. The men's very characters and life histories must be commodified—they must be remembered simply as individuals who took bad risks.

The family members' version of what it would be to achieve accountability after Westray carries radical implications, drawn from most ordinary social expectations. *Settlement* after Westray will be achieved only when the publicly admissible aspects of the family members' demand for accountability hit a familiar rhythm and so no longer have the power to jar public thinking out of comfortable patterns.

# ENDNOTES

## CHAPTER ONE

1. "Union Carbide Says Bhopal Plant Should Have Been Closed," *Wall Street Journal*, March 21, 1985: 18.
2. "Judge Rejects Exxon Alaska Spill Pact," *Wall Street Journal*, April 25, 1991: A3.
3. "Comment on oil spill disavowed," *New York Times*, May 20, 1994: A18; "Apology delivered for Valdez spill," *Washington Post*, March 25, 1999; "Alaska oil executive threatened to call Bush," *Washington Post*, November 27, 1992: A11; "Exxon slides by," *Village Voice*, April 30, 1991: 35; "$9.7 million land damages won in Valdez case," *New York Times*, September 26, 1994: A12.
4. "Spain begins massive cleanup of devastating toxic waste spill," Halifax *Chronicle-Herald*, May 4, 1998; [no title] *Globe and Mail*, June 12, 1998: B5.
5. "Guyanese hope to sue Cambior in Canada," *Financial Post*, May 29, 1998.
6. "A watery grave," *Outside*, January 1997.
7. "Canada muzzles story on mine. Financier wins Summitville round," *Denver Post*, [1993]; "Friedland gets court OK to sue US in Ontario court," *Financial Post*, [no date]; "Man with the Midas touch linked to mercenary bosses," Sydney *Morning Herald*, April 7, 1997.
8. "Tragedy at Westray," Halifax *Chronicle-Herald*, May 11, 1992: C1.
9. "Call of the coal," Halifax *Chronicle-Herald,* May 16, 1992: B1.
10. "Nova Scotia coal mining fuelled by politics of need," *Toronto Star*, May 16, 1992: A1.
11. "Mine tragedy in pictures," Halifax *Chronicle-Herald,* May 12, 1992: M37.
12. Headings indicate the name of the witness, the day, the date and the page numbers of the Inquiry transcript.
13. "How Canada has dug itself into a miner role," Toronto *Globe and Mail*, June 29, 1993: A9.
14. *Transcript of the Westray Mine Public Inquiry, Day 1*, November 6, 1995.
15. "Westray ends without an ending," Toronto *Globe and Mail*, July 5, 1999: A12.

## CHAPTER TWO

1. Shaun's story was commissioned especially for this volume and Shirley's arrived as a surprise. I had asked Shaun if he would write specifically about what it was like to testify at the Inquiry. This chapter, interspersed with extracts from testimony at the Inquiry, is the result.
2. Clifford Frame was chief executive officer of Curragh Resources.

## CHAPTER THREE

1. Patrick Whiteway's chapter was commissioned especially for this volume "as a favour" to me, the editor. When I first heard about the explosion and I mentioned it to Patrick, he exclaimed "why were they there to begin with!" Several years later when I was trying to organize this book, I asked him if he would write a

chapter around that theme.

2. Note from the Editor—This image of the stratigraphic section indicates that the New Glasgow/Stellarton area is a coal-rich geological environment. Even though the Foord Seam is situated at a considerable depth, it is the thickest of the near-surface seams, thus making it amenable to large-scale, mechanized underground mining.

3. Note from the Editor—I am indebted to the Westray Public Inquiry for including a "Glossary of Coal Mining Terminology" from which these definitions have been reproduced.

4. "Room-and-pillar" is a system of mining coal in which the distinguishing feature is the extraction of 50 percent or more of the coal in the first working. The coal is mined by advancing parallel rooms connected by cross drives, leaving supporting coal as rectangular supporting pillars. The coal in the pillars may be subsequently extracted, usually allowing the roof to cave in following the mining. This method is applicable to coal that occurs in relatively flat and shallow deposits.

5. "Longwall" is a method of working coal seams, that is believed to have originated in Shropshire, England, towards the end of the 17th century. A panel is removed in one operation by means of a working face, or wall, that may be several hundred metres long—hence, the name. The roof of the "gob," or space from which coal has been removed, is usually allowed to collapse or cave.

6. This cartoon from the Halifax *Daily News* is reproduced with the permission of Theo Moudakis; but the content has been altered.

7. In January 1999, the federal government announced that it was going to shut down these Devco mining operations after 32 years and subsidies of $1.7 billion, putting approximately 1200 miners out of work.

8. A "fault" is a break in a body of rock that has caused movement of rock on the other side. A "fault zone" is a zone of numerous interlacing small faults, as opposed to a single, clean fracture.

9. A "dip" is the angle at which a bed, stratum, or vein is inclined from the horizontal; the direction of decline from the horizontal.

10. This photo depicts a drum-type continuous mining machine.

11. "Fly ash" is composed of very fine particles of incombustible ash resulting from the burning of fuels like coal.

12. A "panel" is a large rectangular block or pillar of coal identified to be mined, usually separated from other panels by large pillars.

13. The continuous miner cuts or rips coal directly from the face, without the use of explosives, and loads it into conveyors or shuttle cars in a continuous manner.

14. Shuttle cars take coal from the continuous miner to an underground coal breaker; roof bolters install ground support in panels.

15. A "roof bolter" is a machine used to place roof bolts, which are steel bolts or cables secured into place in the roof or rib of a mine opening for the purpose of pinning layers of rock together. Roof bolting is a common form of roof control. Other forms are steel arches (curved lengths or steel, usually H-section, either rigid or yielding, used for long-term roof support in mine roadways and intersections) and steel sets (a traditional passive support system used in main entries of coal mines for ground support, usually consisting of I-beams for caps and H-beams for posts or wall plates. The term "passive" derives from the fact that steel sets and arches do not interact with the rock the way that roof bolts do).

16. A "feeder-breaker" is a mobile crusher into which coal is dumped. The feeder-breaker then loads the coal onto a conveyor.
17. A "roadheader" is a type of continuous miner.
18. Methane is an odourless, tasteless, colourless, and non-poisonous gas formed by the decomposition of organic matter. The most common gas found in coal mines, it is also called firedamp and marsh gas. Methane is lighter than air and highly flammable.
19. Stonedust is an incombustible dust (usually limestone) used to reduce the danger of potentially explosive coal dust. Stonedust is mixed with coal dust on mine roadways to create a non-flammable, non-explosive mixture.
20. In 1995, the Peabody Group produced 136.9 million tonnes (MT); Cyprus Amax Coal, 73.5 MT; Powder River Coal, 68.4 MT; Consol Coal Group, 64.8MT; Arco Coal, 41.4 MT; Kennecott Energy, 39.6 MT; Thunder Basin Coal, 32.7 MT; Zeigler Coal, 31.8 MT; Kerr-McGee Coal, 28.2 MT; A.T. Massey Coal, 26 MT; North American Coal Corp., 24.5 MT; Arch Mineral Corp., 24.2 MT.
21. For example, Consol Pennsylvania Coal operates the underground coal mine in Enlow Fork, Pennsylvania (producing 7.3 million tonnes per year), and also in Bailey, Pennsylvania (6.6 million tonnes annually). The mine in West Elk, Colorado, produces 4.7 million tonnes (operated by Mountain Coal); Kerr-McGee Coal operates Galatia in Illinois (5 million tonnes); Camp No. 11, in Kentucky (4.6 million tonnes, Peobody Coal); Mountaineer, West Virginia (4.5 million tonnes, Mingo Logan); McElroy, West Virginia (3.7 million tonnes, McElroy Coal); Powhatan No. 6, Ohio (3.6 million tonnes, Ohio Valley Coal); Conant, Kentucky (3.5 million tonnes, Arch of Kentucky); Blacksville 2, West Virginia (3.4 million tonnes, Consolidated Coal).

## CHAPTER FOUR

1. Originally published as "Working Paper Series No. 3" for the Centre for Research on Work and Society, York University, Toronto, November 1992. Adapted for this volume with permission.
2. These recurring episodes came to an end only when the incidence of coal mining declined sharply during the 1960s. Almost all of the coal mining that led to these "accidents" took place in Pictou County as investors sought to take advantage of a particularly rich deposit there, known as the Foord seam. Westray was the most recent adventurer to seek to extract profit from that treacherous seam.
3. George E. Wimpey of Canada Limited explored the option of open pit mining in 1979, and the Nova Corporation conducted tests between 1979 and 1987 to determine whether methane extraction was commercially viable. See Placer Development Limited, 1987: Vol. 1, 2.
4. Placer Development Limited, 1987: Vol. 2, 2. One parameter is that there should be isolation of units to permit sealing off of worked-out areas to minimize the risk of spontaneous combustion. Another is that the layout should permit advance proving of mining panels before depillaring.
5. This kind of "neutral" expertise serves players and governments very well when making plans and, even more so, when confronted with disaster. For instance, when Westray mine manager Gerald Phillips was asked about the risk of methane explosions prior to the opening of the mine, he said that the history of deaths in

the Pictou coalfields had "more to do with the old mining methods" and that the mine would use "modern monitoring systems ... [so] you can detect a problem [methane gas] before it becomes a real problem," Halifax *Chronicle-Herald*, May 9, 1989: 2.

6. One of the techniques they expected to be satisfactory was roof-and-pillar mining, something which would require skilled and experienced miners who could exercise a good deal of on-the-spot judgment. Typical of technology enthusiasts, they assumed they could find the right workers and ignored any pressures that might affect these workers' judgment calls.

7. *Coal Mines Regulation Act.* Revised Statutes of Nova Scotia. 1989: c. 73, s.104(1)(b).

8. The former chair of Devco, Ms. Teresa MacNeil, has been quoted as saying that Devco's opposition "was around economics, not safety. We would all like to think today that we were all preaching safety. Safety was a factor, it was mentioned (only)[sic]" *(Canadian Press,* May 13, 1992).

9. Halifax *Chronicle-Herald*, May 9, 1989: 35.

10. Halifax *Chronicle-Herald*, August 18, 1989: 1–2.

11. For Nova Scotia, see *Environment Assessment Act,* Statutes of Nova Scotia (1988), c. 11. The federal Environmental Assessment Review Process (EARP) was created by Cabinet directives.

12. For instance, see Curragh Resources Incorporated, *1990 Annual Report,* which states: "For the mining industry, protection of the environment is a priority.... At Curragh we are always searching for new technologies to help us minimize impact on the ecology" [no page].

13. CANMET's reviewer described the arrangement with Nova Scotia Power Corporation as "particularly attractive," (Canadian Centre for Mineral and Energy Technology [no date]: 9).

14. *Canadian Press,* June 8, 1992.

15. Many of the dealings are shrouded in secrecy. The Nova Scotia Power Corporation, with the support of the government, refused to disclose the details of its contract with Westray to the Public Accounts Committee of the legislature; *Canadian Press,* May 3 & 31, 1989. The details of the government's "take or pay" deal with Westray is the subject of a freedom of information action brought in court by Bernie Boudreau, a member of the Liberal opposition in the Nova Scotia legislature ("Curragh Resources Incorporated has joined the government in fighting disclosure," *Canadian Press,* November 5, 1991, February 17, 1992).

16. *Canadian Press,* September 2, 1988.

17. *Canadian Press,* April 11, 1989. The failure to reach an agreement with the federal government subsequently caused construction of the mine to be halted in late July, not resuming until January 1990 *(Canadian Press,* August, 31 1989, January 4, 1990).

18. *Canadian Press,* December 14, 1990. The links between Eric Barker, the owner of Satellite Equipment, and Don Cameron, and the fact that the contract with Westray was awarded without tender became the subject of an expose on the Canadian Broadcasting Corporation's national investigative news show, *The Fifth Estate,* aired December 11, 1990. Clifford Frame, in defending the contract, was quoted as saying, "I'd give a contract to the devil if he could do the job cheaper than somebody else" *(Canadian Press,* December 11, 1990).

19. *Canadian Press*, May 19, 1992.
20. Toronto *Globe and Mail*, November 1, 1985: B1; and September 1, 1986: B6.
21. Stevie Cameron, Toronto *Globe and Mail*, June 8, 1992: A4.
22. *Canadian Press*, May 11, 1992.
23. Earlier that month, thousands of fish were killed when Satellite Construction discharged a chlorine-based solution it had used to flush out water pipes at the Westray mine into a nearby river. The work had been approved by Westray. In contrast to the way violations of health and safety laws were handled, Satellite was charged and convicted of offences under the Nova Scotia Water Act and Environmental Protection Act *(Canadian Press*, June 4, 7, 12, 1991; *Canadian Press*, April 2, 1992).
24. *Canadian Press*, May 13, 1992.
25. Claude White, Director, Mine Safety, memorandum to Executive Director, Ministry of Labour, October 21, 1991.
26. *Canadian Press*, May 28, 1992.
27. *Canadian Press*, May 23, 1992.
28. Kevin Cox, Toronto *Globe and Mail*, July 30, 1992; *Coal Mines Regulation Act*, op. cit. n.23, ss. 72 & 85, n.46.
29. *Coal Mines Regulation Act*, op. cit. n.23, s. 70(5).
30. *Canadian Press*, May 12, 1992.
31. *Canadian Press*, May 25, 1992.
32. *Canadian Press*, May 23, 1992.
33. *Canadian Press*, May 18, 1992.
34. *Canadian Press*, May 11, 1992.
35. Kevin Cox, Toronto *Globe and Mail*, July 30, 1992.
36. Safety and Health and Work (Robens Report) [UK] 1972; Report of the Royal Commission on the Health and Safety of Workers in Mines (Ham Report) [Ontario] 1976; Report of the Joint Federal-Provincial Inquiry Commission into Safety in Mines and Mining Plants in Ontario (Burkett Report) 1981; Report of the Commission of Inquiry into Occupational Health and Safety, (N.S.W., Australia) (Williams Report) 1981.
37. This is not to say that such a scheme could not be administered more vigorously, as can happen when labour-friendly political parties generate this kind of pressure. Such an event occurred in Saskatchewan from 1974 to 1982 when, under an NDP government, Bob Sass served as director of the occupational health and safety branch of the Department of Labour and introduced many progressive reforms, and in Ontario when the New Democratic Party was able to influence a minority Liberal Party government. But the underlying assumptions remain the same, and the more usual slack enforcement is likely to return as soon as the pressure is reduced. This does not require formal changes in the regulatory mechanism. The example of Saskatchewan in the period following the defeat of the NDP is instructive. See Sass, 1987: 143–47.
38. Revised Statutes of Nova Scotia 1989, c.73, ss. 142 & 146.
39. Statutes of Nova Scotia 1985, c.3, s.49 and S.P.E.I. 1985, c.36.
40. The highest fine, $500,000, is set in Ontario. Alberta is next at $150,000. Manitoba is closer to Nova Scotia with a maximum fine of $15,000.
41. Compiled from Province of Nova Scotia, *Annual Reports* (Department of Labour) 1985–86 to 1989–90. In the 1988–89 report, only the total amount of fines levied

was reported ($8700 from four convictions), making it impossible to ascertain the highest fine. In another tabulation of prosecution data, a total of 97 charges were laid between the fiscal years 1987–88 and 1991–92, resulting in 42 convictions and fines totalling $69,750 (Jim LeBlanc, Director, Occupational Health/Safety Training, Nova Scotia Department of Labour, letter to Eric Tucker, August 19, 1992). The discrepancy between the number of companies charged and the number of charges may result from the fact that any one company may be charged with a number of offences at the same time.

42. Province of Nova Scotia, *Assembly Debates*, July 10, 1991.

43. Province of Nova Scotia, *Annual Report* (Department of Mines and Energy), (1988–89), 138. The mine produced less than 36,000 tonnes annually and employed 45 people.

44. *Financial Times of Canada*, April 15, 1991: 20.

45. Allan Robinson, "Won't Gamble Again, Curragh Head Says," Toronto *Globe and Mail*, May 6, 1992, B6.

46. *Canadian Press*, September 5, November 29, 1991.

47. *Canadian Press*, October 30, 1991.

48. *Canadian Press*, May 11, 1992.

49. *Canadian Press*, May 11, 1992.

50. Nova Scotia, *Occupational Health and Safety Act*, 1985, s. 25, c.3, s.1.

51. *Canadian Press*, May 28, 1992.

52. *Canadian Press*, May 22, 1991.

53. It is worth pointing out that when Curragh Resources began its endeavours in the Yukon, again with federal government guarantees and territorial hand-outs, one of the attractions for it was that the workforce was not unionized. Eventually it did become a unionized enterprise, as did Westray in the aftermath of the disaster.

54. *Canadian Press*, May 28, 1992.

55. Again we want to underscore that what happened at Westray was normal. Two independent studies in two jurisdictions have found that the ratio of unreported to reported claims is 3:1. See Harpur, 1991: 6 (reporting on HSE study); and Brickey and Grant, 1992.

56. *Canadian Press*, May 28, 1992.

57. *Globe and Mail*, September 1, 1986: B6.

58. The other 26 percent of the shares in Frame Mining Corporation were divided equally between a Swedish company called Boliden Canada Limited and a Japanese company called Mitsui and Co. (Canada) Limited They were to be responsible for marketing of lead and zinc concentrates in Europe, the latter in the Far East, on behalf of Curragh Resources Incorporated The pre-existing links between Curragh Resources, Curragh Resources Incorporated, C.H. Frame and the Westray coal project are manifest.

59. The Westray Mining Corporation (70 percent of whose shares were owned by C.H. Frame) owned 519,737 of the multiple voting shares in Curragh Resources Incorporated At the same time, Frame Mining Corporation (in which Westray Mining Corporation held 74 percent of the shares) held 678,887 of the multiple voting shares in Curragh Resources Incorporated Finally, 630902 Ontario Incorporated, wholly-owned by Frame Mining Corporation, held 14,521,113 of the multiple voting shares in Curragh Resources Incorporated.

60. When Curragh Resources Incorporated bought an interest in the Westray Coal

Project by dealing with 630902 Ontario Incorporated, it bought only 90 percent of the holdings, leaving 630902 Ontario Incorporated with the option of retaining a 10 percent interest in the mining lease and exploration licences and entering into a joint venture with Curragh Resources Incorporated to further develop the property or to convert its interest into a 5 percent cash flow royalty, which included a royalty totalling approximately $15 million which would be paid before any other royalty was paid out. This is known as a back-in deal and is relatively common in the industry. It is not the unusual nature of the deal, then, to which attention is drawn, but the fact that, once again, an arrangement was made which would profit a major promoter and shareholder in this web of dealings.

61. *National Union News*, May, 1992.

62. In this regard, it is interesting to note that the *Cape Breton Development Corporation Act*, R.S.C. 1985, C-25, which created Devco as a crown corporation for the purpose of conducting mining in Cape Breton, states (at s. 15) that the object of the Coal Division is "to conduct coal mining and related operations in the Sydney coalfield on a basis that is consistent with efficient mining practice and good mine safety." This inclusion of safety as an independent objective stands in marked contrast to the approach we saw earlier by private coal developers. Of course, statements of legislative intent do not necessarily get translated into action, but the possibilities and advantages of public investment over those of private investment are symbolically underlined.

## CHAPTER FIVE

1. This chapter originally appeared as "Risk Awareness and Risk Acceptance at the Westray Coal Mine: An Attempt to Understand Miners' Perceptions, Motivations and Actions Prior to the Accident," a report submitted to the Westray Public Mine Inquiry, [New Glasgow], 1997. It was published electronically at www.pavlov.psyc.queensu.ca/faculty/wilde/westray.html and has been adapted for this volume. In the following endnotes, the page numbers refer to pages in the hearing transcripts or the exhibits, and in the case of the former, the author has cited the day and witness.

2. Transcript of the Westray Inquiry, February 20, 1996: 7264/65, testimony of Randy Facette.

3. Exhibits 120.034 (Inter-Office Memorandum, announcing the production bonus scheme), 120.040 (Inter-Office Memorandum, regarding incentive system implementation), 120.044 (Underground Bonus Plan, March 1992), and 120.049 (Interoffice Memorandum, regarding incentive bonus for April 1992).

4. Note from the Editor: The final transcript is approximately 17,000 pages long.

5. Exhibit: office\wpwin\dol\intervws\CHAPMAN.DOL: 32/3]; transcript of the Westray Inquiry, March 19, 1996: 7737/9, testimony of Fraser Agnew.

6. Exhibit: office\wpwin\transcpt\intervws\TAJE: 14–15; transcript of the Westray Mine Inquiry, March 20, 1996: 7917/8, testimony of Donald Dooley, Westray Mine Overman.

7. Transcript of the Westray Public Mine Inquiry, February 14, 1996: 7053, testimony of Thomas MacKay, Westray Miner.

8. Transcript of the Westray Public Mine Inquiry, April 1, 1997: 9422, testimony of Bryce Capstick, Westray Mine Overman.

9. Transcript of the Westray Public Mine Inquiry, January 18, 1996: 4195, testimony of Michael Franks, Westray Miner.

10. An employee testified having received payment from the mine's administration in return for not reporting a lost-time accident to Workers' Compensation, (office\wpwin\transcpt\intervws\MACDONNL, p. 18/19).

11. Transcript of the Westray Public Mine Inquiry, March 20, 1996: 7774, testimony of Donald Dooley, Westray Mine Overman.

12. The relationship between the amount of production over 500 tonnes and the size of the bonus per tonne expressed in cents has been graphed in Figure 1. In Figure 2, the effect of the productivity bonus system on the monthly earnings of an employee working at a Miner 1 hourly rate is shown as a curve.

13. Transcript of the Westray Mine Public Inquiry, February 6, 1996: 5562, testimony of John Lanceleve, Westray Miner.

14. Transcript of the Westray Public Mine Inquiry, February 12, 1996: 6424, testimony of Buddy Robinson, Westray Miner.

15. Exhibit office\wpwin\dol\intervws\MACKAY.DO: 28/29; Exhibit office\wpwin\dol\intervws\MACIN-CJ.DOL August 21, 1992: 27; Exhibit office\wpwin\dol\intervws\JOHNSTON.DOL July 8, 1992: 13/14; Exhibit office\wpwin\RCMP\statemnt\NOTES.GIN May 12, 1992.

16. See, for instance, Transcript of the Westray Public Mine Inquiry, March 25/6, 1996, testimony of James Dooley, Westray Mine Overman; March 20, 1996, testimony of Donald Dooley, Westray Mine Overman; February 13, 1996, testimony of Rick Mitchell, Westray Miner; and February 14, 1996, testimony of Thomas MacKay, Westray Miner.

17. See Transcript of the Westray Public Mine Inquiry, January 23, 1996: 4466, testimony of Harvey Martin, Westray Miner.

18. Transcript of the Westray Public Mine Inquiry, March 25, 1996: 8474, testimony of James Dooley, Westray Mine Overman.

19. See for instance Exhibit: office\wpwin\trancpt\intervews\REGLPALM, page 40/1. "Once the mine got along a little ways, we would be able to get a union in there, and we'd be able to have a little bit of say and maybe change things around a little bit, you know," (Transcript of the Westray Public Mine Inquiry, January 18, 1996: 4195, testimony of Michael Franks, Westray Miner).

20. Transcript of the Westray Public Mine Inquiry, January 25, 1996: 5115, testimony of Steven Cyr, Westray Miner; February 13, 1996: 846, testimony of Rick Mitchell, Westray Miner; February 6, 1996: 5466, testimony of John Lanceleve, Westray Miner.

21. "The men had absolutely no training," Transcript of the Westray Public Mine Inquiry, February 12, 1996: 6426–7, testimony of Buddy Robinson, Westray Miner; "And the electrician wasn't experienced in a coal mine before either." Exhibit: p.37/8 from office\wpwin\transcpt\intervws\REGLPALM.

22. "… Corners were taken to make it easier and people started to slough off and the cogging procedures weren't going according to the book, we'll say. They weren't being done right. They were just kind of being slapped together for the sake of getting the job out of the bloody way." Exhibit: office\wpwin\transcpt\intervws\TAJE: 61/2.

23. The miners often mentioned being intimidated Exhibit: office\wpwin\transcpt\ intervws\ ROBINSON: 68/9; being told by management "to quit being a shit disturber" Exhibit: office\wpwin\RCMP\ statemnt\EVANS.STA: 4.

    "They'd pound you into submission pretty well, you know, like verbally," transcript of the Westray Public Mine Inquiry, January 18, 1996, testimony of Michael Franks, Westray Miner;

    "Yes, he said that he could put in a good word for me and that if I went over and apologized and geared up and went back underground and kept my mouth shut, that I'd—I had that option or walking the streets." Transcript of the Westray Mine Public Inquiry, February 8, 1996, testimony of Carl Guptill, Westray Miner.

24. "They got back at you, you know, if you complained too much or asked too many questions or ever—whatever I did, they got back to me by banning me from overtime." Exhibit: office\wpwin\transcpt\intervws\ BARDAUSK: 1078.

25. Transcript of the Westray Mine Public Inquiry, February 6, 1996, testimony of John Lanceleve, Westray Miner.

26. "He told me that according to the Coal Mines Regulation Act, which I had never read to this point, that there was no methanometer required on the miner, so I didn't have a leg to stand on and that I would go and get myself fired for nothing, right?" Transcript of the Westray Public Mine Inquiry, January 18, 1996, testimony of Wayne Cheverie.

27. "Yes, when he [i.e., the mine inspector] was in the mine, he was very closely accompanied by the mine management. You couldn't separate him from mine management in order to bring a concern to his attention. If you did say anything, mine management would be right there to hear everything." Transcript of the Westray Mine Public Inquiry, February 6, 1996, testimony of John Lanceleve, Westray Miner.

28. Transcript of the Westray Public Mine Inquiry, January 18, 1996, testimony of Wayne Cheverie, Westray Miner; transcript of the Westray Public Mine Inquiry February 13, 1996, testimony of David Matthews, Westray Miner.

29. Exhibit: office\wpwin\dol\intervews\MALONE.DOL: 25/6; Exhibit: office\wpwin\ transcpt\intervws\ROBINSON: 68/9; Exhibit: office\wpwin\transcpt\intervws \BARDAUSK: 108/9; Exhibit: office\wpwin\trancpt\intervws\WRICE: 37/8.

30. Transcript of the Westray Public Mine Inquiry, February 7, 1996, testimony of Aaron Conklin, Westray Miner; and from February 5, 1996, testimony of Jonathan Knock.

31. "We complained to them, it didn't do us any good and I guess we felt that the government was probably with them as well. And if the inspectors weren't going do to anything about it, I mean, we felt that was our backup." Exhibit: office\wpwin\dol\intervws\MACIN-CJ.DOL: 28/9.

    "Well, the Inspection Department didn't seem too interested...." Transcript of the Westray Public Mine Inquiry, January 18, 1996, testimony of Michael Franks, Westray Miner.

32. Exhibit: office\wpwin\RCMP\statemnt\EVANS.STA: 2.

33. "... They did not want to take men from there to — because it would look bad on them, reflect bad on them." Transcript of the Westray Public Mine Inquiry, February 6, 1996, testimony of John Lanceleve.

34. Transcript of the Westray Public Mine Inquiry, March 19/ 21, testimony of Fraser Agnew, Westray Mine Overman.

35. See Transcript of the Westray Public Mine Inquiry, February 8, 1996, testimony of Carl Guptill, Westray Miner.

36. "There was no point in complaining to the company. After trying several times, and being told that either you work there or someone else would, you tend to keep quiet. The turn-over at the mine is a reflection of this attitude. Men have gone there and worked one shift, some worked a full week but few last too long." Exhibit: office\wpwin\RCMP\statemnt\WENTZELL.UIC: 2.

37. See Transcript of the Westray Public Mine Inquiry, March 19, 1996, testimony of Fraser Agnew, Westray Mine Overman.

38. Transcript of the Westray Public Mine Inquiry, February 20, 1996, testimony of Randy Facette, Westray Miner; Transcript of the Westray Public Mine Inquiry, February 6, 1996, testimony of John Lanceleve; Exhibit: office\wpwin\transcpt\intervws\POIRIER: 22/3.

39. "I said I left for unsafe conditions. And I had—January 2, I went before what they call a board of referees, which is an independent board. And I explained to them about the unsafe conditions, mostly about the ground conditions. And they interviewed somebody from the company as well, and I guess between the company and myself they said that they more or less believed the company.... I said I don't really think it's fair. I said, I got a nine-week penalty, you know...." Exhibit: office\wpwin\transcpt\intervws\WRICE: 37/8;

"And don't forget this, there were men quitting that rat hole, they'd go to UI and say 'I quit because of coal dust, bad ground conditions, and methane,' and UI used to phone the mine and say 'What's the situation? No problem.'. The guy gets denied UI which is—I think there's some—I think that should be checked out. So, a person can't quit because—you walk away, you get nothing, and you also don't get UI." Transcript of the Westray Public Mine Inquiry, January 22, 1996, testimony of Ray Savidge, Westray Miner;

"I would contribute that fact [namely of continuing to work at Westray] to manpower telling me that I would be not getting my unemployment for a period of couple of months, and I didn't relish the fact of applying for welfare." Transcript of the Westray Public Mine Inquiry January 24, 1996, testimony of Leonard Bonner, Westray Miner;

"I would have quit there, I should have quit there, but I didn't. I stayed working there because I would have been waiting 5 or 8 weeks for unemployment...." Exhibit: office\wpwin\ dol\intervws\WALSH2.DOL: 256/6.

40. See p. 68/9 of office\wpwin\transcpt\intervws\MARSHALL.

41. "I went back because I needed the work and because my buddies were there and I felt things could be more secure if I was there with them." Exhibit: office\wpwin\RCMP\statemnt\RYAN.STA;

"Well, then what do you do, and if I quit, it's not going to make any difference. I'm not going to help the guys who are still working there, if I quit, and a lot of guys did quit, but it didn't make any difference in the situation in the mine." Exhibit: office\wpwin\transcpt\intervws\ ROBINSON: 68/9.

42. "I want to help the mine. Like, the mine, not Curragh [i.e., the company owning Westray Coal]. Like, the mine for the miners, is separate for the company that I worked for. You felt for the mine. Like, I wanted to help the mine as the entity itself. Like, I wanted to keep—I wanted to see the mine keep going. Like, I wanted to help the physical structure of the mine.... They [i.e., the miners] have

the problem with the management, but they still need their baby when they go back." Transcript of the Westray Public Mine Inquiry, March 20, 1996, testimony of Donald Dooley, Westray Mine Overman.

43. See Transcript of the Westray Public Mine Inquiry, January 16, 1996, testimony of Andrew Liney, Mine Ventilation Expert.

## CHAPTER SIX

1. This chapter was originally published in the *Journal of Management Studies* 34 (1997) by Blackwell Publishers. It has been adapted and revised with permission for this volume.

2. Data sources examined in this chapter are: (1) transcripts of provincial public inquiry headed by Justice Peter Richard; (2) the *Nova Scotia Coal Mines Regulation Act*; (3) the *Nova Scotia Mining Code*; (4) various newspaper reports and features from the Toronto *Globe and Mail,* the Halifax *Chronicle-Herald,* the Montreal *Gazette,* the *Toronto Star,* the Calgary *Herald,* and articles from *Maclean's Magazine.*

3. "Westray hearings on two fronts," Montreal *Gazette*, July 20, 1993: A5.

## CHAPTER SEVEN

1. This chapter originally appeared as part of a master of journalism thesis entitled "The Cost of Coal" (Carleton University, 1994), subsequently published as "The Westray Mine Explosion: An Examination of the Interaction Between the Mine Owner and the Media," in *Canadian Journal of Communication*, vol. 21, no. 3, (1996). It has been revised with permission for this volume.

2. Giacomo Capobianco, Former President, Coal Association of Canada, Calgary, AB, personal communication, March 11, 1994; Jacques Hudon, Director of Communications, Mining Association of Canada, Ottawa, ON, personal communication, June 16, 1993.

3. Tom Reid, President, Reid Management, Toronto, ON, personal communication, November 12, 1993.

4. Robert Irvine, President, The Institute for Crisis Management, personal communication, January 25, 1994.

5. Joseph Scanlon (1993, May 7–9), *Covering Disasters* [audio tape], a panel discussion at the Canadian Association of Journalists annual meeting, Toronto, ON.

6. The Nova Scotia government provided a $12 million loan. The federal government guaranteed 85 percent of a $100 million loan from the Bank of Nova Scotia and also agreed to an additional interest buydown of $8.75 million.

7. Betsy Chambers, former legislative reporter, New Glasgow *Evening News, Cape Breton Post* and Truro *Daily News*, NS, personal communication, December 3, 1993; Bruce Wark, journalism professor, University of King's College, and former reporter, Halifax, NS, personal communication, October 26, 1993.

8. Kevin Cox, reporter, Halifax bureau, Toronto *Globe and Mail*, personal communications, February 25, 1993 and November 24, 1993; Dean Jobb, reporter, Halifax *Chronicle-Herald*, personal communications, February 26, 1993, and December 6, 1993.

9. Kathy Dobbs, mental health worker, Aberdeen General Hospital, New Glasgow, NS, personal communication, February 19, 1993.

10. Tom Reid, President, Reid Management, Toronto, personal communication, November 12, 1993.

11. Kevin Cox, reporter, Halifax bureau, Toronto *Globe and Mail*, personal communications, February 25, 1993 and November 24, 1993.

12. Neale Bennet of Bennet Communications in Halifax was hired to advise Curragh officials on the scene. He declined to participate in this study, citing client confidentiality.

13. Tom Reid, President, Reid Management, Toronto, personal communication, November 12, 1993.

14. Paul Curley, President, Advance Planning and Communications, Toronto, ON, personal communication, March 19, 1993; Elizabeth Hoyle, Vice-President, Advance Planning and Communications, Toronto, ON, personal communication, March 19, 1993; Tom Reid, President, Reid Management, Toronto, ON, personal communication, November 12, 1993.

15. Bob Allison, CBC-TV, personal communication, February 15, 1993.

16. Kevin Cox, reporter, Halifax bureau, Toronto *Globe and Mail*, personal communications, February 25, 1993 and November 24, 1993.

17. In March 1979, for example, when the Three Mile Island nuclear energy plant leaked radiation into the atmosphere, journalists who were in Harrisburg, Pennsylvania, to cover the story also had trouble getting information they could understand. The *Columbia Journalism Review* paraphrased Jim Panyard of the *Philadelphia Bulletin* this way: "Sources seemed to speak a foreign language.... You asked them a straight question about how much radiation is escaping and they answered with mumbo-jumbo about millirems, manrems, rads and picocuries." Peter M. Sandman, Mary Paden, Mary Ann Griffin and Greg Miles, "At Three Mile Island." *Columbia Journalism Review*, July 1979: 43–58.

18. Bob Allison, Senior Producer, *First Edition*, CBC-TV, Halifax, personal communication, February 15, 1993; Kevin Cox, reporter, Halifax bureau, Toronto *Globe and Mail*, personal communications, February 25, 1993 and November 24, 1993.

19. Isabel Gillis, widow of deceased miner, Myles Gillis, personal communication, June 30, 1993.

20. Tom Reid, President, Reid Management, Toronto, ON, personal communication, November 12, 1993.

21. Kevin Cox, reporter, Halifax bureau, Toronto *Globe and Mail*, personal communications, February 25, 1993 and November 24, 1993; Dean Jobb, reporter, *Chronicle-Herald*, Halifax, NS, personal communications, February 26, 1993 and December 6, 1993.

22. Kevin Cox, reporter, Halifax bureau, *Globe and Mail*, personal communications, February 25, 1993, and November 24, 1993; Michael Lightstone, reporter, the *Daily News*, Halifax, NS, personal communication, February 24, 1993.

23. Tom Reid, President, Reid Management, Toronto, personal communication, November 12, 1993.

24. Kevin Cox, "Holding on to hope." Toronto *Globe and Mail*, 1992, May 11: A1, A4.

25. Rob Gordon, reporter, *First Edition*, CBC-TV, Halifax, NS, personal communication, February 25, 1993.

26. Tom Reid, President, Reid Management, Toronto, ON, personal communication, November 12, 1993. The literature reflects Reid's observations.
27. Lorne Seifred, Manager, Shaw Cable, New Glasgow, NS, personal communication, February 18, 1993.
28. Doug MacNeil, Editor, *Evening News*, New Glasgow, NS, personal communication, February 8, 1994.
29. David Glenen, reporter, *Evening News*, New Glasgow, NS, personal communication, March 31, 1993; Doug MacNeil, Editor, *Evening News*, New Glasgow, NS, personal communication, February 8, 1994; Wilkie Taylor, reporter, New Glasgow bureau, *Chronicle-Herald*, personal communication, June 28, 1993.
30. John Hault, Former Director, Nova Scotia Museum of Industry, Stellarton, NS, personal communication, May 5, 1994; Bob Allison, Senior Producer, *First Edition*, CBC-TV, Halifax, personal communication, February 15, 1993; Michael Lightstone, reporter, the *Daily News*, Halifax, NS, personal communication, February 24, 1993.
31. Kevin Cox, reporter, Halifax bureau, the *Globe and Mail*, personal communications, February 25, 1993 and November 24, 1993.
32. Curragh Incorporated. *Statement to the press,* May 10, 1992. Unpublished news release.
33. Kevin Cox, reporter, Halifax bureau, the *Globe and Mail*, personal communications, February 25, 1993 and November 24, 1993.
34. Michael Lightstone, reporter, the *Daily News*, Halifax, NS, personal communication, February 24, 1993.
35. Isabel Gillis, widow of deceased miner, Myles Gillis, personal communication, June 30, 1993.
36. Genesta Halloran, widow of deceased miner, John Halloran, personal communication, June 29, 1993.
37. Isabel Gillis, widow of deceased miner, Myles Gillis, personal communication, June 30, 1993; Genesta Halloran, widow of deceased miner, John Halloran, personal communication, June 29, 1993.
38. Mayor Mary Daley, Westville, NS, personal communication, February 26, 1993; Kathy Dobbs, mental health worker, Aberdeen General Hospital, New Glasgow, NS, personal communication, February 19, 1993; Genesta Halloran, widow of deceased miner, John Halloran, personal communication, June 29, 1993.
39. Colin Benner, President of Operations, Curragh Incorporated, Plymouth, NS, news conference broadcast live on CBC *Newsworld*, May 10, 1992.
40. Kevin Cox, reporter, Halifax bureau, the *Globe and Mail*, personal communications, February 25, 1993 and November 24, 1993.
41. Michael Lightstone, reporter, the *Daily News*, Halifax, NS, personal communication, February 24, 1993.
42. Michael Lightstone, reporter, the *Daily News*, Halifax, NS, personal communication, February 24, 1993.
43. Rob Gordon, reporter, *First Edition*, CBC-TV, Halifax, NS, personal communication, February 25, 1993.
44. Dean Jobb, reporter, the *Chronicle-Herald*, Halifax, NS, personal communication, February 26, 1993.
45. Bob Allison, Senior Producer, *First Edition*, CBC-TV, Halifax, personal communication, February 15, 1993; Kevin Cox, reporter, Halifax bureau, the *Globe and*

*Mail,* personal communications, February 25, 1993 and November 24, 1993; Michael Lightstone, reporter, the *Daily News,* Halifax, NS, personal communication, February 24, 1993.

46.  Rob Gordon, reporter, *First Edition,* CBC-TV, Halifax, NS, personal communication, February 25, 1993.

47.  Genesta Halloran, widow of deceased miner, John Halloran, personal communication, June 29, 1993.

48.  Reverend Glen Matheson, First Presbyterian Church, New Glasgow, NS, personal communication, February 26, 1993.

49.  Mayor Mary Daley, Westville, NS, personal communication, February 26, 1993.

50.  Ron Peers, Staff Sergeant, RCMP, New Glasgow, NS, personal communication, June 30, 1993.

51.  Bob Allison, Senior Producer, *First Edition,* CBC-TV, Halifax, NS, personal communication, February 25, 1993.

52.  Rob Gordon, reporter, *First Edition,* CBC-TV, Halifax, NS, personal communication, February 25, 1993.

53.  Rob Gordon, reporter, *First Edition,* CBC-TV, Halifax, NS, personal communication, February 25, 1993.

54.  Genesta Halloran, widow of deceased miner, John Halloran, personal communication, June 29, 1993.

55.  "Sensitivity Required," New Glasgow *Evening News,* 14 May, 1992: 4.

56.  Dean Jobb, reporter, *Chronicle-Herald,* Halifax, NS, personal communications, February 26, 1993, and December 6, 1993.

57.  Bob Allison, Senior Producer, *First Edition,* CBC-TV, Halifax, personal communication, February 25, 1993.

58.  Kevin Cox, reporter, Halifax bureau, the *Globe and Mail,* personal communications, February 25, 1993, and November 24, 1993.

59.  Bob Allison, Senior Producer, *First Edition,* CBC-TV, Halifax, personal communication, February 15, 1993.

60.  Curragh Incorporated, *Statement to the press,* May 15, 1992. Unpublished news release.

## Chapter Eight

1.  This chapter was commissioned especially for this volume.

2.  "Justice system derailed," Halifax *Chronicle-Herald,* June 24, 1995: B1–2.

3.  Bell died June 10, 1998, three years to the day after his comment appeared in print. Bell's family and friends blamed his death on the stress of the Westray ordeal. "He's always been there like a stalwart," noted Ray Wagner, a lawyer for the Westray families. "He's been one of the pillars and he just couldn't take it anymore." Halifax *Chronicle-Herald,* June 11, 1998: D11; interview with Wagner, October 28, 1998.

4.  "Westray: The torture continues," Halifax *Chronicle-Herald,* June 10, 1995: B3.

5.  Richard was one of the court's most senior trial judges. Appointed by the federal Liberals in 1978, he was counsel to a royal commission into the sinking of the oil tanker *Arrow* off the Nova Scotia coast in the early 1970s.

6.  These investigations are summarized in *The Westray Story* 1997: vol 2, 580–93.

7.  Note from the Editor: It was not until 1991 that the Supreme Court in Stinchcombe

required disclosure by prosecutors to defendants. The N.S. review of the Public Prosecution Service was conducted by Fred Kaufman, QC, who also conducted the review in the Guy Paul Morin Inquiry.

8. For a detailed account of the explosion and its immediate aftermath, see Jobb, 1994: ch. 3–5.

9. *Debates of the House of Assembly of the Province of Nova Scotia*, May 15, 1992: 9291. Justice Richard was given a dual mandate as a commissioner under the *Public Inquiries Act*, R.S.N.S. 1989, c. 372, and as a special examiner under the *Coal Mines Regulation Act*, R.S.N.S. 1989, c. 73.

10. Order in Council 92-504, cited in *Phillips et al.* v. *Richard, J.* (1993) 116 N.S.R. (2d) at 37.

11. *Coal Mines Regulation Act*, sections 70(3)(a), 72(3), 85.

12. By 1992, there were only two underground coal mines operating under the jurisdiction of the Nova Scotia Department of Labour—Westray and Cape Breton's Evans Coal Company. Two Cape Breton Development Corporation (Devco) collieries were governed by federal safety laws and inspected by Labour Canada officials.

13. For a detailed examination of the department's handling of Westray, see Jobb, 1994: ch 11.

14. *Debates of the House of Assembly*, May 21, 1992: 9392–93.

15. Interview with John Smith, May 31, 1994; Jobb 1994: 212.

16. *Debates of the House of Assembly*, May 20, 1992: 9317; May 21, 1992: 9393.

17. "Westray site under control of Mounties," Toronto *Globe and Mail*, May 22, 1992: A4; "Mounties deny order to seize papers," Halifax *Daily News*, May 22, 1992: 3. The RCMP later determined that there was no evidence mine records had been among the documents shredded. *The Westray Story*, 1997: vol. 2, 581–82.

18. "Westray mine has new manager," Halifax *Chronicle-Herald*, May 22, 1992: D20. Results of the Curragh investigation were never made public.

19. *Debates of the House of Commons*, May 20, 1992: 10926–27, 10929; May 21, 1992: 1018-19; May 22, 1992: 11072, 11075–76; June 1, 1992: 11158; June 9, 1992: 11652.

20. *Criminal Code of Canada*, Section 220.

21. Jobb, 1994: 233–34; "RCMP eyes charging Westray," Halifax *Chronicle-Herald*, September 12, 1992: A1.

22. *Coal Mines Regulation Act*, section 67(e).

23. *Starr et al.* v. *Holden et al.* (1990) 68 D.L.R. (4th) 641; *Re Nelles et al. and Grange et al.* (1984) 9 D.L.R. (4th) 79. Before the Westray case, the Supreme Court of Canada's precedent in *Starr* was used to strike down a Saskatchewan inquiry into allegations of fraud against officials of a provincial Crown corporation. *Castle* v. *Brownbridge* (1990) 6 W.W.R. 354.

For an analysis of the impact of provincial and federal jurisdiction on the scope of public inquiries in Canada, see Ontario Law Reform Commission, *Report on Public Inquiries*, (Toronto, 1992): 68–103.

24. *Canadian Charter of Rights and Freedoms, Constitution Act, 1982*, sections 7, 11(d).

25. *Phillips et al.* v. *Richard, J.* (1993) 116 N.S.R. (2d) 30.

26. Note from the Editor: Gerald Phillips and Roger Parry applied to the Nova Scotia Supreme Court for a declaration that the Order in Council establishing the

commission was outside the province's jurisdiction, and that it infringed their rights under the *Canadian Charter of Rights and Freedoms*, specifically sections 7 (the right to security of the person), 8 (the right to be secure against unreasonable search and seizure) and 11(d) (the presumption of innocence and the right to a fair trial). The judge ruled that the terms of the Inquiry encroached upon the federal criminal law power. That decision was appealed and was eventually set aside, and the Inquiry's public hearings were ordered stayed pending the resolution of the charges against the individual respondents.

27. *Report on Public Inquiries*, (Toronto, 1992): 1.
28. *Report on Public Inquiries*, (Toronto, 1992): 196–97, 214.
29. Nova Scotia's Court of Appeal discussed the differing practices in *Phillips et al. v. Richard, J.* (1993) 117 N.S.R. (2d) at 247-48.
30. Jobb, 1994: 238; *Occupational Health and Safety Act,* S.N.S. 1986, c. 3, section 49.
31. *The Westray Story,* 1997: vol. 4, 6–8, 11.
32. "The larger lessons of Westray are obvious, but unmentioned," Halifax *Chronicle-Herald*, December 12, 1997: C1.
33. Jobb, 1994: 240–41. The legal problems created by the wording of the Inquiry's terms of reference prompted one writer to suggest a conspiracy to squelch the Inquiry. "The sequence of events that has put the inquiry into limbo and the disaster at a safe political distance has unfolded like a well-crafted plot," journalist Richard Starr noted in 1993 *(Canadian Forum* [May 1993]: 5).
34. *Phillips et al.* v. *Richard, J.* (1993) 116 N.S.R. (2d) 34.
35. *Phillips et al.* v. *Richard, J.* (1993) 117 N.S.R. (2d) 218.
36. "Two department mergers to save money—premier," Halifax *Chronicle-Herald*, April 6, 1993: A3.
37. *Report of the Royal Commission on the Donald Marshall, Jr., Prosecution*, vol. 1 (Halifax: Queen's Printer, 1989) recommendation 35, pp. 286–7. *An Act to Provide for an Independent Director of Public Prosecutions*, S.N.S. 1990, c. 21.
38. "Province a 'suspect' in Westray," Dean Jobb. Halifax *Chronicle-Herald*, May 5, 1993: A1.
39. "Province a "suspect" in Westray." Dean Jobb. Halifax *Chronicle-Herald*, May 5, 1993: A1.
40. "Prosecutor in Westray case criticized by own staff—memos," Halifax *Chronicle-Herald*, May 11, 1994: A7.
41. *Criminal Code*, section 490(2).
42. "Judge orders evidence returned," Halifax *Chronicle-Herald*, March 27, 1993: A2.
43. "Burying Westray." Stevie Cameron and Andrew Mitrovica. *Saturday Night*, May 1994: 83.
44. "RCMP lay charges in Westray deaths," Halifax *Chronicle-Herald*, April 21, 1993: A1.
45. *Criminal Code,* sections 220, 234, 236, 719.
46. *R.* v. *Syncrude Canada Limited* (1984) 1 W.W.R. 355; *R.* v. *Kuhle* (1988) 3 C.O.H.S.C. 53.
47. *R.* v. *Union Colliery Company* (1900) 3 C.C.C. 523; 31 S.C.R. 81; See also *The Halifax Mail*, August 18, 1898:. 1; the Cumberland *News*, Cumberland, B.C., August 20, 1898: 1; August 30, 1989: 1; September 3, 1898: 1; September 6,

1989: 1; September 10, 1898: 2; the *Nanaimo Free Press*, August 17, 1898: 1–2; August 19, 1898: 1.

48. The case is eerily similar to that of Westray; Brazeau's lawyers even asked a judge to quash the charge as too vague but they were turned down. Unlike the Westray case, however, no mine managers were singled out in the charges.

   The evidence against Brazeau Collieries was damning. Miners had complained repeatedly to their bosses about poor ventilation and high levels of methane. An Alberta government inspector had detected explosive levels of gas during an August 1941 tour, in the area where the blast occurred three months later. He had reported his findings to the mine's general manager, but nothing was done to correct the problem.

   Coal was a crucial commodity for the war effort and the goal of Brazeau management was to produce as much as possible. In the words of C.S. Blanchard, the lawyer who prosecuted the case, "the consideration of getting the coal out came first and the interests of the safety of the men came next." *R.* v. *Brazeau Collieries Limited* (1942) 3 W.W.R. 570; the *Calgary Herald*, January 16, 1943: 1, 10; the *Halifax Herald*, November 1, 1941: 1; November 3, 1941: 1; January 16, 1943: 1.

49. "Government still bears responsibility for Westray—Boudreau," Halifax *Chronicle-Herald*, April 21, 1993: A2.

50. *R.* v. *Curragh Incorporated et al.* (1994), 124 N.S.R. (2d) 59.

51. *R.* v. *Curragh Incorporated et al. (No. 2)*(1994) 125 N.S.R. (2d) 185.

52. "Public prosecutor lands new job," Halifax *Chronicle-Herald*, April 12, 1994: A1; "Ghiz to conduct review of public prosecution," Halifax *Chronicle-Herald*, May 4, 1994: A4.

53. Joseph A. Ghiz and Bruce P. Archibald, *Independence, Accountability and Management in the Nova Scotia Public Prosecution Service: A Review and Evaluation* (Halifax: Queen's Printer, 1994). For an overview of the prosecution service's problems and government response to the Ghiz/Archibald report, see "Tarnished Crown," Halifax *Chronicle-Herald*, April 22, 1995: C1.

54. The following account of the trial is based on "Judging Westray," Halifax *Chronicle-Herald.*, March 18, 1995: B1–2; and "Justice system derailed," Halifax *Chronicle-Herald*, June 24, 1995: B1–2.

55. *R.* v. *Curragh Incorporated* (1995) 1 S.C.R. 900.

56. *R.* v. *Curragh Incorporated et al.* (1995) 146 N.S.R. (2d) 163.

57. *R.* v. *Curragh Incorporated et al.* (1996) 146 N.S.R. (2d) 161.

58. "'93 memo warned of document crush at Westray trial," Halifax *Chronicle-Herald*, May 22, 1995: A1.

59. *Phillips* v. *Nova Scotia Commission of Inquiry into Westray Mine Tragedy* (1995) 2 S.C.R. 97. Also reported as *Phillips* v. *Nova Scotia (Westray Inquiry)* (1995) 124 D.L.R. (4th) 129.

60. *Canada (Attorney General)* v. *Canada (Commission of Inquiry on the Blood System)* (1997) 3 S.C.R. 440.

61. The contrast is explored in "Two Inquiries Reveal Two Approaches: Scathing Analysis, Leaden Prose," *Toronto Star,* December 5, 1997: A36.

62. *The Westray Story*, 1997: vol. 4, viii, 12.

63. "N.S. apologizes for Westray," Halifax *Chronicle-Herald*, December 19, 1997: A1; "New mining rules on way," Halifax *Chronicle-Herald*, December 4, 1998: A7.

64. For an overview of the Inquiry's findings, see Jobb, 1998a.

65. *R. v. Curragh Incorporated* (1997) 113 C.C.C. (3d) 481. Despite the harsh findings and their lofty source, a disciplinary committee of the Nova Scotia Barristers' Society dismissed a complaint of unethical conduct against six prosecutors involved in the trial. "Westray Crowns absolved," Halifax *Chronicle-Herald*, February 18, 1998: A5.

66. "Documents reveal split," Halifax *Chronicle-Herald*, November 11, 1998: A3; "Westray prosecution 'unfair'," Halifax *Chronicle-Herald*, December 16, 1998: A7.

67. "Westray charges stayed," Halifax *Chronicle-Herald*, July 1, 1998: A1; Brian Bergman, "A case abandoned: Nova Scotia stays charges in the Westray disaster," *Maclean's,* vol. 111 (July 13, 1998): 28.

68. Prosecutions of individuals or companies for safety-related crimes are "exceedingly rare and convictions almost impossible to obtain," one observer has noted. Of eight such prosecutions in this century in Canada, only one conviction—the Brazeau Collieries case—withstood appeal. Tucker, 1995.

69. "Special prosecutions head picked," Halifax *Chronicle-Herald,* October 29, 1998: A7.

70. "Crown asset." Dean Jobb. *Canadian Lawyer* (January 1998): 20.

71. "Westray case points to flaws in justice system," Halifax *Sunday Herald*, July 5, 1998: A6; Jobb, 1998c.

72. "Ex-judge to probe prosecution service," Toronto *Globe and Mail*, July 11, 1998: A3. For the review's terms of reference, see "Kaufman to keep open mind," Halifax *Chronicle-Herald*, July 18, 1998: A1–2; "Probe to consider Westray," Halifax *Chronicle-Herald*, October 15, 1998: A10.

73. *Phillips v. Nova Scotia (Westray Inquiry)* (1995) 124 D.L.R. (4th) at 170.

74. *Occupational Health and Safety Act,* S.N.S. 1996, c.7. The new act, brought into force in January 1997, improves workplace safety committees and creates stronger rights to refuse dangerous work. Penalties for violations have been increased to a maximum fine of $250,000 and up to two years in jail. See sections 27, 29–31, 43–46, 74.

75. "NDP, families target corporate negligence," Halifax *Chronicle-Herald*, August 5, 1998: A1; "MP urges feds to follow Westray recommendations," Halifax *Chronicle-Herald*, September 30, 1998: A4; "Federal NDP wants tougher penalties for safety violations," Halifax *Chronicle-Herald*, December 2, 1998: A3; "New mining rules on way," Halifax *Chronicle-Herald,* December 4, 1998: A7.

## CHAPTER NINE

1. This chapter was commissioned especially for this volume. It is adapted from an honours thesis in sociology by Sherman Hinze, in collaboration with John McMullan.

2. "Media should do soul-searching over Westray mine disaster role," Halifax *Daily News*, May 17, 1992: 2.

3. "Wait Beginning to Wear on Families," Halifax *Mail-Star*, May 13, 1992: A1; "First 11 Died Quick, Painless Deaths, Says Medical Examiner," Halifax *Mail-Star,* May 15, 1992: B3; "Tearful Draegermen Describe Their Ordeal," Halifax *Mail-Star*, May 15, 1992: A2.

4. "Tragedy at Westray," Halifax *Chronicle-Herald*, May 11, 1992: C1; "Call of the Coal," Halifax *Chronicle-Herald*, May 16, 1992: B1; "Westray Miner Says He'd Return to Pit," Halifax *Mail-Star*, May 11, 1992: A14.

5. "'No Person' will escape mine probe—Cameron," Halifax *Daily News*, May 16, 1992: 5.

6. "Curragh Incorporated Replaces General Manager," Halifax *Mail-Star*, December 26, 1992: A6.

7. "3,000 Expected at Memorial Service for Miners," Halifax *Mail-Star*, October 3, 1992: D2.

8. "Mine Closure Rings Up Coal Order for Devco," Halifax *Mail-Star*, October 8, 1992: A2.

9. "Will We Know the Truth," Halifax *Mail-Star*, November 4, 1995: B1.

## CHAPTER TEN

1. This chapter was an invited contribution for this volume.

2. *About the Interviews:* I conducted eleven interviews with members from eight of the twenty-six bereaved families. In all twenty-six people participated: mothers, fathers, brothers, sisters, wives, children, cousins, and in-laws, in whatever combinations suited them. Most interviews were held in the families' homes, and all but one were tape-recorded. Many of the people I interviewed have become public figures in a small locale so anonymity is difficult to guarantee. None-the-less, I change details about relations to the lost man where it does not distort the speakers' particular vantage. To open each interview I asked, "Can you tell me something about the way the explosion changed your life?" Some laughed sadly, shaking their heads; others cried a minute, then they plunged in. From that point on, the interviews were unscheduled. I intervened as little as possible but was drawn occasionally to reflect on my family's experience, as all knew beforehand that my own brother had died fifteen years ago in the *Ocean Ranger* sinking of February 15, 1982 (see Dodd, 1993, 1995; Dodd et al., 1993).

3. By "family" I mean close domestic relations that may or may not include blood ties and formal marriages. Most of the family members I interviewed shared a "traditional" family relationship with the Westray worker, but the wives in particular insisted that "family" included unmarried partners, in-laws, and in some cases extremely close friends.

4. *Acknowledgments:* In Nova Scotia, my visits with family members were made possible through the hospitality of Carolyn and Mary Alice Chisholm in St. Andrews; John and Dolores Campbell in Sydney; and Linda, James, Jordan, Brittany, and Victoria Smith in Halifax. The Nova Scotia New Democrat Caucus Office gave me access to their excellent research files. And, as always, my parents Joyce and Ed Dodd supported me in everything from the loan of their car to a much needed couple of days rest after the interviews. At York, my work benefited immeasurably from discussions with Chad Thompson, Norma Jo Baker, Larry Patriquin (who transcribed some of the interviews), Bill Swanson, Janice Newson, and the Sunday brunch crowd. I am indebted, further, to a number of people who commented extensively on drafts: at York, John O'Neill, Brian Singer, Bryan Green, and Gordon Darroch; and at King's, Bruce Wark. Finally, Kenton Teasdale, from the Westray Families' Group, made sure I had contact with a variety of

families, often with divergent opinions. I'm sorry I didn't have the time or emotional stamina to talk to more. I thank everyone who spoke with me for their kindness, openness, and their faith.

5. An analogous four-term claim can be seen to ground the social critique currently being articulated by hemophiliacs who have been infected with HIV through the Canadian blood system: a breach of the sacredness of the body fuels the search for a causal and intentional chain and consequent attributions of blame. Social resistance to these claims pushes sufferers deeper into social critique at every turn.

6. This was one topic in a panel discussion in Halifax, June 1996, entitled "Westray: The Story the Media Missed." It is often noted that journalist Betsy Chambers wrote a number of articles raising questions about the safety conditions at Westray. In a structural similarity, a journalist in Bhopal wrote desperate articles about the dangers at Union Carbide in the months before the 1986 catastrophe. Neither journalist was able to communicate the urgency of the situation.

7. Hannah Arendt's *Eichmann in Jerusalem: A Report on the Banality of Evil* is a classic analysis of arguments claiming moral neutrality for functionaries. This works closely with management interpretations of the causes of the explosion.

8. I wonder if family members who identify more closely with liberal–democratic norms of truth-telling and promise-honouring take more time to move to critique than do those family members who always presuppose a conflictual relation between workers and management. In other words, middle-class families may suffer a more sudden, violent movement from estrangement to critique than working-class family members.

9. This family, one of the Westray families who were Cameron's constituents, recalls that Cameron skipped their house while canvassing in his successful bid for re-election in June 1993, one year after the fatal explosion.

10. The issue of physical evidence came up a number of times in the interviews. Family members felt that as they were paralyzed, first with false hopes of finding the men alive and then in the initial days of the deaths, Curragh Resources' agents were strategically destroying documents. The RCMP didn't seal off the companies' offices for a full twelve days after the explosion. During that time, Curragh Resources' personnel were free to come and go from the offices (Jobb, 1994: 216, 217).

11. After the report of the Westray Inquiry, White and McLean were fired. This was not because the Inquiry had the power to demand such things. Rather, they were fired because the Nova Scotia government, on hearing the conclusions of the report, accepted the firings as a manageable aspect of family members' demand that changes be made so this "never happens again." This admission of government guilt coincided with a formal apology from the government (that is, from a Liberal government now in power, as opposed to the Progressive Conservative government that was in power at the time of the deaths. John Hamm, then leader of Nova Scotia's PCs issued his party's apology on December 3, 1997, a couple of weeks before the release of Richard's report).

The Nova Scotia Department of Labour has undergone a number of reviews, most notably the Plummer Report, but the hiring of more occupational health and safety inspectors has been slow indeed. Some occupational health and safety activists are critical of Plummer's report and its emphasis on the OHS division of the Department of Labour as a sick social environment rather than as an under-staffed regulatory agency that lacks the legal power and autonomy to be effective and to fine offending businesses on the spot. The Canadian government has made no move to look into possible routes for holding directors criminally responsible for corporate negligence causing workplace deaths.

12. I have been unable to confirm this point, but a number of family members mentioned that Clifford Frame discussed having lost a brother in a mining accident.

13. This suffering corresponds loosely to the discomfort cause by "coding problems," by the unsettled "fourth corner" in Greimas' semiotic square, as discussed in Green (1993; 1992).

14. I am arguing against a therapeutic account that would reduce the continued suffering of family members to an inadequately healed wound. Simplistic trauma talk would diagnose family members as having failed to complete the process of mourning as if this were a failure of each individual psyche (Butler, 1997).

15. This refers to Kenton Teasdale, long-time spokesperson for the Westray Families Group, whose son-in-law Myles Gillis was killed in the mine. Myles was an electrician, and therefore one of the men considered by some most technically able to tamper with methanometers. Kenton Teasdale is a former teacher, and I believe his pedagogical orientation as well as the fact that he is an "in-law" rather than a blood relative have worked to make him central to the cohesion of the Westray Families Group. Family members comment on Teasdale's patience—his relentless determination to make sure that everyone understands the legal and technical complexities of any given point. Some find this condescending, others rely on it, yet all agree that Teasdale's commitment and remarkable capacity to learn, then teach, have been crucial to the Families Group's survival to date. The Families Group is by no means monolithic and has its history of strife and division—largely around issues of body retrieval. The writing of the history of their organization I leave to them.

16. Isabel Gillis, in Jobb, 1994: 41.

17. The *Daily News* reported that former Westray manager, Gerald Phillips, was hired by a Vancouver-based mining company shortly after the release of Richard's report, despite an outstanding attempted homicide charge against him in Hondu-ras. "Honduran authorities say 18-year-old Wilmer Hernandez suffered a broken pelvis when Phillips drove a bulldozer into a water tower, knocking it over. The tower was surrounded by residents protesting the razing of their village to make way for the mine." (October 18, 1998).

18. "Undaunted Frame maps new empire. 1992 tragedy, ensuing report fail to brake Westray boss," Halifax *Chronicle-Herald*, December 17, 1997: C4.

19. Focusing on the "settlement" process that characterizes the aftermath of death-by-industry is an aspect of what Frankfurt School thinker, Theodor Adorno, would call "non-identity thinking." As David Held explains: "Marx's analysis exposed, Adorno maintained, the prime source of illusion in capitalism and the necessity of imminent criticism to overcome it. Through the exchange process and its subsequent fetishization, unlike phenomena are equated. This occurs in two ways: social phenomena are reified on the one hand and, on the other, inanimate things are treated as if they had the qualities of the social. As a result of reification definite relations between human beings appear in the form of charac-

teristics of, or relations between, material objects, and concepts of things are applied to social relations. With the attribution of properties of social relations to 'things,' a deceptive equation of concept and object also occurs. It is important not to conceive of these phenomena as simple errors of consciousness. They are socially created illusions which project images about the world which contain both truth and error. They contain truth in so far as they reflect the process of commodity exchange, a process which does equate unlike things: 'the exchange principle, the reduction of human labour to its abstract universal concept of average labour-time, is fundamentally related to the principle of identification. Identification has its social model in exchange and exchange would be nothing without it.' It is through the universalization of exchange that the dissimilar becomes comparable" (Held 1980: 220).

20. That is, the families' version draws on moral sources held in what Habermas would call the life-world (in distinction from the "amoral," functionalist systems of the market economy and political realm) or in a "moral economy" as elaborated from E.P. Thompson: "No other term seems to offer itself to describe the way in which, in peasant and in earlier industrial communities, many 'economic' relations are regulated according to non-monetary norms. These exist as a tissue of customs and usages until they are threatened by monetary rationalizations and are made self-conscious as a 'moral economy.' In this sense, the moral economy is summoned into being in resistance to the 'free market'" (1991: 340).

21. The news of the explosion is a temporal breach that alters family members' way of looking at the past, present, and future. This is the first move in what will become a shift in conscious awareness of family members' relationships with social institutions. The move into critique is a move into an uncomfortable position of deep questioning. The role of risk perception is crucial in making this point: both workers and family members have always been aware, in some way, of their antagonistic relationship with Curragh. The move to an explicit articulation of this antagonism is one that passes through the uncanny collapse of fundamental distinctions between life and death, truth and falsehood, coercion and community. "Nobody knew that this stuff was going on and nobody knew what to think if they knew." The family members' demand for accountability is an ongoing process of articulating critique; it holds the experience of the strategic manipulation of "truth" accountable to the conditions necessary to the project of *seeking* truth.

22. Philosopher Paul Ricoeur (1980: 170) describes the participation of readers or listeners in the "configurational dimension" of narratives that gather events into memorable stories: "rather than being predictable, a conclusion must be acceptable. Looking back from the conclusion to the episodes leading up to it, we have to be able to say that this ending required these sorts of events and this chain of actions. But this backward look is made possible by the teleological movement directed by our expectations when we follow the story. This is the paradox of contingency, judged 'acceptable after all', that characterizes the comprehension of any story told."

23. Hannah Arendt would call this the "whoness" of the men, which is accomplished by a fundamentally social synthesis of the contiguous events of a lifetime—the "whatness" of a life—into a personal identity.

24. The concept of "balancing accounts" opens the books to economies of exchange,

via Marx, Smith, Freud, Mauss and Adorno. The concept of "giving accounts" raises concerns about recognition, communication, and the need for a public place of appearance, via Hegel, Taylor, Habermas and Arendt. It raises the question of the background commonalties that make such interpretive "coming into whoness" possible: grammar, for instance. And the idea that there are competing accounts of any events brings concepts of "authoritative" versions of causation into play: ways of "settling" contingency into rational or manageable order, via Ricoeur and other theories of narration and textuality.

# REFERENCES

Ackerlof, George A., and William T. Dickens. 1982. "The Economic Consequences of Cognitive Dissonance." *American Economic Review*, 72.

Alvesson, M. 1987. *Organization Theory and Technocratic Consciousness: Rationally, Ideology and Quality of Work.* New York: Walter de Gruyter.

Aranoff, Craig. 1975. "Newspapermen and Practitioners Differ Widely on PR Role." *Public Relations Journal*, August: 24–25.

Arendt, Hannah. 1963. *Eichmann in Jerusalem: A Report on the Banality of Evil.* New York: Penguin.

Ashforth, B.E., and B.W. Gibbs. 1990. "The Double Edge Sword of Organizational Legitimation." *Organization Science*, 1: 177–94.

Awad, J. 1985. *The Power of Public Relations.* New York: Praeger.

Barak, G. 1994. *Media, Process, and the Social Construction of Crime: Studies in Newsmaking Criminology.* New York: Garland.

Beck, Ulrich. 1992. *Risk Society: Towards a New Modernity.* Trans. Mark Ritter. London: Sage.

_____. 1994. "Risk Society and the Provident State." In S. Lash, B. Szerszynski, and B. Wynne (eds.), *Risk, Economy, and Modernity: Towards a New Ecology.* London: Sage.

Berger, P., and T. Luckman. 1967. *The Social Construction of Reality: A Treatise in the Sociology of Knowledge.* Garden City, NY: Doubleday.

Bergman, Brian. 1998. "A Case Abandoned: Nova Scotia Stays Charges in the Westray Disaster." *Maclean's*, 111(July 13): 28.

Blishen, B.R., W.K. Carroll, and C. Moore. 1987. "The 1981 Socioeconomic Index for Occupations in Canada." *Canadian Review of Sociology and Anthropology*, 24: 465–88.

Blyskal, Jeff, and Marie Blyskal. 1985. *PR: How the Public Relations Industry Writes the News.* New York: William Morrow.

Blythe, Bruce T. 1992. "HR ... Home Run or Strikeout? HR Focus *American Medical Association*, April.

Bonner, K. [no date]. "Crime in the Media: The Underreporting of Wife-battery in the Press." Unpublished.

Bourdieu P. 1977. *Outline of a Theory of Practice.* Cambridge: Cambridge University Press.

_____. 1980. "The Production of Belief." *Media, Culture and Society*, 2(3).

Bowman, E., and H. Kunreuther. 1988. "Post-Bhopal Behavior at a Chemical Company." *Journal of Management Studies*, 25: 387–402.

Box, S. 1983. *Power, Crime and Mystification.* New York: Routledge.

Boyle, Theresa. 1992. "Why Did Safety System Fail: Sad Questions Grow Louder." *Toronto Star*, May 11: A1.

Braithwaite, John. 1985. *To Punish or Persuade: Enforcement of Coal Safety.* Albany: State University of New York Press.

Brantlinger, P. 1990. *Crusoe's Footprints: Cultural Studies in Britain and America.* New York: Routledge.

Brickey, Stephen, and Karen Grant. 1992. "An Empirical Examination of Work-Related Accidents and Illnesses in Winnipeg." *Manitoba Federation of Labour Conference on Workplace Health and Safety.* Winnipeg.

Brodie, Janine. 1990. *The Political Economy of Canadian Regionalism.* Toronto: Harcourt.

Brown, Jane Delano, Carl R. Bybee, Stanley T. Wearden, and Dulcie Murdock Straughan. 1987. "Invisible Power: Newspaper News Sources and the Limits of Diversity." *Journalism Quarterly,* 64(Spring): 45–54.

Burrill, Gary, and I. McKay, eds. 1987. *People, Resources, and Power: Critical Perspectives on Underdevelopment and Primary Industries in the Atlantic Region.* Fredericton: Acadiensis.

Butler, Judith. 1997. *The Psychic Life of Power.* Stanford: Stanford University Press.

Cameron, James M. 1974. *The Pictonian Colliers.* Halifax: Nova Scotia Museum.

Cameron, Stevie. 1992a. "Throwing Light on Westray Financing." *Globe and Mail,* June 8: A7.

_____. 1992b. *Globe and Mail,* June 8: A4.

_____. 1995. *On the Take.* Stoddart.

Cameron, Stevie, and Andrew Mitrovica. 1994. "Burying Westray," *Saturday Night,* May: 54–60, 83–84.

Campbell, Mary, and Susan Dodd. 1993. "Lessons of Disaster," *New Maritimes,* May: 17–20.

Canadian Centre for Mineral and Energy Technology, [no date]. *Westray Coal Incorporated Pictou County Coal Project: Technical Review.*

Canadian Electrical Association. 1998. *Guide to Canada's Electric Utilities.* Montreal: Canadian Electrical Association.

Carson, Kit, and Cathy Henenberg. 1988. "The Political Economy of Legislative Change: Making Sense of Victoria's New Occupational Health and Safety Legislation." *Law in Context,* 6: 2.

Carson, W.G. [no date]. *The Other Price of Britain's Oil.* Oxford: Martin Robertson.

_____. 1979. "The Conventionalization of Early Factory Crime." *International Journal of the Sociology of Law,* 37(July).

_____. 1984. "Ocean Ranger: Still More Questions to Come." *At the Centre,* 7(4): 15.

_____. 1989. "Occupational Health and Safety: A Political Economy Perspective." *Labour & Industry,* 2.

Casey, J. 1992. "Corporate Crime and the Canadian State: Anti-Combines Legislation, 1945–1986." *Journal of Human Justice,* 3(2): 22–36.

Caudill, Harry M. 1977. "Manslaughter in a Coal Mine." *The Nation,* April 23.

Chajet, Clive, and Tom Schachtman. 1991. *Image by Design: From Corporate Vision to Business Reality.* Reading, MA: Addison-Wesley.

Charron, Jean. 1989. "Relations between Journalists and Public Relations Practitioners: Cooperation, Conflict and Negotiation." *Canadian Journal of Communication,* 14(2): 41–45.

Chasse, John Dennis, and David A. LeSourd. 1984. "Rational Decisions and Occupational Health: A Critical View." *International Journal of Health Services,* 14: 443.

Chibnall, S. 1977. *Law-and-Order News.* London: Tavistock.

Clancy, James. 1992. *National Union News.* May.

Clarke, D. 1981. "Second-hand News: Production and Reproduction at a Major Ontario Television Station." In L. Salter (ed.), *Communication Studies in Canada.* Toronto: Butterworths.

Clinard, Marshall. 1990. *Corporate Corruption: The Abuse of Power.* New York: Praeger.

Clinard, Marshall, and Richard Quinney. 1973. *Criminal Behaviour Systems: A Typology.* New York: Holt.

Clinard, Marshall, and Peter Yeager. 1980. *Corporate Crime.* New York: Free.

Clow, Michael. 1993. *Stifling Debate: Canadian Newspapers and Nuclear Power.* Halifax: Fernwood.

*Coal Age.* "[Mining in] Russia." *Coal Age.* October 1996: 26.

Coal Association of Canada. 1995. *Guidebook.* Calgary: Coal Association of Canada.

Coffey, Amanda, and Paul Atkinson. 1996. *Making Sense of Qualitative Data: Complementary Research Strategies.* London: Sage.

Cohn, Robin J. 1991. Pre-Crisis Management. *Executive Excellence,* 8, 10, 19(October).

Coleman, J. 1989. *The Criminal Elite: The Sociology of White-Collar Crime.* New York: St. Martin's.

Comish, Shaun. 1993. *The Westray Tragedy: A Miner's Story.* Halifax: Fernwood.

Counihan, T.M. 1975. "Reading Television: Notes on the Problem of Media Content." *Australian and New Zealand Journal of Sociology,* 11(2): 31–36.

Cox, Kevin. 1992a. "Documents on Westray Raise Concerns." *Globe and Mail,* July 30: A6.

_____. 1992b, "Coal Mine Experienced Serious Safety Problems." *Globe and Mail,* May 21, A5.

_____. 1992c. "Holding on to Hope." *Globe and Mail,* May 11: A1, A4.

Creighton, Breen, and Neil Gunningham. 1985. "Is There an Industrial Relations of Occupational Health and Safety?" In Breen Creighton and Neil Gunningham (eds.), *The Industrial Relations of Occupational Health and Safety.* Sydney: Croom Helm.

Croall, H. 1992. *White Collar Crime.* Buckingham: Open University Press.

Cullen, Robert. 1993. "Environment: The True Cost of Coal." *The Atlantic Monthly,* 272(6): 38, 40, 48.

"Curragh Inc. Replaces General Manager." 1992. *Mail-Star,* December 26: A6.

Curragh Resources Incorporated, 1990. Annual Report. Toronto.

Curran, Daniel J. 1984. "Symbolic Solutions for Deadly Dilemmas: An Analysis of Federal Coal Mine Health and Safety Legislation." *International Journal of Health Services,* 14(5).

Dennis, John, Chasse, and David A. LeSourd. 1984. "Rational Decisions and Occupational Health: A Critical View." *International Journal of Health Services,* 14(433).

Dodd, Susan. 1993. "Reflections of a Family Member." *New Maritimes,* May–June: 19.

_____. 1995. "Restitching Reality: How TNCs Evade Accountability for Industrial Disaster." *Alternate Routes,* 21: 23–63.

Dodd, Susan, with Mary Campbell. 1993. "The Ocean Ranger: Lessons of Disaster." *New Maritimes,* May–June: 17–19.

Donovan, Arthur L. 1988. "Health and Safety in Underground Coal Mining, 1900–1969: Professional Conduct in a Peripheral Industry." In Ronald Bayer (ed.), *The Health and Safety of Workers: Case Studies in the Politics of Professional Responsibility.* New York: Oxford University Press.

Douglas, Mary. 1986. *How Institutions Think.* Syracuse: Syracuse University Press.

_____. 1992. *Risk and Blame: Essays in Cultural Theory.* New York: Routledge.

Douglas, Mary, and Aaron Wildavsky. 1982. *Risk and Culture: An Essay on the Selection of Technical and Environmental Dangers*. Berkeley, CA: University of California Press.

Dowling, J., and J. Pfeffer. 1975. "Organizational Legitimacy: Social Values and Organizational Behavior." *Pacific Sociological Review*, 18: 122–36.

Drabek, Thomas E., and Gerry Hoetmer. 1991. *Emergency Management: Principles and Practice for Local Government*. Washington, DC: International City Management Association.

Dunbar and Goldberg. 1978. "Crisis Development and Strategic Response in European Corporations." In Carol F. Smart and W.T. Stanburg (eds.), *Studies in Crisis Management*. Toronto: Institute for Research on Policy.

Eco, U. 1979. *The Role of the Reader*. London: Hutchison.

Elias, R. 1986. *The Politics of Victimization: Victims, Victimology and Human Rights*. New York: Oxford University Press.

Ellis, Desmond. 1987. *The Wrong Stuff: An Introduction to the Sociological Study of Deviance*. Toronto: Collier Macmillan.

Ellis, Desmond, and Walter DeKeseredy. 1996. *The Wrong Stuff: An Introduction to the Sociological Study of Deviance*. Second edition. Scarborough: Allyn and Bacon.

Elsbach, K.D., and R.L. Sutton. 1992. "Acquiring Organizational Legitimacy through Illegitimate Actions: A Marriage of Institutional and Impression Management Theories." *Academy of Management Journal*, 35: 699–738.

Ericson, Richard V., Patricia M. Baranek, and Janet B.L. Chan. 1987. *Visualizing Deviance: A Study of News Organization*. Toronto: University of Toronto Press.

_____. 1989. *Negotiating Control: A Study of News Sources*. Toronto: University of Toronto Press.

_____. 1991. *Representing Order: Crime, Law and Justice in the News Media*. Toronto: University of Toronto Press.

Evans, S., and R. Lundman. 1983. "Newspaper Coverage of Corporate Price Fixing." *Criminology*, 21(4): 529–41.

_____. 1987. "Newspaper Coverage of Corporate Crime." In David Ermann and R. Lundman (eds.), *Corporate and Governmental Deviance*. New York: Oxford University Press.

Ewald, Francois. 1991. "Insurance and Risk." In Graham C. Burchell and Gordon P. Miller (eds.), *The Foucault Effect: Studies in Governmentality*. Chicago: University of Chicago Press.

Felstiner, W.L.F., and Peter Siegelman. 1989. "Neoclassical Difficulties: Tort Deterrence for Latent Injuries." *Law & Policy*, 11: 309.

Fishman, M. 1980. *Manufacturing the News*. Austin: University of Texas Press.

_____. 1981. "Police News: Constructing an Image of Crime." *Urban Life*, 9: 371–94.

Fitzpatrick, J. 1974. "Underground Mining: A Case of an Occupational Subculture of Danger." Unpublished doctoral dissertation. Columbus: Ohio State University.

Fitzpatrick, Kathy R., and Maureen Shubow Rubin. 1995. "Public Relations vs. Legal Strategies in Organizational Crisis Decisions." *Public Relations Review*, 21(1): 21–33.

Fox, D.K., B.L. Hopkins, and W.K. Anger. 1987. "The Long-Term Effects of a Token Economy on Safety Performance in Open-Pit Mining." *Journal of Applied Behaviour Analysis*, 20: 215–24.

Francis, D. 1986. *Controlling Interest: Who Owns Canada?* Toronto: Macmillan.

Frank, David. 1992. "Blood on the Coal: A Deadly History." *Globe and Mail*, A15.

_____. 1994. "Westray: Two Years After." *New Maritimes*, June: 16–17.

Freud, A. 1946. *The Ego and the Mechanisms of Defense*. London: Hogarth.

Friedrichs, D. 1996. *White Collar Crime: Trusted Criminals in Contemporary Society*. Belmont: Wadsworth.

Fritz, Charles. 1961. "Disaster." In Robert K. Merton and Robert E. Nisbet (eds.), *Contemporary Social Problems*. New York: Harcourt.

Gans, Herbert J. 1980. *Deciding What's News: A Study of CBS Evening News, NBC Nightly News, Newsweek and Time*. New York: Vintage.

Garnham, N. 1973. *Structures of Television*. London: British Film Institute.

Gavin, MacKenzie. 1993. *Lawyers and Ethics: Professional Responsibility and Discipline*. Scarborough: Carswell.

Geis, Gilbert. 1984. "White-Collar and Corporate Crime." In Robert Meier (ed.), *Major Forms of Crime*. Beverly Hills: Sage.

Gephart, R.P. 1984, "Making Sense of Organizationally Based Environmental Disasters." *Journal of Management*, 10: 205–25.

_____. 1987. "Organization Design for Hazardous Chemical Accidents." *Columbia Journal of World Business*, 22: 51–58.

_____. 1993. "The Textual Approach: Risk and Blame in Disaster Sensemaking." *Academy of Management Journal*, 36: 1465–514.

Gephart, R.P., and R. Pitter. 1993. "The Organizational Basis of Industrial Accidents in Canada." *Journal of Management Inquiry*, 2: 238–52.

Gephart, R.P., L. Steier, and T. Lawrence. 1990. "Cultural Rationalities in Crisis Sensemaking: A Study of a Public Inquiry into a Major Industrial Accident." *Industrial Crises Quarterly*, 4: 27–48.

Gerbner, G., L. Gross, M. Morgan, and N. Signorielli. 1984. "Political Correlates of Television Viewing." *Public Opinion Quarterly*, 48: 283–300.

Gerbner, G., L. Gross, N. Signorielli, M. Morgan, and M. Jackson-Beeck. 1980. "The Mainstreaming of America: Violence Profile No. 11." *Journal of Communication*, 30.

Ghiz, Joseph A., and Bruce P. Archibald. [no date]. *Independence, Accountability and Management in the Nova Scotia Public Prosecution Service: A Review and Evaluation*. Halifax: Queen's Printer.

Giddens, A. 1987. *Social Theory and Modern Sociology*. Cambridge: Polity.

Girard, Rene. 1977. *Violence and the Sacred*. Trans. Patrick Gregory. Baltimore: Johns Hopkins University Press.

_____. 1986. *The Scapegoat*. Trans. Yvonne Freccero. Baltimore: Johns Hopkins University Press.

Gitlin, T. 1979. "Prime-Time Ideology: The Hegemonic Process in Television Entertainment." *Social Problems*, 26(3): 251–66.

Glasbeek, H.J. 1989. "A Role for Criminal Sanctions in Occupational Health and Safety." In *Meredith Memorial Lectures 1988, New Developments in Employment Law*. Cowansville, PQ: Yvon Blais.

Glasbeek, Harry, and Eric Tucker. 1992. *Death by Consensus: The Westray Story*. North York: York University Press.

_____. 1993. "Death by Consensus: The Westray Mine Story." *New Solutions*, 14(Summer).

Goff, C., and C. Reasons. 1980. *Corporate Crime in Canada: A Critical Analysis of Anti-Combines Legislation*. Englewood Cliffs, NJ: Prentice-Hall.

_____. 1986. "Organizational Crimes Against Employees, Consumers, and the Public." In B. Maclean (ed.), *The Political Economy of Crime: Readings for a Critical Criminology*. Scarborough: Prentice-Hall.

Gordon R., and I. Coneybeer. 1991. "Corporate Crime." In M. Jackson and C. Griffiths (eds.), *Canadian Criminology*. Toronto: Harcourt.

Gordon, Raymond L. 1987. *Interviewing, Strategy, Techniques and Tactics*. Chicago: Dorsey.

Gouldner, Alvin. 1954. *Patterns of Industrial Bureaucracy*. New York: Free.

Graber, D. 1980. *Crime News and the Public*. New York: Praeger.

Graber, D., J. Sheley, and C. Ashkins. 1981. "Crime, Crime News, and Crime Views." *Public Opinion Quarterly*, 45: 492–506.

Graebner, William. 1988. "Private Power, Private Knowledge, and Public Health: Science, Engineering, and Lead Poisoning, 1900–1970." In Ronald Bayer (ed.), *The Health and Safety of Workers: Case Studies in the Politics of Professional Responsibility*. New York: Oxford University Press.

Gray, James G. Jr. 1986. *Managing the Corporate Image: The Key to Public Trust*. Westport: Quorum.

Green, Bryan. 1992. *Gerontology and the Construction of Old Age*. New York: Aldine de Gruyter.

_____. 1993. *Knowing the Poor*. Brookfield, VT: Gregg Revivals.

Grunberg, Leon. 1983. "The Effects of the Social Relations of Production on Productivity and Workers' Safety: An Ignored Set of Relationships." *International Journal of Health Services*, 13: 621.

Grunig, James E., and Todd Hunt. 1984. *Managing Public Relations*. New York: CBS.

Guastello, S.J. 1991. "Do We Really Know How Well our Occupational Accident Prevention Programs Work?" *Safety Science*, 16: 445–63.

Gunningham, Neil. 1984. *Safeguarding the Worker*. Sydney, Aus.: Law Book.

Habermas, Jurgen. 1979. *Communication and the Evolution of Society*. Boston: Beacon.

Hackett, R., R. Pinet, and M. Ruggles. 1992. "From Audience-Commodity to Audience-Community: Mass Media in BC." In H. Holmes and D. Taras (eds.), *Seeing Ourselves: Media Power and Policy in Canada*. Toronto: Harcourt.

Hale, A.R., and M. Hale. 1970. "Accidents in Perspective." *Occupational Psychology*, 44: 115–21.

Hall, Alan. 1996. "The Ideological Construction of Risk in Mining: A Case Study." *Critical Sociology*, 1: 93–116.

Hall, S., J. Clarke, C. Critcher, T. Jefferson, and B. Roberts. 1978. *Policing the Crisis*. London: Macmillan.

Hambling, Skip. 1992. "Westray: A View from Afar." *New Maritimes*, September.

Harpur, Keith. 1991. "Work Accidents 'Three Times Reported Rate'." *Guardian*, Dec. 12: 6.

Harris, Michael. 1986. *Justice Denied: The Law versus Donald Marshall*. Toronto: Macmillan.

Hartley, J. 1982. *Understanding News*. London: Methuen.

Hartley, J.F. 1994. "Case Studies in Organizational Research." In C. Cassell and G. Symon (eds.), *Qualitative Methods in Organizational Research*. London: Sage.

Hatty, S. 1991. "Police, Crime and the Media: An Australian Tale." *International Journal of the Sociology of Law*, 19(1): 171–91.

Held, David. 1980. *Introduction to Critical Theory: Horkheimer to Habermas*. Berkeley: University of California Press.

Hills, S. 1988. *Corporate Violence: Injury and Death for Profit*. Totowa, NJ: Rowman & Littlefield.

Hopkins, Andrew. 1984. "Blood Money? The Effect of Bonus Pay on Safety in Coal Mines." *Australia and New Zealand Journal of Sociology*, 23.

_____. 1989. "Crime Without Punishment: The Appin Mine Disaster." In Peter Grabosky and Adam Sutton (eds.), *Stains on a White Collar*. Sydney, Aus.: Hutchinson.

Hopkins, Andrew, and Nina Parnell. 1984. "Why Coal Mine Safety Regulations in Australia Are Not Enforced." *International Journal of the Sociology of Law*, 12: 179–94.

Hynes, Timothy, and Pushkala Prasad. 1997. "Patterns of 'Mock Bureaucracy' in Mining Disasters: An Analysis of the Westray Coal Mine Explosion." *Journal of Management Studies*, 34: 4.

Jackall, R. 1988. *Moral Mazes: The World of Corporate Managers*. New York: Oxford University Press.

Jermier, J., J.W. Slocum, L.W. Fry, and J. Gaines. 1991. "Organizational Subcultures in a Soft Bureaucracy: Resistance Behind the Myth and Facade of an Official Culture," *Organizational Science*, 2: 170–94.

Jobb, Dean. 1992. "52 Charges Laid in Westray Probe." *Chronicle-Herald*, October 6: A1, A2.

_____. 1994. *Calculated Risk: Greed, Politics and the Westray Tragedy*. Halifax: Nimbus.

_____. 1998a. "The Westray Conundrum." *OHS Canada*, 14(April/May): 24–31.

_____. 1998b. "Crown Asset." *Canadian Lawyer*, 22(January): 18–21.

_____. 1998c. "A Legal Minefield." *Elm Street*, November: 71, 73.

*John Deutsch Round Table on Economic Policy, Tax Expenditures and Government Policy*. 1988. November 17–18. Kingston: Queen's University.

Kappeler, V., M. Bluberg, and G. Potter. 1993. "Myths that Justify Crime: A Look at White Collar Criminality." *The Mythology of Crime and Criminal Justice*. Prospect Heights: Waveland.

Kellner, D. 1990. *Television and the Crisis of Democracy*. Boulder: Westview.

Kilborn Limited. [no date]. *Technical and Cost Review of the Pictou County Coal Project Nova Scotia*.

Kirby, Sandra, and Kate McKenna. 1989. *Experience, Research, Social Change: Methods from the Margins*. Toronto: Garamond.

Knight, S. 1980. *Form and Ideology in Crime Fiction*. Bloomington: Indiana University Press.

Kopenhaver, Lillian Lodge, David L. Martinson, and Michael Ryan. 1984. "How Public Relations Practitioners and Editors in Florida View Each Other." *Journalism Quarterly*, 61(4).

Kreps, Gary A. 1980. "Research Needs and the Westray Tragedy: Police Issues on Mass Media Disaster Reporting." In *National Research Council, Disasters and the Mass Media*. Washington, DC: National Academy of Sciences.

Kuklan, H. 1988. "Crisis Confrontation in International Management: Consequences and Coping Actions." *Management International Review*, 28: 21–30.

Labour Canada. 1990. *Employment Injuries and Occupational Illnesses, 1985–87*. Ottawa: Ministry of Supply and Services.

Langille, Brian. 1981. "The Michelin Amendment in Context." *Dalhousie Law Journal*, 6: 523.

Law Reform Commission of Canada. 1986. "Workplace Pollution." Working paper no. 53. Ottawa: Law Reform Commission of Canada.

Lawrence, A.C. 1974. "Human Error as a Cause of Accidents in Gold-Mining." *Journal of Safety Research*, 6: 78–88.

Lester, M. 1980. "Generating Newsworthiness: The Interpretive Construction of Public Events." *American Sociological Review*, 45: 984–94.

Levi-Strauss, Claude. 1987. *Introduction to the Work of Marcel Mauss*. Trans. Felicity Baker. London: Routledge.

Lewis, O. 1966. "The Culture of Poverty." *Scientific American*, 215: 19–35.

*Liaison*. 1993. (20). Ottawa: Labour Canada.

Lichter, S., and S. Rothman. 1981. "Media and Business Elites." *Public Opinion*, 4: 42–46.

MacKenzie, Gavin. 1993. *Lawyers and Ethics: Professional Responsibility and Discipline*. Scarborough: Carswell.

MacLean, Brian. 1986. *The Political Economy of Crime*. Scarborough: Prentice Hall.

MacLean, Brian C. 1996. *Crime in Society: Readings in Critical Criminology*. Toronto: Copp Clark.

Macleod, Donald. 1983. "Colliers, Colliery Safety and Workplace Control: The Nova Scotia Experience, 1873 to 1910." *Canadian Historical Association Historical Papers*, 226.

MacPherson, Colin. 1962. *The Political Theory of Possessive Individualism: Hobbes to Locke*. London: Oxford University Press.

Marcus. 1987. "Preventing Corporate Crises: Stock Market Losses as a Deterrent to the Production of Hazardous Products." *Columbia Journal of World Business*, 22: 33–42.

Marcuse, Herbert. 1955. *Eros and Civilization*. Boston: Beacon.

Marx, Karl. 1970. "Commodities." In I. Howe (ed.), *Essential Works of Socialism*. Binghamton: Vali-Ballou.

Mater, M. 1994. "'Am I the Only One Who Wants to Launch?' Corporate Masculinity and the Space Shuttle Challenger Disaster." *Masculinities*, 1: 34–45.

Mauss, Marcel. 1990. *The Gift: The Form and Reason for Exchange in Archaic Societies*. London: Norton.

McAfee, R.B., and A.R. Winn. 1989. "The Use of Incentives/Feedback to Enhance Work Place Safety." *Journal of Safety Research*, 20: 7–19.

McCormick, Chris. 1995. *Constructing Danger: The Mis/representation of Crime in the News*. Halifax: Fernwood.

_____. 1999. *Criminology in Canada*. Toronto: ITP Nelson.

McKay, Ian. 1985. "The Provincial Workmen's Association: A Brief Survey of Several Problems of Interpretation." In W.J.C. Cherwinski and Gregory S. Kealey (eds.), *Lectures in Canadian Labour and Working-Class History*. St. John's: CCLH & NHP.

_____. 1987. "Springhill 1958." In Gary Burrill and McKay (eds.), *People, Resources, and Power: Critical Perspectives on Underdevelopment and Primary Industries in the Atlantic Region*. Halifax: Gorsebrook.

McManus, P. 1992. "Westray Tragedy: Mysteries of the Deep." *Atlantic Lifestyle Business*, 3(3), August 29: 9–60.

McMullan, John L. 1992. *Beyond the Limits of the Law: Corporate Crime and Law and Order*. Halifax: Fernwood.

Mechanic, D. 1991. "Some Modes of Adaptation: Defense." In A. Monat and R.S. Lazarus (eds.), *Stress and Coping: An Anthology*. New York: Columbia University Press.

Messner, M. 1990. "When Bodies are Weapons: Masculinity and Violence in Sport." *International Review of the Sociology of Sport*, 25: 203–21.

Milburn, T.W., R.S. Schuler, and K.H. Watman. 1983. "Organizational Crises. Part I: Definition and Conceptualization." *Human Relations*, 36: 1141–1160.

Miller, John. 1990. "Rethinking Old Methods." *Content*, September: 23–25.

Miller, Peter. 1994. "Accounting as Social and Institutional Practice: An Introduction." In P. Miller and A.G. Hopwood (eds.), *Accounting as Social and Institutional Practice*. Cambridge: Cambridge University Press.

Miller, Peter, and Ted O'Leary. 1994. "Governing the Calculable Person." In P. Miller and A.G. Hopwood (eds.), *Accounting as Social and Institutional Practice*. Cambridge: Cambridge University Press.

Mitroff, I.I., and R.H. Kilman. 1984. *Corporate Tragedies: Product Tampering, Sabotage and Other Catastrophes*. New York: Praeger.

Mokhiber, Russell. 1988. *Corporate Crime and Violence: Big Business Power and the Abuse of the Public Trust*. San Francisco: Sierra.

Moon, P. 1993. "Alarm Preceded Westray Explosion." *Globe and Mail*, March 27: Al, A6.

Moore, Michael J., and W. Kip Viscusi. 1990. *Compensation Mechanisms for Job Risks*. Princeton: Princeton University Press.

Murdock, G. 1974. "The Press Coverage of Militant Political Demonstrations." In P. Rock and M. McIntosh (eds.), *Deviance and Social Control*. Tavistock: London.

_____. 1980. "Misrepresenting Media Sociology."*Sociology*, 14: 457–68.

_____. 1982. "Disorderly Images." In C.S. Sumner (ed.), *Crime, Justice and the Mass Media*. Cambridge: Institute of Criminology.

Murray, Eileen, and Saundra Shohen. 1992. "Lessons from the Tylenol Tragedy on Surviving a Corporate Crisis." *Medical Marketing & Media*, 27(2): 14–19.

Murty, K., and Y. Siddiqi. 1991. "Government Subsidies to Industry." *Canadian Economic Observer*, 4(May).

National Safety Council. (various years). *Accident Facts*. Chicago.

Navarro, Vincente. 1983. "The Determinants of Social Policy—A Case Study: Regulating Health and Safety at the Workplace in Sweden." *International Journal of Health Services*, 14: 517.

Newman. [no date]. "Exxon's Lessons for Other Managers." *Business and Economic Review*, 35: 8–10.

Noble, Charles. 1986. *Liberalism at Work: The Rise and Fall of OSHA*. Philadelphia: Temple.

Novek, Joel, et al. 1990. "Mechanization, the Labour Process, and Injury Risks in the Canadian Meat Packing Industry." *International Journal of Health Services*, 20: 281.

O'Keefe, Betty. 1984. "Public Relations in the Mining Industry." In Walter B. Herbert, John R.D. Jenkins (eds.), *Public Relations in Canada: Some Perspectives*. Markham, ON: Fitzhenry and Whiteside.

O'Malley, Pat. 1996. "Risk and Responsibility." In Andrea Barry, Thomas Osborne and Nikolas S. Rose (eds.), *Foucault and Political Reason: Liberalism, Neo-liberalism and Rationalities of Government.* Chicago: University of Chicago Press.

O'Neill, John.1976. "Critique and Remembrance." In John O'Neill (ed.), *On Critical Theory.* New York: Seabury.

_____. 1994. *The Missing Child in Liberal Theory: Towards a Covenant Theory of Family, Community, Welfare and the Civic State.* Toronto: University of Toronto Press.

O'Reilly-Fleming, Thomas. 1996. *Post-Critical Criminology.* Scarborough: Prentice-Hall.

Olive, David. 1992. "A Discourse on Events." *Globe and Mail*: May 16, 1992: D4.

Pauchant, T.C., and I.I. Mitroff. 1992. *Transforming the Crisis-Prone Organization.* San Francisco: Josey-Bass.

Perrow, C. 1984. *Normal Accidents: Living with High Risk Technologies.* New York: Basic.

Perry, Charles S. 1982. "Government Regulation of Coal Mine Safety." *American Politics Quarterly*, 10: 303.

Peters, R.H. 1991. "Strategies for Encouraging Self-Protective Employee Behaviour." *Journal of Safety Research*, 22: 53–70.

Picard, J. 1992. "The Pictonian Colliers." *Globe and Mail*, May 12: A4.

*Pictou Project Feasibility Study.* Vol. 1, Mining, 6.

Pinsdorf, Marion K. 1987. *Communicating When Your Company Is Under Siege, Surviving Public Crisis.* Lexington, MA: DC Heath.

Placer Development Limited. 1987. *Pictou Project Feasibility Study, Vol. 1. Geology*, July.

Prasad, A. 1995. "Institutional Ideology and Corporate Legitimation: A Critical Hermeneutic Study of the US Petroleum Industry." Working Paper #94-01, Faculty of Management. Calgary: University of Calgary.

Province of Nova Scotia. 1988. *Environment Assessment Act.* Halifax: S.N.S.

_____. 1989. *Coal Mines Regulation Act.* Halifax.

_____. 1992. Debates of the House of Assembly. Transcript. May 15, 1992: 291; May 21, 1992: 9392-93.

_____. 1996. *Occupational Health and Safety Act.* Halifax: S.N.S.

_____. 1997. *The Westray Story: A Predictable Path to Disaster. Report of the Westray Mine Public Inquiry.* 3 vols. Halifax: Queens Printer.

Province of Nova Scotia, Department of Labour. 1985–90. *Annual Reports.*

Province of Nova Scotia, Department of Mines and Energy. 1988–89. *Annual Report.*

Province of Ontario. 1976. *Report of the Royal Commission on the Health and Safety of Workers in Mines.* (Ham Report.) Attorney General of Ontario.

Reasons, C., L. Ross,. and C. Patterson. 1981. *Assault on the Worker; Occupational Health and Safety in Canada.* Toronto: Butterworths.

Regester, Michael. 1989. *Crisis Management: What To Do When the Unthinkable Happens.* London: Business.

*Report of the Commission of Inquiry, Explosion in No. 26 Colliery Glace Bay, Nova Scotia on February 24, 1979.* 1979. Ottawa.

*Report of the Commission of Inquiry into Occupational Health and Safety* (Williams Report). 1981. NSW, Australia.

*Report of the Royal Commission on the Donald Marshall, Jr., Prosecution, Vol. 1.* 1989. Halifax: Queen's Printer.

*Report of the Westray Public Mine Inquiry.* Executive Summary.

*Report on Public Inquiries.* 1992. Toronto: Ontario Law Reform Commission.

Richards, Trudie. 1994. "The Cost of Coal: The Westray Mine Explosion, May 9, 1992." Unpublished masters thesis. Ottawa: Carleton University.

Ricoeur, Paul. 1980. "Narrative Time." In W.J. Thomas, *On Narrative.* Chicago: University of Chicago Press.

_____. 1981. *Hermeneutics and the Human Sciences.* Cambridge: Cambridge University Press.

Risk, R.C.B. 1983. "'This Nuisance of Litigation': The Origins of Workers' Compensation in Ontario." In David Flaherty (eds.), *Essays in the History of Canadian Law, Vol. 2.* Toronto: University of Toronto Press.

Robb, Nancy. 1992. "The History of Westray." *Occupational Health and Safety Canada,* July/August: 43.

Robinson, Allan. 1992. "Won't Gamble Again, Curragh Head Says," *Globe and Mail,* May 6: B6.

Rock, P. 1973. "News as Eternal Recurrance." In S. Cohen and J. Young (eds.), *The Manufacture of News.* London: Constable.

Roshier, B. 1973. "The Selection of Crime News by the Press." In S. Cohen and J. Young (eds.), *The Manufacture of News.* London: Constable.

Royal Commission of Newspapers. 1981. *The Newspaper and Public Affairs.* Ottawa: Research Studies on the Newspaper Industry, Ministry of Supply and Services.

Ryan, Judith Hoegg. 1992. *Coal in Our Blood: 200 Years of Coal Mining in Nova Scotia's Pictou County.* Halifax: Formac.

*Safety and Health and Work.* Robens Report. 1972. U.K. Cmnd. 5034.

Sandman, Peter M., Mary Paden, Mary Ann Griffin, and Greg Miles. 1979. "At Three Mile Island." *Columbia Journalism Review.* July: 43–58.

Sass, Robert. 1987. "The Tory Assault on Labour in Saskatchewan." *Windsor Yearbook of Access to Justice,* 7: 133.

_____. 1989. "The Implications of Work Organization for Occupational Health Policy: The Case for Canada." *International Journal of Health Services,* 19: 163.

_____. 1991. "A Critique: Canadian Public Policy in Workplace Health and Safety." *New Solutions.*

Scanlon, Joseph. 1993. *Covering Disasters* (audio tape). A panel discussion at the Canadian Association of Journalists annual meeting. Toronto, ON.

Scanlon, Joseph, Suzanne Alldred, Al Farrell, and Angela Prawzick. 1985. "Coping with the Media in Disasters: Some Predictable Problems." *Public Administration Review,* 45: 123–33.

Schiller, D. 1986. "Transformations of News in the US Information Market." In P. Golding, G. Murdock and P. Schlesinger (eds.), *Communicating Politics.* Leiceister: Leicester University Press.

Schrager, Laura, and James Short. 1978. "Toward a Sociology of Organizational Crime." *Social Problems,* 25: 415–25.

Schwartz, H. 1990. "The Symbol of the Space Shuttle and the Degeneration of the American Dream." In P. Gagliardi (ed.), *Symbols and Artifacts: Views of the Corporate Landscape.* New York: Aldine de Gruyter.

Sethi, S.P. 1987. "Inhuman Errors and Industrial Crises." *Columbia Journal of World Business,* 22(1): 101–10.

Sheley, J., and C. Ashkins. 1981. "Crime, Crime News, and Crime Views." *Public Opinion Quarterly*, 45: 492–506.

Shristava, P., I. Mitroff, D. Mieler, and A. Miciani. 1988. "Understanding Industrial Crises." *Journal of Management Studies*, 25: 285–303.

Shrivastava, P. 1987. *Bhopal, Anatomy of a Crisis*. Cambridge, MA: Ballinger.

Sigal, Leon V. 1973. *Reporters and Officials: The Organization and Politics of Newsmaking*. Lexington, MA: DC Heath.

Simon, D., and S. Eitzen. 1990. *Elite Deviance*. Boston: Allyn and Bacon.

Smith, C. 1992. *Media and Apocalypse: New Coverage of the Yellowstone Forest Fires, Exxon Valdez Oil Spill, and Loma Prieta Earthquake*. Westport: Greenwood.

Smith, C.P. 1992. *Motivation and Personality: Handbook of Thematic Content Analysis*. New York: Cambridge University Press.

Smith, Conrad. 1992. "How News Media Cover Disasters: The Case of Yellowstone." In Philip S. Cook, Douglas Gomery and Lawrence W. Lichty (eds.), *The Future of News: Television, Newspapers, Wire Services, Magazines*. Washington, DC: Woodrow Wilson Center; Baltimore, MD: John Hopkins University Press.

Smith, Daryn. [no date]. "Westray Mine Incident Report." Prepared for the Emergency Measures Organization. Unpublished.

Snider, Laureen. 1993. *Bad Business: Corporate Crime in Canada*. Scarborough: Nelson.

Soloski, John. 1989. "Sources and Channels of Local News." *Journalism Quarterly*, 66: 864–70.

Sparks, R. 1990. "Dramatic Power: Television, Images of Crime and Law Enforcement." In C.S. Sumner (ed.), *Censure, Politics and Criminal Justice*. Milton Keynes: Open University Press.

Stake, R.E. 1993. "Case Studies." In N. Denzin and Y. Lincoln (eds.), *Handbook of Qualitative Research*. Thousand Oakes, CA: Sage.

Starr, C. 1969. "Social Benefit versus Technological Risk." *Science*, 165: 1232–38.

Starr, Richard. 1992. "Where Was the Warning at Westray?" *Content*, December: 10–13.

_____. 1993. "Blood on the Coal." *Canadian Forum*, 72(May): 5–9.

Statistics Canada. 1996. "Income and Work; Education; Families and Dwellings; and Population." *Statistical Community Profile, 1996 Census*. Ottawa: Statistics Canada.

Stegall, Sandra Kruger, and Keith P. Sanders. 1986. "Coorientation of PR Practitioners and News Personnel in Education News." *Journalism Quarterly*, 63: 2.

Stowers Carr, T. 1991 "Underground Mine Disasters: History, Operations and Prevention." *Professional Safety*, 36: 28–32.

Sumner, C.S. 1979. *Reading Ideologies*. London: Academic.

_____. 1982. *Crime, Justice and the Mass Media*. Cambridge, MA: Cambridge Institute of Criminology, Cropwood Series, 14.

_____. 1990. "Rethinking Deviance: Towards a Sociology of Censure." In C.S. Sumner (ed.), *Censure, Politics and Criminal Justice*. Milton Keynes: Open University Press.

Sumner, C.S., and S. Sandberg. 1990. "The Press Censure of 'Dissident Minorities': The Ideology of Parliamentary Democracy, Thatcherism and Policing the Crisis." In C.S. Sumner (ed.), *Censure, Politics and Criminal Justice*. Milton Keynes: Open University Press.

Surrette, R. 1992. *Media: Crime and Criminal Justice: Images and Realities*. Pacific Grove: Brooks/Cole.

Swinton, Katherine E. 1983. "Enforcement of Occupational Health and Safety Legislation: The Role of the Internal Responsibility System." In Kenneth Swan and Katherine E. Swinton (eds.), *Studies in Labour Law*. Toronto: Butterworths.

Synnett, R.J. 1992. "Construction Safety: A Turnaround Program." *Professional Safety*, 37: 33–37.

Szasz, Andrew. 1986. "The Reversal of Federal Policy Toward Worker Safety and Health." *Science & Society*, 50: 25.

Taras, D. 1992. "Defending the Cultural Frontier: Canadian Television and Continental Integration." In H. Holmes and D. Taras (eds.), *Seeing Ourselves: Media Power and Policy in Canada*. Toronto: Harcourt.

Taylor, Ian, Paul Walton, and Jock Young. 1975. *Critical Criminology*. London: Routledge.

Taylor, S.E., and J.D. Brown. 1988. "Illusion and Well-Being: A Social Psychological Perspective on Mental Health." *Psychological Bulletin*, 103: 193–210.

Thompson, E.P. 1963. *The Making of the English Working Class*. London: Penguin.

_____. 1991. *Customs in Common*. New York: New.

Tibbets, J. 1992. "Westray's Last Day," Halifax *Chronicle-Herald*, July 29, Al-A2.

Toscano, G., and J. Windau. 1993. "Fatal Work Injuries: Results from the 1992 National Census." *Monthly Labor Review*, 116: 39–48.

*Towards Safe Production*. 1981. Report of the Joint Federal–Provincial Inquiry Commission into Safety in Mines and Mining Plants in Ontario. Burkett Report.

Trebilcock, M. 1985. *The Political Economy of Business Bailouts*. Toronto: Ontario Economic Council.

Trotter, R.C., S.G. Day, and A.E. Love. 1989. "Bhopal, India and Union Carbide." *Journal of Business Ethics*, 8: 439–54.

Tucker, Eric. 1984. "The Law of Employers' Liability in Ontario 1861–1900: The Search for a Theory." *Osgoode Hall Law Journal,* 22: 213.

_____. 1990. *Administering Danger in the Workplace: The Law and Politics of Occupational Health and Safety Regulation in Ontario, 1850–1914*. Toronto: University of Toronto Press.

_____. 1992. "Worker Participation in Health and Safety Regulation: Lessons from Sweden." *Studies in Political Economy*, 37: 95.

_____. 1995. "The Westray Mine Disaster and its Aftermath: The Politics of Causation." Canadian Journal of Law and Society, 10(1): 91–123.

Turner, B.A. 1976. "The Organizational and Interorganizational Development of Disasters." *Administrative Science Quarterly*, 21: 378–97.

United States Department of Labor. [no date]. *Number of Fatalities in Underground Coal Mines in the US 1978–92*.

United States Mine Health and Safety Accident statistics, various years.

Vaught C., and D. Smith. 1980. "Incorporation and Mechanical Solidarity in an Underground Coal Mine." *Sociology of Work and Occupations*, 7: 159–87.

Vaught, C., and W.J. Wiehagen. 1991. "Escape from a Mine Fire: Emergent Perspective and Work Group Behavior." *Journal of Applied Behavioral Science*, 27: 452–74.

Vieira, Paul. 1992. "Perilous Industry Vital to Province." *Globe and Mail*, May 11: A4.

Viscusi, W. Kip. 1983. *Risk by Choice*. Cambridge: Harvard University Press.

Wallace, Michael. 1987. "Dying for Coal: The Struggle for Health and Safety Conditions in American Coal Mining, 1930–82." *Social Forces*, 66(336): 343.

Walters, L., L. Wilkins, and T. Waters. 1989. *Bad Tidings: Communication and Catastrophe*. Hillsdale: Lawrence Erlbaum.

Walters, Vivienne. 1991. "State Mediation of Conflicts over Work Refusals: The Role of the Ontario Labour Relations Board." *International Journal of Health Services*, 21: 717.

Walters, Vivienne, and Ted Haines. 1988. "Workers' Use and Knowledge of the 'Internal Responsibility System': Limits to Participation in Occupational Health and Safety." *Canadian Public Policy*, 14: 411.

Ward, B. 1992. "Safety Violations Documented." *Chronicle-Herald*, May 29: A12.

Wardell, M., C. Vaught, and D. Smith. 1985. "Underground Coal Mining and the Labor Process: Safety at the Coal Face." In C. Bryant, D. Shoemaker, J. Skipper and W. Snizek (eds.), *The Rural Work Force: Non-agricultural Occupations in America*. South Hadley, MA: Bergin & Garvey.

Weinstein, N.D. 1984. "Unrealistic Optimism about Future Life Events." *Journal of Personality and Social Psychology*, 39: 806–912.

Wells, Jennifer. 1992. "The Fault Line." *Report on Business*, December: 33–52.

*The Westray Story: A Predictable Path to Disaster*. 1997. Halifax: Westray Mine Publis Inquiry.

White, Jon. 1991. *How to Understand and Manage Public Relations*. London: Business.

Wilde, G.J.S. 1994. *Target Risk: Dealing with the Danger of Death, Disease and Damage in Everyday Decisions*. Toronto: PDE.

_____. 1996. "Improving Trucking Safety and Profitability through Safety Incentive Schemes." In F.F. Saccomanno and J.H. Shortreed (eds.), *Truck Safety: Perceptions and Reality*. Waterloo, ON: Institute for Risk Research.

_____. 1997. "The Concept of Target Risk and its Implications for Accident Prevention Strategies." In A.M. Feyer and A. Williamson (eds.), *Occupational Injury: Risk, Prevention and Intervention*. London: Taylor and Francis.

_____. 1998a. "Accident Models: Risk Homeostasis." In Jeanne M. Stellman, *ILO Encyclopaedia of Occupational Health and Safety*. 4th edition. Geneva, CH: International Labour Office.

_____. 1998b. "Safety Incentive Programmes." In Jeanne M. Stellman *ILO Encyclopaedia of Occupational Health and Safety*. 4th edition. Geneva, CH: International Labour Office.

Wilkins, Lee. 1989. "Conclusion: Accidents Will Happen." In Lynne Masel Walters, Lee Wilkins and Tim Walters (eds.), *Bad Tidings: Communication and Catastrophe*. Hillsdale, NJ: Lawrence Erlbaum.

Williams, R. 1974a. "Communications as Cultural Science." *Journal of Communication*, 23(4): 17–25.

_____. 1974b. *Television: Technology and Cultural Form*. London: Fontana.

_____. 1977. *Marxism and Literature*. Oxford: Oxford University Press.

Wright, Chris. 1986. "Routine Deaths: Fatal Accidents in the Oil Industry." *Social Review*, 34: 265.

Wright, Erik Olin. 1978. *Class, Crisis and the State*. London: New Left.

Wright, G. 1984. *Behavioural Decision Theory*. Harmondsworth: Penguin.

Yates, J.F. 1992. *Risk-taking Behaviour*. New York: Wiley.

Young, J. 1981. "The Manufacture of News: A Critique of the Present Convergence in Mass Media Theory." In European Group for the Study of Deviance (eds.), *State Control of Information in the Field of Deviance and Social Control*. Leuven: Working papers in European Criminology No 2.

Young, K. 1993. "Violence, Risk, and Liability in Male Sports Culture." *Sociology of Sport Journal*, 10: 373–96.

Zataman, J. 1992. "UIC Decision 'Madness.'" The Halifax *Chronicle-Herald*, August 22: A3.

Zizek, Slavoj. 1994. *Mapping Ideology*. New York: Verso.

# LEGAL REFERENCES

*Canada (Attorney General)* v. *Canada (Commission of Inquiry on the Blood System)*, [1997] 3 SCR 440.

Canadian Charter of Rights and Freedoms, Constitution Act, 1982.

*Castle* v. *Brownbridge* (1990); 6 WWR 354.

Nelles et al. and Grange et al. 1984. 9 D.L.R. (4th) 79.

*Phillips et al.* v. *Richard, J.* (1993), 116 N.S.R. (2d) 30.

*Phillips et al.* v. *Richard, J.* (1993), 117 N.S.R. (2d) at 247-8.

*Phillips* v. *Nova Scotia* (Westray Inquiry) (1995), 124 D.L.R. (4th) 129.

*Phillips* v. *Nova Scotia* (Westray Inquiry) (1995), 124 D.L.R. (4th) 170.

*Phillips* v. *Nova Scotia Commission of Inquiry into Westray Mine Tragedy,* [1995] 2 SCR 97.

*R.* v. *Brazeau Collieries Limited* (1942), 3 WWR 570

*R.* v. *Curragh Incorporated* (1997), 113 C.C.C. (3d) 481

*R.* v. *Kuhle* (1988), 3 C.O.H.S.C. 53.

*R.* v. *Syncrude Canada Limited* (1984), 1 WWR 355.

*R.* v. *Union Colliery Company* (1900), 3 C.C.C. 523; 31 SCR 81

*Starr et al.* v. *Holden et al.* (1990), 68 D.L.R. (4th) 641.

Statutes of Nova Scotia. 1990. *An Act to Provide for an Independent Director of Public Prosecutions*. Halifax: S.N.S.